Lecture Notes in Computer Science 13318

More information about this series at https://link.springer.com/bookseries/558

Jessie Y. C. Chen · Gino Fragomeni (Eds.)

Virtual, Augmented and Mixed Reality

Applications in Education, Aviation and Industry

14th International Conference, VAMR 2022
Held as Part of the 24th HCI International Conference, HCII 2022
Virtual Event, June 26 – July 1, 2022
Proceedings, Part II

Editors
Jessie Y. C. Chen
U.S. Army Research Laboratory
Aberdeen Proving Ground, MD, USA

Gino Fragomeni
U.S. Army Combat Capabilities
Development Command Soldier Center
Orlando, FL, USA

ISSN 0302-9743   ISSN 1611-3349 (electronic)
Lecture Notes in Computer Science
ISBN 978-3-031-06014-4   ISBN 978-3-031-06015-1 (eBook)
https://doi.org/10.1007/978-3-031-06015-1

This Springer imprint is published by the registered company Springer Nature Switzerland AG
The registered company address is: Gewerbestrasse 11, 6330 Cham, Switzerland

Foreword

Human-computer interaction (HCI) is acquiring an ever-increasing scientific and industrial importance, as well as having more impact on people's everyday life, as an ever-growing number of human activities are progressively moving from the physical to the digital world. This process, which has been ongoing for some time now, has been dramatically accelerated by the COVID-19 pandemic. The HCI International (HCII) conference series, held yearly, aims to respond to the compelling need to advance the exchange of knowledge and research and development efforts on the human aspects of design and use of computing systems.

The 24th International Conference on Human-Computer Interaction, HCI International 2022 (HCII 2022), was planned to be held at the Gothia Towers Hotel and Swedish Exhibition & Congress Centre, Göteborg, Sweden, during June 26 to July 1, 2022. Due to the COVID-19 pandemic and with everyone's health and safety in mind, HCII 2022 was organized and run as a virtual conference. It incorporated the 21 thematic areas and affiliated conferences listed on the following page.

A total of 5583 individuals from academia, research institutes, industry, and governmental agencies from 88 countries submitted contributions, and 1276 papers and 275 posters were included in the proceedings to appear just before the start of the conference. The contributions thoroughly cover the entire field of human-computer interaction, addressing major advances in knowledge and effective use of computers in a variety of application areas. These papers provide academics, researchers, engineers, scientists, practitioners, and students with state-of-the-art information on the most recent advances in HCI. The volumes constituting the set of proceedings to appear before the start of the conference are listed in the following pages.

The HCI International (HCII) conference also offers the option of 'Late Breaking Work' which applies both for papers and posters, and the corresponding volume(s) of the proceedings will appear after the conference. Full papers will be included in the 'HCII 2022 - Late Breaking Papers' volumes of the proceedings to be published in the Springer LNCS series, while 'Poster Extended Abstracts' will be included as short research papers in the 'HCII 2022 - Late Breaking Posters' volumes to be published in the Springer CCIS series.

I would like to thank the Program Board Chairs and the members of the Program Boards of all thematic areas and affiliated conferences for their contribution and support towards the highest scientific quality and overall success of the HCI International 2022 conference; they have helped in so many ways, including session organization, paper reviewing (single-blind review process, with a minimum of two reviews per submission) and, more generally, acting as goodwill ambassadors for the HCII conference.

This conference would not have been possible without the continuous and unwavering support and advice of Gavriel Salvendy, founder, General Chair Emeritus, and Scientific Advisor. For his outstanding efforts, I would like to express my appreciation to Abbas Moallem, Communications Chair and Editor of HCI International News.

June 2022   Constantine Stephanidis

HCI International 2022 Thematic Areas and Affiliated Conferences

Thematic Areas

- HCI: Human-Computer Interaction
- HIMI: Human Interface and the Management of Information

Affiliated Conferences

- EPCE: 19th International Conference on Engineering Psychology and Cognitive Ergonomics
- AC: 16th International Conference on Augmented Cognition
- UAHCI: 16th International Conference on Universal Access in Human-Computer Interaction
- CCD: 14th International Conference on Cross-Cultural Design
- SCSM: 14th International Conference on Social Computing and Social Media
- VAMR: 14th International Conference on Virtual, Augmented and Mixed Reality
- DHM: 13th International Conference on Digital Human Modeling and Applications in Health, Safety, Ergonomics and Risk Management
- DUXU: 11th International Conference on Design, User Experience and Usability
- C&C: 10th International Conference on Culture and Computing
- DAPI: 10th International Conference on Distributed, Ambient and Pervasive Interactions
- HCIBGO: 9th International Conference on HCI in Business, Government and Organizations
- LCT: 9th International Conference on Learning and Collaboration Technologies
- ITAP: 8th International Conference on Human Aspects of IT for the Aged Population
- AIS: 4th International Conference on Adaptive Instructional Systems
- HCI-CPT: 4th International Conference on HCI for Cybersecurity, Privacy and Trust
- HCI-Games: 4th International Conference on HCI in Games
- MobiTAS: 4th International Conference on HCI in Mobility, Transport and Automotive Systems
- AI-HCI: 3rd International Conference on Artificial Intelligence in HCI
- MOBILE: 3rd International Conference on Design, Operation and Evaluation of Mobile Communications

List of Conference Proceedings Volumes Appearing Before the Conference

1. LNCS 13302, Human-Computer Interaction: Theoretical Approaches and Design Methods (Part I), edited by Masaaki Kurosu
2. LNCS 13303, Human-Computer Interaction: Technological Innovation (Part II), edited by Masaaki Kurosu
3. LNCS 13304, Human-Computer Interaction: User Experience and Behavior (Part III), edited by Masaaki Kurosu
4. LNCS 13305, Human Interface and the Management of Information: Visual and Information Design (Part I), edited by Sakae Yamamoto and Hirohiko Mori
5. LNCS 13306, Human Interface and the Management of Information: Applications in Complex Technological Environments (Part II), edited by Sakae Yamamoto and Hirohiko Mori
6. LNAI 13307, Engineering Psychology and Cognitive Ergonomics, edited by Don Harris and Wen-Chin Li
7. LNCS 13308, Universal Access in Human-Computer Interaction: Novel Design Approaches and Technologies (Part I), edited by Margherita Antona and Constantine Stephanidis
8. LNCS 13309, Universal Access in Human-Computer Interaction: User and Context Diversity (Part II), edited by Margherita Antona and Constantine Stephanidis
9. LNAI 13310, Augmented Cognition, edited by Dylan D. Schmorrow and Cali M. Fidopiastis
10. LNCS 13311, Cross-Cultural Design: Interaction Design Across Cultures (Part I), edited by Pei-Luen Patrick Rau
11. LNCS 13312, Cross-Cultural Design: Applications in Learning, Arts, Cultural Heritage, Creative Industries, and Virtual Reality (Part II), edited by Pei-Luen Patrick Rau
12. LNCS 13313, Cross-Cultural Design: Applications in Business, Communication, Health, Well-being, and Inclusiveness (Part III), edited by Pei-Luen Patrick Rau
13. LNCS 13314, Cross-Cultural Design: Product and Service Design, Mobility and Automotive Design, Cities, Urban Areas, and Intelligent Environments Design (Part IV), edited by Pei-Luen Patrick Rau
14. LNCS 13315, Social Computing and Social Media: Design, User Experience and Impact (Part I), edited by Gabriele Meiselwitz
15. LNCS 13316, Social Computing and Social Media: Applications in Education and Commerce (Part II), edited by Gabriele Meiselwitz
16. LNCS 13317, Virtual, Augmented and Mixed Reality: Design and Development (Part I), edited by Jessie Y. C. Chen and Gino Fragomeni
17. LNCS 13318, Virtual, Augmented and Mixed Reality: Applications in Education, Aviation and Industry (Part II), edited by Jessie Y. C. Chen and Gino Fragomeni

http://2022.hci.international/proceedings

Preface

With the recent emergence of a new generation of displays, smart devices, and wearables, the field of virtual, augmented, and mixed reality (VAMR) is rapidly expanding, transforming, and moving towards the mainstream market. At the same time, VAMR applications in a variety of domains are also reaching maturity and practical usage. From the point of view of the user experience, VAMR promises possibilities to reduce interaction efforts and cognitive load, while also offering contextualized information, by combining different sources and reducing attention shifts, and opening the 3D space. Such scenarios offer exciting challenges associated with underlying and supporting technologies, interaction and navigation in virtual and augmented environments, and design and development. VAMR themes encompass a wide range of areas such as education, aviation, social, emotional, psychological and persuasive applications.

The 14th International Conference on Virtual, Augmented and Mixed Reality (VAMR 2022), an affiliated conference of the HCI International conference, provided a forum for researchers and practitioners to disseminate and exchange scientific and technical information on VAMR-related topics in various applications. The presentations covered a wide range of topics, centered on themes related to interaction techniques, development issues, underlying technologies, and user experience and performance. With recent advances in robotics and artificial intelligence-based systems, topics of interest have expanded to include VAMR-based techniques for human-robot interaction and human interaction with intelligent systems. There are several emerging trends that are noteworthy. Increasingly, multimodal techniques are utilized to enhance VAMR effectiveness – ranging from interaction modalities to prediction of user behaviors. Multi-user and multi-platform paradigms are also explored in several studies.

Two volumes of the HCII2022 proceedings are dedicated to this year's edition of the VAMR conference, entitled Virtual, Augmented and Mixed Reality: Design and Development (Part I) and Virtual, Augmented and Mixed Reality: Applications in Education, Aviation and Industry (Part II). The first focuses on topics related to developing and evaluating VAMR environments, gesture-based, haptic, and multimodal interaction in VAMR, and social, emotional, psychological, and persuasive aspects in VAMR, while the second focuses on topics related to VAMR in learning, education and culture, VAMR in aviation, and industrial applications of VAMR.

Papers of these volumes are included for publication after a minimum of two single-blind reviews from the members of the VAMR Program Board or, in some cases, from members of the Program Boards of other affiliated conferences. We would like to thank all of them for their invaluable contribution, support, and efforts.

June 2022

Jessie Y. C. Chen
Gino Fragomeni

14th International Conference on Virtual, Augmented and Mixed Reality (VAMR 2022)

Program Board Chairs: **Jessie Y. C. Chen,** U.S. Army Research Laboratory, Aberdeen Proving Ground, USA and **Gino Fragomeni,** U.S. Army Combat Capabilities Development Command (DEVCOM) Soldier Center, Orlando, USA

- Shih-Yi Chien, National Chengchi University, Taiwan
- Tamara Griffith, U.S. Army DEVCOM Soldier Center, Orlando, USA
- Sue Kase, U.S. Army Research Laboratory, Aberdeen Proving Ground, USA
- Daniela Kratchounova, Federal Aviation Administration (FAA), Oklahoma City, USA
- Fotis Liarokapis, CYENS, Cyprus
- Phillip Mangos, Adaptive Immersion Technologies, USA
- Jose San Martin, Universidad Rey Juan Carlos, Spain
- Andreas Schreiber, German Aerospace Center (DLR), Germany
- Sharad Sharma, Bowie State University, USA
- Simon Su, National Institute of Standards and Technology (NIST), USA
- Denny Yu, Purdue University, USA

The full list with the Program Board Chairs and the members of the Program Boards of all thematic areas and affiliated conferences is available online at

http://www.hci.international/board-members-2022.php

HCI International 2023

The 25th International Conference on Human-Computer Interaction, HCI International 2023, will be held jointly with the affiliated conferences at the AC Bella Sky Hotel and Bella Center, Copenhagen, Denmark, 23–28 July 2023. It will cover a broad spectrum of themes related to human-computer interaction, including theoretical issues, methods, tools, processes, and case studies in HCI design, as well as novel interaction techniques, interfaces, and applications. The proceedings will be published by Springer. More information will be available on the conference website: http://2023.hci.international/.

General Chair
Constantine Stephanidis
University of Crete and ICS-FORTH
Heraklion, Crete, Greece
Email: general_chair@hcii2023.org

http://2023.hci.international/

Contents – Part II

VAMR in Aviation

Industrial Applications of VAMR

Contents – Part I

Evaluating VAMR Environments

Gesture-Based, Haptic and Multimodal Interaction in VAMR

VAMR in Learning, Education and Culture

User Movement for Safety Training in a Virtual Chemistry Lab

Daniel Ben-Zaken, Abdelwahab Hamam$^{(\boxtimes)}$ ⓘ, and Doga Demirel ⓘ

Florida Polytechnic University, Lakeland, FL 33805, USA
{dbenzaken4421,ahamam,ddemirel}@floridapoly.edu

Abstract. Virtual Reality (VR) has become a large area of focus especially after the effects of COVID-19. During the lockdown students had to partake in different methods of learning outside of the traditional face-to-face classroom setting. In this paper, we focus on the type of locomotion that students would utilize when traversing in a virtual environment. We studied the effectiveness of two types of movement the first being Embodied Movement, or movement through the Head Mounted Display (HMD) device such as the Oculus Quest, or the HTC VIVE, and the second form of movement being Joystick Movement through the use of a thumb stick on an attached controller. To test these movements, we implemented a scenario in a virtual chemistry lab, where the user's vision is impaired, and they would need to navigate throughout the scene to reach a safety shower that once activated would restore their vision. Our results show that using the joystick controller was more suitable for this type of experiment in terms of user preference and the speed of which the user completed the task. Our results also show that for some subjects when partaking in the study, mild cyber-sickness was prevalent and further investigation is needed on how to mitigate its effects.

Keywords: Virtual reality · Education · Locomotion

1 Introduction

In recent years, after overcoming previous restraints, intake on virtual reality (VR) technology has been on a stark rise. However as stated by [1], inconsistencies in implementation of perceived optimal movement strategies have led to mixed insights of the use of VR entirely. Until recently, difficulties in navigation of 3D virtual spaces made 1st person movement to be a high cognitive load task on most systems. This was solved through the discovery that limiting degrees of freedom could increase the performance of system tasks such as visualization and rendering [2, 3]. Results of this discovery led to the formation of three primary forms of movement in VR: Embodied Movement, or the movement being reflected by the user in a confined three-dimensional space into VR, Joystick Movement, or movement using an external controller, and Teleportation which abruptly changes the movement vector of the user to a new point instantaneously. Although each movement solution solved the initial problem and gave boon to different benefits, more problems began to arise along with the issue of inconsistency.

© Springer Nature Switzerland AG 2022
J. Y. C. Chen and G. Fragomeni (Eds.): HCII 2022, LNCS 13318, pp. 3–13, 2022.
https://doi.org/10.1007/978-3-031-06015-1_1

Although each movement solution solved the initial problem and gave boon to different benefits, more problems began to arise along with the issue of inconsistency. As stated by Smith and Neff [4] the use of Embodied Movement in virtual reality complimented the nonverbal communication, such as slight head-nods or arm waving, between users alongside that of physical movement. This led to users being able to perform cooperative tasks without the use of verbal communication, such as talking through a microphone. Embodied Movement is also believed to be more natural, as the user is more interactable and has a greater sense of motion when compared to other forms of locomotion [5, 6]. The problem that arose from this method of locomotion was that due to being in a confined space, the area to which the user can move virtually was also confined. As such if the virtual area was not configured to match the specifications of the user's confined space, some parts of the virtual environment would thus be labeled as inaccessible to the user.

Joystick Movement, as expressed by Kison and Hashernian [5], is a more comfortable and precise form of locomotion when compared to other types of virtual movement. As this type of locomotion is more akin to traditional methods of control and movement in virtual spaces, it is easily adaptable, and responsive. When paired with a virtual headset however, a problem that arose was that the user will begin to feel motion sickness when stationary in the real world but moving in VR [7]. Kison and Hashernian [5] believed this problem could be solved by incorporating small physical motions from the user, to help express that movement is occurring.

Teleportation is described by Bozgeyikli and Raij [8] as users simply being able to point where they want to be in the virtual world, and they are teleported to that position. Because this action is instant, motion sickness is reduced as no transition is occurring. The method is not without its challenges as of the three options mentioned, Teleportation gives the user less control, and can lead to issues with collision detection and placing the user out-of-bounds in the virtual environment.

1.1 Virtual Reality Chemistry Lab

The Florida Polytechnic Virtual Reality Chemistry Lab project is a work focusing on providing adaptive remote learning techniques comparable to that of traditional face-to-face learning [9]. Due to prior restrictions from COVID-19 the transition to remote learning has proved to be difficult, but most courses have translated over without any problems. Unfortunately, the same cannot be said for the lab courses, which traditionally have students conduct hands-on experiments. This greatly hampered the instruction of chemistry labs, where students typically conduct experiments using chemicals and instruments. Instead, students watch videos of experiments, write lab reports on provided data, perform at-home experiments, and use virtual simulations [10]. The long-term goal of this work is to develop a complete immersive Virtual Reality (VR) chemistry lab.

In the VR lab space, the student can handle chemicals and equipment to simulate an actual chemistry lab. Using a VR headset and haptic gloves, the user will be able to freely move and interact with the virtual lab, fellow students, and their teacher. Benefits of a virtual lab would also extend beyond the end of the current pandemic. Students who cannot attend lab because they are pregnant, in the military, or are handicapped would benefit from alternative lab experiences that still adequately prepare them for working in a lab [11]. Even before the pandemic began, the utility of undergraduate labs for General Chemistry courses was called into question [10, 12, 13]. Labs are expensive to conduct [14], and many academic institutions were already experiencing a strained budget. Furthermore, it was questionable if students were actually learning the intended goals [10, 12, 13].

However, despite the cost and questions about learning, if done correctly, labs can be a vital part of the General Chemistry learning experience. Our solution to remote lab instruction is to use virtual reality (VR) head-mounted displays (HMDs) with haptic gloves. VR is beneficial for student learning for multiple reasons including making abstract ideas seem tangible and making students be actively engaged [15]. Our simulation will allow students to explore a realistic lab setting while handling machinery and chemicals. The haptic gloves will allow the students to feel the weight of the glassware and to handle the lab equipment and chemicals in a safe and controlled manner.

VR has been used in classroom instruction for decades. Computer simulations have been used to augment lab instruction as far back as 1980 [16]. VR-haptic surgery training has been used since 1998 [17, 18] and remains an important tool for training doctors and surgeons before practicing on patients. VR has been used to train surgeons in how to do laparoscopies, carotid stenting, and ophthalmology [15]. VR-trained surgeons were 29% faster and six times less likely to make mistakes while performing laparoscopic cholecystectomy gallbladder dissection than surgeons with traditional training [15, 19]. These studies show that VR training is effective at preparing doctors. We believe that it can be equally as effective as preparing students for their chemistry courses.

2 Methodology

2.1 Background

This study is intended to evaluate the movement through a learning environment where students can experience classes in a VR setup. The user study tested the two movement types Embodied Movement, and Joystick Movement. Teleportation Movement was excluded from this testing as that mode of movement is designed to traverse large distances and after finding the size of the virtual space being too small for its applicable use. To increase the size of the virtual space would be to lessen the realism the room would hold when comparing the virtual classroom to real world counterparts.

2.2 Application

Our virtual scenario consists of two main components: the HMD and the virtual scene itself. The virtual scene has two capabilities: a classroom and a lab. The HMD used for running our user study was the Oculus Quest 2 tethered to a Personal Computer using the Oculus Link Cable. For a realistic rendering of the scene, we used High-Definition Render Pipeline and Physically based Rendering (PBR) [20, 21] in the Unity Game Engine using the HurricaneVR software package. PBR uses bi-directional reflectance distribution function (BRDF) [22, 23] to approximate accurate light-flow models. We placed an interactive menu on the wall in our scene that would act to begin the scenario (Figs. 1 and 2).

Fig. 1. View of the interactive menu in the virtual scene

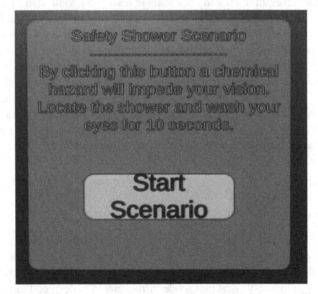

Fig. 2. A close-up of the interactive menu inside the virtual scene that users will use to begin the scenario

Before we begin the testing scenario, we had the user get acquainted to the virtual scene and the different movement types by freely traversing the scene and discovering the VR chemistry lab. They took as much time as needed. Once the scenario begins all, but one safety shower on the other side of the scene is disabled, and a volume box is enabled that would impair the vision of the user by adjusting the color and adding a film grain, vignette, and motion blur to the camera (Fig. 3). Once the vision is impaired the user will try to navigate to the safety shower and pull a lever to activate it (Fig. 4). Once the shower is activated the user must stand underneath it and not move for ten seconds for their vision to be repaired. If the user were to move out of the zone of the safety shower, they must repeat the process of pulling the lever and standing underneath the shower again. This process of starting the scenario and navigating to the safety shower

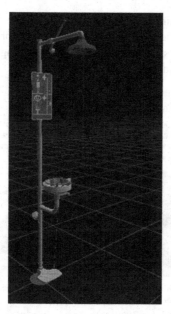

Fig. 3. The model of the safety shower used in the virtual scene

is repeated four more; two times using just embodied movement and two times using joystick movement only, the order of which was randomized to each user. As a way to measure the effectiveness of each trial, we recorded how long it would take the user to complete the task, relating how fast the trial took to how comfortable the movement type was to the user.

Fig. 4. Version of the scene with the impaired vision

2.3 Questionnaire

The questionnaire began by giving the user a general description on what the user would be experiencing in this virtual scenario. This was followed by a pre-questionnaire about the user's background in chemistry and experience with using a VR headset.

The background questionnaire consists of simple multiple-choice questions (as seen in Fig. 5) followed by questions about the user's demographic data such as the user's department of study. The questions comprise of understanding the user's VR knowledge, and experience in chemical lab safety procedures.

Usability Study – Virtual Reality Learning Framework

This user study is intended to evaluate the movement through a learning environment where students can experience classes in a virtual reality (VR) setup. We will be testing two movement types in VR, the first being Lean-In / Head Mounted Display (HMD) movement where the movement from the VR headset is translated to movement in the Virtual World, and the second being Joystick movement with a controller.

This study aims to evaluate the vision, and movement of the user where visibility will be impaired, and the user will navigate to the safety shower in order to clear their eyesight.

PRE- Background Questions

Q1- Do you have any Virtual Reality Experience:

    a) Experienced VR user
    b) Moderate Experienced
    c) I have tried it a few times
    d) Novice to VR

Q2- Have you taken a chemistry course in either high school or college:

    a) Yes
    b) No

Q3- Do you have any experience with lab safety procedures:

    a) Experienced
    b) Moderate experience
    c) Never been taught

Do you have any experience in VR education (yes/no)? If yes, please explain:

In which department/area is your field of study/work:

Fig. 5. The Pre-Questionnaire given to the users partaking in the study

After partaking in the scenario, the users were given a post-evaluation questionnaire with open-ended and Likert-like questions which outlined how the user's experience was using the two different types of movement being studied in VR. The Likert-like questions for the post-evaluation asked the user about their comfortability using embodied movement and joystick movement while running the scenario. The open-ended questions focused on if the user felt any nausea or dizziness while performing the tasks and asked about their opinions regarding the experiment (Fig. 6).

POST – Evaluation

What is your preferred movement in VR:

    a) Head Mounted Display / Lean In
    b) Joystick
    c) Depends on the task

Explain:

How difficult was it to navigate using the Head Mounted Display?

(Easy)   (Hard)

1   2   3   4   5

How difficult was it to navigate using the Joystick?

(Easy)   (Hard)

1   2   3   4   5

How difficult was it to locate the showers with impaired vision using the Head Mounted Display?

(Easy)   (Hard)

1   2   3   4   5

How difficult was it to locate the showers with impaired vision using the Joystick?

(Easy)   (Hard)

1   2   3   4   5

How was your experience performing this experiment?

(Bad)   (Great)

1   2   3   4   5

Did you experience any form of dizziness or nausea while performing the tasks? (Please explain your answer):

If so, what type of movement caused this?

Do you expect VR classes to become available in the future? (Please explain your answer):

Did you find any positive/negative experiences while doing the tasks?

Any additional comments for improvement?

Fig. 6. The Post-Evaluation Questionnaire given to the users after the study

3 Results

Seven participants performed the experiment: six males and one female. All the subjects are students at Florida Polytechnic University. The participants are between the ages of 18 and 24. Regarding the multiple-choice questions of the pre-background questionnaire, when asked if they had prior experience regarding Virtual Reality, six of the seven answered "I have tried it a few times" with the remaining student being a "novice to VR." All students participating had previously taken a chemistry course, with four students being experienced in lab safety procedures, and three students having some moderate experience regarding lab safety. When asked if the participants had any education in VR such as taking a course or having VR incorporated into a previous subject two of the seven students expressed "yes" they had, while the remaining five did not. Out of the seven students five students belonged to the Computer Science department of Florida Polytechnic University, one was part of the Mechanical Engineering department, and the final student belonged to Analytics and Logistics.

Five of the subjects did complete the experiment fully while the other two did not complete it for the following reasons. One subject (female) experience Virtual Reality induced symptoms in the form of nausea and we had to stop the experiment. The other person was not able to complete the experiment because of technical issues where the Quest 2 room guardian settings, in the form of a virtual border that prevents the user from colliding with real life obstacles, prevented the subject's ability to reach and grasp the shower head. Thus, for that subject we only recorded the joystick results. For the remaining subjects we have disabled the guardian settings and we kept an eye on their movement in case they got close to an obstacle.

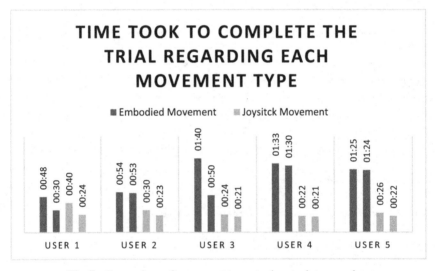

Fig. 7. Comparison of movement types to time took to complete

The results from Fig. 7 are from the five students who were able to complete the scenario. Across all users the time it took to complete the scenario with regards to a particular movement type have remained consistent with the second trial of both Embodied Movement, and Joystick Movement being faster than the first. Due to this fact, we could assume that the randomization of the shower's location did not affect the speed it took to complete the trials. The results also show that movement using the Joystick is significantly faster than movement with the HMD.

During the post-scenario questionnaire, six of the seven students agreed that navigating with the joystick was easier to perform than using Embodied Movement and everyone agreed that although their vision was impaired it was easy to locate the safety showers. Three of the seven students had some form of dizziness or nausea from partaking in the scenario one student when moving with the joystick, another when using Embodied

Movement, and the last student expressed getting dizzy when using both movement types. Regarding the open questioned portion of the questionnaire all students agreed they can expect VR to be used in classes to some degree in the future.

A common issue that was expressed was the complications students had when partaken in the scenario using embodied movement due to the tethering of the headset to the PC. Due to the cable's length, students' movement were heavily restricted, and as such additional time was needed to reposition.

4   Conclusion

In this paper we presented two ways of moving users in a virtual lab. The first being Embodied Movement through the use of an HMD, for our purposes we used the Oculus Quest 2, and the second type being Joystick Movement where locomotion is controlled in part by a thumb stick on the controller. We also performed this user study to evaluate the speed it would take the user to complete the scenario, and their preferred method of movement. We also took in to account any cyber-sickness such as dizziness or nausea when partaking in activities related to VR.

For our safety training scenario, the preferred method of locomotion was the use of Joystick Movement. This was evident to the user's responses to the post-scenario questionnaire where we asked the user how difficult using each type of locomotion was, and their experience participating in the scenario. This could also contribute to the user's speed of completion in relation to the type of movement being tasked for the users that completed the experiment.

For future trials, work will be done into untethering the HMD from the PC, such as using the Oculus Quest's AirLink feature in order to better enhanced the experience of the user using Embodied Movement and negate any complications with restricting the user movement. Untethering the PC will also enhance the VR learning experience by having a more life-like interpretation where actions could be incorporated to real world use. The only setback is that not every headset has this option, and to be more universal tethering options would always be accounted for when working with VR.

In addition, we would like to implement Teleportation Movement for rooms of greater size in order to traverse larger distances. Due to the area utilized for chemistry labs and the tight spaces between equipment teleportation may not be effective but is something we would be willing to test. Furthermore, we want to further investigate the effects of cyber-sickness on the user, and how it relates to the movement being done in our virtual scene.

References

1. Simpson, M., Zhao, J., Klippel, A.: Take a Walk: Evaluating Movement Types for Data Visualization in Immersive Virtual Reality. Immersive Analytics: Exploring Future Interaction and Visualization Technologies for Data Analytics (2017)
2. Elmqvist, N., Dragicevic, P., Fekete, J.: Rolling the dice: multidimensional visual exploration using scatterplot matrix navigation. IEEE Trans. Visual Comput. Graph. **14**(6), 1539–1148 (2008). https://doi.org/10.1109/TVCG.2008.153

3. Amini, F., Rufiange, S., Hossain, Z., Ventura, Q., Irani, P., McGuffin, M.J.: The impact of interactivity on comprehending 2D and 3D visualizations of movement data. IEEE Trans. Visual Comput. Graph. **21**(1), 122–135 (2015). https://doi.org/10.1109/TVCG.2014.2329308

4. Smith, H.J., Neff, M.: Communication behavior in embodied virtual reality. In: Proceedings of the 2018 CHI Conference on Human Factors in Computing Systems (2018)

5. Kitson, A., Hashemian, A.M., Stepanova, E.R., Kruijff, E., Riecke, B.E.: Lean into it: exploring leaning-based motion cueing interfaces for virtual reality movement. In: 2017 IEEE Virtual Reality (VR), pp. 215–216 (2017). https://doi.org/10.1109/VR.2017.7892253

6. Gillies, M.: What is movement interaction in virtual reality for? In: Proceedings of the 3rd International Symposium on Movement and Computing (2016)

7. Gresty, M.A., Waters, S., Bray, A., Bunday, K., Golding, J.F.: Impairment of spatial cognitive function with preservation of verbal performance during spatial disorientation. Curr. Biol. **13**(21) (2003)

8. Bozgeyikli, E., Raij, A., Katkoori, S., Dubey, R.: Point teleport locomotion technique for virtual reality. In: Proceedings of the 2016 Annual Symposium on Computer-Human Interaction in Play (2016)

9. Demirel, D., Hamam, A., Scott, C., Karaman, B., Toker, O., Pena, L.: Towards a new chemistry learning platform with virtual reality and haptics. In: Zaphiris, P., Ioannou, A. (eds.) Learning and Collaboration Technologies: Games and Virtual Environments for Learning, HCII 2021. LNCS, vol. 12785. Springer, Cham (2021). https://doi.org/10.1007/978-3-030-77943-6_16

10. Henry, A.C.: Questioning the value of general chemistry labs. Chem. Eng. News **98**(18) (2020). https://cen.acs.org/education/undergraduate-education/Questioning-value-general-chemistry-labs/98/i18

11. Jo, C.C.: Virtualizing Organic Chemistry Labs. DELTA News (2018). https://delta.ncsu.edu/news/2018/12/19/virtualizing-organic-chemistry-labs/

12. Bretz, S.L.: Evidence for the importance of laboratory courses. J. Chem. Educ. **96**(2), 193–195 (2019). https://doi.org/10.1021/acs.jchemed.8b00874

13. Hofstein, A., Lunetta, V.N.: The laboratory in science education: foundations for the twenty-first century. Sci. Educ. **88**, 28–54 (2004)

14. Nicola, J.: Simulated labs are booming. Nature **562**, S5–S7 (2018). https://doi.org/10.1038/d41586-018-06831-1

15. Slater, M., Sanchez-Vives, M.V.: Enhancing our lives with immersive virtual reality. Front. Robot. AI **3**, 74 (2016). https://doi.org/10.3389/frobt.2016.00074

16. Moore, C., Smith, S., Avner, R.A.: Facilitation of laboratory performance through CAI. J. Chem. Educ. **57**(3), 196 (1980). https://doi.org/10.1021/ed057p196

17. Krummel, T.M.: Surgical simulation and virtual reality: the coming revolution. Ann. Surg. **228**(5) (1998). https://journals.lww.com/annalsofsurgery/Fulltext/1998/11000/Surgical_Simulation_and_Virtual_Reality__The.2.aspx

18. Marescaux, J., et al.: Virtual reality applied to hepatic surgery simulation: the next revolution. Ann. Surg. **228**(5) (1998). https://journals.lww.com/annalsofsurgery/Fulltext/1998/11000/Virtual_Reality_AppAppl_to_Hepatic_Surgery.1.aspx

19. Seymour, N.E., et al.: Virtual reality training improves operating room performance: results of a randomized, double-blinded study. Ann. Surg. **236**(4) (2002). https://journals.lww.com/annalsofsurgery/Fulltext/2002/10000/Virtual_Reality_Training_Improves_Operating_Room.8.aspx

20. Pharr, M., Jakob, W., Humphreys, G.: Physically Based Rendering: From Theory to Implementation (2016)

21. Schlick, C.: An inexpensive BRDF model for physically-based rendering. Comput. Graph. Forum **13**(3), 233–246 (1994)

22. Ashikhmin, M., Shirley, P.: An anisotropic phong BRDF model. J. Graph. Tools 5(2), 25–32 (2000)
23. Ashikmin, M., Premože, S., Shirley, P.: A microfacet-based BRDF generator. In: Proceedings of the 27th Annual Conference on Computer Graphics and Interactive Techniques, pp. 65–74 (2000). https://doi.org/10.1145/344779.344814

Development of an Educational AR Tool for Visualization of Spatial Figures and Volume Calculation for Vocational Education

Simone Dalager[✉] [iD] and Gunver Majgaard[iD]

SDU Game Development and Learning Technology, Mærsk Mc-Kinney Møller Institute, University of Southern Denmark, Campusvej 55, 5230 Odense M, Denmark
simonedalager@hotmail.com, gum@mmmi.sdu.dk

Abstract. This paper describes the development of a prototype for an AR application, which supports volume calculation and spatial understanding for mathematics in vocational educations in Denmark. Teaching of spatial shapes and their properties are done mainly in a two-dimensional space on paper. To mitigate the inherent contradiction of learning about 3D-figures on paper, we set forth to develop an application, which focus on visualizing 3D-objects with the use of handheld AR. The application is developed with the iterative design process where the development of low- and high-fidelity prototypes have been essential for improving and testing the product. From testing it was noted that there was expressed excitement for the visualization of the 3D-objects through AR and how real they seemed. Especially the visualizations of the figures size and the size compared to its volume. From test results the AR visualization of 3D-objects and interaction with them helped test subjects to better understand the spatiality of the shown object. With the application they were able to "see the unseen" [6], which helped their understanding of spatial objects. We propose the use of AR technology to be further utilized as a natural tool in relevant subjects, where a visualization can promote or enhance a better understanding of a topic. On the top of this, AR contributes to the learning experience, which will vast and remain with the users.

Keywords: Augmented Reality · Spatial understanding · Volume calculation · Volume · Image based · Mathematics · Learning · Unity

1 Introduction

We have all been taught mathematics in school and drawn several geometrical shapes as well as calculated the volume of them. The concern and question here is, can you remember volume and explain it as well? It is very likely that you have been taught about three dimensional shapes on a piece of paper and with the perspective of the shape "seen" it in 3D. This challenges you to imagine the three dimensions in your head, which can be a challenge. Students seem to have difficulty with understanding spatial knowledge with complex phenomena [3, 16] such as volume. Here teachers and educators must find new ways to teach and present spatial concepts, which will aid their existing understanding of the subject matter. We claim Augmented Reality (AR) can assist such a challenge substantially. AR offers the ability to see and manipulate virtual 3D-objects in real time

© Springer Nature Switzerland AG 2022
J. Y. C. Chen and G. Fragomeni (Eds.): HCII 2022, LNCS 13318, pp. 14–30, 2022.
https://doi.org/10.1007/978-3-031-06015-1_2

on top of the physical world. It also enables you to bring your 2D-understanding into the 3D-space. The use of AR in mathematics has the possibility to support students spatial understanding by connecting their already existing knowledge with an understanding of volume in a 3D-space.

This application is made in collaboration with a mathematics teacher at a vocational education. The teacher explains how students have troubles understanding volume and size of volume. The target group of this application is the students of the first-year introductory course at Danish vocational educations. These students age from 15 years and up. The age range in these classes can then vary a lot.

The purpose of the application is to give the students a better spatial understanding when working with spatial objects and shapes. Additionally, the application can support the calculations they have to do in classes when doing assignments. Potentially the application could also work for teaching students of volume calculation in the entire education system, probably more relevant in the upper grades of primary school. The application is developed for Danish vocational educations and the language for the app is in Danish.

The reason for choosing AR is that it intertwines the physical and virtual world and enables interaction between them [4, 5, 11]. AR can be seen as a continuum between these worlds, the physical and the augmented content (see Fig. 1). AR becomes a layer on top of reality and makes it possible to see a world of virtual objects on top of the physical world. This is all done in real time [4, 10].

Fig. 1. The application showing the cylinder shape next to a coffee mug in the physical world.

AR afford and encourage the user to investigate object(s). Users can freely orientate themself and inspect the 3D object(s) from different perspectives [4]. This is somewhat like one's perception of holograms. It invites the user to interact and reflect over spatial concepts [4]. To be able to manipulate spatial objects creates more opportunities for understanding features and "behaviour" of objects while still encouraging creativity [15]. AR can "illustrate the temporal relationships between objects" [10] and afford the spatial abilities and can extend the practical skills [4]. Furthermore, AR affordances the ability to make the otherwise invisible visible as Dunleavy [6] describes it, "see the unseen".

With the use of AR on smartphones the user can see through an AR lens which Dunleavy [6] describes can allow you to view content, which would otherwise be beyond an everyday experience [10]. The phone goes from being the simple screen to shifting into a lens, where one can see the previously unseen [6].

These reflections led to the choice of developing the AR application "Rumlige figurAR", which translated into English is "Spatial figurARs".

This project is developed in spring 2021. The preliminary test result was affected by the COVID-19 pandemic.

2   Related Work

The use of AR as an educational tool is quite new and the latest research with use of AR is mainly focused and tested on/with pupils/students in elementary school [3, 15]. Limited research has been found with students in the same target group, but research have been found with undergraduate students. Similar research focus more on geometry and/or 3D thinking skills and not on the visualization and understanding of volume [3, 15, 16].

Shelton and Hedley [16] researched an AR tool to help undergraduate geography students about the relationship between the earth and the sun. The AR system was a Head mounted display (HMD) and students completed a pre- and post-assessment. Shelton and Hedley realized students quickly experienced the virtual objects as part of the physical environment. They pointed and referred to the virtual objects when wearing the HMD AR system as if people outside the "AR world" could all see what they saw in AR. The students' "belief was temporarily suspended" [16]. By manipulating the 3D objects students got a better sense of the earth-sun relationship. Shelton and Hedley believe 3D spatial phenomena and concepts taught in similar subjects can benefit from AR and the visualization it brings.

The Geo+ application [15] help children in 3rd and 4th grade learn and explore solid geometry figures. Rossanno et al. [15] research aim to use AR to support geometry teaching in primary schools. The students felt drawn into their AR app, had fun using it and teachers pointed out their students were more focused on the task. They conclude AR allows users an immersive virtual world. Furthermore, the students did improve from the pre-test to the post-test which was statistically confirmed with a t-test.

In the study from Cahyono et al. [3] they designed and developed apps for interactive education model for various geometry objects as a way for teachers to learn mathematics to elementary school students. From there results they conclude there is strong support that AR has potential to be a helpful tool used in studying what they call "formal content (mathematics)" [3]. They consider their geometry app to be able to improve students in elementary school "understanding of mathematics subjects in 3D space building materials" [3]. Likewise, it can make the ordinary learning of mathematics more interactive by creating a new atmosphere.

Different from these works, which address the use for younger children or in a different subject, "Spatial FigurARs" focuses on vocational students' volume understanding of geometrical objects and the spatial visualization AR can offer the students.

3   Methodology

The different uses of methodologies in the development of the app are inspired by the methods utilized within game development and game design [8]. Especially the iterative process, as well as systematic testing and prototyping throughout the process of the project development, characterize the methods within game development and game design.

3.1 The Iterative Process

The iterative design process was chosen to create structure in the project development. The iterations meant that each prototype in the development was designed, tested, results were evaluated and so on throughout the development process. To iterate is important "to the playcentric process" [8]. The focus of the playcentric approach/process is to involve the user in the design process in all steps from conceptualization to the result. It means to always mind the user experience and test with users in all the iterative phases in the development [8]. To put the application in focus it was important to make continual development and make use of the stepwise iterative process (see Fig. 2).

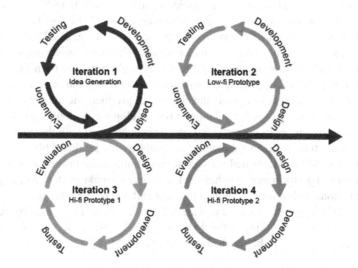

Fig. 2. The iterative design processes.

The iterative design process helped design the application continuously and the testing and feedback located which areas of the application were troublesome for users. The continual testing of the application prevented the project from being sidetracked. To test and redesign continually aided in ironing out problems early in the process. When testing was done the test results were evaluated followed by evaluation, which would tie together the iteration and initiate a path toward a new iteration.

3.2 Prototyping

There has been heavily worked with prototypes in this project. From simple low fidelity (low-fi) to more advanced high fidelity (hi-fi) prototypes. Physical prototypes allowed for fluid exploration of the design and the arrangement while keeping the budget in check [8, 14]. The physical prototypes forced us to think the design elements through and constrain them [8]. This was relevant to focus on to create the boundaries and maintain a project plan.

3.3 Iterative Test

To ensure a useable product, testing was a focus point in the iterative development process. The testing was made to ensure for "gaining useful feedback from players to improve the overall experience (…)" [8]. It was mostly the functionality of the application which needed testing. In this project different testing methods have been utilized. Because of the COVID-19 pandemic at the time of development testing is preliminary and limited.

Testing is time consuming, and this led to a lot of self-testing regarding functionality and finding common bugs in the system. This is mostly useful in the early stages of prototyping, where experimentation with fundamental ideas is still ongoing. The objection is to get a working prototype and an approximation of the product. Further in the development process focus was on outside test subjects [8]. Functionality testing was effective through the entire process to ensure different operations were working as intended.

Testing with close contacts can be helpful in the beginning stages. When a playable prototype is ready it can be tested on close contacts. They can come with a fresh look at the product and draw attention to details, which might not have been thought of as written by Fullerton [8]. The intension is to test a version which can be "played" with no or little interference from developer. In developing the product, one must step back from this test form since the test subject relation to the developer can cloud their objectivity.

Usability testing is about how user friendly a product is and with the target group in mind it was important to focus on making an easily usable product [14]. A controlled environment should be established for such tests to limit social influence, which could impact test subject performance or behavior. The focus is to make the test subject perform preset instructions and observe how they perform and where stops happen.

Wizard of Oz is a method where you are the "wizard" who make the product work. You presume to have a working software prototype. The user tester then interact with this user interface as was it the finished software product [14].

3.4 Technical Platforms

For the development of the application the game engine Unity [19] and AR Software Development Kit Vuforia [21] have been used.

The application is developed with image targets. Image targets are photos which the Vuforia Engine detects and can follow. The engine detects the photo by comparing it to its natural features from the photo against the known image target from the database in the Vuforia Target Manager [23]. The AR content is then "projected" down on top of the image target. The Target Manager lets one administrate and set up image target databases. It is important that the image target(s) has/have many natural feature points to enable the best possible tracking of the image. Feature points are "sharp, spiked, chiseled detail in the image" [22].

The Unity engine supports multiple platforms including iOS and Android [20] where development is possible for both 2D and 3D content. Unity has included a set of simple objects such as cube and sphere, which have eased the required modelling skills and enables energy to be focused elsewhere. It is also possible to import 3D models into a Unity project as well.

Since not all the required shapes for the app were available in Unity, these shapes were modelled in Blender 3D [2]. The pyramid, prism and cone objects were 3D-modelled using Blender 3D.

For testing the app, different smartphone models were used which are Samsung J5, Samsung Galaxy S10e and Oneplus 5t.

4 Product Development of "Spatial figurARs"

The basic idea of the application was to implement the 6 fundamental shapes for volume calculation: cube, sphere, cylinder, cone, pyramid, and a triangular prism. With these shapes the user can edit its values, define which unit, and then calculate the volume of the shape in the set unit. For instance, for the cube shape the user can change the length, width, and height, specify the unit, and calculate the volume from the set values in the specified unit. To develop the application image targets were chosen as the AR technology. This would later turn out to be a favorable decision.

4.1 Iteration 1 – Idea Generation

With the basic idea in place the idea generation for further features began. This idea generation (see Fig. 3) would bring new ideas to functions and features which could create more value for the current idea state for the application. The focus was to find functions which could be implemented later.

The ideas were prioritized accordingly when it became clear that not all ideas would be possible to implement. This created an overview of the features to be implemented but also produced in which order each feature should be implemented. The list at the time of making became the following:

1. A single shape with image target (preferably the cube)

    a. Able to change length, width, and height (not necessarily the unit as well)
    b. Calculate the volume of the shape

2. Add one more shape (preferably the sphere)

    a. Change radius
    b. Correct the dimensions to the physical world
    c. Add 1–2 units (one unit for all values)
    d. Calculate volume with correct unit
    e. Add the same new functionality to the previous shape

3. Experiment with editing values and shape in real time
4. Add the last missing shapes

    a. Add same functionality to all shapes

5. Experiment with calculating density

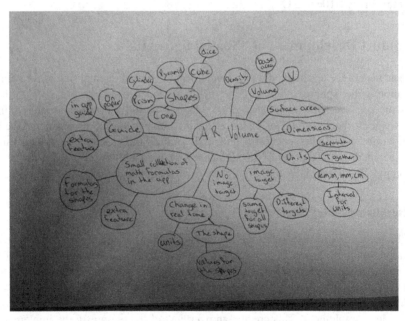

Fig. 3. Translated version of the original brainstorm.

Other than the prioritized list, there was also made a *nice to have* list and in unpri-oritized form. This included a "mini" mathematics collection of formula, which could be implemented in the app or made on paper; no tracking with image target; a guide on how to use the application either in the app or in written form with pictures on paper; add surface area calculation to all shapes and lastly a start menu. These lists turned out to be fluid in the development and the actual development did deviate from these them.

4.2   Iteration 2 – Low-Fi Prototype

The first design ideas were sketched on paper. From these sketches a low-fi paper prototype was produced with cardboard, paper, and sticky track. The paper prototype was made to test functionality and clarify how users understand the interface for the product.

Design

A physical prototype made it possible to let the thoughts and ideas become tangible. To sit down with something physical ensures others get an understanding of the vision of the product [8]. This visualization made the foundation for a common understanding with the collaborating teacher. With image targets chosen as the tracking technology this was relevant to bring into the prototyping phase as also seen in Fig. 4.

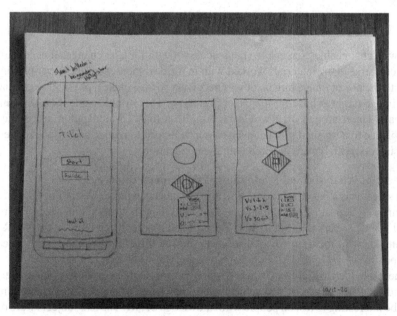

Fig. 4.   One of the first sketches of an idea to a prototype. Left: start menu, Middle: sphere, right: cube with calculations. The small box with calculations is placed at the bottom of the "screen" to make it less disturbing and make the 3D object as visible as possible.

Development

The paper prototype is developed from sketches seen in Fig. 4. A paper phone was made and from this, different possible screenshots were sketched on paper. The prototype was

Fig. 5. Development of the paper prototype.

made with changeable "screens" to make it easy to edit for later changes if necessary. In Fig. 5 can be seen the materials worked with in the development of the paper prototype.

With the use of image targets, it was necessary to also make a physical resemblance of the image target to have for the paper prototype. This would enable the user to move the image target around as it would be done in a finished application and make the resemblance to a finished product even closer. It helped to realize and visualize the real image targets, which were to come with the application.

Test Results, Analysis, and Evaluation of the Paper Prototype

The first test was a paper prototype tested on 3 subjects with the Wizard of Oz method. They answered a set of predefined questions and then the test commenced. Their age ranged from 23 years to 60 years old. They all had no preceding knowledge of AR and only one knew of the term AR. All subjects showed difficulties "typing" the values on the paper.

The test helped to highlight, where to put focus for future iterations as well as identify future difficulties. Since no test subjects had knowledge of AR for future iterations, it could be interesting to test on people with knowledge of AR. The test subjects were older than the target audience and in the future test subjects should be younger and closer to the main target group.

4.3   Iteration 3 – High-Fi Prototype 1: Spatial Cube and Sphere

From the paper prototype a hi-fi prototype was developed. The goal of this iteration was to develop a working software prototype with the functionality described in the earlier prioritized list of features.

Design

Firstly, a prototype with the cube as the visualized shape was developed. The values for the cube were changeable and had to be typed in. In the beginning only the unit meter was implemented and the volume calculation in the corresponding unit cubic meters as well. It was relevant to test the prototype with more units for the shape. The units m, dm, cm and mm was added as well as the corresponding cubic unit. Lastly the sphere shape was added with the same functionality as for the cube.

In anticipation of later development, all image targets for the 6 different shapes were established in this iteration. This presented a limitation for the project since we have no or very limited knowledge of digital drawing, especially for image targets. Image targets need to have great amount of feature points for best possible detection of the image [22]. These feature points were difficult to make while keeping a resemblance to the object to be visualized on the image target. It was decided that time would be better spend on further developing the app instead of drawing image targets.

Fig. 6. Screenshot from the application. To the left is the early stage of the prototype and to the right the final stage for the application.

Development

Through the development of this iteration, there were small internal improvements on new or existing features. The cube looked heavy and compact (see left on Fig. 6) and as a solution the cube and later shapes were made transparent (see right on Fig. 6). This was done to have a uniform impression on the shapes and make a clear distinction between the physical and virtual world. Among this was also an improvement on the interface as it was very simplistic in the beginning as seen on the left of Fig. 6 compared to the final developed interface seen on the right on Fig. 6.

Test Results, Analysis, and Evaluation of Hi-Fi Prototype 1

This test was the first test of the software prototype. The cube and sphere shape were implemented for this test. The test was conducted on 2 siblings at the age of 15 and 17 years referred to as test subject 5 and 4. The test was conducted individually and there was first asked some pre-defined questions. None of them knew of AR and both had trouble explaining what volume was. When testing the app test subject 5 said, what is translated to "okay this is quite cool" and they both expressed positive to the thought of using this for teaching in school. Tester 4 expressed "it might even help". In that regard tester 5 stated what is translated to "I actually think it would give a better understanding of how it looks and so". For this tester 4 also stated what is translated to "I think it is quite smart (…). It would certainly help some. (…) again, it would be really cool to have an app where you can like visually get to see a figure/shape and calculate all". There were troubles typing in the input fields, which could be designed to be bigger and easier to utilize.

Considering their age, it seems unlikely they don't know AR since it is used in apps like Snapchat [12] and Pokémon GO [13]. The thought is they know of AR and have encountered it but are unaware of what it is. The trouble of explaining volume indicates there is a problem understanding the concept of volume. With both testers being positive toward using this app in teaching volume and support the visual aspect of it as well, it is considered valuable to work further with this type of visualization.

4.4   Iteration 4 – High-Fi Prototype 2: Designing Meaningful Image Targets

In the fourth iteration focus has been on design of image targets and implementing the last shapes (cylinder, cone, triangular prism, and pyramid).

Design

In addition to the design of image targets there was made further experimentation on changing the sphere to have a slider function instead of typing in the values. This was done to get an idea of what a change of the shape in real time could offer of functionality. The sphere was chosen because it only has one changeable variable, which would simplify the interface instead of 2–3 sliders to change different values on the other shapes (see Fig 7).

 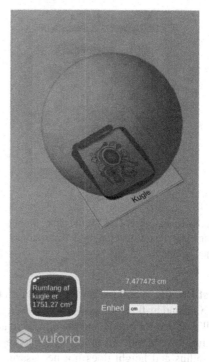

Fig. 7. Interface for the sphere with the slider functionality.

Development

To give the different image targets meaningful use, new designs were made for each figure to better support their usage and physicality. Since physical interaction with the environment support learning [1] this design decision was decided on. Small image target cards (ITC) were developed where the front of the card was the image target with written text of what shape it represents. The back of the ITC is a line drawing of the corresponding shape, which is like what students know from their mathematics formula collection. On the back is also written the formula for volume calculation for the corresponding shape. To anticipate for further implementation the formula for surface area was also added. In Fig. 8 is the ITC for the cube shape.

With the new design from just an image representing the shape to the ITC, there was developed a closer connection between the app and the physical image target. We as humans experience the world with our bodies through physical interactions, thus would physical elements injected into the design of learning encourage embodied learning [1]. The physical ITC have recognizable line drawing and formulas of the corresponding shape. The use of a physical representation in the ITC assists the shape to manifest in the physical world in combination with AR.

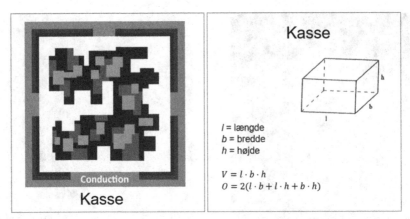

Fig. 8. Image target card for the cube. Front of the image target is on the left and the back of the image target card is to the right. Translations: kasse = cube, længde = length, bredde = witdh, højde = height.

Test Results, Analysis, and Evaluation of Hi-Fi Prototype 2

The second hi-fi prototype is tested on the collaborating mathematics teacher whom we call Z. Z knows of AR and have participated in a course of development with AR, but he has never applied it in his own teaching. He wants to show students that the change in radius and height does not necessarily make the same change in the volume of a shape. Z sees it is possible to use the app for visualization, but it can also assist with calculations. Overall Z is very positive and committed towards the app. When using the app and moving physically around the ITC he expresses the app provide an excellent spatial sense/feeling. He is very positive to see and recognize elements form mathematics formula collection and he believes it will benefit the students to see familiar drawings etc. on the ITC.

When testing the sphere with the slider (as shown in Fig. 7) functionality Z points out the slider works well on the sphere because only one value is changing but also emphasizes it is imprecise if the user needs a specific radius. What Z compliments is the "simplicity" in the design. He states, "one can really sense the depth in it". "It" referring to the shape.

To test with someone who is familiar with AR was positive and minimized small confusion of the AR technology. The physical ITC was confirmed to be a great choice to have implemented. The trouble of understanding units should be looked further into whether it is the app which is confusing, or testers existing knowledge of units is conflicting with the use of the app. The slider function for the sphere is kept and works very well for shapes with only one changeable value though the implementation need adjust- and refinements. The choice of a physical object to represent a spatial shape was confirmed to be a great way to combine the AR and students existing knowledge of volume as well as the recognition of known formulas and drawings.

5   Discussion

By examining the feedback from the test subjects in the 3 tests we discovered a lack of knowledge and understanding of the concept volume.

5.1   AR, Phones, and Teaching

To make use of AR in classrooms can turn out to be a challenge. The fact that students don't seem to know what AR is, but most likely already know of it and are using it on daily basis, will influence the experience for the students. The app offers a different form of AR compared to what they might see or use in i.e., Snapchat [12], where you can put augmented content in a 2D form such as cat ears etc. on top of your face. "Spatial figurARs" can on the other hand show a 3D-object in the physical world as the augmented content, which differs from the usual experience. This could be why students seem to not recognize or have knowledge of AR. The term AR should be explained to students before they try the app to broaden likely already existing knowledge on the subject.

A second challenge for the app will be to get teachers and educators to use it in their teaching. To ensure this, the app should have clear instruction for them to easily work with the app in teaching. The app should be available on all capable mobile platforms/phones to allow students with different platforms to try the app.

One thing to consider is the use of mobile phones in classrooms. Generally, phones are not acceptable during class for various reasons. The use of phones in teaching situations can distract students if they receive notifications, when using the app in a teaching setting. It can potentially lead to some students having difficulties distinguishing when the phone is for teaching and when it is not. This can lead to a blurred line between teaching and spare time. Possibly it can cause confusion for some students, which would have to concentrate on the teaching and not the notification(s) they might receive while using the app. The phone should not hinder learning but rather work as an educational tool and add quality to the learning situation [18].

5.2   Limitations

Development of this preliminary project during the COVID-19 pandemic made a great impact on the possibility of testing in general as well as testing on the target group. This has led to preliminary data results instead of more accurate result as desired.

There have been limitations to the project regarding the technology of image targets. It was very difficult to find relevant and useable image target in good quality and featurepoints with the available tools and software. It is clear new image targets with representation to the corresponding shape should be made and added to the ITC. This could bring greater value to the product.

With the project extending over a period of 5 months, time has been limited which led to a need to prioritize the developed features as well as balancing practical and theoretical needs for the project. Though the time was short, we succeeded to implement almost all features from the list of prioritized ideas. Only the last idea on the list "experiment with calculating density" was not touched upon because of time limitations.

The project is preliminary, and the developed app is an early prototype and need further development to be at an acceptable finished state.

5.3 Reflections on the Development

When in development you don't just implement without regard. You learn in the process and get smarter along the way.

In retrospective the use of the Wizard of Oz method would be reconsidered and not utilized with test subjects unfamiliar with AR. The method confused test subjects by the imitation of a real app done on paper. The usage of this method will be further considered in the future.

As for data gathering, sound recordings work great, when documenting answer for questions, but for gathering data on the user's experience of the application sound data is limiting. For future tests, video recording should be considered further if possible whether it be recordings of the user or as screen recordings in similar cases. Overall, much knowledge and applicable experiences have been gained through the testing of users, which has led to better knowledge, understanding and positively better testing setups and experiences for future work and testing.

The physical image targets and later ITC turned out to have a positive impact on the use of the app. The physical target and resemblance of an augmented geometrical shape made it possible to connect the virtual and physical world. It also made it possible to physically move and walk around the 3D augmented shape and look at it from multiple angles and viewpoints.

The sphere was redeveloped with the slider functionality because of the single changeable value. This was a decision made later in the development and it turned favorable. Though it should be further investigated the pros and cons for this type of functionality.

6   Conclusion and Future Work

The project's goal was to develop an educational AR tool to use in the introductory course for vocational schools in Denmark. A prototype was developed through 4 iterations and can show 6 different geometrical shapes using AR technology and image targets.

The testing showed only a few people had any knowledge of AR, what it is capable of, and all test subjects had difficulties explaining/remembering what volume calculation is. There were problems understanding the units, but the subjects were positive about the app, and they could see it as tool to help visualization.

Thus, the critical lack of testing on the main target group, we found sufficient data from the preliminary test with test subjects and mathematics teacher to conclude; AR, and the application have potential to help learners' visualization and understanding the concept of volume and size of spatial shapes. Especially the positive comments and feedback from the mathematics teacher validates our findings.

We propose to continue to develop AR technology for three-dimensional visualization, which can provide a better understanding of the subject and spatiality. The AR technology has the capability to improve learning experiences as well, in this area of mathematics, which should be considered for future work. We suggest for future research, the use of AR to be developed even further as a tool applied for visualization.

This project is innovative in the use of AR compared to previous mention AR applications because of the use of three dimensional augmented content to help see spatial shapes. The use of AR visualization to help vocational students' understanding of volume and volume calculation could help broaden their understanding. To work with AR in this manner gets closer to an imitation of holograms but through the phone.

Future work on the project would include further testing of the app in its current state with the target group. The slider functionality for the sphere should be further improved on. To get the app working in relation to teaching, a course should be planned with the use of the app into consideration. It should be investigated if it is possible to nudge the user to investigate the augmented spatial shapes further by i.e., walking around the shape.

Acknowledgments. Thank you to teacher Søren Damgaard for the basic idea for the application. Thank you to co supervisor Patricia Bianca Lyk, for supervising the project and project report. A big thank goes to Simone's dear friend Nina Weilbaecher for doing the graphical work on Fig. 2. Special thanks to Lasse Juel Larsen for internal perusal and proofreading in the writing of this paper.

References

1. Anderson, S.P.: Chapter 1. Learning and thinking with things. In: Designing for Internet of Things. O'Reilly Media (2015). https://www.oreilly.com/library/view/designing-for-the/978 1491971468/ch01.html. Accessed 15 Jan 2022
2. Blender Foundation, Blender 3D. https://www.blender.org/. Accessed 19 Feb 2022
3. Cahyono, B., Firdaus, M.B., Budiman, E., Wati, M.: Augmented reality applied to geometry education. In: The 2nd East Indonesia Conference on Computer and Information Technology (2018). https://doi.org/10.1109/EIConCIT.2018.8878553
4. Cheng, K.H., Tsai, C.C.: Affordances of augmented reality in science learning: suggestions for future research. J. Sci. Educ. Technol. **22**, 449–462 (2013). https://doi.org/10.1007/s10 956-012-9405-9
5. Coimbra, T., Cardoso, T., Mateus, A.: Augmented reality: an enhancer for higher education students in math's learning? Procedia Comput. Sci. **67**, 332–339 (2015). https://doi.org/10. 1016/j.procs.2015.09.277
6. Dunleavy, M.: Design principles for augmented reality learning. TechTrends **58**(1), 28–34 (2013). https://doi.org/10.1007/s11528-013-0717-2
7. Giant Lazer Seeing the world of geometry with Augmented Reality. https://giantlazer.com/ seeing-the-world-of-geometry-with-augmented-reality/. Accessed 2 Feb 2022
8. Fullerton, T.: Game Design Workshop. 2nd edn. Elsevier, United States (2008). https://doi. org/10.1201/b13172
9. Klopfer, E.: Augmented Learning: Research and Design of Mobile Educational Games. The MIT Press, London (2008)
10. Majgaard, G., Larsen, L.J., Lyk, P., Lyk, M: Seeing the unseen – spatial visualization of the solar system with physical prototypes and augmented reality. international J. Des. Learn. **8**(2), 95–109 (2017). https://doi.org/10.14434/ijdl.v8i2.22368
11. Milgram, P., Takemura, H., Utsumi, A., Kishino, F: Augmented reality: class of displays on the reality-virtuality continuum. Telemanipulator and telepresence technologies SPIE **2351**, 282–292 (1994). https://doi.org/10.1117/12.197321
12. Murphy, B., Spiegel, E.: Snapchat, Snapchat Inc. https://www.snapchat.com/. Accessed 25 Jan 2022

13. Niantic, Pokémon GO. https://pokemongolive.com/en/. Accessed 25 Jan 2022
14. Preece, J., Rogers, Y., Sharp, H.: Interaction Design Beyond Human-Computer Interaction, 4th edn. WILEY, Chichester (2015)
15. Rossano, V., Lanzilotti, R., Cazzolla, Antonio., Roselli, T.: Augmented reality to support geometry learning. IEEE Access **8**, 107772–107780 (2020). https://doi.org/10.1109/ACC ESS.2020.3000990
16. Shelton, B.E., Hedley, N.R.: Using augmented reality for teaching earth-sun relationships to undergraduate geography student. In: The First IEEE International Workshop Augmented Reality Toolkit (2002). https://doi.org/10.1109/ART.2002.1106948
17. Song, E., Susub, N., Sihes, A.J., Alwee, R., Yonos, Z.M.: Design and development of learning mathematics game for primary school using handheld augmented reality. OP Conf. Ser. Mater. Sci. Eng. **979**(1), 1–10 (2020). https://doi.org/10.1088/1757-899X/979/1/012014
18. Pedersen, J.B., Andersen, S., Majgaard, G.: Design of trigonometry apps for vocational education. In: IASTED International Conference. HCI (2012). https://doi.org/10.2316/P.2012. 772-020
19. Unity Technologies, Unity. https://unity.com/. Accessed 19 Jan 2022
20. Unity Technologies, Multiplatform. https://unity.com/features/multiplatform. Accessed 19 Jan 2022
21. Vuforia Engine. https://developer.vuforia.com/. Accessed 19 Jan 2022
22. Vuforia Developer Library, Best Practices for Designing and Developing Image-Based Targets. https://library.vuforia.com/features/images/image-targets/best-practices-for-designing-and-developing-image-based-targets.html. Accessed 13 Jan 2022
23. Vuforia Developer Library, Vuforia Target Manager. https://library.vuforia.com/articles/Tra ining/Getting-Started-with-the-Vuforia-Target-Manager.html. Accessed 19 Feb 2022

An Extended Reality Simulator for Advanced Trauma Life Support Training

Nikitha Donekal Chandrashekar[1], Mark Manuel[1], Juwon Park[1],
Alicia Greene[2], Shawn Safford[2], and Denis Gračanin[1(✉)]

1 Virginia Tech, Blacksburg, VA 24060, USA
{nikitha,mmark95,juwon8,gracanin}@vt.edu
2 Penn State Health, Hershey, PA 17033, USA
{agreene6,ssafford1}@pennstatehealth.psu.edu

Abstract. We describe the design and development of an Extended Reality Advanced Trauma Life Support (ATLS) simulator that incorporates several ATLS scenarios. ATLS is a training program developed by the American College of Surgeons for teaching medical practitioners a systematic approach to treating trauma patients. The ATLS simulator is based on case-level data, which helps create reusable medical training scenarios. The simulation consists of three components, namely, incident history, initial assessment and resuscitation, and a secondary survey. It provides several scenarios for medical practitioners to perform the tasks from the ATLS checklist and practice diagnosing patients. The simulator can also predict the requirement of an ICU room, ventilator and the length of stay for a given trauma patient based on the type and severity of their injury. With our ATLS simulator we aim to provide medical practitioners a comprehensive training module for practicing emergency trauma response.

Keywords: Extended Reality · Medical simulation · Education and training · Machine Learning

1 Introduction

Extended Reality (XR) is an umbrella term used to describe immersive technologies that merge physical and virtual worlds. It comprises the entire spectrum of augmented reality (AR), virtual reality (VR), and mixed reality (MR). The recent advances in XR technologies and head-mounted display devices have resulted in several new educational, collaborative, and gaming applications. Medical training, however, is increasingly complex and imposes financial, ethical, and supervisory constraints. Digitizing training helps medical trainees with evidence-based solutions to enhance their skills and supplement the traditional curriculum.

In the ATLS simulator, the trainee is immersed in an XR environment and asked to correctly diagnose a virtual patient following the ATLS guidelines

© Springer Nature Switzerland AG 2022
J. Y. C. Chen and G. Fragomeni (Eds.): HCII 2022, LNCS 13318, pp. 31–44, 2022.
https://doi.org/10.1007/978-3-031-06015-1_3

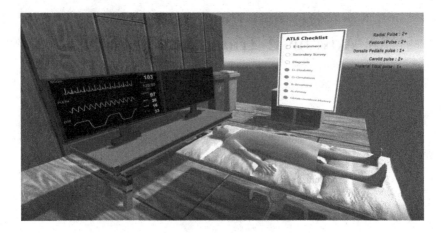

Fig. 1. Trauma room scene.

(Fig. 1). At the start of the simulation, the trainee is provided with a brief about the Mechanism, Injury patterns, Signs, and Preliminary Treatment (MIST) of the patient. The trainee then performs the Airway, Breathing, Circulation, Disabilities, and Exposure (ABCDE) steps of the ATLS procedure as listed on the checklist in the scene.

Sudden interruptions and stressful situations could lead to failure in following the ATLS guidelines. Therefore, we created a checklist in our XR simulator to facilitate adherence to the ATLS guidelines. The ATLS checklist in the XR simulator provides visual feedback about the trainee's progress in the scene and helps to ensure that all the ATLS steps are performed in the correct sequence. The steps in the simulation require the trainee to attach additional devices, like a pulse oximeter or a blood pressure cuff, for receiving and monitoring the patient's vitals. After completing a thorough examination of the patient, the trainee diagnoses them and makes appropriate arrangements for transferring them to Definitive Care. The MIST information of the patient and the outcomes of the ABCDE steps vary in each scenario, providing the trainee with several trauma cases to diagnose.

Artificial Intelligence (AI) and Machine Learning (ML) methods have been used to improve the interactions of XR users and evaluate their performance in training modules. The ATLS simulator includes a resource prediction model that supplements trainee medical diagnosis and can help manage hospital resources. The predictor model uses a random forest algorithm to predict the requirement of hospital resources like ventilators, ICU rooms and hospital beds for a trauma patient with a given set of injuries and vitals data.

We used the Pennsylvania State Trauma Registry as our dataset for training [2]. The trauma registry was created by the Pennsylvania Health Department to collect information about injured patients from all accredited trauma centers and to develop a mechanism to review the quality of care provided by the state's trauma system. The Pennsylvania Trauma Outcome Study (PTOS) registry has entries of more than one million trauma patients, including the demographic data, pre-hospital data, the process of acute care, clinical data, and outcomes data of the patient. Along with the advantages of creating reusable scenarios for medical training, our ATLS simulator with AI assistance will help medical trainees provide patients with more data-driven and personalized healthcare treatment.

2   Related Work

The advantages of using XR in healthcare training is immense and includes reduced training cost and repeatable standardized practice scenarios. These simulators typically have a one-time development and equipment cost, followed by minimal runtime cost per session [9]. Zweifach et al. discuss the needs and benefits of realistic XR simulation methods over the traditional training opportunities with real patients [33]. In their work, they also describe a framework to help medical schools adopt the mixed reality tools into their school's anatomy and procedural curricula. De et al. observed that the majority of students who attended online training sessions were satisfied with their virtual, interruption-free medical training experience and gave positive feedback to the perceived quality [8]. This suggests that virtual training modules can be successfully developed to enhance vocational training.

The examples of simulators for healthcare training include an ultrasound-guided vascular access simulator [4], a cardiac simulator [12], an orthopedic surgical training simulator [5] and ophthalmoscopy simulators [23] that help medical students improve their diagnostic skills and offer superior clinical findings. Sheik-Ali et al. investigated the role of these devices in the acquisition of technical skills during surgical education. They observed a positive correlation between the usage of XR in surgical education and improvement in procedural accuracy, hand-eye coordination, and the surgeon's ability to multitask [24]. Harrington et al. demonstrated validity criteria for a VR-based medical training simulator. Their simulator was successfully tested for its ability to distinguish decision-making skills between the different levels of expertise [16]. Handosa et al. similarly developed a mixed reality training program for CNA students [15]. These simulators indicate the feasibility of using XR for practical medical training.

2.1   Intelligent XR Simulators

AI and XR are two prominent and growing fields of Computer Science with different focus areas and applications. However, these two fields can be synergistically combined to create advanced training modules for various disciplines. Studies have been conducted to understand and investigate the AI-XR continuum applications, including training AI, conferring intelligence to XR, and interpreting XR-generated data [7,22].

ML models have recently been seeing increased use in supporting medical diagnoses. Stanney et al. observe that XR simulators driven by AI offer a unique opportunity to decrease time to proficiency and extend trainee retention significantly [26]. ML models can be used to predict hospital admission from patient medical history and triage data [17]. Patient mortality, hospital stay duration, and readmission likelihood can also be predicted using patient information at admission [6,18,29].

Adding Natural Language Processing (NLP) and ML helps improve XR experiences. For example, Talbot et al. created an AI Dialogue system to integrate XR models with the ability to understand human speech and hold a conversation. Such ML models are trained on large datasets consisting of patient hospital data [28]. In addition to this, ML models can be trained to teach XR simulators to make decisions by identifying patterns and analyzing historical data. In this paper, we present an approach to using ML algorithms to augment medical trainee diagnosis in an XR ATLS simulator. Hospital data from the Penn State trauma unit was used as the training data.

2.2 Advanced Trauma Life Support

Patients with trauma injuries are not easy to manage and can cause anxiety even for expert clinicians. The ATLS course was developed to solve this issue. All trauma surgeons and ED physicians working at trauma centers are reuired to complete this course. Several studies show the importance of the ATLS courses in emergency rooms. Williams et al. reviewed the value of ATLS training for medical staff in a major incident situation [32]. 13 simulated casualties were treated by eight doctors with different experience levels. Williams et al. awarded scores to these doctors based on whether they took the critical treatment criteria into account while making their diagnoses. Their research shows that medical staff who had undertaken ATLS training scored higher than those who had not. Wang et al. compared the severe trauma care effect before and after the ATLS training [31]. From their experiment, they observed that the mortality of the patients in the emergency department decreased significantly post-ATLS training.

Trauma-related injuries are extremely common. They are a leading cause of death in children and adults below 45 years. Severely injured patients are resuscitated by a trauma team, who perform a predefined set of tasks in a sequence determined by the ATLS. Stressful situations can make it difficult to correctly follow through with the ATLS protocol. In order to address this issue, a checklist was created to help medical practitioners adhere to ATLS guidelines. Maarseveen et al. reviewed the effects of applying a checklist during the resuscitation process of trauma patients [30]. They observed that the average adjusted time to task completion was 9 s faster with the application of a checklist.

Several studies have been conducted to evaluate the effects of a checklist during trauma resuscitation. Smith et al. developed a standardized pre-procedural checklist to assist clinicians in ensuring adequate preparation for intubation [25]. They also studied its effectiveness for reducing intubation-related complications in emergency department (ED) trauma patients. For this study, 141 patients were considered, including 76 patients in the pre checklist period and 65 in the post checklist period. A 7.7% absolute risk reduction of intubation-related complications was observed from the pre checklist period to the post checklist period. There was only a 12 s decrease in the time associated with the process of intubation, which may not directly result in the improvement of patient outcomes.

3   Problem Definition

The ongoing pandemic has also reinforced the importance of healthcare training and education. Typically, training is conducted by having actors enact certain conditions that medical trainees need to diagnose. Physically recreating each reuired training scenario with actors and equipment can cost institutions around $63,000 per trainee [1]. This expense can be brought down significantly with XR-based training modules.

The medical field demands accurate and precise procedures to be performed by doctors, with no room for error. Traditional training methods involve the trainer demonstrating the technique and the student repeating it, which increases the risk of medical errors [21]. The memory recall, ease of use, and novel learning modality offered by immersive environments benefit the using XR technologies in medical education. XR also provides risk-free, immersive, reproducible environments that help improve physicians' performances for various surgical and medical tasks.

The majority of the existing simulators are in VR. VR being fully-immersive leads to a phenomenon called VR sickness. In VR sickness, the users often forget where they actually experience a visually induced perception of self-motion that leads to disorientation, discomfort, headache, and nausea [10].

Lastly, having the ability to place the user within an augmented world, with the option to interact with both physical and digital objects simultaneously, has many advantages. The inclusion of MR will also make it possible for physicians and educators to incorporate real-world medical instruments into training modules. Using tools like Vuforia [11], or Microsoft's Mixed Reality Toolkit [20], physical objects can be detected in MR applications and made to interact with virtual content. This will provide realistic training environments for new medical trainees to practice the ATLS curriculum.

4   Proposed Approach

In this section, we present an XR ATLS training simulator that is developed in conjunction with Penn State Health. Our goal is to create reusable training modules for medical students to practice trauma diagnosis. These modules can be designed to simulate several different trauma scenarios, including accidental injury, poisoning, drowning, and burn injuries. These scenarios can be used not only for training but also for evaluating medical student performance as part of their educational curriculum.

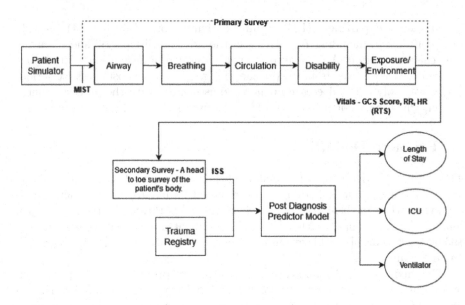

Fig. 2. System flow diagram

4.1 ATLS Scenario

Our ATLS simulator was developed for the Microsoft HoloLens 2 using the Unity Game Engine. ATLS protocol dictates that students perform a medical evaluation of trauma patients in a specific sequence, scanning for injuries in areas of importance first and then proceeding to lower priority areas. The ATLS procedure consists of two assessments, a primary survey and a secondary survey (Fig. 2). The primary survey is the most important part of assessing a trauma patient where life-threatening injuries are identified and resuscitation steps are taken. After completing this survey, patient vitals are recorded, and a secondary survey is conducted. The secondary survey is a head-to-toe examination of the trauma patient, including a complete physical inspection and reassessment of all vital signs.

We created a practice scenario involving a young male patient injured in an automobile accident. The patient is rolled into the trauma bay, and the trainee student (HoloLens 2 user) is provided with the MIST (Mechanism, Injury, Signs, Treatment) information. This information is provided in audio format to the user and varies with each trauma scenario. After receiving background MIST information about the patient, the medical student performs the ATLS procedure. A checklist is provided to the student to help them identify the correct sequence of actions to perform.

Primary Survey: The primary survey comprises of 5 ABCDE steps namely Airway, Breathing, Circulation, Disability and Exposure:

1. **Airway**: The first step of the primary survey is to assess the airway. If the patient is able to state their name clearly, the airway is considered to be patent.
2. **Breathing**: In the second step, the chest of the trauma patient must be examined by inspection, palpation, percussion and auscultation.
3. **Circulation**: In the next step, the trainee connects the cardiac monitor and pulse oximeter to the patient. The goal of this step is to identify all possibilities of hemorrhage, as it the predominant cause of preventable trauma-related deaths. After connecting the devices, the trainee notes the vitals of the patient which includes Blood Pressure (BP), heart rate (HR), respiration rate (RR) and oxygen saturation (SpO2).
4. **Disability**: In this step, the patient's level of consciousness is assessed by using the Glasgow coma scale (GCS), pupil size and reaction, and lateralizing signs.
5. **Exposure**: The last step of the primary survey is to ensure that no physical injuries were missed. Body temperature and critical skin conditions must be examined.

The checklist contains all the steps of the ATLS guidelines in sequential order. Each step of the primary survey is marked completed on the checklist after successfully executing the tasks involved.

Secondary Survey: A secondary survey is performed once the patient has been resuscitated and stabilized. After the primary survey, the patient is examined head-to-toe to identify significant but not immediately life-threatening injuries. The purpose of the secondary survey is to evaluate and treat injuries not found during the primary survey. It helps prioritize continued evaluation and management. In our ATLS simulator, the medical trainee examines the head, neck, chest, abdomen, and musculoskeletal system of the patient. Additionally, radiographs might be requested depending on the observed injuries.

4.2   Hospital Resource Management

Currently, in the COVID-19 pandemic, hospital resources like ICU rooms, ventilators, and hospital beds are severely strained. Increased patient volumes make the allocation of these resources a grave problem. This has direct consequences on hospital costs and patient satisfaction. To address this issue, we developed a NLP-based ML model for predicting the requirements of ICU rooms, ventilators, and patient length of stay based on the MIST information of the patient and diagnosis made by the trainee.

For training the model, we considered the Pennsylvania State Trauma Registry. The registry contains records of all trauma patients from January 2018 to July 2021 reported at the trauma centers in Pennsylvania. A random forest algorithm was used to make predictions as it is simple to implement, fast in operation, and has proven to be successful in various domains (Fig. 3).

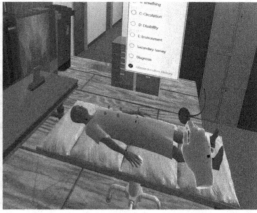

Fig. 3. Left: Participant wearing HoloLens 2. Right: Participant's point of view.

The input parameters for training the model include:

1. **MIST information:** Standard NLP preprocessing techniques like removing stop words, lower casing, tokenization were applied to the MIST text to prepare the text data for the model building. The top 200 keywords from the entire corpus were selected using the TF-IDF (Term Frequency - Inverse Document Frequency) score.
2. **Injury type:** An integer value ranging from 1 to 4. The values represent the different categories of injury, namely: blunt, penetrating, burn, and skin disease. It helps medical practitioners identify the type of force applied to the body.
3. **Revised Trauma Score (RTS):** A physiological score ranging from 1 to 12 based on the GCS Score, Blood Pressure, Respiratory Rate of a trauma patient as recorded during the primary survey [14]. A patient with an RTS score of 12 is labeled delayed, 11 urgent, 3–10 immediate, and a score below 3 is declared dead.
4. **Injury Severity Score (ISS):** A medical score ranging from 3 to 75 that helps assess trauma severity [27]. It is based on the Abbreviated Injury Scale (AIS) severity code of the three most severely injured ISS body regions. It correlates with mortality, morbidity, and hospitalization time after trauma.

To predict the patient's length of stay, a KNN model was trained on the above-mentioned input parameters of the PTOS registry. The model identifies the 5 nearest cases (neighbors) to the test case and uses them to predict the length of the stay. After successfully completing the secondary survey, the model predicts the requirement of an ICU room, ventilator for the trauma patient and the length of stay of the patient. This prediction is based on the MIST information and the evaluation of the medical trainee.

4.3   Study Procedure

We conducted a pilot study with five participants to test our XR ATLS simulator. All participants were familiar with XR technology and Human-Computer Interaction concepts. Participants performed the ABCDE steps of the ATLS with minimal assistance.

For the pilot study, a situation was given, and participants followed the checklist to complete the simulation. At the start of the pilot study, the simulator states the background MIST information about the patient. Participants were asked to probe the patient's airway by having them state their name. Next, participants were asked to examine the patient's breathing sounds. Breathing sounds were heard using a virtual stethoscope. Blue bubbles were used to indicate locations where participants were required to measure breathing.

Following this, participants noted the patient's HR and pulse vitals from the cardiac monitor. They assessed the radial, femoral, posterior, tibial and dorsalis pedis pulses of the patient bilaterally. Pulse reading locations were indicated using yellow bubbles.

Next, in the Disability step, participants determined the patient's consciousness level and assessed the patient's motor control. This was done by making the patient blink their eyes, wiggle their toes, and state their current location.

The last step of the ATLS simulator involved examining the patient and ensuring that no physical injuries were missed during the previous stages. Participants assessed the right leg of the patient and observed deformity in the lower right leg. They also noted that no open wound was present. Participants asked for x-rays of the right knee, leg, and ankle, following which they applied a splint and requested an orthopedic consult.

5   Results

After completing the pilot study, the participants were asked to fill out a System Usability Scale (SUS) Questionnaire. The SUS was developed by John Brooke in 1986 [3]. It is a popular tool for evaluating the usability of software, websites and applications. It consists of a 10-item questionnaire. Each question is multiple choice with five answer choices ranging from "Strongly Agree" to "Strongly Disagree". Odd numbered questions corresponded to "positive affect" questions, while even numbered questions corresponded to "negative affect" questions. Participants were asked to respond to these ten questions based on their experience with the ATLS simulator. An additional free response question was also included in the questionnaire for participants to provide feedback.

5.1   SUS Results

All ten question item responses were assigned raw numeric values, with 1 = "Strongly Disagree" and 5 = "Strongly Agree". These raw scores were converted to weighted scores based on their effect. The weighted scores range from 0 to 4.

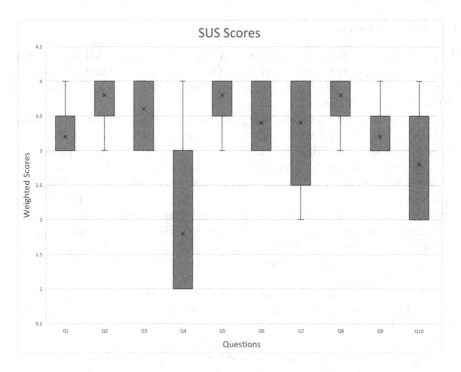

Fig. 4. Pilot study SUS scores

Each participant's weighted score was added, and the total was multiplied by 2.5 to get a composite score out of 100. A score of over 68 is considered to indicate good usability [19]. The average SUS score we observed through our pilot study was 82. It indicates that the participants considered our ATLS simulator to have high usability. The SUS scores for all 5 participants can be seen in Fig. 4.

Limitations of the ATLS Simulator: Our pilot study also highlighted certain limitations of the ATLS simulator that we need to improve on in future iterations. Two of these limitations can be observed in the SUS scores graph (Fig. 4). The score for Question 4 is significantly lower than the scores. This question corresponds to the "I think that I would need the support of a technical person to use this system." prompt of the SUS questionnaire. We believe that participants gave low scores in response to this prompt because of their inexperience with real-world ATLS scenarios and unfamiliarity with the ATLS protocol.

The second lowest score was given in response to the "I needed to learn a lot of things before I could get going with this system" prompt (Question 10). This could also be attributed to the participant's lack of experience with ATLS terminology. Testing our ATLS simulator with actual medical practitioners would help us re-evaluate these two usability scores.

During the study, a participant found it difficult to pick the virtual stethoscope using the default hand-interaction technique (select-and-drag). The participant also commented that the voice commands used in our ATLS simulator were too specific and could be improved further.

5.2 Model Prediction Results

The models predict three hospital resource values. Two of the predicted values (ICU bed requirement and ventilator requirement) are binary, and one value (the length of stay of the patient in days) is numeric. We use Accuracy and F1 scores as metrics to evaluate the binary predictions. To evaluate the predictions for the numeric values of the model, we use Mean Absolute Percentage Error (MAPE). The dataset was split in the following manner: 70% of the data was used for training, and 30% of the data was used to test the random forest model. The metrics used to evaluate the classification problem were accuracy and F1 score. The F1-score combines the precision and recall of the classifier into a single metric by taking their harmonic mean. We performed a 5-fold evaluation of the trained models and observed the following results (Table 1):

Table 1. ML model prediction results.

Patient requirement	Accuracy	F1 score
ICU	0.907	0.790
Ventilator	0.974	0.915

Similarly, to predict the length of stay of the patient, a KNN model was trained on the same input parameters of the dataset. The patient's length of stay varies from 0 days to 365 days. The model was evaluated using the MAPE metric. MAPE is the average percentage error and measures how accurate a forecast system is.

$$MAPE = \frac{1}{n} * \sum_{t=1}^{n} |\frac{PredictedValue - ActualValue}{ActualValue}|$$

A prediction model with MAPE value between 10% to 20% is considered good, and this varies with the type of industry and application. [13] The average MAPE value calculated over 5-fold cross-validation of the model is 0.129, which implies that the average difference between the predicted value and the actual value is 12.9%. The percentage error also indicates that the trained model is effective and acceptable.

6 Conclusion

Medical training is expensive and laborious to set up. To address this problem, we developed an XR medical training application for ATLS. In addition to this, we also used ML models to predict the requirement of hospital resources by incoming trauma patients.

We conducted a pilot study with five participants to evaluate our ATLS simulator. The System Usability Scale was used to evaluate the usability of our simulator application. We observed an average SUS score of 82, indicating that most of our participants found the XR ATLS simulator easy to use. However, additional improvements to the user interface and interaction modes can help further increase the usability of our ATLS simulator.

Our future work will include making the simulator more realistic by incorporating real-world objects in it and conducting a more comprehensive user study with healthcare professionals. Lastly, we also plan to add haptic feedback to enhance the realism of the ATLS simulator.

References

1. The cost of medical VR training. https://axonpark.com/the-cost-of-medical-vr-training/. Accessed 11 Nov 2021
2. Trauma registry resources (2022). https://www.ptsf.org/trauma-registry/trauma-registry-resources. Accessed 11 Jan 2022
3. Brooke, J., et al.: SUS–a quick and dirty usability scale. Usability Eval. Ind. **189**(194), 4–7 (1996)
4. de Carvalho Fürst, R.V., Polimanti, A.C., Galego, S.J., Bicudo, M.C., Montagna, E., Corrêa, J.A.: Ultrasound-guided vascular access simulator for medical training: proposal of a simple, economic and effective model. World J. Surg. **41**(3), 681–686 (2017)
5. Cecil, J., Gupta, A., Pirela-Cruz, M.: An advanced simulator for orthopedic surgical training. Int. J. Comput. Assist. Radiol. Surg. **13**(2), 305–319 (2017). https://doi.org/10.1007/s11548-017-1688-0
6. Daghistani, T.A., Elshawi, R., Sakr, S., Ahmed, A.M., Al-Thwayee, A., Al-Mallah, M.H.: Predictors of in-hospital length of stay among cardiac patients: a machine learning approach. Int. J. Cardiol. **288**, 140–147 (2019)
7. Dasgupta, A., Manuel, M., Mansur, R.S., Nowak, N., Gračanin, D.: Towards real time object recognition for context awareness in mixed reality: a machine learning approach. In: 2020 IEEE Conference on Virtual Reality and 3D User Interfaces Abstracts and Workshops (VRW), pp. 262–268 (2020). https://doi.org/10.1109/VRW50115.2020.00054
8. De Ponti, R., Marazzato, J., Maresca, A.M., Rovera, F., Carcano, G., Ferrario, M.M.: Pre-graduation medical training including virtual reality during COVID-19 pandemic: a report on students' perception. BMC Med. Educ. **20**(1), 1–7 (2020)
9. Farra, S.L., et al.: Comparative cost of virtual reality training and live exercises for training hospital workers for evacuation. Comput. Inform. Nurs. CIN **37**(9), 446 (2019)
10. Farshid, M., Paschen, J., Eriksson, T., Kietzmann, J.: Go boldly!: explore augmented reality, virtual reality, and mixed reality for business. Bus. Horiz. **61**(5), 657–663 (2018)
11. Frantz, T., Jansen, B., Duerinck, J., Vandemeulebroucke, J.: Augmenting Microsoft's HoloLens with Vuforia tracking for neuronavigation. Healthc. Technol. Lett. **5**(5), 221–225 (2018)

12. Gauthier, N., et al.: Does cardiac physical exam teaching using a cardiac simulator improve medical students' diagnostic skills? Cureus **11**(5) (2019)
13. Gilliland, M.: The Business Forecasting Deal: Exposing Myths, Eliminating Bad Practices, Providing Practical Solutions. Wiley, Hoboken (2010)
14. Gilpin, D., Nelson, P.: Revised trauma score: a triage tool in the accident and emergency department. Injury **22**(1), 35–37 (1991)
15. Handosa, M., Schulze, H., Gračanin, D., Tucker, M., Manuel, M.: Extending embodied interactions in mixed reality environments. In: Chen, J.Y.C., Fragomeni, G. (eds.) VAMR 2018. LNCS, vol. 10909, pp. 314–327. Springer, Cham (2018). https://doi.org/10.1007/978-3-319-91581-4_23
16. Harrington, C.M., et al.: Development and evaluation of a trauma decision-making simulator in oculus virtual reality. Am. J. Surg. **215**(1), 42–47 (2018)
17. Hong, W.S., Haimovich, A.D., Taylor, R.A.: Predicting hospital admission at emergency department triage using machine learning. PLoS ONE **13**(7), e0201016 (2018)
18. Hosseinzadeh, A., Izadi, M., Verma, A., Precup, D., Buckeridge, D.: Assessing the predictability of hospital readmission using machine learning. In: Twenty-Fifth IAAI Conference (2013)
19. MeasuringU: Measuring usability with the system usability scale (SUS) (2011). https://measuringu.com/sus. Accessed 10 Jan 2022
20. Microsoft: What is the mixed reality toolkit (2021). https://docs.microsoft.com/en-us/windows/mixed-reality/mrtk-unity/?view=mrtkunity-2021-05. Accessed 14 Jan 2022
21. Patel, D., Hawkins, J., et al.: Developing virtual reality trauma training experiences using 360-degree video: tutorial. J. Med. Internet Res. **22**(12), e22420 (2020)
22. Reiners, D., Davahli, M.R., Karwowski, W., Cruz-Neira, C.: The combination of artificial intelligence and extended reality: a systematic review. Front. Virtual Reality 114 (2021)
23. Ricci, L.H., Ferraz, C.A.: Ophthalmoscopy simulation: advances in training and practice for medical students and young ophthalmologists. Adv. Med. Educ. Pract. **8**, 435 (2017)
24. Sheik-Ali, S., Edgcombe, H., Paton, C.: Next-generation virtual and augmented reality in surgical education: a narrative review. Surg. Technol. Int. **33** (2019)
25. Smith, K.A., High, K., Collins, S.P., Self, W.H.: A preprocedural checklist improves the safety of emergency department intubation of trauma patients. Acad. Emerg. Med. **22**(8), 989–992 (2015)
26. Stanney, K.M., et al.: Performance gains from adaptive extended reality training fueled by artificial intelligence. J. Def. Model. Simul. 15485129211064809 (2021)
27. Stevenson, M., Segui-Gomez, M., Lescohier, I., Di Scala, C., McDonald-Smith, G.: An overview of the injury severity score and the new injury severity score. Inj. Prev. **7**(1), 10–13 (2001)
28. Talbot, T.B., Sagae, K., John, B., Rizzo, A.A.: Sorting out the virtual patient: how to exploit artificial intelligence, game technology and sound educational practices to create engaging role-playing simulations. Int. J. Gaming Comput.-Mediated Simul. (IJGCMS) **4**(3), 1–19 (2012)
29. Taylor, R.A., et al.: Prediction of in-hospital mortality in emergency department patients with sepsis: a local big data-driven, machine learning approach. Acad. Emerg. Med. **23**(3), 269–278 (2016)

30. Van Maarseveen, O.E., Ham, W.H., Van de Ven, N.L., Saris, T.F., Leenen, L.P.: Effects of the application of a checklist during trauma resuscitations on ATLS adherence, team performance, and patient-related outcomes: a systematic review. Eur. J. Trauma Emerg. Surg. **46**(1), 65–72 (2020)
31. Wang, P., et al.: Comparison of severe trauma care effect before and after advanced trauma life support training. Chin. J. Traumatol. **13**(6), 341–344 (2010). www.scopus.com
32. Williams, M., Lockey, A., Culshaw, M.: Improved trauma management with advanced trauma life support (ATLS) training. J. Accid. Emerg. Med. **14**(2), 81–83 (1997). https://doi.org/10.1136/emj.14.2.81. https://europepmc.org/articles/PMC1342874
33. Zweifach, S.M., Triola, M.M.: Extended reality in medical education: driving adoption through provider-centered design. Digit. Biomark. **3**(1), 14–21 (2019)

Virtual Access to STEM Careers: Two Preliminary Investigations

Elham Ebrahimi[✉], Brittany Morago, James Stocker, Amelia Moody,
Amy Taylor, Toni Pence, Matthew Jarrett, and Blake Blackport

University of North Carolina Wilmington, Wilmington, NC 28403, USA
{ebrahimie,moragob,stockerj,moodym,taylorm,pencet,mdj7111,
bab1228}@uncw.edu

Abstract. Virtual Access to STEM Careers (VASC) is a technology-rich, inquiry and problem-based curriculum designed to expose and stimulate student interest in marine, environmental, computer, and geological sciences. Intended for 3rd through 5th grade students, VASC builds academic momentum at the intermediate level to prepare students for STEM opportunities later in middle school and high school. Our program is aligned with "Next Generation Science Standards" and "Common Core State Standards" and immerses students in rigorous, high-interest learning modules where students are introduced to and take on the roles of different STEM occupations. We are specifically developing and testing virtual reality-based modules that place students in a coastal environment where they learn about the sea turtle life-cycle. Students also practice the types of measurements and conservation tasks that park rangers and marine scientists regularly perform. The investigations focused on the design of a user interface that meets the needs of students and their teachers. We collected feedback on user interface design and knowledge gained by the users from the simulation. Additionally, we compared two different virtual reality head-mounted displays; i) HTC Vive and ii) Oculus Quest 2, to identify the pros and cons of each technology in future classroom settings. Our investigations yielded valuable information about how instructions should be presented to users, how the interface should provide immediate feedback for user error, how surveys should be administered, what equipment is most efficient for transporting and setting up large scale experiments in schools, and what types of interactions students and teachers want to experience in VASC.

Keywords: Virtual reality · HCI · Usability testing · K-12 STEM education

1 Introduction

Consider the value of elementary school students being able to take on the roles and responsibilities of STEM occupations by completing authentic, problem-

Supported by NSF Award #1850430.

J. Y. C. Chen and G. Fragomeni (Eds.): HCII 2022, LNCS 13318, pp. 45–58, 2022.
https://doi.org/10.1007/978-3-031-06015-1_4

based collaborative tasks set in immersive 3-D environments - all within a traditional classroom. The Virtual Access to STEM Careers (VASC) project does this by synthesizing cutting-edge virtual technologies and problem-based learning instructional practices to develop an innovative curriculum that: (1) removes traditional barriers (e.g., lack of school resources; geographic distance; poverty; disability) that prevent under-served students from participating in authentic STEM learning opportunities; (2) sparks interest in pursuing a STEM career in marine, environmental, geological, and computer sciences; (3) embeds effective gamification and reward systems to increase and maintain motivation and focus; (4) ensures students have the academic foundation to transition to STEM coursework at the middle school level; and (5) provides educators with tools and professional development to effectively implement this innovative method of instruction. To achieve the aforementioned goals, we have created several virtual reality environments that introduce the sea turtle life cycle to students. Through these virtual environments, students learn about different activities that park rangers and marine scientists regularly perform in real life. Figure 1 shows an example of one such activity students can take part in with VASC.

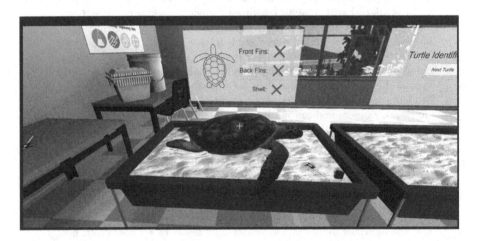

Fig. 1. Measuring Sea Turtle Exercise within VASC. Students practice using a tape measure and calipers while taking measurements of a sea turtle. Progress panel above turtle tells students what measurements they still need to complete.

Although virtual technologies are becoming more commonplace in formal and informal learning environments, there is still a paucity of research on how to effectively synthesize virtual technologies and problem based learning in STEM curriculum [20]. Challenges posed in the literature include transferring and expanding knowledge and skills aligned to standards learned in the classroom to virtual worlds. It is also a challenge to strategically sequence virtual learning experiences that increase and maintain student engagement and motivation. Synthesizing virtual activities and STEM curriculum that yield meaningful observable and measurable outcomes can also be a challenge. Finally, the lack of educator training to effectively utilize virtual technologies in formal and informal learning environments can be an obstacle. In efforts to address some of these challenges, VASC focuses on the following research questions: (1) What learning experiences involving emerging technologies effectively enable diverse populations of students to gain familiarity and relevant competencies with these technologies, (2) What factors influence the outcomes of the learning experiences?, and (3) Does the type of hardware alter the accessibility, learning outcome, and effectiveness of learning through virtual environments?

Our research team completed an initial round of development in which we built a virtual environment for learning about different types of sea turtles featuring tasks such as measuring turtles, counting eggs, and relocating nests. Our environment includes an indoor classroom (i.e., training environment) with sand tables for students to become acquainted with virtual reality interactions and movements as well as learn the fundamental tools and skill sets applied by scientists and park rangers. This iteration of VASC also includes an outdoor beach scene in which students can explore the actual environment sea turtles inhabit and where STEM professionals do their work in the field. Future iterations will have the students transfer skill sets learned in the indoor classroom to "grand challenges" that occur in the outdoor beach scene. Examples of the scenes and tasks that make up VASC are shown in Figs. 1 and 2. Having completed development for the indoor classroom, we invited students and teachers to test out our system in two separate investigations using two different types of hardware. The investigations gathered information about how quickly and easily the participants adapt to the immersive virtual environment, evaluate the type of instructions necessary for guiding users through the system, and document the overall impressions of students and teachers using the technology. The results will inform our next round of development related to the selection of equipment, methods of interaction, delivering immediate feedback at different points of the simulation, and creating new surveys.

1.1 Paper Organization

The remainder of this paper is organized as follows. Section 2 discusses related research in integrating virtual technologies into the classroom, Sect. 3 details the design of our investigations including hardware used, participant demographics, and administered surveys. Sections 4 and 5 discuss our formal survey results, general observations of the two investigations, lessons learned for the next stages of development, and conclusion.

Fig. 2. Examples of different activities within VASC. *Left to right, top down:* 1) Measuring a turtle with calipers. 2) Exploring outdoor environment. 3) Identifying turtle species by tracks in sand. 4) Laying cage around eggs on beach.

2   Background

Legislation including the Next Generation Science Standards [7] and Common Core State Standards for Mathematics [15] promote the integration of STEM by offering in depth connections between the STEM domains. STEM is grounded in situated cognition theory which suggests that an individual's knowledge is rooted in the activity, context, and culture in which it was learned [26]. This theory operates under the understanding that how STEM knowledge is applied is as important as how and where the knowledge is applied because the learning is authentic and representative of a real world experience.

As real-world applications continue to gain momentum across K-12 settings, efforts to promote research and practice in STEM education have increased to ameliorate the roadblocks that separate the four disciplines through authentic, Problem-Based Learning [2]. Problem-Based Learning has garnered positive outcomes for students in the areas of collaboration [23], student engagement [1,3], critical thinking, and problem-solving skills [21]. Problem Based Learning can offer students the type of scaffolding that enriches inquiry and increases student motivation [10,30,31]. The integration of technology into Problem Based Learning assists teachers because it can promote independence [17], especially for students with disabilities [6,12] and English Language Learners [11].

Despite growing evidence of effective instructional STEM practices, recent research asserts students become disenfranchised with STEM due to cost, content rigor, time barriers, and lack of access to resources and opportunities [4]. However, proper integration of technologies into the science curriculum has been shown to overcome some of these obstacles [13,14,19,25]. One of the available technologies that has a significant impact on learning, training and education is through Immersive Virtual Environments [8,22,25].

Immersive Virtual Environments synthesized in a Problem-Based Learning framework has the potential to support underserved and underrepresented students in accessing STEM curriculum as well as stimulating interest in pursuing later academic and career opportunities. Within Immersive Virtual Environments, students can visualize abstract concepts and complete related hands-on tasks rather than imagining them [5,16,32]. For example, Trindade et al. [32] utilized virtual environments to explain the atomic and molecular structures and behaviors of water when taking different forms; gas, liquid or solid. After observing *virtual water*, students' conceptual understanding of the aforementioned concepts increased. Students showed the most significant improvements with the tasks that had the highest interactivity. Rousseou et al. [28] created a *virtual playground* for students to address a set of tasks involving arithmetical fraction problems. Their results indicate that the fully interactive virtual environment significantly improved students' problem solving skills. In general, a growing body of research indicates that when students interact and control events in virtual environments, they become more actively involved in constructing knowledge through an immersive experience rather than learning by lecture and reading dense expository text [9,27,28].

Contemporary STEM classrooms offer students problem-based learning opportunities embedded in real world contexts [18,24] versus traditional learning activities [29]. Research suggests STEM programs aim to incorporate more technology, experiential learning opportunities, and student-centered projects [29]. Through the problem-based learning process, students develop a line of inquiry, collaborate with peers, and research relevant topics to design solutions to problems. For instance, within the VASC Curriculum there is a focus on why a turtle nest requires emergency relocation (e.g., predators, high tide). Then when confronted with the pressing issue of relocation, students develop an action plan using the problem-based learning approach. After developing the action plan, the students practice discrete skills in cooperative learning activities that prepare and mimic the activities that will occur in immersive virtual environments. The activities occurring in the immersive virtual environments reflect the actual practices of STEM professionals operating in the field. Given the novelty of implementing immersive technologies in variety of classroom settings and may include 20–25 students, teachers need a streamlined process where they can independently facilitate learning activities efficiently and effectively. Incongruity between technology, curriculum, and the learning environment can lead to issues with fidelity of implementation, social validity, and teachers abandoning the project.

3   Experimental Design

To test the current state and usability of VASC, we ran two investigations using different HMD's. Different groups of students and teachers were invited to participate in both investigations. The research team used both pre- and post-surveys and structured observation to collect data. The first investigation was deployed on the HTC Vive at a local school and the second on the Oculus Quest 2 in a university research lab. Figure 3 shows participants interacting with VASC during each investigation. While the physical locations and type of HMD changed between investigations, participants saw and experienced the exact same virtual environment and were asked to complete the same pre- and post-surveys.

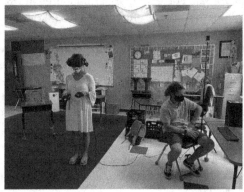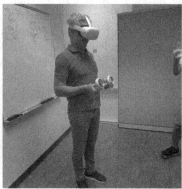

Fig. 3. Participants testing VASC on the HTC Vive (left) and the Oculus Quest 2 (right).

3.1   Equipment Used

The following list of equipment was set-up and used during the first investigation:

- 2× HTC Vive Headsets
- 4× Towers/Sensors for the Vive
- 2× Desktops capable of running the project
- 2× monitors for the computer
- cables and peripherals for the computers

This hardware was packed up, loaded into a vehicle, hauled to a local school, and set-up in the classroom on the day of the investigation. Our team had to determine on the day how best to set-up this equipment in the classroom to make sure each testing station had enough room.

For the second investigation our equipment list was simply an Oculus Quest 2 and a computer for users to complete the pre- and post-surveys.

3.2   Demographics

There were 10 participants in the first investigation. All participants were either students in the target grade range or were teachers working in or near the target grade range for VASC:

- 2 students - each in grade 4
- 8 teachers - 1 in kindergarten and 7 in grades 2–5

There were 8 participants in the second investigation. While the students and educators in this group were mainly outside of VASC's target grade range, their feedback still offers extra perspectives to consider:

- 2 students - 1 in grade 5 and 1 in grade 10
- 6 teachers - 2 elementary school teachers (1 in special education) and 4 university professors

The sample size and demographics of each investigation reflects the logistical limitations presented from **Covid-19** *protocols involved in IRB approval and state mandates.*

3.3 Survey Design

We administered surveys at the beginning and end of each investigation. The purpose of the pre-survey was to gather participants' demographic information and background with gaming and virtual reality. The post-surveys were designed to gauge how comfortable participants had been understanding given directions, navigating the system, performing tasks, and what they would like to see added or improved. We have designed one set of surveys for students and another for teachers. All surveys were created and administered using Qualtrics, an experience management software.

Survey for Students. The goal of the student survey is to solicit feedback from the students' perspective, as they will be the primary users of the simulation. Since VASC is designed for students between 3rd and 5th grades, the survey was kept simple with the two following sections:

- *Demographics* - basic demographic and video game familiarity questions
- *User Experience* - questions on user's enjoyment, immersion, and understanding of the simulation

Questions on the student survey are presented in different formats, including written and pictorial questions, examples of which are shown in Fig. 4. The goal is to keep these surveys short overall and for questions to be easy to understand and answer for all elementary age students.

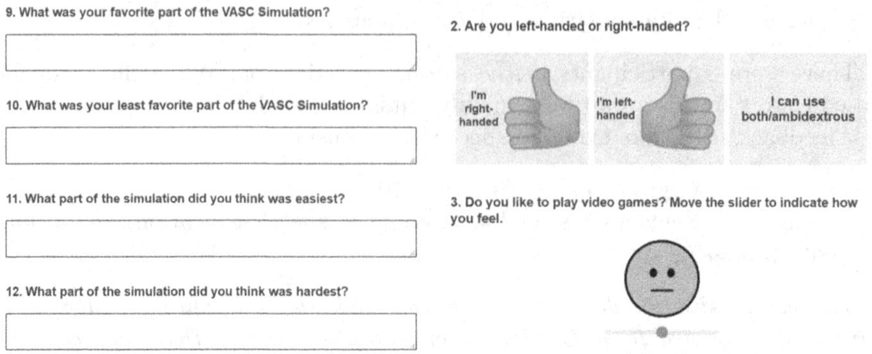

9. What was your favorite part of the VASC Simulation?

2. Are you left-handed or right-handed?

10. What was your least favorite part of the VASC Simulation?

I'm right-handed   I'm left-handed   I can use both/ambidextrous

11. What part of the simulation did you think was easiest?

3. Do you like to play video games? Move the slider to indicate how you feel.

12. What part of the simulation did you think was hardest?

Fig. 4. Examples of formats used for written (left) and pictorial (right) questions on student survey.

Survey for Teachers. The goal of the teacher survey is to solicit feedback on the functionality and usability of the simulation. It is important to our design process that teachers easily understand the VASC system so that they can seamlessly use it in their classrooms. We also need to ensure that the system is compatible to content learned "in-person" and is accessible to the diverse needs of learners. The pre-survey had the following two sections:

- *Demographics* - general demographic information and user's familiarity and comfort level with video games
- *Technology Acceptance* - user's general familiarity with and how closely they follow emerging technology

   The post-survey had the following three sections:

- *User Experience* - user's experience and feedback on the content and functionality of the simulation
- *Slater-Usoh-Steed Questionnaire* - user's sense of immersion in the simulation
- *NASA-TLX* - questions on the simulation's difficulty

We administered the teacher survey to all participants in our two investigations, including the students as all participants experienced the exact same simulation. Eventually teachers and students will use different simulations that are more targeted toward their roles in the classroom and the different surveys will take this into account. The time taken and difficulties encountered during our investigations did emphasize the need to give students different, shorter, and more pictorial surveys as shown in Fig. 4.

4   Results

Data from the investigation was collected in two different fashions. The first was the administering of surveys before and after the participants tested VASC. The second was our research team documenting general observations about the running of the overall investigation including how equipment was set-up, participant behavior, and back-end data collection.

4.1 Survey Results

Table 1. Summary of Pre- and Post-Survey Results for Students (*S*) and Teachers (*T*) over two investigations. Yellow (left side): Investigation 1 on HTC Vive. Blue (right side): Investigation 2 on Oculus Quest 2.

Question	S1	S2	T1	T2	T3	T4	T5	T6	T7	T8	S1	S2	T1	T2	T3	T4	T5	T6
Daily hrs spent gaming	3-5	3-5	0-1	0-1	0-1	0-1	0-1	0-1	0-1	0-1	0-1	3-5	0-1	0-1	0-1	0-1	1-2	0-1
Used VR before?	N	Y	N	Y	N	N	N	Y	N	N	N	Y	Y	Y	N	N	N	Y
Time (min) in experiment	70	38	21	89	28	26	36	55	26	31	46	20	54	24	23	21	21	17
Easy to understand VASC	y	Y	Y	y	y	y	y	Y	Y	Y	Y	Y	Y	n	y	n	y	y
Fully completed all tasks	Y	Y	y	y	y	n	y	Y	y	y	y	Y	Y	n	y	n	y	n
Completed tasks efficiently	Y	y	Y	y	y	n	y	Y	y	Y	y	Y	Y	n	yn	N	Y	N
Interface easy to use	y	Y	y	y	Y	y	Y	y	Y	Y	y	Y	Y	n	y	n	Y	Y
VASC is mentally demanding	L	L	L	M	M	L	M	M	M	M	Y	L	M	M	L	Y	L	N
VASC is frustrating	N	N	N	L	L	L	N	N	N	L	N	N	N	M	L	Y	L	M

Y: *Yes/Strongly Agree*, **y**: *Somewhat Agree*, **yn**: *Neither Agree nor Disagree*, **n**: *Somewhat Disagree*, **N**: *No/Strongly Disagree*, **L**: *a Little*, **M**: *a Moderate amount*

Table 1 summarizes the types of data collected in our pre- and post-surveys. Both students and teachers were asked a number of questions measuring their familiarity with gaming and VR and how comfortable and successful they were using all aspects of the VASC system. Overall the participants reported that they were able to successfully complete all tasks tested in the VASC system and enjoyed doing so with few problems. All of the students in our test groups reported being able to understand how to use the simulation and complete all tasks, and had little trouble doing so. This group also wanted to explore the system in greater detail and tended to request that more open-world exploration and interactions be added to VASC. Adults in our tests tended to have a little more trouble getting comfortable and navigating the simulation. This may indicate that when our system is expanded to have one version for students and one for teachers that a different level and type of instructions should be made available for each group. Our testing also showed that participants moved through the tasks faster on average when using the Quest 2 over the Vive.

The administered surveys also included several open-ended questions asking for more detailed opinions and suggestions on different aspects of the system. These questions helped us to identify what aspects of VASC are working well and are on the right track and what areas need improvement. Participants wrote that they were impressed with the realism of the scene, the overall accuracy of moving within the environment, and the ability to interact with objects. They felt that the way in which they interacted with tools made sense. Many participants felt they had enough information throughout the investigation to successfully use the program. However, some participants felt they needed more directions whether they be auditory or visual and requested they be placed throughout the simulation to explain each individual task. Some responses also said it took time to learn how to interact with the environment and said having a period to learn and practice at the beginning would be very helpful. The tasks that were most commonly reported as being difficult were holding objects, shoveling, picking up and moving objects, teleporting, and teleporting while doing a second task (like holding an object or scrolling). Dropping objects and trying to pick them back up also caused frustration for several participants. These results are inline with the data collected from NASA-TLX which indicates that users were mainly concerned about their performance when no time constraint was present. Users' physical demands were one of the lowest workload factors which indicates the tasks were not physically demanding and were easy to perform in virtual reality (Fig. 5). We did not do a factor analysis to see whether the six items represent a single dimension or multiple dimensions for this initial study. As far as requests for expanding the system, several participants requested the simulation include animations showing baby turtles hatching from shells and walking toward the ocean. Students wanted to be able to interact with even more objects and buildings in the environment to add to the sense of immersion and realism.

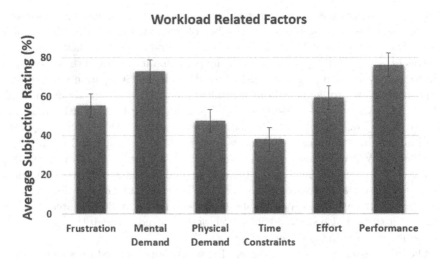

Fig. 5. Average scores for the six workload factors. Lowest are Time Constraints at 38 and Physical Demand at 48 and highest are Performance at 76 and Mental Demand at 73.

4.2   General Observations

In addition to data collected from surveys, our team made several general observations while setting up and running the investigations that will be used to modify and improve future investigations.

First, it took too long for participants, especially students, to complete the survey. Some students needed assistance from parents to complete the surveys and had trouble staying focused through the whole process. The surveys will be condensed in future investigations to only include the most relevant questions. Additionally, students will be given different surveys that are formatted in a way more targeted for grades 3–5 as discussed in Sect. 3.3.

We also decided that the equipment we used in the first investigation is impractical for future tests. It took too long to move and set-up all the computers and sensors required for using the HTC Vive. This particular set of equipment also requires too much space to be practical for having several testing stations in a standard classroom. We were only able to use 2 out of the 3 sets of hardware we brought for this experiment as the towers interfered with each other. For the second investigation, we used the Oculus Quest 2 which does not require any towers or any connection to computers. We also did not have the problem of separate units interfering with each other when using the Quest 2. We will only run future investigations and experimental manipulations on the Quest 2 so that the only equipment that will need to be transported to classrooms are the headsets and we will be able to perform larger scale tests.

As far as the actual running of the investigations went, we observed that users need more guidance throughout the testing process and more feedback from the UI. We will add written and auditory instructions especially when users complete or fail to complete a task as the current feedback method was not intuitive to all users. Additionally, we need to include instructions when users fail a task multiple times so they can reach their goals via step-by-step guidance as needed. We are also updating our environment so that once a user picks up an object it snaps to his or her hand. Several users dropped objects, became frustrated, and lost focus on the primary goals of the program. Our next iterative investigation will explore whether or not this change improves user satisfaction with the program and decreases the time it takes them to complete activities.

5   Conclusion

We are developing a virtual environment to expose students in 3rd through 5th grades to STEM careers in marine, environmental, computer, and geological sciences. At a recent stage of our process we ran two investigations with teachers and students to gain feedback on the usability of our system and gather information to inform design decisions in the next stages. By having 18 participants pick up VASC for the first time, complete a number of virtual tasks, and fill out surveys about their experiences, we learned several things that we will take into account in both our system design and future experimental set-ups. We will add more instructions through both visual and auditory means inside the simulation to guide participants through the exact steps of the system. We will examine exactly what level of detail is necessary and at what point instructions can be taken away or made optional so that participants can be successful and still have freedom to explore. We are also updating how participants interact with objects used to complete measuring tasks so that they do not waste time and become frustrated dropping, searching for, and picking up virtual tools. To maximize how much data can be collected in each investigation we will use Oculus Quest 2 that are easier to transport and a higher number of which can be used by multiple people in a tight space. We will also shorten our surveys and administer different surveys to students and teachers that are more targeted at their age ranges.

We have found that VASC was well-received by students and teachers and with enthusiasm. Our system has the potential to be a powerful tool in the classroom to engage students in a unique way and educate them on STEM concepts and career opportunities. We will continue to develop, test, and solicit educator feedback on VASC to ensure it is accessible to students and teachers and meets STEM learning objectives and national standards.

Acknowledgement. The project is supported by NSF Award #1850430. The authors would like to acknowledge the following students who have also contributed to the development and testing of VASC: Daniel Vaughn, Jacob Thomas, Lauren Rota, Kenneth McMillan, Patricia Beeksma, Grant Hitson, Alexandra Gonzales, Kayla Dorsey, Cameron Detig, Mogran Davis, Emily Crumpler, Bryson Harlee, Seth Angell, and Elijah Tripp.

References

1. Belland, B.R., Ertmer, P.A., Simons, K.D.: Perceptions of the value of problem-based learning among students with special needs and their teachers. Interdiscipl. J. Probl. Based Learn. **1**(2), 1 (2006)
2. Breiner, J.M., Harkness, S.S., Johnson, C.C., Koehler, C.M.: What is stem? A discussion about conceptions of stem in education and partnerships. School Sci. Math. **112**(1), 3–11 (2012)
3. Brush, T., Saye, J.: The effects of multimedia-supported problem-based inquiry on student engagement, empathy, and assumptions about history. Interdiscipl. J. Probl. Based Learn. **2**(1), 4 (2008)
4. Center, P.R.: Women and men in stem often at odds over workplace equity (2018)
5. Christou, C.: Virtual reality in education. In: Affective, interactive and cognitive methods for e-learning design: creating an optimal education experience, pp. 228–243. IGI Global (2010)
6. Cote, D.: Problem-based learning software for students with disabilities. Interv. School Clin. **43**(1), 29–37 (2007)
7. Council, N.R., et al.: Next generation science standards: For states, by states (2013)
8. Daily, S.B., Leonard, A.E., Jörg, S., Babu, S., Gundersen, K., Parmar, D.: Embodying computational thinking: Initial design of an emerging technological learning tool. Technol. Knowl. Learn. **20**(1), 79–84 (2015)
9. Dewey, J.: Democracy and education. Courier Corporation (2004)

10. Ertmer, P.A., Simons, K.D.: Jumping the PBL implementation hurdle: supporting the efforts of k-12 teachers. Interdiscipl. J. Probl. Based learn. **1**(1), 5 (2006)
11. Foulger, T.S., Jimenez-Silva, M.: Enhancing the writing development of English language learners: Teacher perceptions of common technology in project-based learning. J. Res. Child. Educ. **22**(2), 109–124 (2007)
12. Hernández-Ramos, P., Paz, S.D.L.: Learning history in middle school by designing multimedia in a project-based learning experience. J. Res. Technol. Educ. **42**(2), 151–173 (2009)
13. Hew, K.F., Cheung, W.S.: Use of three-dimensional (3-D) immersive virtual worlds in k-12 and higher education settings: a review of the research. Br. J. Educ. Technol. **41**(1), 33–55 (2010)
14. Hsieh, P., Cho, Y., Liu, M., Schallert, D.: Examining the interplay between middle school students' achievement goals and self-efficacy in a technology-enhanced learning environment. Am. Second. Educ. **36**(3), 33–50 (2008)
15. Initiative, C.C.S.S., et al.: Common core state standards for mathematics (2010). http://www.corestandards.org/assets/CCSSI_MathStandards.pdf
16. Javidi, G.: Virtual reality and education (1999)
17. Krajcik, J., Codere, S., Dahsah, C., Bayer, R., Mun, K.: Planning instruction to meet the intent of the next generation science standards. J. Sci. Teach. Educ. **25**(2), 157–175 (2014)
18. LaForce, M., et al.: The eight essential elements of inclusive stem high schools. Int. J. STEM Educ. **3**(1), 1–11 (2016)
19. de Marcos, L., Garcia-Lopez, E., Garcia-Cabot, A.: On the effectiveness of game-like and social approaches in learning: comparing educational gaming, gamification & social networking. Comput. Educ. **95**, 99–113 (2016)
20. Merchant, Z., Goetz, E.T., Cifuentes, L., Keeney-Kennicutt, W., Davis, T.J.: Effectiveness of virtual reality-based instruction on students' learning outcomes in k-12 and higher education: a meta-analysis. Comput. Educ. **70**, 29–40 (2014)
21. Mergendoller, J.R., Maxwell, N.L., Bellisimo, Y.: The effectiveness of problem-based instruction: a comparative study of instructional methods and student characteristics. Interdiscipl. J. Probl. Based Learn. **1**(2), 5 (2006)
22. Parmar, D., et al.: Programming moves: design and evaluation of applying embodied interaction in virtual environments to enhance computational thinking in middle school students. In: Virtual Reality (VR), 2016 IEEE, pp. 131–140. IEEE (2016)
23. Penuel, W.R.: Implementation and effects of one-to-one computing initiatives: a research synthesis. J. Res. Technol. Educ. **38**(3), 329–348 (2006)
24. Peters-Burton, E.E., Lynch, S.J., Behrend, T.S., Means, B.B.: Inclusive stem high school design: 10 critical components. Theory Pract. **53**(1), 64–71 (2014)
25. Potkonjak, V., et al.: Virtual laboratories for education in science, technology, and engineering: a review. Comput. Educ. **95**, 309–327 (2016)
26. Putnam, R.T., Borko, H.: What do new views of knowledge and thinking have to say about research on teacher learning? Educ. Res. **29**(1), 4–15 (2000)
27. Roussou, M.: Learning by doing and learning through play: an exploration of interactivity in virtual environments for children. Comput. Entertain. (CIE) **2**(1), 10–10 (2004)
28. Roussou, M., Oliver, M., Slater, M.: The virtual playground: an educational virtual reality environment for evaluating interactivity and conceptual learning. Virtual Real. **10**(3–4), 227–240 (2006)
29. Sias, C.M., Nadelson, L.S., Juth, S.M., Seifert, A.L.: The best laid plans: educational innovation in elementary teacher generated integrated stem lesson plans. J. Educ. Res. **110**(3), 227–238 (2017)

30. Tamim, S.R., Grant, M.M.: Definitions and uses: case study of teachers implementing project-based learning. Interdiscipl. J. Probl. Based Learn. **7**(2), 3 (2013)
31. Thomas, J.W., Mergendoller, J.R.: Managing project-based learning: Principles from the field. In: Annual Meeting of the American Educational Research Association, New Orleans (2000)
32. Trindade, J., Fiolhais, C., Almeida, L.: Science learning in virtual environments: a descriptive study. Br. J. Educ. Technol. **33**(4), 471–488 (2002)

Me, Myself, and the (Virtual) World: A Review of Learning Research in 4E Cognition and Immersive Virtual Reality

Gregory McGowin[1]([✉]) [iD], Stephen M. Fiore[1] [iD], and Kevin Oden[2] [iD]

[1] University of Central Florida, Orlando, FL 32816, USA
gmcgowin@knights.ucf.edu
[2] Lockheed Martin, Orlando, FL 32819, USA

Abstract. This paper examines how the principles of 4E cognition can be used to interpret, and potentially improve, immersive virtual reality (I-VR). A selection of relevant 4E + I-VR studies are reviewed to illustrate this relationship. Towards this end, this paper provides: 1) an overview of Immersive Virtual reality (I-VR), 2) a summary of 4E cognition (embodied, enacted, embedded, extended), and 3) a discussion relevant literature in 4E cognition applied to learning in I-VR. The paper concludes with a series of recommendations that may offer possible routes of research that could expand this important area of inquiry.

Keywords: 4E cognition · Immersive virtual reality · Learning · Training

1 Introduction

With the growing affordability and presence of immersive virtual reality (I-VR), there has been a dramatic increase in the interest in exploring how the technology can be leveraged to promote learning for both training and education (e.g., Meyer et al. 2019, Kaplan et al. 2021). When leveraged correctly, I-VR may be a powerful training tool that can replicate real-world experiences while allowing learners to engage in a highly interactive multimedia environment (Castro-Alonso and Fiorella 2019; Hamilton et al. 2021, Wang et al. 2021). I-VR also provides learners the opportunities to practice complex skills and procedures through experiential learning that would otherwise be too impractical or dangerous (Hilfert and König 2016; Kaplan et al. 2021), and has shown improved learning outcomes in education (Radianti et al. 2020; Hamilton et al. 2021), or at least, equal learning outcomes as compared to traditional training methods (Kaplan et al. 2021). As such, I-VR provides a safe and cost-effective place to perform learning activities that would otherwise be too expensive, improbable, or dangerous (Slater and Sanchez-Vives 2016; Kaplan et al. 2021). With this increased interest in the immersive technology, I-VR research will continue to shape how we learn, teach, and share information.

Despite increasing adoption, there is still little attention on how learning theory can be leveraged to improve I-VR applications. The perspective from 4E cognition offers an important avenue of inquiry into how I-VR may be applied to both learning and training.

J. Y. C. Chen and G. Fragomeni (Eds.): HCII 2022, LNCS 13318, pp. 59–73, 2022.
https://doi.org/10.1007/978-3-031-06015-1_5

We do so by using the learning affordances offered by I-VR (i.e., immersion & presence, engagement, abstract ideas made concrete) (Bailenson 2018; McGowin et al. 2021; Slater and Sanchez-Vives 2016), coupled with the person + environment centric view of 4E cognition (Christ et al. 2021; Schiavio and Van der Schyff 2018). 4E Cognition can loosely be described as how a person's body or avatar (embodied cognition) interacts (i.e., sensorimotor) with its environment (extended cognition) through active actions within the environment (enactive cognition), with the additional capability to utilize situated cognition in that environment (embedded cognition) (Christ et al. 2021; Pouw et al. 2014).

Recent research into 4E and I-VR has yielded promising findings as it relates to learning. For example, König et al. (2020) found that participant's judgments of spatial directions were more accurate after exploration of an I-VR environment (i.e., *embodied*) compared to that of top-down map exploration. Additionally, another I-VR study conducted by Thompson et al. (2021) found improvements in biological learning. Participants were better able to recall and draw biological diagrams after being embodied into biological cells and being provided with an integrated information tool (i.e., *extended cognition*). Andreasen et al. (2019) examined the interaction between media and method (e.g., media comparison) coupled with *enactment*, which resulted in improvements in both procedural knowledge and transfer in the I-VR group, in comparison to the video group. While the literature for *extended* cognition inside I-VR is limited, Pillai (2017) provides a look into how they believe extended cognition may be utilized by examining the interaction between autonomous vehicles and pedestrians.

While virtual reality has long been studied in application, the theory and methods of the learning sciences have yet to be fully studied with immersive virtual reality. Because of this, an interdisciplinary approach to research is needed to investigate the means more completely in which immersive virtual reality can augment conventional training. Towards that end, in this paper we will first describe what we consider immersive virtual reality. We then summarize key findings from 4E cognition research that has, or can be, adapted to immersive virtual reality.

2   Immersive Virtual Reality (I-VR)

While Virtual Reality (VR) has often been defined differently across domains (e.g., LaValle 2019; Briggs 1996), it is generally understood to be a system that uses 3D graphic systems to digitally simulate or replicate a real or imaginary environment (Makransky and Lilleholt 2018) to provide the psychological effect of presence (Slater 2017a, b) inside an interactive virtual environment (Pan et al. 2006). These computer-simulated environments induce "targeted behavior in an organism by using artificial sensory stimulation, while [optimally] the organism has little or no awareness of the interference" (LaValle 2019, p. 1).

What makes VR such a compelling tool for researchers across domains is what Johnsen-Glenberg (2018) refers to as the 'two profound affordances' of VR, namely presence [and immersion] and embodiment. At a high level, presence is defined as the psychological feeling of one's body existing in a different world (Waterworth and Waterworth 2003). Presence in VR can be delineated into three characteristics: the feeling of *being* inside the virtual environment (VE), the magnitude that the VE becomes the prominent locus of attention (i.e., VE events become as, or more, important than the real-world for a user), and the extent to which users recall the VE (Slater 1999).

Presence is often conflated with the term immersion, but care should be taken to distinguish between the two. While presence deals with the psychological effect of 'being there', immersion describes the technological ability of the system to induce presence. Slater and Wilbur (1997) phrase it as "the extent to which the computer displays are capable of delivering an inclusive, extensive, surrounding and vivid illusion of reality to the senses of a human participant" (p. 604). To achieve this, a user must be represented in the VE (i.e., an embodied form), and be allowed to engage or interact with the environment (i.e., interactivity) (Slater and Wilbur 1997). Thus, immersion can be thought of as the extent to which VR systems stimulate the senses to replicate the real world into the virtual. Phrased another way, immersion is the *technological* aspect of the experience that facilitates the *psychological* feeling of presence" (Mestre et al. 2006; Bowman and McMahan (2007). Immersion can be thought of as the degree to which a system is capable of technologically both replicating the real world and then 'shutting out' the outside world, while allowing the learner to retain a psychological presence in the virtual environment (Makransky and Petersen, 2021).

What makes it Immersive VR, as opposed to VR, is the technology used to enter the virtual environment. While some scholars (e.g., Makransky and Petersen, 2021) take the stance that VR can be accessed through several different types of display technology, such as a desktop computer, a head-mounted display (HMD), or a cave automatic virtual environment (CAVE) (Chittaro and Buttussi 2019), we argue that, of the current technology, only HMDs provide a true representation of I-VR. These are currently the only technology that allows for a fully embodied state (i.e., self-avatar) inside the virtual environment. We tend to agree with Johnsen-Glenberg's rather blunt statement regarding other forms of VR when they state, "A three-dimensional object or avatar moving on a regular-sized computer monitor is never 'VR'; we hope that educators soon stop conflating the terms and phenomena" (2018). To add further comment, we recommend practitioners and scholars should, instead, use the term virtual environments as the broad umbrella term for any digital environment one may find themselves in, and reserve VR to mean I-VR.

I-VR is also categorically different than mixed or augmented reality as its defining characteristic is that it blocks out the real world while maintaining a psychological presence in the virtual environment (Loomis et al. 1999; Makransky and Petersen, 2021). By shutting out the 'outside' world, I-VR enables a user to assume a form other than their own (e.g., embody a six-legged creature vs the four limbs we normally have). Another defining characteristic of I-VR is that its high level of interaction compared to traditional multimedia methods such as PowerPoint, or even mouse + keyboard Interactivity in I-VR is usually at least partially bodied, meaning a person uses their limbs (i.e., hands, arms) to interact with the environment.

While this paper will not go into depth on what we consider the qualifications of I-VR to be (see McGowin et al. 2021 for a more detailed reading of I-VR) we now briefly outline the technologies we believe are required to be considered to be the minimum requirements for I-VR.

Head Mounted Display (HMD). A HMD with a large Field of View (FOV), Field of Regard (FOR), and stereoscopic vision that has both a responsive viewing source (e.g., frame rate) and head tracking to mitigate the effects of simulation/cyber sickness.

Six Degrees of Freedom (DOF). The ability for the body and head to move in six degrees of freedom (i.e., forward/backward, up/down, left/right pitch, roll, yaw) within the VE.

Sufficiently Natural User Interface. The ability for the user to intuitively navigate and manipulate objects in the VE. Included in this category are body movements (e.g., gestures) and congruence of actions (Johnson-Glenberg 2018).

Auditory Stimulation. Spatialized sound with a user being able to approximate the location in 3D space (Lavalle 2019).

2.1 Summary

This brief review was meant to highlight some of the key concepts and technologies relevant to I-VR. Noting that technology produces the capability for immersion, and the psychological response to this immersion can create a sense of presence, we outlined a set of key technologies we believe are minimally needed for I-VR. We next describe how theory from the cognitive sciences can be adapted to help turn this technology into a powerful learning tool.

3   4E Cognition (Embodied, Embedded, Enactive, Extended/External)

The nature of the mind and body and how they interact with the environment has been a long-standing debate among philosophers (Newen et al. 2018). In recent years, researchers have been influenced by Clark and Chalmers (1998) seminal work, "The Extended Mind", which helped pave the way for the emergence of 4E cognition. The 4E paradigm argues that cognition occurs extra-cranially (i.e., outside the head), or in other words, does not occur exclusively within the head (Rowlands 2010). Instead, it is dynamically interconnected between a body, the environment (Schneegans and Schöner 2008) and to a series of separate entities including both technological and social (Aagaard 2021). Put another way, 4E cognition assumes that cognition is shaped by how the brain, body, and physical and social environments interact (Newen et al. 2018). While not all 4E scholars agree on the exact nature of the philosophy, most 4E researchers share the basic tenet that human cognition is not siloed solely inside the 'inner world', neither from the established Cartesian philosophy, nor in the modern-day intracranial sense (Aagaard 2021). In its place, it is believed the human cognitive processes are intrinsically interconnected with our surroundings (Aagaard 2021).

The wellspring of 4E cognition centers around the seminal work Varela and Colleagues (1993) on the embodied mind, and by Clark and Chalmers (1998) relating to the extended mind. These scholars argued what was, at the time, a controversial view, that human cognition is not limited to just inside the head. Rather, cognition arises with and from a body, and extends to technological artifacts and social interactions in a person's neighboring environment (Aagaard 2021). From this, the philosophy can be categorized into four separate yet interconnected theories of 4E cognition.

It should be noted that, while the 4Es are distinctly different, they will inevitably blend into one another (Carney 2020). As such, exact definitions vary by theorists. However, generally the four types of cognition can be described as embodied, embedded, extended, and enactive (Carney 2020; Gonzalez-Grandon and Froese 2018; Newen et al. 2018).

In the following set of definitions, it can be seen that each stresses considerable emphasis on embodied action (i.e., perception is action-oriented) (Newen et al. 2018). As mentioned earlier, there are multiple definitions for 4E cognition, and here we offer Schiavio and Van der Schyff's (2018) succinct definition for each:

- **Embodied:** Cognition cannot be fully described in terms of abstract mental processes (i.e., in terms of representations). Rather, it must involve the entire body of the living system (brain and body).
- **Embedded:** Cognition is not an isolated event separated from the agent's ecological niche. Instead, it displays layers of co-determination with physical, social, and cultural aspects of the world.
- **Extended:** Cognition is often offloaded into biological beings and non-biological devices to serve a variety of functions that would be impossible (or too difficult) to be achieved by only relying on the agent's own mental processes.
- **Enactive:** Cognition is conceived of as the set of meaningful relationships determined by an adaptive two-way exchange between the biological and phenomenological complexity of living creatures and the environments they inhabit and actively shape" (p. 2).

It should be noted that there can be gradients of the 4Es, such that they exist on a continuum from weak to strong, and each of the 4Es should not be considered binary or exclusionary. Now that we have defined the aspects of 4E cognition, we will expand upon it from the relevant literature and provide representational research on each 'E'.

3.1 Embodiment

Cognition generally involves perceiving the situated environment and acting upon the environment with the body that is immersed in it (Schneegans and Schöner 2008). If we are to understand what these cognitive processes entail, we must first understand the close link between the motor surfaces that generate action and to the sensory systems that provide sensory signals about the environment (Schneegans and Schöner 2008). One way to view embodiment is through a Gibsonian lens, in that we have a body which contains senses (e.g., sight, touch) that detect the environment around us, and we make sense (i.e., sense-making) of the environment through these perceptions. How we understand the world is inherently dependent on the types and kinds of senses we have. This can be thought of as a feedback process between the brain, body, and environment (Varela et al. 1993).

A simple example of embodied cognition would be using gestures to articulate a point or referencing your own height to gauge the height of someone else. A classic example of embodiment, recently reviewed through the lens of neuroscience, is the rubber hand illusion (Della Gatta et al. 2016). In this study a realistic rubber hand is placed in front of a participant and lined up to their shoulder. The participant's hand is obscured except for the fingers. The illusion is induced by having a researcher lightly stroke the finger of the participant's real hand while concurrently stroking the same finger on the rubber hand. As the visual-temporal sensation of touch is paired over time, the participant's brain will erroneously accept that the rubber hand is part of the person's body. The researchers next used transcranial magnetic stimulation to send electrical impulses from the motor-cortex region (i.e., part of the brain that controls hand movement), to the hand where they were recorded as muscle twitches. They found that, as the strength of the illusion increased, the strength of electrical pulses decreased, such that the brain had effectively reduced the availability or readiness to use the real hand. This is both an example of embodiment and disembodiment, as the embodied self accepts the rubber hand as its own and discards the 'real' hand.

In terms of embodiments in the learning sciences, Kontra et al. (2015) examined how the activation of sensorimotor systems (i.e., body and brain) impacted STEM learning (i.e., physics knowledge gains). They compared groups studying angular motion and the corresponding changes in torque. Groups either physically held a spinning wheel and changed the orientation of its axis (i.e., horizontal to vertical) or observed said movement. Those who had a kinesthetic experience outperformed those who only observed on later knowledge tests, implying those who had an embodied experience outperformed those who did not.

Additionally, Kontra et al. (2015) used functional MRI (fMRI) to examine the level of the blood-oxygen-level-dependent (BOLD) signal in the motor regions of the brain and found that those individuals who had a higher BOLD signal (i.e., more activation in the motor regions) performed better on the knowledge test (Kontra et al. 2015).

3.2 Embedded

4E cognition includes not only extracranial processes, but the active engagement of a person with their environment (Varela et al. 1993). Put another way, the embodied brain does not exist in a vacuum distinct from its environment. Instead, it is readily embedded in the context (i.e., environment) around it (Gonzalez-Grandon and Froese 2018). This environment, or context, provides Gibsonian affordances to the available 'possible' actions/interactions in the environment, for which an agent (i.e., person) is able to directly perceive in a meaningful fashion (Gonzalez-Grandon and Froese 2018). It is a continuous interaction between the existing states of the brain, body, and the environment (Clark 2008; Pouw et al. 2014). It is worth noting that, "under certain conditions, perceptual and interactive richness can alleviate cognitive load imposed on working memory by effectively embedding the learner's cognitive activity in the environment" (Pouw et al. 2014, p. 52). Or, as Robbins and Aydede (2009) phrase it, "cognitive activity routinely exploits structure in the natural and social environment" (p. 3). A simple example of embedded cognition is how to pack groceries efficiently, with the ideal structure being to place heavy items on the bottom, and lighter or more delicate items on the top. A person could mentally calculate the best possible location of each item as it enters their work area from the conveyor belt, or the worker could use the provided external physical cues (e.g., size, weight) of the items and organize them into categories (e.g., heavy, intermediate, delicate) and place them in distinct spatial locations prior to packing (Robbins and Aydede 2009).

3.3 Enactive

Enactive cognition deals with the coupling between the human and environmental systems as they work jointly to help navigate the world (Varela et al. 1991; revised 2016) and are sometimes thought of as the structural coupling of an autonomous (i.e., living) system with their environment. This theory emphasizes patterns within dynamical interaction and the active embodied engagement to the environment, versus internal representations (Gonzalez-Grandon and Froese 2018). In other words, it is cognition that is extended to *active* action within the individual and among the environment (Gonzalez-Grandon and Froese 2018).

A simple example of enactive cognition would be catching a ball based on the relevant environmental factors apparent to the catcher (i.e., size, speed) as they move through an environment to actively perceive the ball. A relevant example of enactive cognition in the learning sciences comes from Lindgren et al. (2016) in which they examined how mixed reality (MR) technology can be used to provide an enactive/embodied interaction with scientific content (i.e., the physics related to orbital mechanics). In this study, they compared learning between two groups, one who used a whole-body interaction coupled with a simulator against another group who used a traditional desktop (i.e., mouse and keyboard) simulation. Those in the whole-body group were required to enact the concepts of gravity and planetary motion and outperformed those in the disembodied and non-active desktop learning. Results of the study indicate that "enacting concepts and experiencing critical ideas in physics through whole-body activity leads to significant learning gains, higher levels of engagement, and more positive attitudes towards science" (Lindgren et al. 2016, p. 174).

3.4 Extended

The final 'E' in four E cognition is *extended*, which moves from the idea that cognition is embedded, to the idea that cognition is the interactions between humans natural, technical, and social environments (Hutchins 1995), and that they enhance the cognitive capacities of the human through a larger cognitive system (e.g., artifact, social-technical system) (Clark and Chalmers 1998; Menary 2008). To be extended, it needs to be at least partially composed of an extracranial system not comprised of the body (Newen et al. 2018). Gonzalez-Grandon and Froese (2018) succinctly define it as cognition that is extended beyond the boundaries of the person, thus being intrinsically connected with the respective physical or socio-cultural environment. It is worth noting that some scholars believe that embedded and extended cognitions are the same since both reference how the cognitive system depends on the environment through "cultural artifacts, including language and technological tools, in order to free limited cognitive abilities" Gonzalez-Grandon and Froese 2018, p. 190). Simple examples of extended cognition include working math formulas with paper and pencil (as opposed to doing the calculations solely inside the head).

A relevant example of extended cognition in the learning sciences comes from Newton, Fiore and LaViola (2017), in which they explored how visualization of information (i.e., visual artifact in the form of color mapping) could be used to extend cognition. Here they constructed an artifact that helped users offload as well as scaffold information of a cognitively challenging event, decision-making under uncertainty.

3.5 Summary

In the above we reviewed some of the key concepts of 4E cognition to provide a foundation for viewing them through the lens of I-VR. We additionally related them to studies in the learning sciences to show the relationship between 4E cognition and learning. Next, we discuss examples of research in I-VR that directly, or indirectly, can be linked to 4E cognition.

4 I-VR and 4E Learning Studies

4.1 Embodied I-VR and Learning

König and Colleagues (2020) examine how embodiment affects knowledge acquisition in spatial tasks. They created a virtual environment of a European style village. Two groups were compared against each other, A) an I-VR group, and B) a computer display group (i.e., desktop). Participants in the I-VR condition were able to wander and explore the town (i.e., embodied state). In the desktop group, a top-down interactive map was used, similar to Google maps. Three types of spatial knowledge were tested, 1) cardinal directions (e.g., turn north at this juncture), 2) building-to-building orientation (e.g., the church is oriented perpendicular to the inn), and 3) judgment of direction be-tween buildings in a pointing task (e.g., from your location point to where X building is). In the *embodied* state (i.e., I-VR), participants outscored the desktop group in the judgment of direction (i.e., pointing to where objects/buildings are within the village). However, the I-VR group performed worse when it came to cardinal directions and building-to-building orientation. The authors determined that these results imply that the *source* of spatial exploration (i.e., in-person vs top-down) differently influences spatial knowledge acquisition.

4.2 Enactive I-VR

Andreasen et al. (2019) examined the instructional efficacy of I-VR compared to traditional video for learning about STEM knowledge. Additionally, they explored the effectiveness of enactment in combination with both I-VR and video instruction. It should be noted, this study used a lower immersion I-VR system, with only head movement tracking in 3DOF (i.e., no hand/arm usage was tracked). This study used a 2 × 2 between subjects design, breaking each group into video, I-VR, video + enactment, and I-VR + enactment. Learning outcomes were knowledge acquisition of both declarative and procedural knowledge, as well as a transfer task, and perceived enjoyment. In this study, participants learned about DNA polymerase chain reaction (PCR) laboratory procedures, either through video or I-VR coupled with or without an enactive learning strategy completed in the 'real' world (i.e., 'interacting' with paper mock-ups of the lab equipment). This enactment involved users participating in task-relevant actions (i.e., PCR laboratory procedures) during the learning phase by "manipulating respective objects in coordination with the lesson content" (p. 840). This encompassed 'acting out' a PCR lab sequence by pointing to printed props (i.e., models) of lab tools to perform a task. In their results, the researchers found no differences across groups for declarative knowledge or transfer. However, they did find a significant interaction in the I-VR group between those who enacted the procedure in the real world and those who did not (i.e., increase in procedural knowledge).

4.3 Embedded I-VR

Thompson and Colleagues (2021) examined the differences between I-VR and desktop PC learning. Participants were required to diagnose a cell by examining and searching the virtual cell for clues to indicate what type of illness is present (i.e., one of five types of cystic fibrosis). Assessment were pre/post knowledge (primarily declarative) tests, a procedural knowledge test about translation from RNA to amino acids, as well as drawing a diagram, used as a measurement tool for participant's mental model of translation. Both the I-VR and desktop conditions played the game moving about the virtual environment and then 1) selecting organelles, 2) identifying them, and 3) sampling them by using a virtual 'evidence' clipboard. Once sampled, the information was added to their 'evidence' board. The clipboard served as an extended information source allowing users to view and review information found. Overall, both groups improved their knowledge of the cell environment and translation. The I-VR condition had stronger positive learning gains as compared to the desktop group in addition to a more well-developed mental model of translation, as measured via diagram drawings. The authors conclude that the improvements in recall of the cell system in drawings suggest that information that was embedded or integrated into the environment (e.g., being inside the cell with the organelles) aided the recall process, and may be evidence of embedded cognition in a I-VR setting.).

4.4 Extended I-VR

Unfortunately, we are not currently able to report on a 4E + I-VR study that explicitly examines extended cognition. Although these researchers searched extensively, there does not appear to be many (if at all) studies that explicitly explore the coupling of extended cognition to I-VR. That being said, we can report upon a study that makes the claim of extended cognition used in an I-VR setting, although the argument for it being extended cognition is tenuous. Pillai (2017) explores how humans and autonomous vehicles may interact with each other through the extension of the human mind. In their study, they examined the relationship between autonomous vehicles and pedestrians crossing a crosswalk (i.e., how do humans interact with an autonomous agent). They present a series of interactions to participants in I-VR, such as high and low visibility of the pedestrian crosswalk, and examine the interactions (e.g., wave through the vehicle). The author's primary claim is that, as perceived by the pedestrian, a human + vehicle is a type of extended mind (i.e., extended cognition). Therefore, when a pedestrian views an autonomous vehicle, it views that as another extended cognitive system. Their findings show that, even though a pedestrian cannot always visually see a vehicle, they can hear the vehicle (via the engine and tire noise), and consider it to be an approaching cognitive system and process this information to derive approximate distance to the vehicle. They found that in general, this claim was supported, such that participants used their senses (i.e., visual and auditory channels) to determine when/if it was safe to cross the pathway with an approaching autonomous vehicle.

5 Discussion

Across this set of studies relevant to 4E + I-VR and learning, we found an important pattern that should guide the future of research in this area. Although some scholars are looking at various aspects of 4E cognition and I-VR, there is clearly a lack of *integration* of the 4E concepts into I-VR. In this closing section of the paper, we briefly review this and offer potential routes of research that could expand this important area of inquiry.

König and Colleagues (2020) examined how embodiment affects the development of spatial knowledge. They showed that those embodied in I-VR outperformed those on traditional desktop PCs (i.e., non-embodied, non-I-VR) in judgment of direction between buildings (a specific type of spatial knowledge). While users in the I-VR condition were embodied (e.g., HMD, 6DOF), they had limited natural mobility. Specifically, users sat in a swivel chair, and conveyed movement in the VE via button press (e.g., pushing forward on the controller to move forward in the VE), which is not a strong form of embodiment. Also, while not explicitly mentioned by König and Colleagues, the I-VR task could also be considered an embedded cognition task, as learners were situated in an environment that most resembles how someone would navigate in the 'real' world. Additionally, as users moved closer or further to a built structure, the buildings would dynamically change their relative size to the user (i.e., a building closer to the user appears larger than one in the distance). This, it could be argued, is a weak form of enactive cognition. However, as the users are not physically walking or using their bodies in a particularly natural way, it is only partially enactive, that is, visual changes are associated with virtual movement. But the body's actions are tremendously limited.

Andreasen et al. (2019) explored the effectiveness of enactment by comparing it within both an I-VR environment as well as video (2D) instruction format. They found that those in the enactive plus I-VR group outperformed those in the non-enactive groups in regard to procedural knowledge. Unlike most other I-VR studies, all enactive experimental groups, regardless of I-VR or video, performed the enactment tasks while in the real world (i.e., interaction using paper props). It should be noted that the I-VR equipment used in this study was limited (i.e., 3DOF, non-natural user interface), which presumably prevented enactment of the tasks inside the VR environment. While the study did not explicitly reference embodiment or embeddedness, we can infer there to be a weak form of both. For embodiment, learners were inside the virtual environment and had a limited amount of agency (i.e., could move their head to look around). But they could not manipulate objects in a natural fashion with their hands. For embedded cognition, the learners were inside a 'realistic' representation of a PCR laboratory with tools that would be used in said lab.

Thompson and Colleagues (2021) examined the effectiveness of I-VR vs desktop learning. They found that both groups showed improvements over pre-test scores with the I-VR group generally performing better. However, there was no significant effect found as measured by content assessment (i.e., declarative and procedural knowledge). That being said, learners in the I-VR condition did develop a more advanced mental model, as measured by translation drawings. Here we see that this study had multiple forms of 4E cognition, primarily embedded and extended, with a weak form of embodiment. Learners were embedded not in a real world, but in an environment that transformed the abstract into concrete (e.g. Slater and Sanchez-Vives 2016). More specifically, learners were inside the cell where they could view the interactions of cell organelles and translation from RNA to amino acids. For extended cognition, learners used the 'clipboard' to store and review information, which allowed them to offload cognition or extend their cognition to the tool. Additionally, learners were embodied into the VR environment (i.e., 6DOF, natural controllers) and able to move within and interact with parts of the VE. It should be noted though, that those in the I-VR environment did not have a body per se (i.e., avatar); but they did have hands, and ways of interacting in the environment.

Unfortunately, there is a dearth of scholarly material that explicitly examines extended cognition and I-VR. While Pillai (2017) did explore some elements of extended cognition in I-VR, we'd argue that extended cognition is a poor fit to the scholarly material. As such, we suggest that the material is more in line with embodied and enactive cognition, as no offloading of cognition occurred. Instead, the participants relied on their embodied state and the visual and auditory feedback provided by the vehicle to make decisions of when it is safe to cross the pedestrian walkway.

By identifying these gaps, we can recommend how research in studies like this might be able to incorporate additional elements of 4E cognition in I-VR. These provide representative illustrations of how to build a more integrative body of literature in the study of learning and I-VR by taking into account the body and all its sensory-cognitive capabilities.

5.1 Recommendations

Recommendation 1. Researchers need to examine each of the 4E's individually in regard to I-VR and learning. As 4E concepts are known for blending into each other, it is difficult to explicitly study a single concept at a time. However, we suggest that, to be diagnostic of where/when/what types of 4E are needed to enhance learning in I-VR, it would be prudent to create a context in which to study each concept individually.

Recommendation 2. Related to #1, is the need to examine the *integration* of 4E concepts such that we are explicitly examining a combination of multiple Es. This could simply be integration of embodied and enactive, or extended and embedded cognition within a study, or some combination across a series of studies using the same learning context. Christ et al. (2021) began this process for the 4Es; however, a single article is not nearly broad enough. Additionally, they performed the study in a retro-active manner (e.g., made a determination on a series of studies as to what category of 4E the study fit into). This brings us to our third recommendation.

Recommendation 3. Researchers need to explicitly state which forms of 4E theory they are examining in regard to I-VR. While reflecting upon previous I-VR studies, and binning them into categories of 4E, is a productive way to help understand how well the field is examining this conceptual space, a more fruitful and productive approach would be for researchers to actively and explicitly state which of the 4Es they are examining. This allows for more objective assessment of studies and would also facilitate more careful meta-analytic methods to be used as the field grows.

6 Limitations

As with any research there are limitations to this work. For this paper, although there was a search for studies explicitly linking I-VR with the 4E's (i.e., embodied, embedded, enactive, extended), a more nuanced approach may provide additional literature to examine. For example, searching each of the 4E's by their component parts (e.g., embodiment –> gesture, self-avatar; embedded -> situated, experiential, in situ). Additionally, only a few illustrative examples of 4E + I-VR are provided in this paper. However, as costs in I-VR decrease, empirical research will increase, providing a stronger body of knowledge to interpret the relationship between theory and technology.

7 Future Research

Future areas of research are ripe for this field, as is evidenced by the fact that when reviewing scholarly material for this paper, the majority of the focus of 4E + immersive VR research is almost exclusively dedicated to embodiment, relegating embedded and enactive to the proverbial backseat of the vehicle, and almost forgetting or ignoring extended/external cognition. As mentioned in the limitations, searching for the component parts of 4E may provide additional scholarly resources. Additionally, while this paper did not cover distributed systems theory, we believe it may link with enactive cognition + I-VR in a meaningful way. Lastly, while believe Christ et al.'s (2021) approach to binning existing I-VR research into 4E categories is a fruitful endeavor we believe it's research base should be extended, we believe a more objective assessment of 4E + I-VR studies will facilitate more careful meta-analytic methods to be used as the field grows.

Acknowledgments. This study was supported by funding from Lockheed Martin Corporation to Stephen M. Fiore and Gita Sukthankar, with Kevin Oden as program manager. The views and opinions contained in this article are the authors' and should not be construed as official or as reflecting the views of the University of Central Florida or Lockheed Martin Corporation.

References

Aagaard, J.: 4E cognition and the dogma of harmony. Philos. Psychol. **34**(2), 165–181 (2021)

Andreasen, N.K., Baceviciute, S., Pande, P., Makransky, G.: Virtual reality instruction followed by enactment can increase procedural knowledge in a science lesson. In: 2019 IEEE Conference on Virtual Reality and 3D User Interfaces (VR), pp. 840–841. IEEE (2019)

Bailenson, J. (2018). Experience On Demand: What Virtual Reality Is, How It Works, and What It Can Do. WW Norton and Company

Briggs, J.C.: The promise of virtual reality. Futurist **30**(5), 13–18 (1996)

Bowman, D.A., McMahan, R.P.: Virtual reality: how much immersion is enough? Computer **40**(7), 36–43 (2007)

Castro-Alonso, J.C., Fiorella, L.: Interactive science multimedia and visuospatial processing. In: Castro-Alonso, J.C. (ed.) Visuospatial processing for education in health and natural sciences, pp. 145–173. Springer, Cham (2019). https://doi.org/10.1007/978-3-030-20969-8_6

Christ, O., Sambasivam, M., Roos, A., Zahn, C.: Learning in immersive virtual reality: how does the 4E cognition approach fit in virtual didactic settings? In: Ahram, T., Taiar, R. (eds.) IHIET 2021. LNNS, vol. 319, pp. 790–796. Springer, Cham (2021). https://doi.org/10.1007/978-3-030-85540-6_100

Clark, A.: Supersizing the Mind: Embodiment, Action, and Cognitive Extension. OUP USA (2008)

Clark, A., Chalmers, D.: The extended mind. Analysis **58**(1), 7–19 (1998).

Chittaro, L., Buttussi, F.: Exploring the use of arcade game elements for attitude change: two studies in the aviation safety domain. Int. J. Hum. Comput. Stud. **127**, 112–123 (2019)

Carney, J.: Thinking avant la lettre: a review of 4E cognition. Evolu. Stud. Imagin. Cult. **4**(1), 77–90 (2020)

Della Gatta, F., Garbarini, F., Puglisi, G., Leonetti, A., Berti, A., Borroni, P.: Decreased motor cortex excitability mirrors own hand disembodiment during the rubber hand illusion. Elife **5**, e14972 (2016)

Gonzalez-Grandón, X., Froese, T.: Grounding 4E cognition in Mexico: introduction to special issue on spotlight on 4E cognition research in Mexico (2018)

Hamilton, D., McKechnie, J., Edgerton, E., Wilson, C.: Immersive virtual reality as a pedagogical tool in education: a systematic literature review of quantitative learning outcomes and experimental design. J. Comput. Educ. **8**(1), 1–32 (2020). https://doi.org/10.1007/s40692-020-00169-2

Hilfert, T., König, M.: Low-cost virtual reality environment for engineering and construction. Visual. Eng. **4**(1), 1–18 (2016). https://doi.org/10.1186/s40327-015-0031-5

Hutchins, E.: Cognition in the Wild. MIT Press, Cambridge, Mass (1995)

Johnson-Glenberg, M.C.: Immersive VR and education: embodied design principles that include gesture and hand controls. Front. Robot. AI **5**, 81 (2018)

Kaplan, A.D., Cruit, J., Endsley, M., Beers, S.M., Sawyer, B.D., Hancock, P.A.: The effects of virtual reality, augmented reality, and mixed reality as training enhancement methods: a meta-analysis. Hum. Factors **63**(4), 706–726 (2021)

König, S.U., Keshava, A., Clay, V., Ritterhofer, K., Kuske, N., König, P.: Embodied Spatial Knowledge Acquisition in Immersive Virtual Reality: Comparison to Map Exploration. *bioRxiv* (2020)

Kontra, C., Lyons, D.J., Fischer, S.M., Beilock, S.L.: Physical experience enhances science learning. Psychol. Sci. **26**(6), 737–749 (2015)

Shumaker, R. (ed.): ICVR 2007. LNCS, vol. 4563. Springer, Heidelberg (2007). https://doi.org/10.1007/978-3-540-73335-5

LaValle, S.: Virtual Reality (2019). Retrieved from http://vr.cs.uiuc.edu/

Lindgren, R., Tscholl, M., Wang, S., Johnson, E.: Enhancing learning and engagement through embodied interaction within a mixed reality simulation. Comput. Educ. **95**, 174–187 (2016)

Loomis, J.M., Blascovich, J.J., Beall, A.C.: Immersive virtual environment technology as a basic research tool in psychology. Behav. Res. Methods Instrum. Comput. **31**(4), 557–564 (1999)

Makransky, G., Lilleholt, L.: A structural equation modeling investigation of the emotional value of immersive virtual reality in education. Educ. Tech. Res. Dev. **66**(5), 1141–1164 (2018). https://doi.org/10.1007/s11423-018-9581-2

Makransky, G., Petersen, G.B.: The cognitive affective model of immersive learning (CAMIL): a theoretical research-based model of learning in immersive virtual reality. Educ. Psychol. Rev. **33**(3), 937–958 (2021)

Meyer, O.A., Omdahl, M.K., Makransky, G.: Investigating the effect of pre-training when learning through immersive virtual reality and video: a media and methods experiment. Comput. Educ. **140**, 103603 (2019)

McGowin, G., Fiore, S.M., Oden, K.: Learning affordances: theoretical considerations for design of immersive virtual reality in training and education. In: Proceedings of the Human Factors and Ergonomics Society Annual Meeting, vol. 65, no. 1, pp. 883–887. SAGE Publications, Los Angeles, CA (2021)

Menary, R.: Embodied narratives. J. Consciou. Stud. **15**(6) (2008)

Mestre, D., Fuchs, P., Berthoz, A., Vercher, J.L.: Immersion et présence. Le traité de la réalité virtuelle. Paris: Ecole des Mines de Paris, pp. 309–38 (2006)

Newen, A., De Bruin, L., Gallagher, S.: 4E cognition: Historical roots, key concepts, and central issues. The Oxford Handbook of 4E Cognition, pp. 2–16 (2018)

Newton, O.B., Fiore, S.M., LaViola Jr, J.J.: An external cognition framework for visualizing uncertainty in support of situation awareness. In: Proceedings of the Human Factors and Ergonomics Society Annual Meeting, vol. 61, no. 1, pp. 1198–1202. SAGE Publications, Los Angeles, CA (2017)

Pan, Z., Cheok, A.D., Yang, H., Zhu, J., Shi, J.: Virtual reality and mixed reality for virtual learning environments. Comput. Graph. **30**(1), 20–28 (2006)

Pillai, A.: Virtual reality based study to analyse pedestrian attitude towards autonomous vehicles (2017)

Pouw, W.T., Van Gog, T., Paas, F.: An embedded and embodied cognition review of instructional manipulatives. Educ. Psychol. Rev. **26**(1), 51–72 (2014)

Radianti, J., Majchrzak, T.A., Fromm, J., Wohlgenannt, I.: A systematic review of immersive virtual reality applications for higher education: design elements, lessons learned, and research agenda. Comput. Educ. **147**, 103778 (2020)

Robbins, P., Aydede, M.: A short primer on situated cognition (2009)

Rowlands, M.J.: The New Science of the Mind: From Extended Mind to Embodied Phenomenology. MIT Press (2010)

Schiavio, A., Van der Schyff, D.: 4E music pedagogy and the principles of self-organization. Behav. Sci. **8**(8), 72 (2018)

Schneegans, S., Schöner, G.: Dynamic field theory as a framework for understanding embodied cognition. Handbook of Cognitive Science, pp. 241–271 (2008)

Slater, M.: Measuring presence: a response to the Witmer and Singer presence questionnaire. Presence **8**(5), 560–565 (1999)

Slater, M., Sanchez-Vives, M.V.: Enhancing our lives with immersive virtual reality. Front. Robot. AI **3**, 74 (2016)

Slater, M., Wilbur, S.: A framework for immersive VEs (FIVE): speculations on the role of presence in VEs. Pres. Teleoper. VEs **6**(6), 603–616 (1997)

Slater, M.: Implicit learning through embodiment in immersive virtual reality. In: Liu, D., Dede, C., Huang, R., Richards, J. (eds.) Virtual, augmented, and mixed realities in education. SCI, pp. 19–33. Springer, Singapore (2017). https://doi.org/10.1007/978-981-10-5490-7_2

Smart, P.: Extended cognition and the internet. Philosop. Technol. **30**(3), 357–390 (2017)

Thompson, M., et al.: Immersion positively affects learning in virtual reality games compared to equally interactive 2d games. Inf. Learn. Sci. **122**, 442–463 (2021).

Varela, F.J., Thompson, E., Rosch, E.: The Embodied Mind: Cognitive Science and Human Experience. MIT Press (1993)

Wang, A., Thompson, M., Uz-Bilgin, C., Klopfer, E.: Authenticity, interactivity, and collaboration in virtual reality games: best practices and lessons learned. Front. Virtual Real. **130** (2021)

Waterworth, J.A., Waterworth, E.L.: The meaning of presence (2003)

Using AR Headset Camera to Track Museum Visitor Attention: Initial Development Phase

Nikolay Sargsyan[✉] and Cheryl Seals

Auburn University, Auburn, USA
nzs0067@auburn.edu

Abstract. Augmented Reality (AR) has become one of the mainstream media volumes. In museums, AR applications are being implemented to enhance visitor experience. Analyzing the museum visitor experience is crucial for a museum to provide better service to society. Head-mounted cameras and eye-tracking headsets can be used to analyze visitor experience. With the AR headsets becoming part of museum exhibitions, one can utilize these headsets to track and analyze visitor experience. This research aims to improve on the existing work on tracking museum visitor experience using AR headsets. Specifically, this paper discusses an experiment performed at the Jule Collins Museum of Fine Arts at Auburn, Alabama. Visitors' attention towards exhibits was measured using an AR headset camera. Visitor exit surveys were collected reflecting on the visitor experience. This paper illustrates the applicability and failures of analyzing visitor experience with AR headset camera for different exhibits and scenarios. This paper also provides insight into the following issues: privacy concerns with using AR headsets in museums and the ways AR headsets affect visitor experience and behavior.

Keywords: History and culture · Alternative computing environments · Tracking technologies · Consumer products and experience

1 Introduction

The traditional role of museums as institutions is to collect, preserve, research artifacts. Modern museum are also locations for leisure and recreation, knowledge and education delivery. A post-modern sustainable museum adds educational and entertainment value to society and is economically and commercially successful [9]. Nick Merriman identifies museum sustainability dimensions as social sustainability, economic sustainability, and environmental sustainability [13]. He stresses that a fully sustainable museum must fulfill all three dimensions. Social sustainability is the value-added to society (e.g., providing entertainment and recreation environments, informal and lifelong learning environments).

© Springer Nature Switzerland AG 2022
J. Y. C. Chen and G. Fragomeni (Eds.): HCII 2022, LNCS 13318, pp. 74–90, 2022.
https://doi.org/10.1007/978-3-031-06015-1_6

Economic sustainability implies financial stability and describes the environmental contribution by preserving artifacts and landscapes, using renewable power sources, and decreasing air pollution.

The visitor experience must be analyzed to support a museum's social sustainability. The first systematic approach to visitor experience evaluation was introduced by the acclaimed museum consultant Beverly Serrell [19]. She researched the connection between visitors' attention and their behavior patterns inside the museum. There is a direct correlation between the time spent at an exhibit, the number of stops at all exhibits, and a positive visitor experience.

Another insightful measure is the attention the visitor pays to certain areas of an exhibit, known as areas of interest (AOI, or regions of interest, ROI). E.g, an example of AOI is a particular detail in a painting.

Traditionally, insights into visitor behavior are obtained by observing visitors in combination with visitor exit surveys. A visitor can also be tracked by being asked to wear eye-tracking headsets or head-mounted cameras during the visit. Although eye-tracking headsets are best utilized inside controlled laboratory environments, there is limited yet productive research illustrating the applicability of eye-tracking headsets to analyze visitor attention towards exhibits and exhibit AOIs [1,5,6,16,22]. The head-mounted cameras cannot provide the depth of data gathered by eye-tracking headsets. Head-mounted cameras follow only head direction but cannot provide insight into the eye gaze. There is evidence that the visitor's head is directed towards the exhibit when the visitor is paying attention to the exhibit. Both eye-tracking and head-tracking may provide false positives, as gaze direction towards an object does not necessarily imply mental engagement with that object.

Today, Augmented Reality (AR) and Mixed Reality (MR) are widely accepted media volumes applied in many different fields and scenarios. This includes AR apps developed to enhance the experience of museum visitors [3,4] for both mobile and headset platforms.

AR and MR headsets can be used to gather and analyze the visitor experience by recognizing visitor patterns and measuring the attention towards exhibits. Hololens 2 by Microsoft [14] and Magic Leap One by MagicLeap [11] are the only available headsets that feature eye-tracking technologies. The eye-tracking in these devices is tuned specifically to map the user's gaze direction within the virtual world and is not readily suitable for real-world behavioral research purposes requiring custom setup and plugins [2,10]. Unlike the eye-tracking headsets dedicated to behavior analysis that track the gaze of both eyes, Hololens 2 and Magic Leap One report only the estimated intersection of the gaze. The dynamic environment of a visitor traversing through a museum exhibition poses additional challenges for eye-tracking and can affect its accuracy since the eye-tracking works the best in calibrated static environments. The eye-tracking also comes with a price tag, e.g., the Lynx R-1 MR headset that is currently under development by Lynx [21] has reported a price drop of about $500 after the eye-tracking feature was removed [8].

With the current limitations of eye-tracking inside AR and MR headsets, it is worth investigating the headset cameras' capabilities to track the visitor's attention. While human head and eye directions do not necessarily correlate [7], co-occurrence takes place during observation tasks [12,17], and head direction can be used to infer attention direction [20].

The existing research on applying eye-tracking glasses and head-mounted cameras to analyze museum visitors' experience provides evidence that footage from a head-mounted camera can be used to track visitors' attention [1,5,6,16, 18,22]. However, the existing research does not specifically focus on the viewpoint of utilizing AR and MR headsets to track visitors' attention. The existing research also features issues such as the lack of an exhibition with diverse content and visitor exit surveys to verify results.

The research describes an experiment on tracking visitor experience and attention with the camera of an AR headset in a diverse museum environment. The paper provides evidence on the applicability of head-tracking in a museum environment and discusses a set of issues to be considered if developing a system to analyze visitor experience with an AR headset.

2   Related Work

Despite the limited research on applications of eye-tracking and head-tracking to analyze museum visitor experience, the existing research provides a solid basis for new developments. In this section, a few existing research with direct connection to the goals of this research is presented.

The research performed by Daniel Wessel et al. [22] focused on exploring the advantages of eye-tracking over visitor interviews and surveys. The data obtained from the eye-tracking device were analyzed, with visitor exit interviews to support the analysis since eye-tracking data does not provide a full description of the visitor's mental and cognitive processing of the exhibition. An artificial poster exhibition was created for the purposes of the research. The researchers had utilized the ASL Mobile eye tracker. Daniel Wessel et al. validated the applicability of eye-tracking technologies used along with exit interviews to derive visitor behavior data.

The research performed by Ali S. Razavian, et al. [18] explore the possibilities of utilizing a head-mounted camera to track visitors' attention level in an exhibition. A photo poster exhibition was created in a two-room area for the experiment. Participants were asked to attend the exhibits while wearing a head-mounted camera. A classifier was then trained to recognize the photos appearing in a video frame under different perspectives. This classifier was successfully used to determine the position of the exhibit in a video frame and the time it remained there. A visitor was considered to have paid attention to an exhibit when it was focused on the central part of the video frame. A sequence of such frames was named a focus shot. The time an exhibit spent being focused was used to determine the attention level of the visitor for that exhibit.

Although not performed in a museum environment, Michael Barz, et al. [2] has performed research that has a direct implication in terms of museum visitor experience tracking with AR headsets. Utilizing Microsoft Hololens 2 MR headset and Augmented Reality Eye-Tracking Toolkit (ARETT) developed by Sebastian Kapp et al. [10], they have implemented a system that aggregates the attention to the defined object in real-time.

3 Research Method

The research was performed at the Jule Collins Smith Museum of Fine Art, located in Auburn, Alabama. The Jule Collins Smith Museum features a wide range of art in its exhibition, including paintings, posters, photography, video materials, sculptures, clothing, furniture, chandelier, and an AR-enabled exhibit. At the moment of the experiment, there were over 100 exhibits on display in the museum. Some were displayed standalone, and some were united into installations.

The main point of this research is to illustrate the applicability of measuring visitors' attention using an AR headset camera.

Hypothesis 1 (H1): *There is a correlation between the time spent at an exhibit derived from the headset camera footage and the visitor's self-assessment of the attention paid to the exhibit.*

Hypothesis 2 (H2): *The AR camera can detect the AOI within an exhibit that a visitor paid the most attention to.*

Wearing an AR headset may alter the visitor's behavior due to expectations of virtual interaction. Visitor behavior could have been affected because they knew it was being recorded.

Hypothesis 3 (H3): *Wearing AR headset affects the visitor behavior.*

Given the weight and form factor of modern AR headsets and the presence of the virtual user interface, they may annoy the visitors and obstruct them from their experience.

Hypothesis 4 (H4): *The AR headset does obstruct the visitor experience.*

Usage of AR technologies is known for personal privacy violation concerns. Privacy violation concerns may hinder the adoption of AR technologies in museums.

Hypothesis 5 (H5): *The museum visitors do not have privacy concerns associated with AR headset camera.*

Additionally, with the input from the curators of the Jule Collins Smith Museum of Fine Art, the following questions about the quality of the current exhibition were identified:

1. The museum exhibition halls are interconnected, creating a loop. No signage of which direction to start from are provided to the visitors. Is there a preference in the start direction among the visitors?
2. Do visitors engage with the AR experience of exhibit A10?
3. Do visitors pay attention to exhibit A24?
4. Do visitors pay attention to the installation A27?
5. What part of the installation A27 is the most popular among the visitors?
6. Do visitors have a preference between the two paintings in the installation A31?
7. The exhibits A32 and A38 are next to each other and share a similar color pattern. Exhibit A38 is the first to be viewed when entering the exhibition hall. Is exhibit A32 neglected?
8. Do visitors pay attention to exhibit A59?
9. Do visitors pay attention to exhibit A60?

4   Research Design

18 individual exhibits and exhibit installations were selected to be included in the experiment. The list of these exhibits can be found in Table 1.

Two headsets were employed during the experiment. The first headset, an AR smart glasses Epson Moverio Bt-350, produced by the Epson Moverio, has the camera placement in the right endpiece. This kind of positioning can be found in all of the smartglasses available in the market. Epson Moverio Bt-350 has a constantly present virtual user interface. The second headset, a modified non-brand camera eyeglass, had a camera placed in the glasses' bridge. Such cameras are available in high-end MR headsets such as Hololens 1&2 and Magic Leap One.

Visitors were approached at the museum entrance and offered to participate in the research. The participants were asked to wear the headset during the whole duration of their visit. Upon exit, the participants were asked to complete a survey consisting of two sections.

An exit survey consisting of two sections was created to gather the visitors' reflections on their museum visit.

The first section assessed the participant demographic and the experience with the headset during the current visit. This section included questions about visitors' age, education level, and if they had previously visited the museum.

To address Hypothesis 3, this section included the following question: "Did the head-mounted camera affect your behavior during visit?", and the following scale: "Strongly disagree (0) - Somewhat disagree (1) - Neither agree not disagree (2) - Somewhat agree (3) - Somewhat disagree (4)".

To address Hypothesis 4, this section included the following question: "Was the head-mounted camera obstructing?", and the following scale: "Definitely not (0) - Probably not (1) - Might or might not (2) - Probably yes (3) - Definitely yes (4)".

Table 1. The list of exhibits and installations included in the experiment (total of 18) with descriptions.

Exhibit code	Type	Exhibit description
A1	Painting	A painting of the museum founder
A2	Glass figure	A glass figure attach to the wall, with a large description text
A4	Sculpture, Freestanding	A lightweight circular sculpture with leafs
A10	Painting, AR-enabled	A modern art painting accompanied by a QR code The visitors are prompted to scan the QR code, download the associated app, and engage into an AR experience with the painting
A11	Installation, Wall-sized	An art installation of books occupying a whole wall
A16	Clothing	A manikin wearing the exhibited clothing piece
A20	Installation, Table	A table with an installation of books on it
A24	Informative texts, Wall-sized	A set of descriptions of the current exhibitions and the artists behind it Occupies half of the wall in height and width
A27	Installation, Room-Sized	A room with an installation depicting process of creation of electric guitars on it's walls The walls were divided into 3 logical sections, each section was treated as an individual exhibit (A27-A, A27-B, A27-C)
A31	Installation, Paintings, Two	Two paintings (A31-A, A31-B) next to each other, sharing a common theme
A32	Painting	A large painting
A38	Blanket	A large blanket hanging on a wall, with artistic paintings
A49	Sculpture, Freestanding	A modern art sculpture, requiring to get very close to it for a full experience
A51	Sculpture, Under glass	A sculpture of a human hand
A55	Installation, Paintings, Three	Three paintings (A55-A, A55-B, A55-C) next and under each other, united by a single theme
A58	Installation, Furniture, Table and Chair	Two pieces of concept furniture, a table (A58-A) and a chair (A58-B)
A59	Chandelier	A huge chandelier spanning 2 floors, hanging from the ceiling
A60	Poster, Wall-sized	A large poster occupying a whole wall

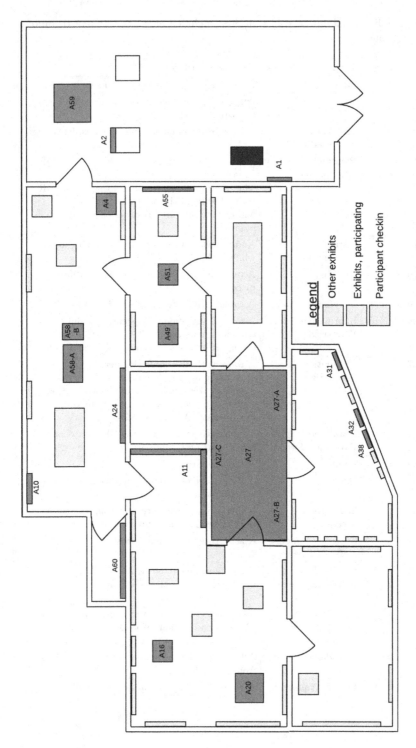

Fig. 1. Schematic representation of the museum floor plan and exhibit locations.

To address Hypothesis 4, this section included the following questions: "Augmented Reality devices rely heavily on cameras. Are you concerned with violating other people's privacy while wearing a device with a camera?"; "Are you concerned with people wearing a device with a camera violating your privacy?", and the following scale: "Not concerned (0) - Somewhat concerned (1) - Strongly concerned (2)".

The second section asked the participants to evaluate the attention paid to the exhibits. The schematic floor map of the museum with the participating and non-participating exhibits can be found in Fig. 1. The exhibits were selected to cover the multitude of different types of exhibits usually found in museum exhibitions.

To address Hypothesis 1, this section included the following question: "How much attention did you pay to this exhibit?", and the following scale: "None at all (0) - A little (1) - A moderate amount (2) - A lot (3) - A great deal (4)" for each exhibit.

To address the Hypothesis 2 the participants were also asked to select which exhibit in an installation they paid the most attention to.

For the AR-enabled exhibit A10, the visitors were asked about their experience with the AR portion of the exhibit.

Similar to [18], the length of focus shot in seconds (focus length) was measured. Unlike [18], the measurement of focus length was performed manually. For exhibits within an installation, both the focus length for individual exhibits and the focus length for the installation were measured (Table 6).

5   Results and discussion

In total, 26 museum visitors agreed to participate in the research. The list of all participant demographics can be found in Table 2. There were 21 valid survey submissions and 14 valid camera footage records. More details about visitor and participant numbers can be found in Table 3.

The average visit length was 1785 s seconds and the visit length standard deviation was 573 s. To normalize the focus length, the adjusted focus length was calculated for each exhibit for each visitor:

$$AdjustedFocusLength = \frac{FocusLength}{VisitLength} \qquad (1)$$

The correlation coefficients between the adjusted focus length and the visitors' self-report of attention paid to the exhibits can be found in Table 7.

Exhibit A1 (painting) was dropped from the research. As seen in Fig. 1, this exhibit is located right next to the participant check-in location. Although exhibit A1 did not appear in any footage, only 6 participants indicated not paying any attention to it at all. This may be due to participants attending exhibit A1 before or after wearing the headset.

As seen in Fig. 1, exhibits A11 (installation) and A24 (wall of text) occupy large portions of the wall and are impossible to bypass during the visit. Hence, these exhibits can be centered in the footage frames without the participants

Table 2. The list of all participants (total of 26).

Participant code	Device	Notes	Visit duration (mm:ss)	Visitor persona	Exploration style	Returning visitor	Age
C1	Camera glasses	Corrupt Data	-	Experience Seeker Recharger	Ant	Yes	60+
E1	Epson Moverio Bt-350	Corrupt Data	-	-	-	-	-
C2	Camera glasses	Corrupt Data	-	Explorer Recharger	Ant Butterfly	Yes	21-29
E2	Epson Moverio Bt-350	No Survey Taken	20:19	-	-	-	-
C3	Camera glasses	Corrupt Data	-	Experience Seeker Professional/Hobbyist	Butterfly	No	40-49
C4	Camera glasses	-	28:18	Experience Seeker Explorer	Ant	No	30-39
E3	Epson Moverio Bt-350	Distracting	-	-	-	-	-
C5	Camera glasses	-	40:34	Experience Seeker Explorer	Ant	Yes	50-59
E4	Epson Moverio Bt-350	-	34:16	Explorer Recharger	Ant Butterfly	No	20-29
E5	Epson Moverio Bt-350	Taking off the headset during the visit	22:51	Experience Seeker Recharger	Fish Butterfly	Yes	21-29
C6	Camera glasses	-	10:26	Explorer Professional/Hobbyist	Ant	Yes	21-29
C7	Camera glasses	-	29:11	Experience Seeker Explorer	Fish	No	18-20
E6	Epson Moverio Bt-350	-	36:22	Explorer Recharger	Ant	Yes	60+
E7	Epson Moverio Bt-350	-	26:11	Explorer Professional/Hobbyist	Fish Butterfly	No	50-59
C8	Camera glasses	-	35:59	Experience Seeker Explorer	Ant Butterfly	No	40-49
E8	Epson Moverio Bt-350	Distracting	-	-	-	-	-
E9	Epson Moverio Bt-350	Corrupt Data	-	Experience Seeker Recharger	Ant Butterfly	Yes	21-29
E10	Epson Moverio Bt-350	Corrupt Data	-	Explorer Professional/Hobbyist	Ant	Yes	21-29
C9	Camera glasses	-	46:00	Experience Seeker Explorer	Fish Butterfly	Yes	21-29
E12	Epson Moverio Bt-350	Corrupt Data	-	Explorer Recharger	Butterfly	Yes	21-29
C10	Camera glasses	-	25:38	Explorer Recharger	Fish Butterfly	No	21-29
E11	Epson Moverio Bt-350	Out of Power	-	-	-	-	-
C11	Camera glasses	-	15:28	Experience Seeker Explorer	Fish	No	21-29
C12	Camera glasses	Optical glasses worn over camera glasses	94:04	Explorer Professional/Hobbyist	Ant Butterfly	Yes	60+
C13	Camera glasses	-	29:45	Explorer Recharger	Butterfly	Yes	18-20
E13	Epson Moverio Bt-350	-	28:40	Experience Seeker Explorer	Butterfly	No	21-29

paying attention. Additionally, participants may observe them with their side eyesight, which is impossible to capture with a head-mounted camera alone.

The AR-enabled exhibit A10 illustrated another issue. With A10, the participants spent a significant amount of time reading the exhibit description compared to viewing the exhibit itself. A similar behavior can be observed for exhibits A31 (installation of two paintings), A32 (painting), and A38 (blanket with paintings).

Table 3. Visitors and participants.

	Number
Total visitors approached	43
Total visitors declining to participate	17
Visitors declining to participate due to videotaping-related privacy concerns	1
Visitors declining to participate due to previous unsatisfying experience with AR in museums	2
Total participants	26
Valid footage extracted from the headset camera	13
Valid survey completed on exit	21

Table 4. Results of survey questions on privacy concerns associated with AR headset camera.

Question	Not concerned (0)	Somewhat concerned (1)	Somewhat concerned (2)
Augmented Reality devices rely heavily on cameras Are you concerned with violating other people's privacy while wearing a device with a camera?	66.6% (14)	33.3% (7)	0% (0)
Are you concerned with people wearing a device with a camera violating your privacy?	76.2% (16)	23.8% (5)	0% (0)

Table 5. Results of survey question on if wearing the AR camera affects their behavior.

Question	Strongly disagree (0)	Somewhat disagree (1)	Neither agree nor disagree (2)	Somewhat agree (3)	Strongly agree (4)
Did the head-mounted camera affect your behavior during visit?	28.6% (6)	4.8% (1)	14.3% (3)	33.3% (7)	9.5% (2)

Table 6. Results of survey question on if wearing the AR camera obstructed their experience.

Question	Definitely not (0)	Probably not (1)	Might or might not (2)	Probably yes (3)	Definitely yes (4)
Was the head-mounted camera obstructing?	23.8% (5)	19.0% (4)	9.5% (2)	28.6% (6)	0% (0)

Table 7. Correlation between adjusted focus length and the visitors' estimation of attention paid to the exhibit in the survey. Green - strong correlation, White - moderate correlation, Yellow - Moderate correlation, but statistically insignificant, Orange - No correlation.

#	Exhibit Code	Correlation to survey reports	Statistical Significance
1	A1	*N/A*	*N/A*
2	A60	$R = 0.62$ Moderate Positive	$p = 0.018$ Significant
3	A2	$R = 0.67$ Moderate Positive	$p = 0.008$ Significant
4	A24	$R = 0.51$ Moderate Positive	$p = 0.062$ Not Significant
5	A59	$R = 0.73$ Moderate Positive	$p = 0.003$ Significant
6	A20	$R = 0.80$ Strongly Positive	$p = 0.0005$ Significant
7	A4	$R = 0.3$ No Correlation	$p = 0.29$ Not Significant
8	A32	$R = 0.61$ Moderate Positive	$p = 0.02$ Significant
9	A49	$R = 0.40$ No Correlation	$p = 0.15$ Not Significant
10	A16	$R = 0.24$ No Correlation	$p = 0.41$ Not Significant
11	A55	$R = 0.79$ Strongly Positive	$p = 0.0007$ Significant
12	A27	$R = 0.61$ Moderate Positive	$p = 0.02$ Significant
13	A23	$R = 0.23$ No Correlation	$p = 0.042$ Significant
14	A31	$R = 0.63$ Moderate Positive	$p = 0.015$ Significant
15	A51	$R = 0.37$ No Correlation	$p = 0.19$ Not Significant
16	A58	$R = 0.51$ Moderate Positive	$p = 0.006$ Not Significant
17	A10	$R = 0.32$ No Correlation	$p = 0.26$ Not Significant
17	A11	$R = 0.26$ No Correlation	$p = 0.2$ Not Significant

The exhibits A49 (sculpture), A16 (clothing exhibits on a manikin), and A4 (sculpture) closely resemble some of the other exhibits in the museum. This can explain the lack of correlation between the captured footage and the survey results. More analysis of the footage is required to draw a conclusion.

Additionally, due to their location, all three exhibits can be observed without being centered in the footage frame.

In Fig. 1 it can be seen that exhibit A51 appears as the first exhibit when a visitor enters the exhibition hall. This had potentially distorted the visitor behavior regarding exhibit A51, hence the lack of correlation.

Exhibit A58 also appears in the center of the exhibition hall. So visitors could potentially view it from a distance or with side eyesight, hence the lack of correlation.

As can be seen in Fig. 1, due to its location, a visitor viewing exhibit A55 is not distracted by other exhibits. Similarly, exhibit A20, being installed on a table, requires the visitor to look down at the table to view the exhibit. In both cases, the visitor behavior is simple, with the head direction being explicitly connected with attention. Hence, the a strong correlation of results.

It can be concluded that Hypothesis 1 holds for some of the exhibits.

The Hypothesis 1 not holding for some of the exhibits illustrates the pitfalls of the simplistic approach towards measuring the focus length. Individual exhibits and installations require a system of weights applied to the focus length based on the position of the exhibit within a frame, its size within a frame, and the speed of the head movement. Further research is required to develop a framework addressing this issue.

Table 8. The percentage of correctly guessed exhibits within an installation that the visitor payed most attention to, and the T-test against the desired guess value of 80%.

Population	Guessed %	T-test
A55	46.15%	$t(13) = -2.35$ $p < 0.05$
A27	50%	$t(13) = -1.98$ $p < 0.05$
A31	23.07%	$t(13) = -4.68$ $p < 0.05$
A58	76.92%	$\mathbf{t(13) = -0.25}$ $\mathbf{p = 0.4}$

For each exhibit in the installation, the one with the longest adjusted focus length was selected. These selections were matched against the visitors' self-report of the exhibit within an installation to which they directed most attention, as seen in Table 8.

The Hypothesis 2 not holding for installations A55 and A31 illustrates the issue that using an AR headset camera between closely located exhibits as an AR headset camera cannot capture the eye movements between these exhibits.

The Hypothesis 2 not holding for installation A27 should be investigated further to understand the visitor behavior towards this particular exhibit and tune the focus length measurement approach.

The installation A58 illustrates an ideal scenario for an AR headset camera. The exhibits within the installation are located relatively far away. Visitors clearly favored exhibit A58-A over the A58-B. So there was no eye movement between the two exhibits.

It can be concluded that Hypothesis 2 holds for certain scenarios.

Table 9. The results of T-tests of the results of the survey question "Did the head-mounted camera affect your behavior during visit?" against the positive scale values "Strongly agree (4)" and "Somewhat agree (3)"

Population	T-test against "Somewhat agree (3)"	T-test against "Strongly agree (4)"
All participants (21)	$t(21) = -3.87$ $p < .05$	$t(13) = -6.88$ $p < .05$
Participants with camera glasses (13)	$t(13) = -4.15$ $p < .05$	$t(13) = -6.5$ $p < .05$
Participants with Epson Moverio Bt-350 smart glasses (8)	$\mathbf{t(8) = -1.18}$ $\mathbf{p = .27}$	$t(8) = -3.54$ $p < .05$

Table 10. The results of T-tests of the results of the survey question "Was the head-mounted camera obstructing?" against the positive scale values "Definitely yes (4)" and "Probably yes (3)"

Population	T-test against "Probably yes (3)"	T-test against "Definitely yes (4)"
All participants (21)	$t(21) = -5.25$ $p < .05$	$t(13) = -9.06$ $p < .05$
Participants with camera glasses (13)	$t(13) = -7.21$ $p < .05$	$t(13) = -10.81$ $p < .05$
Participants with Epson Moverio Bt-350 smart glasses (8)	$\mathbf{t(8) = -1.42}$ $\mathbf{p = 0.2}$	$t(8) = -5.22$ $p < .05$

The results of the survey question "Did the head-mounted camera affect your behavior during the visit?" can be seen in Table 5. The results of T-tests against the positive scale values "Strongly agree (4)" and "Somewhat agree (3)" can be seen in Table 9. The Hypothesis 3 holds for Epson Moverio Bt-350 users against "Somewhat agree (3)". This is supported by the complaints from some of the participants that they constantly expect an AR experience to launch, albeit told that only the camera of the AR headset is enabled. Unlike the camera glasses, the Epson Moverio also had an idle virtual user interface displayed during the

Table 11. The results of T-tests of the results of the survey question "Augmented Reality devices rely heavily on cameras. Are you concerned with violating other people's privacy while wearing a device with a camera?" against the value "Not concerned (0)"

Population	T-test against "Not concerned (3)"
All participants (21)	$t(21) = -3.16$ $p < .05$
Young and middle age adults (15)	$t(15) = 3.05$ $p < .05$
Older adults (6)	$\mathbf{t(6) = 1}$ $\mathbf{p = 0.36}$

Table 12. The results of T-tests of the results of the survey question "Are you concerned with people wearing a device with a camera violating your privacy?" against the value "Not concerned (0)"

Population	T-test against "Not concerned (3)"
All participants (21)	$t(21) = 2.5$ $p < .05$
Young and middle age adults (15)	$t(15) = 2.25$ $p < .05$
Older adults (6)	$\mathbf{t(6) = 1}$ $\mathbf{p = .036}$

experiment. The Hypothesis 3 holds for the case of using Epson Moverio Bt-350 AR headset with the virtual interface.

The results of the survey question "Was the head-mounted camera obstructing?" can be seen in Table 5. The results of T-tests against the positive scale values "Definitely yes (4)" and "Probably yes (3)" can be seen in Table 10. The Hypothesis 4 holds for Epson Moverio Bt-350 users against "Probably yes (3)". This is supported by two participants pausing the participation complaining the AR headset distracts their experience, and two visitors rejecting to participate under the pretext that their previous AR experience at the museum was distracting. Unlike the camera glasses, the Epson Moverio Bt-350 also had an idle virtual user interface displayed during the experiment. The Hypothesis 3 holds for the case of using Epson Moverio Bt-350 Bt-350 AR headset with the virtual interface.

The results of the survey questions "Augmented Reality devices rely heavily on cameras. Are you concerned with violating other people's privacy while wearing a device with a camera?" and "Are you concerned with people wearing a device with a camera violating your privacy?" can be seen in Table 4. The results of T-tests against the value "Not concerned (0)" can be seen in Table 11 and in Table 12. The Hypothesis 5 did hold for older adults, while it is the young and middle-aged adults who are the main target of AR experiences.

The questions by the museum curators were answered as follows based on the footage analysis:

1. *There museum exhibition halls are interconnected creating a loop. No signage of which direction to start from is provided to the visitors. Is there a preference in the start direction among the visitors?* No preferences were indicated, participants split evenly.
2. *Do visitors engage with the AR experience of exhibit A10?* No, the visitors did not.
3. *Do visitors pay attention to exhibit A24?* The visitors spend 10 s at exhibit A24 on average. Given that the text in exhibit A24 takes 80 s to read, it can be safely assumed that the visitors didn't attend exhibit A24.
4. *Do visitors pay attention to the installation A27?* Yes, the visitors spend 2 min at the installation A27 on average.
5. *What part of the installation A27 is the most popular among the visitors?* Based solely on the footage, 61% of visitors attended exhibit C, 23% of visitors attended exhibit B, and 23% of visitors attended exhibit A.
6. *Do visitors have a preference between the two paintings in the installation A31?* Based solely on the footage, both paintings were equally attended by the visitors.
7. *The exhibits A32 and A38 are next to each other and share a similar color pattern. Exhibit A38 is the first to view when a visitor enters the exhibition hall. Is exhibit A32 neglected?* Contrary to the museum curator expectations, visitors spent 3 s longer attending exhibit A32 on average.
8. *Do visitors pay attention to exhibit A59?* It was assumed by the curators that exhibit A59 is neglected. 50% of the visitors paid attention to exhibit A59. On average, the visitors viewed it for 7.2 s. It can be assumed that the visitors do pay attention to exhibit A59.
9. *Do visitors pay attention to exhibit A60?* It was assumed by the curators that exhibit A60 is neglected. 50% of the visitors paid attention to exhibit A60. On average, the visitors viewed it for 9.3 s. It can be assumed that the visitors do pay attention to exhibit A60.

6   Conclusion and Future Work

Hypothesis 1 and Hypothesis 2 hold for some of the exhibits.

The Hypothesis 3 and Hypothesis 4 holds for AR smartglasses with constantly present virtual interface.

The Hypothesis 5 did not hold.

This research illustrates the applicability of AR headset cameras to analyze visitor experience with certain limitations. More research must be performed to address the limitations.

We suggest, that a combination of an image classifier for the exhibits and a focus shot classifier to extract the focus shot for each individual exhibit can be used to overcome the limitations uncovered in this research, enabling automated visitor experience evaluation utilizing an AR headset camera.

Future work will include developing and testing such a system.

References

1. Al-Baddai, S., Ströhl, B., Lang, E.W., Ludwig, B.: Do museum visitors see what educators want them to see? In: Adjunct Publication of the 25th Conference on User Modeling, Adaptation and Personalization (2017)
2. Michael, B., et al.: Automatic recognition and augmentation of attended objects in real-time using eye tracking and a head-mounted display. In: ACM Symposium on Eye Tracking Research and Applications (2021)
3. Desai, N.: Recreation of history using augmented reality. ACCENTS Trans. Image Process. Comput. Vis. **4**(10), 1–5 (2018)
4. Ding, M.: Augmented Reality in Museums, pp. 3–8. Arts Management and Technology Laboratory, Heinz College (2017)
5. Eghbal-Azar, K., Widlok, T.: Potentials and limitations of mobile eye tracking in visitor studies: evidence from field research at two museum exhibitions in Germany. Soc. Sci. Comput. Rev. **31**(1), 103–118 (2013)
6. Raphaela, G., Amrhein, A., Krug, M., Pitsch, K.: Towards using eyetracking data as basis for conversation analysis on real-world museum interaction. In: SAGA-International Workshop on Solutions for Automatic Gaze Data Analysis: Proceedings (2015)
7. Hieronymus, G.H.L.M, Van Opstal, A.J.: Human eye-head coordination in two dimensions under different sensorimotor conditions. Exper. Brain Res. **114.3**, 542–560 (1997)
8. Peter, G.: Mixed Reality Lynx R-1 Gets Huge Price Drop, Launching September Kickstarter. VRFocus (2021). https://www.vrfocus.com/2021/07/mixed-reality-lynx-r-1-gets-huge-price-drop-launching-september-kickstarter/
9. Luiza, P.I., Borza, A.: Factors influencing museum sustainability and indicators for museum sustainability measurement. Sustainability **8.1**, 101 (2016)
10. Sebastian, K., et al.: ARETT: augmented reality eye tracking toolkit for head mounted displays. Sensors **21.6**, 2234 (2021)
11. Magic Leap: Reality Is Just Beginning. Spatial Computing for Enterprise—Magic Leap. www.magicleap.com/en-us
12. Marius't Bernard, H., et al.: Gaze allocation in natural stimuli: comparing free exploration to head-fixed viewing conditions. Vis. Cogn. **17.6–7**, 1132–1158 (2009)
13. Merriman, N.: Museum collections and sustainability. Cultural Trends **17**(1), 3–21 (2008)
14. Microsoft HoloLens: Mixed Reality Technology for Business. Microsoft HoloLens; Mixed Reality Technology for Business. www.microsoft.com/en-us/hololens?icid=SSM_AS_Promo_Devices_HoloLens2
15. Moverio BT-350 Smart Glasses. Moverio BT-350 Smart Glasses; Smart Glasses; Wearables; For Work; Epson US. www.epson.com/For-Work/Wearables/Smart-Glasses/Moverio-BT-350-Smart-Glasses/p/V11H837020#

16. Naspetti, S., Pierdicca, R., Mandolesi, S., Paolanti, M., Frontoni, E., Zanoli, R.: Automatic analysis of eye-tracking data for augmented reality applications: a prospective outlook. In: De Paolis, L.T., Mongelli, A. (eds.) AVR 2016. LNCS, vol. 9769, pp. 217–230. Springer, Cham (2016). https://doi.org/10.1007/978-3-319-40651-0_17

17. Francis, Q., Ehrich, R., Lockhart, T.: As go the feet... on the estimation of attentional focus from stance. In: Proceedings of the 10th International Conference on Multimodal Interfaces (2008)

18. Ali, S.R., et al.: Estimating attention in exhibitions using wearable cameras. In: 2014 22nd International Conference on Pattern Recognition. IEEE (2014)

19. Beverly, S.: Paying attention: the duration and allocation of visitors' time in museum exhibitions. Curator Museum J. **40.2**, 108–125 (1997)

20. Clara, S., et al.: Using a head-mounted camera to infer attention direction. Int. J. Behav. Dev. **37.5**, 468–474 (2013)

21. The Future of Mixed Reality, Now. Lynx. https://lynx-r.com/

22. Wessel, D., Mayr, E., Knipfer, K.: Re-viewing the museum visitor's view. Workshop Research Methods in Informal and Mobile Learning. Institute of Education, London, UK (2007)

Sculpting in Augmented Reality

Redefining Digital Crafts Through Multimodal Interactions

Fabio Scotto[(✉)] [iD]

The University of Edinburgh, Edinburgh EH8 9YL, UK
fabio.scotto1@gmail.com

Abstract. Sculpting is a complex craft that relies on the synergy of multiple factors. The makers' dexterity, material properties and environmental conditions are fundamental in determining a successful sculpting process. Although advanced software solutions emulate this craft through sophisticated interactions and design options, craftsmen and digital makers criticize these interfaces' lack of physical engagement. This study explores augmented reality technology to define an additional method for sculpting processes that links the physical craft with methodologies from 3D modelling software. The research output consists of an augmented reality app - SculptAR - that applies concepts from multimodal interactivity studies to implement gesture and voice recognition methods. The aim is to integrate these inputs and define augmented sculpting as an engaging and interactive experience that merges physical and digital skills. Furthermore, this research wants to highlight the emergence of possibilities for developing interactive experiences that include various human senses.

Keywords: Augmented reality · Augmented sculpting · Multimodal interface · Embodied interactivity

1 Introduction

With the recent decades' growing computer power and visualization technology, artists and craftsmen use digital devices to extend their creative production. In addition to brushes, chisels, and scrapers, they also include software and hardware equipment to expand their toolsets and define novel technology-assisted processes that enhance human creativity (Adzhiev et al. 2003). Sculpting is a craft that involves adding, pushing, and carving material from a block made of clay, stone, or wood. Digital sculpting simulates these operations through a computer interface and replaces the physical object with a digitally-generated mesh. In addition to providing new interactions for free-form 3D modelling (Galyean and Hughes 1991), this digital process allows the manipulation and exploration of form in ways that are not possible when working with physical materials (Treadaway 2009).

In his PhD thesis on the role of technology in the crafts and design practice, Marshall states that craftsmanship is a manual activity and a process of knowledge transfer between the maker and the product. Beyond understanding materials and tools, craftsmen embed their experience, sensitivity, and memory onto the object through manual

© Springer Nature Switzerland AG 2022
J. Y. C. Chen and G. Fragomeni (Eds.): HCII 2022, LNCS 13318, pp. 91–107, 2022.
https://doi.org/10.1007/978-3-031-06015-1_7

work, highlighting 'hand-made' as one of the fundamental characteristics of crafts (Marshall 1999). Therefore, many makers and practitioners criticize digital crafting software for its inability to integrate the makers' bodily intelligence and represent the expressive characteristics that originate from the interactions between hands and material (Treadaway 2009). Furthermore, sculptor and craftsman Gheyselinck argues how the subtlety of handcrafting (fingerprints, tool marks, environments) enrich the sculpted object and promotes its uniqueness. On the contrary, digital software provides a perfectly sculpted 3D model with no imperfections and an unlimited possibility of reproduction (Gheyselinck 2021).

This study uses Augmented Reality (AR) to explore alternative interactions and overcome the limited physical engagement of digital sculpting processes. AR refers to the technology that overlays digital information on the physical environments. Through monitors, projections and head-mounted displays (HMD), this technology continuously registers the surroundings' spatial characteristics, and it layers virtual objects on the physical space (Carmigniani et al. 2010; Azuma 1997). By contextualizing digital artefacts within the user's private environment, research in AR interfaces explore concepts of proximity and familiarity to develop new modes of interactions (Billinghurst et al. 2009). These real-time interactions originate from sophisticated input capturing devices and include physical input as hand gestures, voice commands, and body tracking to pursue a more intuitive integration of human skills (Ehn and Linde 2004).

This paper links physical and digital sculpting to emphasize the emergence of new interactive methods mediated through AR. While standard 3D modelling software provides a vast range of sculpting tools and options, AR offers new possibilities for developing intuitive 3D modelling processes. It allows more natural interactions with the digital artefact, merges physical and digital inputs, and highlights new methodologies for customizing unique design objects. This research uses HoloLens 2, a holographic HMD that integrates sensors to recognize various physical inputs (Microsoft 2021). Furthermore, this study utilizes a custom AR app – *SculptAR* - to validate sculpting approaches that use hand gestures and voice commands as input for mesh manipulation. SculptAR also relies on capturing devices that allow real-time access to the surrounding sound, translating it into a customization parameter for the AR objects.

2 Context

2.1 Physical Sculpting

Sculpting is an ancient craft, and it is a process of shaping a block of material for figurative and realistic three-dimensional representations. The process is either additive or subtractive. The additive method refers to the process of layering material to achieve the desired form. This approach applies primarily to softer materials (clay, modelling wax, paper) and uses hand pressure or tools to shape them. On the contrary, the subtractive process removes material from the main block until its appearance matches the intended depiction. The subtractive process applies when sculpting harder materials like stone, wood, plaster, and it is 'far less forgiving as the wrong move, or the wrong amount of pressure can be disastrous' (Mongeon 2015).

Sculpting describes an artistic approach and a making process, and in this paper, its definition follows the one provided by Marshall (1999) as a craft 'concerned with the processes, technologies and thinking employed in the making of work'. During sculpting, craftsmen use their hands to evaluate the material's properties and actively modify it, conferring to the hand a role that is both information channel and responsive tool (McCullough 1998). Through vision, the sculptor evaluates the proportions of an artefact, identifies material features, and highlights its cultural context with meaningful details and ornamentation (McCullough 1998). Thus, a sculpted artefact represents an immersive multi-sensorial experience that relies on vision and touches synergies and the engagement of the craftsman with material and tools (Nimkulrat 2012).

Furthermore, using the hands as an exploratory tool directly relates to learning and knowledge-acquisition processes. For cognitive psychologists, the sense of touch is a primary source of information, one that builds knowledge and spatial intelligence through physical interactions (Klemmer et al. 2006). Human memory retains this tactile knowledge permanently and can recall it even when 'decoupled from the original situation in which the embodied experience took place' (Novak and Schwan 2020). Makers and design practitioners develop a unique understanding of their crafts through skilful handwork and the use of tools. Craft knowledge builds upon these physical experiences, and it is challenging to translate this understanding into theory, text or mathematical notations (Dormer 1994). Although exploited for commercial value or protectionist policies, craft knowledge is a defining characteristic of sculpting and crafts, and it originates from the maker's rational and physical abilities (Marshall 1999).

This research defines *Embodied Knowledge* as the innate ability to interact with physical objects. It consists of 'knowing' how to respond to one's surroundings without analytical processing. Similarly to sculpting and crafts knowledge, it develops from experience, but it does not require masterful skills. Instead, it is the ability to recognize a particular action and physically react to it, like writing with a pen, opening a door, or holding a cup. This chapter will further discuss Embodied Knowledge to establish a rational link between the physical knowledge of sculpting processes and immersive virtual interactions.

2.2 Digital Sculpting

Digital sculpting refers to manipulating computer-generated geometries either through software or a digital interface. It develops from understanding the characteristics of the craft of sculpting, and it allows the use of (virtual) tools to enable a variety of interactions. Programs such as ZBrush, Mudbox, and Blender are among a large selection of digital sculpting applications which allow options for pushing, pulling, and smoothing the digital meshes to resemble additive (Mongeon 2015) or clay sculpting (Spencer 2011). This section will highlight some of the advantages of digital sculpting compared to physical craft.

The most apparent difference between digital and physical sculpting is the dependency on the material's properties. Stone, clay or other sculptable materials come with a defined set of constraints that determine their ability to create form and shapes. Digital sculpting technology overcomes these limitations by freeing a sculpted artefact from the challenges of physical characteristics (material properties and gravity) and enabling new visual possibilities (Brown 2016). Nevertheless, Gheyselinck (2021) argues that these material constraints do not constitute a deficiency in the sculpting process. On the contrary, they strengthen it by defining a workability range that aid the craftsman in determining the material's design potential. Furthermore, the weightless properties of the virtual object allow the designer to add and remove parts with no consequences on the results (Mongeon 2015), differently from the physical artefact that would require additional armatures to provide support and prevent collapse (Flor and Mongeon 2010).

Another property of digital sculpting is the option to 'undo' a specific operation and reset the geometry to a prior stage. This process is a particular functionality of sculpting software, and it allows correcting errors throughout the design process. On the other hand, physical sculpting requires focused attention from the craftsman to measure each carving and stone mark to avoid irreversible mistakes (Mongeon 2015). Nevertheless, Professor and wood craftsman Pye (1995) argues that this specific risk of failure creates valuable handcrafted objects. The tension between hand and material and the uncertainty of the outcome provides subtlety and delicacy in the work of craftsmen (Pye 1995).

Practice and experience in digital sculpting develop skills specific to the technique, and similarly to embodied knowledge and physical sculpting, contribute to the growth of the digital craftsman. The interaction with software creates knowledge that this paper describes as *Digital Knowledge*. Beyond manual dexterity in controlling the mouse and quick execution of keyboard shortcuts, the interaction with computer interfaces increases mental agility, for example, by switching between view modes (orthogonal or perspective views), constructing mental models, understanding the electronic device's feedback and responses (McCullough 1998), and shifting from detail to full-scale modelling (Alcaide-Marzal et al. 2013). Research in cognitive psychology confirms that exposure to digital technology positively impacts cognition and intellectual abilities (Di Giacomo et al. 2017). However, over-exposure might lead to social isolation, techno-addiction and impaired emotional intelligence (Small et al. 2020).

This study considers Digital Knowledge as the result of learning by (digital) doing. It builds on the familiarity with software interface and computer interactions. Like playing piano or knitting, this type of understanding provides spontaneous responses when facing a digital interface (mouse clicking on an icon to confirm an action or dragging the cursor to increase/decrease the volume level).

2.3 Augmented Reality: Concept and Applications

Augmented Reality (AR) refers to the technology that enables the enhancement of real-world environments through overlaying of digital visualizations. These holographic experiences place computer-generated information onto physical objects and allow interactions through multiple sensory channels - sight, voice, touch (Carmigniani et al. 2010). Computer scientist and technology pioneer Ivan Sutherland developed the first AR head-mounted display in 1968 (Fig. 1). Sutherland's device projects images on semi-transparent mirrors placed in front of the user's eyes to allow the user to simultaneously see the projected graphics and the background objects present in the room (Sutherland

1968). However, it was only in the '90s when Caudell and Mizell used the term 'augmented reality' for the first time. Their research proposes using HMD to project assembly/production information onto real objects to aid technicians and improve aviation manufacturing processes (Caudell and Mizell 1992).

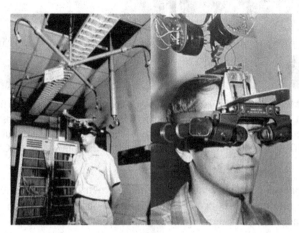

Fig. 1. 'The Sword of Damocles': the first head-mounted display for augmented reality by Ivan Sutherland. 'Sword of Damocles', Elaine.T, 2016. Accessed: http://etsanggarp.blogspot.com/2016/03/01-research-kickstarter-images.html

By contextualizing a digital artefact within the user's immediate surroundings, the interactive characteristics of the represented object must address the physical quality of the experience (Ehn and Linde 2004). Thanks to the advances of AR technology, users can now utilize physical inputs as interactive agents: hand gestures, voice commands, and eye-tracking can directly manipulate a digital artefact through an HMD or other tracking devices (Billinghurst et al. 2009). This multimodal approach to interactivity is one of defining significance for AR applications. One of the first applications of multimodal inputs for the augmentation of physical experiences is Bolt's Media Room (1980). This project uses a custom-built room the size of a personal office (4.8 * 3.3 * 2.4 m approximately), equipped with body tracking sensors and voice-controlled devices. The users can finger-point from a distance to a display to activate functions or use their voice to dictate the commands (Fig. 2). Thus, the Media Room augments interactivity beyond personal space and towards spatially aware augmented experiences.

Similarly, Girbacia (2010) proposes an approach for developing an AR interface through multimodal interactions. In their research, the system relies on synergies among various devices (HMD, data glove) and methods (voice recognition, hand tracking) to define 3D modelling and design strategies for Computer-Aided Design software. This research uses voice-activated commands in addition to gesture recognition to extend interactivity in AR through multiple modalities and promote more intuitive design processes (Girbacia 2010).

AiRSculpt is another AR application that focuses solely on hand gesture recognition to develop free-hand digital sculpting interactions (Jang et al. 2014). The project uses

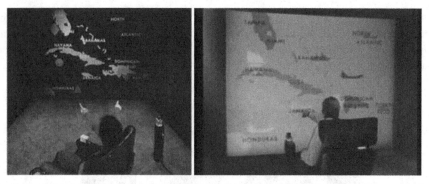

Fig. 2. In Bolt's Media Room, the user can use voice commands and gestures (finger-pointing) to interact with a wall-projected interface. (left) Bolt (1980). Accessed: https://www.media. mit.edu/speech/papers/1980/bolt_SIGGRAPH80_put-that-there.pdf. (right) 'Put That There', VintageCG – (YouTube), 2010. Accessed: https://www.youtube.com/watch?v=sC5Zg0fU2e8.

an HMD and consists of manipulating a digital geometry with properties resembling those of clay. While the HMD provides information on depth between the hand and the headset, an additional camera registers and recognizes the hand gestures (Fig. 3). These hand positions are further compared with a catalogue of pre-recorded hand poses to confirm or access the app's functionalities. In addition to adding/removing volume to simulate sculpting, the users can also access erase, undo, scale, and rotate functions by executing specific hand gestures.

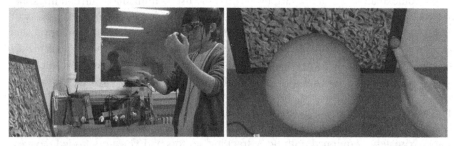

Fig. 3. AiRSculpt: gesture recognition for an augmented sculpting process. AiRSculpt, Jang et al. (2014). Accessed: https://www.researchgate.net/figure/AiRSculpt-evaluation-environment-left-and-users-view-at-startup-right_fig3_290645655

2.4 Augmented Sculpting: Merging Embodied and Digital Knowledge

As observed in the previous section, various research applications exploit the advantages of AR to merge physical inputs and digital interfaces to provide more intuitive augmented experiences. AR technology pulls the virtual world into the physical one and joins them 'to become effectively one continuous interactive space' (Bolt 1980). Furthermore, AR mediates the interactions with digital artefacts through multimodal interfaces to engage users and promote creative thinking (Price et al. 2009). This paper explores multimodal interactivity to link Embodied and Digital knowledge. The aim is to define new sculpting processes centred on the user's experience and skills. It also highlights the emergence of a new craft - Augmented Sculpting that combines physical and digital sculpting characteristics to promote an alternative interacitons and design technique.

3 Implementation

3.1 SculptAR App

The SculptAR App is an AR application that enables sculpting through augmented interactions. It utilizes an HMD to provide immersive visualizations that the users can directly interact with either their hands or voice commands. Similarly to additive and digital clay sculpting, SculptAR integrates methods for mesh manipulation - pushing, pulling, smoothing - to simulate the behaviour of a sculpted object. Furthermore, it allows users to personalize a geometry and create unique artefacts through their voices and surrounding sounds. The HMD is HoloLens 2, a Mixed Reality (MR) device that seamlessly merges digital visualization into reality for immersive augmented experiences. MR and AR are terms commonly used interchangeably. Nevertheless, MR refers to the computing ability to register spatial features and anchor the holographic representations into the physical environment (Milgram and Kishino 1994). Although SculptAR enables interactions that allow the user to manipulate a digital geometry as a tangible object (another MR characteristic), it does not rely on the environment attributes to generate the visualization, hence the definition of SculptAR as an AR application.

As observed in the previous section, research in multimodal interactions requires various devices to sense and collect real-time information. This hardware might include body-tracking sensors, microphones, speakers, and gesture recognition cameras. One of the most functional characteristics of HoloLens (and similar AR-HMDs) is that the device integrates a range of sensors that facilitate its use for detecting physical inputs for multimodal interfaces (Williams et al. 2020). Furthermore, the open-source Mixed Reality Toolkit package provides building blocks for streamlining the development of HoloLens' applications with multimodal interactions in AR (Microsoft 2019). SculptAR utilizes these HMD's features to deliver an immersive AR sculpting experience and enable interactions through the user's physical engagement.

3.2 Geometry Selection and Visualization

SculptAR is developed through Unity, a cross-platform real-time 3D software that, thanks to a large community of developers, provides solutions for various applications - gaming, film, architecture, automotive. In addition, the app uses the C# programming framework to compile the app's basic sculpting functionalities. Before starting the sculpting process, the app offers the users the option of selecting an object from a list of three primary meshes: plane, cube, sphere. In computer graphics, a mesh is a network of vertices, edges and polygonal faces (triangles or quads), and it is the preferred representation method to optimize rendering times (Furht 2006). Although Unity offers the option of importing objects from most 3D modelling software, the geometries must contain a few polygonal faces to minimize the computing effort for the rendering and visualization in portable HMD (Sherman and Craig 2002). For this reason, the three primitive geometries used in SculptAR are developed through procedural meshing, a method that provides control over the number of mesh vertices and faces built within the Unity framework (Flick 2015) (Fig. 4).

Fig. 4. Selection page from SculptAR

Thanks to its ability to contextualize the sculpted geometry in the physical space, AR-HMDs enable users to obtain a high level of engagement with the AR artefact. Thus, the users can freely move around the digital sculpted object and get a complete overview of its features. In addition, SculptAR embeds options for rotating and scaling the digital geometries to provide additional control over the visualization of the artefact.

3.3 Sculpting Interactions

The sculpting interactions build upon the capability of the HMD to track the hands' position continuously. Unity can access this information and determine the relationship (distance, rotation) between the physical hand and the digital object. This process uses a method defined as 'ray casting' that projects a virtual ray from an object to the forward direction, and it allows to detect and identify objects that get in contact with it (Unity Technologies 2020). In SculptAR, two rays project outwards from the user's palms. Whenever these rays recognize the mesh to sculpt, a function will calculate the distance between the hand and the object. This information is fundamental for sculpting since the hand's proximity to the mesh determines the user's intention of pulling/pushing the geometry. Furthermore, the HMD's built-in functionality to recognize hand gestures allows the user to confirm the sculpting by executing a pinch pose (bringing the index and thumb fingers together). The app enables continuous sculpting until the pinch gesture is released (Fig. 5).

SculptAR provides two main sculpting modes that differ primarily by their effect on the sculpted object. The first, *Sculpt Vertices*, provides a more uniform mesh manipulation. This approach iterates, at every frame, through the mesh vertices and determines

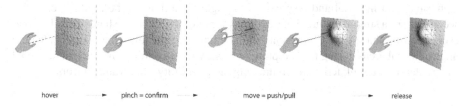

hover   ►   pinch = confirm   ─►   move = push/pull   ►   release

Fig. 5. SculptAR: concept diagram for mesh manipulation

their distance to the user's hand position. Once the program registers the sculpting confirmation, the force applied to the vertices decreases proportionally to their closeness to the manipulated area. On the contrary, the second sculpting option, *Sculpt Faces*, utilizes the ray from the user's hand to determine the position of the selected mesh face. In this operation, the vertices adjacent to the highlighted face react to the same displacement force, creating a more jagged effect, ideal for creating the overall form. Both sculpting operations apply a displacement force perpendicular to the selected vertex/face (normal vector) (Figs. 6 and 7).

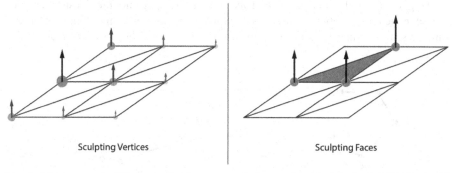

Sculpting Vertices   Sculpting Faces

Fig. 6. Displacement differences in the two sculpting options inside SculptAR. SculptAR manipulation methods - diagram

Fig. 7. SculptAR: vertices (left) and face (right) sculpting. SculptAR manipulation methods - screencast

Furthermore, to aid the sculpting process, SculptAR allows the possibility of switching the geometry's material appearance from shaded to wireframe. The first simulates a physical matt material and responds to the light conditions of the digital scene. The second shows a simple texture that highlights the outlines of the mesh geometries. However, since the shaded view represents realistic light and shadow behaviour, this feature might conceal areas during the sculpting process. On the contrary, the wireframe model shows clearly the sculpted area, minimizing the possibility of unwanted errors.

3.4 Smoothing Operation

Sculpting is a sequential process. It starts with a rough shape, and in stages, the sculptor adds details to the object to represent the envisioned outcome. Similarly, digital sculpting begins with an approximate mesh which the (digital) sculptor manipulates to express the intended shape. When selecting the operation of 'smoothing', the software divides each mesh face into smaller polygons to increase mesh resolution and create more precise details. Nevertheless, this method requires high computer-processing power, a feature found in most desktop computers (Mongeon 2015).

Since SculptAR relies on the more moderate hardware capabilities of the HMD, the smoothing operation uses a different approach. In computer graphics, Laplacian smoothing refers to the process of modifying the positions of each mesh vertex in relation to its neighbours (Vollmer et al. 1999). This method results in smoother meshes with no increase in the total number of polygons. SculptAR integrates this smoothing algorithm within its sculpting interface to extend the users' interactions choices (Figs. 8 and 9).

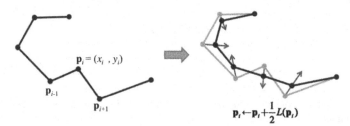

Fig. 8. Laplacian smoothing. Mesh Smoothing. Accessed: http://graphics.stanford.edu/courses/cs468-12-spring/LectureSlides/06_smoothing.pdf

Fig. 9. SculptAR smoothing operation - screencast

The smoothed mesh shows a shrinking behaviour at every iteration. This response is due to the Laplacian algorithm, which affects all points in the mesh to satisfy the smoothing function. Solutions to this behaviour comprise adding other filtering algorithms, constraining the position of the boundary vertices, or applying inflating techniques to re-adjust the position of the vertices after smoothing (Nealen et al. 2006). Nevertheless, the visual representation of the smooth option from the SculptAR app is satisfactory within the purpose of this study.

3.5 Audio Colour

The research review discussed in the previous chapter shows how the use of the voice facilitates interactions with functions of AR interfaces. Nevertheless, the vocal input is often used as a passive agent. For example, the users dictate commands that activate/deactivate features within the program: 'open', 'close', 'next', 'menu', etc. In addition to these interactions, SculptAR uses the input from the HMD's microphone to convert sound into an active manipulation of the mesh. More specifically, the app transforms the user's voice and surrounding audio frequencies into RGB values and assigns them to the sculpted geometry. This method collects input sounds and generates the relative spectrum data to remap into colour values (Figs. 10 and 11).

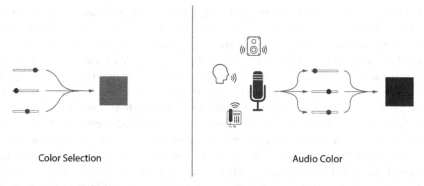

Color Selection   Audio Color

Fig. 10. SculptAR uses audio inputs to define unique colours. SculptAR colour inputs – diagram

Fig. 11. (left) Colour selection through slider values. (right) Colour assigned through audio input. SculptAR colour inputs - screencast

While physical sculpting relies on the bodily relationship between the craftsman and the object to create unique results (Gheyselinck 2021), digital sculpting provides makers with various tools to personalize their virtual products (Masterton 2007). SculptAr wants to explore voice and sound as tools for customizing AR visualizations. Since no two voices or environments sound equal, the audio capturing method provides visualizations that are time and space specific. As a result, the app will produce different colour effects if used in different environments or users.

4 Discussion

The following chapter analyses the research output and relates it to the literature review presented earlier in the text. It also discusses the limitations of the practical application and suggests possibilities for future research. Furthermore, it shows the emergence of unexpected findings and contributions to existing studies. Unfortunately, due to the limited availability of the HMD and the reduced possibility of in-person meetings, the results from this study do not include a comprehensive user study. Instead, the analysis generates from the author's observations and peer's feedback.

4.1 Analysis

SculptAR proves that AR is a highly appropriate technology to enhance sculpting methods and digital modelling processes. The interactive features of this application are engaging, and the results satisfy the aims set for the project. Although the outcome primarily reflects digital sculpting and 3D modelling software characteristics, the physical interactions promote a more intuitive understanding of the mesh manipulation process. Unlike the mouse- and monitor-based interfaces, the user is physically manipulating the geometries, which create a more natural relationship to the object. Furthermore, the learning of the interaction does not require any specialized prior knowledge. Except for the pinch gesture, all interactions are 'known' to the user. For example, seeing a digital object that resembles a physical button does not require an explanation: it activates if pressed. This approach builds upon the concept of Embodied Knowledge, and this project integrates it to develop the interactive physical AR interface. In addition, as for any technique, practice and repetition refine the sensibility to the design possibilities embedded into SculptAR. Quickly, the interactions require no mental processing so that the user's attention can focus on the object instead of the procedure. SculptAR merges this understanding (Digital Knowledge) with physical engagement (Embodied Knowledge) to promote an alternative method for augmented sculpting.

The methodologies for embedding physical inputs and visualizing digital objects are probably the most significant differences between SculptAR and the research projects discussed in the chapter' Context'. These studies rely on a combination of sensors, tracking devices, and displays to register the user's inputs and represent them either through an HMD or a conventional computer monitor. This approach is beneficial for defining specific procedures and control over each device, although the development phase might be challenging. On the contrary, SculptAR takes advantage of the sophisticated technology of HoloLens 2 that integrates all necessary capturing devices and allows a more effective development of AR applications. Furthermore, using the MRTK package and its control functions is straightforward and easily transferable among systems.

The use of the voice input as a parameter for customization develops from the engagement with the literature review. These projects use speech recognition algorithms to detect the vocal instruction and execute the respective operation. For example, in Bolt's Media Room (1980), the users can dictate articulated sentences that include multiple functions - "Move the blue triangle to the right of the green square". Nevertheless, the voice commands remain highly descriptive and do not actively connect with the system. SculptAR, instead, wants to utilize the nuances of the user's voice and surrounding sound to determine a unique outcome. The Audio Color method develops a distinctive colour value and assigns it to the augmented object to differentiate each sculpting experience.

4.2   Reflections and Outlooks

Materiality. Materiality is a highly debated topic that characterizes the physical-digital divide in sculpting processes. For example, in (Brown and Duguid 1994)'s study, the concept of 'demassification' does not only refer to the effect of removing the material mass in a digital artefact. Instead, they argue that technology strips away the social/personal values attached to the physical characteristics of an object and that designers and makers should work closely with communities for more functional translation of crafts into digital processes. The handcrafted products represent the craftsmen's carefully planned manual interactions and reflect their makers' arbitrary judgements, and 'the object itself is the only documentation of the effort' (Zoran and Buechley 2013). Therefore, future applications of AR and MR should capture the craft of sculpting directly from the craftsman's point of view and equip makers with HMD and other tracking devices. This approach will enable real-time recording of the material properties and overlaying this information on the represented sculpted object. The sensing systems of the AR devices allow an immediate reconstruction of the physical artefact into its digital twin and use it for generating a highly representative 3D model. This approach would benefit artisans since their products could be directly used for digital applications (3D models for games, movies) or personal e-commerce interfaces.

The fundamental difference between physical and digital materials reside in their fundamental structures. McCullough (1998, p. 213) explains it as 'bits versus atoms'. Any modifications in the physical microstructures of atoms cause irreversible changes. On the contrary, interactions with the digital material only modify an arrangement of values and bits. The latter are not static and allow continuous reconfiguration and repetition. Hence, augmented sculpting is not a process that compares physical and digital material behaviour in sculpting. Still, it defines a new method based on AR technology, as stated by Gheyselinck during the interview with the author. Gheyselinck indicates that digital methods that emulate crafting processes should not be considered a direct interpretation of the craft but more as additional techniques available for makers and craftsmen. The craftsmen's sensibility and design intention remain the underlying constant in all sculpting processes (Gheyselinck 2021).

Future developments of SculptAR could explore the concept of materiality further. For example, simulating different material properties and adapting the sculpting operations to match them (stone, wood, and metal require different approaches to modelling clay). Furthermore, enabling the customization of material and textures through physical inputs as for the Audio Color option discussed in the previous chapter. Also, the possibility of overlaying physical materials onto the holographic object will enhance their appearance and define realistic features.

Interactivity. Research in Human-Computer Interactions highlights the importance of understanding the relationship between the human body and the physical space to achieve effective digital interfaces. In cognitive science, this relationship is central to human development and determines our understanding of the environments we inhabit (Foglia and Wilson 2013). For example, in the early stages of child development, touch is fundamental to acquiring spatial skills and stimulating cognitive processes. The hands not only allow us to interact with the world around us, but it also enables us to understand it. This bidirectional exchange of information (exerting force and sensing pressure) is what characterizes 'active touch' and distinguishes professions that require complex manual dexterity (sculptors, surgeons, musicians) (Klemmer et al. 2006). Haptic gloves are wearable mechanical devices that simulate the sense of touch in virtual environments. These systems utilize various feedback methods to provide a physical sensation in response to a digital action. For example, the devices use vibrations to highlight a specific interaction or integrate complex robotic systems to constraint hand movements to match the grabbing motion of a virtual object (Bermejo and Hui 2017). Although the sculpting interactions in SculptAR are highly engaging and formative, the integration of haptic devices could enhance the sculpting process and promote a more holistic understanding of the craft. Furthermore, the tactile feedback will improve the perception of material textures and geometrical features.

By researching the use of the hands and the body for enhanced interactivity in augmented sculpting, the author understands how these topics might exclude people with limited physical abilities to use such applications. Thanks to the advances of the HMD to capture different physical inputs, this technology highlights the emergence of new possibilities for more accessible software development and interface design. The use of the voice or eye-gaze methods provide alternatives to create interactions for people with limited upper-body mobility (Mott et al. 2019). Due to the project's time constraints, SculptAR is not an application designed for accessibility. However, early studies pursued the integration of eye-gaze as an additional input for the multimodal interface and proved the possibility of the technology to expand interaction modalities.

5   Conclusions

Augmented reality (AR) is an effective technology for enhancing digital sculpting processes. Tise study explores the capability of AR and multimodal interactivity to link physical skills and digital interfaces. Furthermore, this project argues the advantages of using AR methodologies (hand-tracking, voice recognition) and applying them for developing SculptAR, an interactive sculpting application for AR head-mounted displays (HMD).

The study highlights the challenges of transferring the knowledge from a physical craft to a digital system. A handcrafted object is the result of interactions between various parameters. The maker's knowledge of materials, sensibility and manual dexterity are the factors observed for developing the fundamental understanding of the craft. The research also lists the advantages of current software solutions that simulate sculpting processes through computer-based interactions. This approach, digital sculpting, is highly sophisticated and provides numerous options for design explorations.

This research recognizes that technology is part of the modern craftsman's toolset and identifies the limitation of digital sculpting software to embed the maker's physical knowledge. Primary and secondary research underlines this absence of physicality in digital sculpting programs and sets the basis for arguing the necessity to use alternative methods to mediate the craftsman's skills and the digital outcome. As a result, this paper discusses AR as the solution for merging manual and digital sculpting processes by utilizing physical inputs (hands, eyes, gestures) as agents for manipulating and sculpting digital geometries.

The SculptAR app exploits the functionalities of the HMD (HoloLens 2) and extends interactivity to the natural use of the hands and the voice. This app's AR interface uses multimodal inputs to engage users and facilitate their physical experience. Although the paper discusses projects that use similar approaches in the literature review, the SculptAR's outcome is novel due to the self-contained features of the HMD that does not rely on additional devices for sensing or tracking operations. Further implementation of the app could include using a haptic glove to enhance the sculpting interactions with physical feedback. This approach will refine the sculpting process and extend functionalities for texturing and material representations. Furthermore, the use of alternative physical inputs to the hands (voice, eye-gaze, head-tracking) provides the research with the possibility to explore the design of accessible AR interfaces for creating augmented sculpting systems for individuals with limited physical abilities.

In conclusion, this study wants to provide a new outlook on sculpting processes, which learns from the physical craft and implements it digitally into an interactive experience. AR is the technology that facilitates this knowledge transfer between humans and computers, and it creates possibilities for further exploration and research on the crafts of the future.

References

Adzhiev, V., Comninos, P., Pasko, A.: Augmented sculpture: computer ghosts of physical artifacts. Leonardo **36**(3), 211–219 (2003). https://doi.org/10.1162/002409403321921433

Alcaide-Marzal, J., et al.: An exploratory study on the use of digital sculpting in conceptual product design. Des. Stud. **34**(2), 264–284 (2013). https://doi.org/10.1016/j.destud.2012.09.001

Azuma, R.T.: A survey of augmented reality. Presence Teleoperators Virtual Environ. **6**(4), 355–385 (1997). https://doi.org/10.1162/pres.1997.6.4.355

Bermejo, C., Hui, P.: A survey on haptic technologies for mobile augmented reality. arXiv:1709.00698 (2017). http://arxiv.org/abs/1709.00698. Accessed 13 Aug 2021

Billinghurst, M., Kato, H., Myojin, S.: Advanced interaction techniques for augmented reality applications. In: Shumaker, R. (ed.) VMR 2009. LNCS, vol. 5622, pp. 13–22. Springer, Heidelberg (2009). https://doi.org/10.1007/978-3-642-02771-0_2

Bolt, R.A.: "Put-that-there": Voice and gesture at the graphics interface. ACM SIGGRAPH Comput. Graph. **14**(3), 262–270 (1980). https://doi.org/10.1145/965105.807503

Brown, J., Duguid, P.: Borderline issues: social and material aspects of design. Hum. Comput. Interact. (1994). https://doi.org/10.1207/s15327051hci0901_2

Brown, K.: Journey through the centre_01 (2016). https://digitalartarchive.siggraph.org/artwork/keith-brown-journey-through-the-centre_01/. Accessed 6 Aug 2021

Carmigniani, J., et al.: Augmented reality technologies, systems and applications. Multimedia Tools Appl. **51**, 341–377 (2010). https://doi.org/10.1007/s11042-010-0660-6

Caudell, T., Mizell, D.: Augmented reality: an application of heads-up display technology to manual manufacturing processes. In: Proceedings of the Twenty-Fifth Hawaii International Conference on System Sciences, vol. 2, pp. 659–669 (1992). https://doi.org/10.1109/HICSS.1992.183317

Di Giacomo, D., Ranieri, J., Lacasa, P.: Digital learning as enhanced learning processing? Cognitive evidence for new insight of smart learning. Front. Psychol. (2017). https://doi.org/10.3389/fpsyg.2017.01329

Dormer, P.: The Art of the Maker. Thames and Hudson, London (1994)

Ehn, P., Linde, P.: Embodied interaction - designing beyond the physical-digital divide. In: Futureground - DRS International Conference (2004). https://dl.designresearchsociety.org/drs-conference-papers/drs2004/researchpapers/36

Flick, J.: Procedural Grid, a Unity C# Tutorial (2015). https://catlikecoding.com/unity/tutorials/procedural-grid/. Accessed 10 Aug 2021

de la Flor, M., Mongeon, B.: Digital Sculpting with Mudbox: Essential Tools and Techniques for Artists, 1st edn. Focal Press, Burlington (2010)

Foglia, L., Wilson, R.A.: Embodied cognition. WIREs Cognit. Sci. **4**(3), 319–325 (2013). https://doi.org/10.1002/wcs.1226

Furht, B. (ed.): 'Mesh, 3D', Encyclopedia of Multimedia. Springer, Boston (2006). https://doi.org/10.1007/0-387-30038-4_126

Galyean, T.A., Hughes, J.F.: Sculpting: an interactive volumetric modeling technique. In: Proceedings of the 18th Annual Conference on Computer Graphics and Interactive Techniques (SIGGRAPH 1991), pp. 267–274. Association for Computing Machinery, New York (1991). https://doi.org/10.1145/122718.122747

Gheyselinck, I.: Craftmanship and Technology. (Interview) (2021)

Girbacia, F.: An approach to an augmented reality interface for computer aided design. In: Annals of DAAAM for 2010 & Proceedings of the 21st International DAAAM Symposium. 21st International DAAAM Symposium, DAAAM International (2010). https://www.daaam.info/Downloads/Pdfs/proceedings/proceedings_2010/22853_Annals_1_head.pdf. Accessed 8 Aug 2021

Jang, S.-A., Kim, H., Woo, W., Wakefield, G.: AiRSculpt: a wearable augmented reality 3D sculpting system. In: Streitz, N., Markopoulos, P. (eds.) DAPI 2014. LNCS, vol. 8530, pp. 130–141. Springer, Cham (2014). https://doi.org/10.1007/978-3-319-07788-8_13

Klemmer, S.R., Hartmann, B., Takayama, L.: How bodies matter: five themes for interaction design. In: Proceedings of the 6th ACM Conference on Designing Interactive Systems - DIS 2006. The 6th ACM Conference, p. 140. ACM Press, University Park (2006). https://doi.org/10.1145/1142405.1142429

Marshall, J.: The role and significance of CAD/CAM technologies in craft and designer-maker practice With a focus on architectural ceramics. Open University (1999). https://www.academia.edu/28345437/The_role_and_significance_of_CAD_CAM_technologies_in_craft_and_designer_maker_practice_With_a_focus_on_architectural_ceramics. Accessed 4 Aug 2021

Masterton, D.: Deconstructing the Digital', New Craft Voices (2007). https://www.semanticscholar.org/paper/Deconstructing-the-Digital-Masterton/9923c052bbfd560fb9650155d3d338a4602fd2b8. Accessed 3 Aug 2021

McCullough, M.: Abstracting Craft: The Practiced Digital Hand. MIT Press, Cambridge (1998)

Microsoft: Introducing MRTK for Unity - Mixed Reality (2019). https://docs.microsoft.com/en-us/windows/mixed-reality/develop/unity/mrtk-getting-started. Accessed 16 Aug 2021

Microsoft: Microsoft HoloLens | Mixed Reality Technology for Business (2021). https://www.microsoft.com/en-us/hololens. Accessed 4 Aug 2021

Milgram, P., Kishino, F.: A taxonomy of mixed reality visual displays. IEICE Trans. Inf. Syst. **E77-D**(12), 1321–1329 (1994)

Mongeon, B.: 3D technology in fine art and craft : exploring 3D printing, scanning, sculpting and milling (2015). https://doi.org/10.4324/9781315730455

Mott, M., et al.: Accessible by design: an opportunity for virtual reality. In: 2019 IEEE International Symposium on Mixed and Augmented Reality Adjunct (ISMAR-Adjunct). 2019 IEEE International Symposium on Mixed and Augmented Reality Adjunct (ISMAR-Adjunct), pp. 451–454 (2019). https://doi.org/10.1109/ISMAR-Adjunct.2019.00122

Nealen, A., et al.: Laplacian mesh optimization. In: Proceedings of the 4th International Conference on Computer Graphics and Interactive Techniques in Australasia and Southeast Asia (GRAPHITE 2006), pp. 381–389. Association for Computing Machinery, New York (2006). https://doi.org/10.1145/1174429.1174494

Nimkulrat, N.: Hands-on intellect: integrating craft practice into design research. Int. J. Des. **6**, 1–14 (2012)

Novak, M., Schwan, S.: Does touching real objects affect learning? Educ. Psychol. Rev. **33**(2), 637–665 (2020). https://doi.org/10.1007/s10648-020-09551-z

Price, S. et al.: Technology and embodiment: relationships and implications for knowledge, creativity and communication (2009)

Pye, D.: The Nature and Art of Workmanship, revised Herbert Press, London (1995)

Sherman, W.R., Craig, A.B.: Understanding Virtual Reality: Interface, Application, and Design, 1st edn. Morgan Kaufmann, Amsterdam; Boston (2002)

Small, G.W., et al.: Brain health consequences of digital technology use. Dialogues Clin. Neurosci. **22**(2), 179–187 (2020). https://doi.org/10.31887/DCNS.2020.22.2/gsmall

Spencer, S.: ZBrush Character Creation: Advanced Digital Sculpting, 2nd edn. Sybex, Indianapolis (2011)

Sutherland, I.E.: A head-mounted three dimensional display. In: Proceedings of the December 9–11, 1968, Fall Joint Computer Conference, Part I (AFIPS 1968 (Fall, Part I)), pp. 757–764. Association for Computing Machinery, New York (1968). https://doi.org/10.1145/1476589.1476686

Treadaway, C.P.: Hand e-craft: an investigation into hand use in digital creative practice. In: Proceedings of the Seventh ACM Conference on Creativity and Cognition (C&C 2009), pp. 185–194. Association for Computing Machinery, New York (2009). https://doi.org/10.1145/1640233.1640263

Unity Technologies: Unity - Scripting API: Physics. Raycast (2020). https://docs.unity3d.com/2019.3/Documentation/ScriptReference/Physics.Raycast.html. Accessed 16 Aug 2021

Vollmer, J., Mencl, R., Müller, H.: Improved laplacian smoothing of noisy surface meshes. Comput. Graph. Forum **18**(3), 131–138 (1999). https://doi.org/10.1111/1467-8659.00334

Williams, A.S., Garcia, J., Ortega, F.: Understanding multimodal user gesture and speech behavior for object manipulation in augmented reality using elicitation. IEEE Trans. Visual Comput. Graphics **26**(12), 3479–3489 (2020). https://doi.org/10.1109/TVCG.2020.3023566

Zoran, A., Buechley, L.: Hybrid reassemblage: an exploration of craft, digital fabrication and artifact uniqueness. Leonardo **46**, 4–10 (2013). https://doi.org/10.2307/23468110

Multi-agent Crowd Simulation in an Active Shooter Environment

Sharad Sharma[(⊠)] [iD] and Syed Ali

Department of Computer Science, Bowie State University, Bowie, MD, USA
ssharma@bowiestate.edu, alis0712@students.bowiestate.edu

Abstract. In recent years there has been a sharp increase in active shooter events, but there has been no introduction of new technology or tactics capable of increasing preparedness and training for active shooter events. This has raised a major concern about the lack of tools that would allow robust predictions of realistic human movements and the lack of understanding about the interaction in designated simulation environments. It is impractical to carry out live experiments where thousands of people are evacuated from buildings designed for every possible emergency condition. There has been progress in understanding human movement, human motion synthesis, crowd dynamics, indoor environments, and their relationships with active shooter events, but challenges remain. This paper presents a virtual reality (VR) experimental setup for conducting virtual evacuation drills in response to extreme events and demonstrates the behavior of agents during an active shooter environment. The behavior of agents is implemented using behavior trees in the Unity gaming engine. The VR experimental setup can simulate human behavior during an active shooter event in a campus setting. A presence questionnaire (PQ) was used in the user study to evaluate the effectiveness and engagement of our active shooter environment. The results show that majority of users agreed that the sense of presence was increased when using the emergency response training environment for a building evacuation environment.

Keywords: Virtual reality · Active shooter events · Crowd simulation · Multi-agent simulation

1 Introduction

Crowd simulation has many uses, which include improving traffic flows in busy highways and streets [1], enhancing training and virtual environments, and implementing artificially intelligent (AI) characters in games and movies [2]. Crowd behavior during an active shooter simulation has been an important topic of interest as it aims to reduce casualties during emergency event. In the United States and around the world, reported active shooter incidents have become incredibly common. In the year 2020, there have been over 40 active shooter incidents in the United States, with over 200 fatalities [3]. Due to this, it is critical to find tools and technologies that will allow for the modeling and simulation of human behavior during emergency response training. The law enforcement personnel must be properly trained for an active shooter event so that they

© Springer Nature Switzerland AG 2022
J. Y. C. Chen and G. Fragomeni (Eds.): HCII 2022, LNCS 13318, pp. 108–120, 2022.
https://doi.org/10.1007/978-3-031-06015-1_8

can get a better overview of the situation and perform the best response strategy. VR training environment allows one to perform virtual evacuation drills for different what-if situations without any accompanying risk. Traditional performance-based tests for emergency evacuation drills for fire and active shooter response are expensive to perform due to safety and legal issues.

Fig. 1. Active shooter response environment for a campus building

According to the FBI [4], most of the active shooter incidents have taken place at educational facilities such as high schools or university campuses between the years 2001 and 2015. The 2007 Virginia Tech massacre is a prime example of an active shooter event at a higher educational facility, where 33 individuals lost their lives, along with 127 injured, which is why in this study we propose a system that simulates agent behavior when an active shooter is present at a university campus. This paper presents a VR training module for active shooter events for a campus building emergency response in an institute of higher education (IHE). The VR environment is implemented in Unity 3D where the user has an option to enter the environment as a security personnel or as an occupant in the building. The VR training module offers a unique way of performing virtual evacuation drills for different what-if scenarios. The novelty of our work lies in the implementation of crowd behavior in the VR active shooter environment. We have presented two ways for controlling crowd behavior. First, by defining rules for agents or NPCs (Non-Player Characters). Second, by providing controls to the users as avatars or PCs (Player characters) to navigate around the virtual environment as autonomous agents using a keyboard when an active shooter is present. The rules are developed by implementing behavior trees for the agents. The system is built using the Unity gaming engine. Figure 1 shows our developed VR training environment for active shooter events for the course of action, visualization, and situational awareness.

The rest of the paper is organized as follows: Sect. 2 discusses the existing work that has been done related to crowd simulations, Sect. 3 discusses how the system was implemented in Unity and the hardware specifications used to build the system, Sect. 4

discusses the user studies and evaluation of the system using presence questionnaire (PQ) scheme and lastly, Sect. 5 discusses the drawn conclusions and proposed future work. Finally, Sect. 6 states acknowledgments and references.

2 Related Work

Lately, there has been an increase in active shooter events. As a result, there is a need to learn from past active shooter events and create public awareness for the safety procedures and tactics. Hoogendoorn et al. [5] have demonstrated a behavior system of three interrelated layers:

- Operational layer: It describes the movement of agents such as walking, acceleration, and approaching a point of interest.
- Tactical layer: This is used in pathfinding algorithms, collision evasion, and route preparation.
- Strategic layer: This shows how the agents will choose their next point of interest based on the existing state of the model environment.

Currently, many frameworks can be used to simulate crowd behavior. Most of these frameworks typically share the same set of common operational and tactical models of crowd behavior [6] which includes ORCA (Optimal Reciprocal Collision Avoidance) [7] or GCF (Generalized Centrifugal Force) [8, 9]. These frameworks provide a reliable crowd simulation behavior. The issue with these frameworks is that the behavior patterns are the same for all agents. For example, the agents will always choose the shortest route to their targets, and the behavior only varies when there is an obstacle on the way. Singh et al. [10] have created an agent-centered system that was used for simulating evolving behaviors. It was designed to detect and classify emerging agent behavior to control undesirable actions. Agents in this framework followed an OODA (Observe, Orient, Decide, Act) loop, and their behavior system was based upon an FSM (Finite-State Machine). FSM is a good tool for developing looped behaviors, but the system is restricted and cannot create believable characters.

Agent-centered pedestrian simulation system allows users to implement, test, and develop various behavior models. MomenTUM [11, 12] is a Java-based framework and can expand the set of used models and allows users to add different models in a single simulation. The system also allows users to add different behaviors, such as an awareness system, to their agents. The framework comes with a graphical user interface (GUI) built-in that allows users to configure their simulation environment without coding. Thus, MomenTUM allows users to create a flexible, and generalized approach to crowd simulation and provides a generalized view on agent's movements. The issue with this framework is that it doesn't create an immersive environment to fully simulate everyday life. The agents in this framework cannot interact with everyday objects in the model environment, and there is no support for animation states, which is crucial when creating believable characters.

There has been considerable interest in modeling and simulation of human behavior for emergency response during evacuation [13]. Sharma et al. [14, 15] have created an active shooter response training environment for a building evacuation in a collaborative virtual environment (CVE). Their CVE is implemented in Unity 3D and is based on run, hide, and fight mode for emergency response. The participant can enter the CVE setup on the cloud and participate in the active shooter response training environment. CVE has been used as a training and education tool for many applications such as military, psychological, medical, and education applications, subway evacuation [16–21]. AnyLogic [22] is a crowd simulation modeling framework that supports discrete-event, system dynamics pedestrian simulation, and agent-centered pedestrian simulation systems. This system is widely used to simulate commercial applications such as markets, healthcare, and manufacturing. The system also contains a pedestrian library which is used to envision pedestrian flows in models. The library also can gather statistics on pedestrian traffic (crowd density) in various areas of the model. AnyLogic utilizes flowcharts to set the behavior of the agents. AnyLogic is has a limited set of possible actions, so the agent can only move from one point to another. It is therefore a powerful tool to get statistics about pedestrian activity and was not designed for an immersive pedestrian system [23].

Menge [24] is a widely used open-source crowd movement C++ framework designed for pedestrian dynamics. It allows users to decompose the agent behavior into three sub-categories which include: goal selection, planned computations, and planned variations. Menge utilizes a set of pathfinding algorithms and movement parameters that generates an accurate pedestrian behavior system. Goal selection in Menge is implemented using Finite State Machine (FSM). Modern games use behavior trees [25] for implementing AI to non-playable characters. Most gaming engines such as Unity come with a built-in behavior tree module. This module has a hierarchical structure, where each node on the agent has a specific behavior implemented to it and is executed once it is initialized. This allows users the ability to create complex behaviors on each or group of agents.

3   Crowd Simulation Behavior Framework

Our proposed active shooter VR simulation is created using the Unity gaming engine. Unity provides the ability to achieve complex agent behaviors with high-quality resolution. Our proposed crowd simulation behavior framework includes the following functional requirements:

1. The agents within the system should have the ability to make decisions.
2. The system should be able to simulate crowds, adjust their speeds accordingly and create goal posts or points of interest for the agent to run to when an active shooter is around.
3. System should have the capability of implementing animated non-playable agents.
4. Behavior AI model on one agent should easily be expandable to be used in other models.

Behavior trees have a wide range of applications. A behavior tree is a tree of ranked nodes on an AI object that control the flow of decision making (strategic layers) and forms branches on various types of weighted (utility) nodes that control the agent's intentions. As we progress down the tree, it can reach the sequences of instructions that would be best suited to the situation [26]. When game developers are creating AI for games, they often face situations like what AI path the agent should take next from a given set of possible paths. If developers, for instance, decided to use a utility-based algorithm, then each action must be matched with a utility curve [27]. In our crowd simulation behavior system, agents normally choose a path based on their intention of their inner state. To achieve this, several goal points were added to the model world. To choose the best goal point, behavior trees are implemented to the agent, where the weighted nodes then decide the best path to take. Figure 2 shows how the behavior trees were implemented in our system.

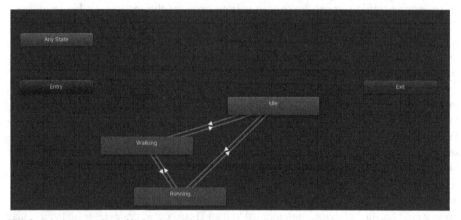

Fig. 2. Implementation of behavior trees in our crowd simulation system. Each node is weighted so that agents can choose the best goal point.

Decision-making is a key component of behavior trees. It allows users to describe how the agent will choose the next state or action. The choice is defined by the agent's utility nodes. Intention based approach [28] has been widely used for defining utility nodes. Intention describes the possible actions taken by the agent. To determine the utility intention node, an "urge" value (weights) was placed for each node in our developed decision-making system. This value determines which intention needs to be done first and is changed over time based on other factors. Intention can be divided into two subcategories:

1) Mandatory: These intentions must be followed by every agent in the model during the simulation and is usually at the parent node of the behavior tree. An example is if there is an active shooter within the vicinity then all agents surrounding the vicinity will run away from the shooter.
2) Standard: These are optional intentions and may or may not be followed by every agent during the simulation. For example, when an active shooter is not present in the vicinity then some agents might be walking, or sitting, or running to catch a bus, and so forth.

Other types of intention include Uninterrupted Intention: Here the agent's behavior will not change. For example, even with an active shooter around the vicinity, some agents will not be running away from the shooter since they will be busy performing a specific task. In our system, the agents are separated into different behavior groups for different intentions. However, common characteristics such as weight, speed, and radius are still shared between all the agents. The behavior group determines how the objects in the model world would behave with the agent. Agents or groups of agents may have different interaction logic implemented when interacting with certain objects. We can consider the whole decision-making process as the brain of each agent since it accumulates and maintains all the agent's intentions. Figure 3 demonstrates our decision-making system:

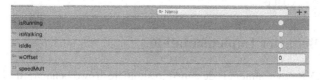

Fig. 3. 3D Data visualization in non-immersive environment

To support the agent's interaction in the model world, certain points of interest or goal posts were added. This allows agents to randomly move around the points of interest or goal posts. Once the agent reaches a certain goal post or interest point, the process of interaction starts. During the interaction process, the agent's behavior tree nodes start to randomly move around. Once the interaction stops the structure of the behavior tree changes, and a new intention state begins.

Fig. 4. An example of an interaction space. Different agents have different behaviors within a small space.

As described by T. Plch, et al. [25], two types of points of interest are added to the model which are interaction objects and interaction areas. Interaction objects are objects that are placed into the model world and allow agents to interact with the object using intention (animation) states. In our system, a specified number of agents can only interact with one object, and their interaction time is also limited. Interaction areas are an expansion of interaction objects where agents occupy a small space within the model and interact with that space a certain way. Figure 4 shows an example of an interaction space where agents have different behaviors. Thus, our system's whole decision-making process of an agent can be described as follows:

- Creating a behaviour tree with all possible intentions.
- Placing weights for each intention.
- Choosing an intension with the highest weight.
- Picking the appropriate goal post.
- Moving to that goal post.

4 Crowd Behavior Implementation

Our proposed VR environment is designed to simulate crowd behavior during an active shooter event at the university campus. We have built a scenario to simulate an active shooter response inside the building. The environment is built using the Unity game engine and used the behavior tree module within the engine for building the character's AI framework. Before to the active shooter arriving on the scene, the agents move around to random points of interest.

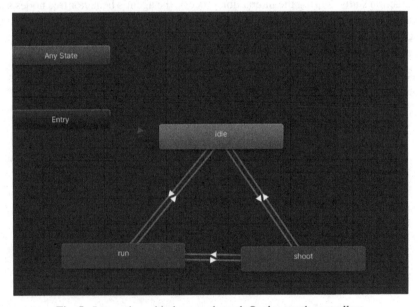

Fig. 5. Interacting with the map through Oculus touch controllers.

We have implemented several goal points or points of interest in Unity, and the agents tend to pick random goal points while moving around the environment. While they are moving around random points of interest, the intention is set to a "walk and talk" state. We have also implemented an audio functionality for the agents so that they can talk while moving around to different goal states in the environment. The audio functionality adds an extra layer of immersion to the simulated environment. Once the user presses the "Q" key on the keyboard it spawns in the active shooter. The intention state for the active shooter is set to "idle", however, the intention state for the crowd changes from "walk and talk" state to "run and talk" state, and we notice that the crowd moves away from the active shooter. We also notice that after a certain distance, the crowd's intention changes back from "run and talk" state to "walk and talk state". When the active shooter spawns in the agents pick random points of interest away from the active shooter. An example of the active shooter's intention state is shown in Fig. 5. However, the intention state for the agent changes for example "talk" state, to "hide" state.

Table 1. Framework characteristics summary

CHARACTERISTICS	FRAMEWORK
ENGINE	Unity
PROGRAMMING LANGUAGE	C#
DECISION-MAKING SYSTEM	✓
DYNAMIC AGENTS	✓
INTENSION SUPPORT	✓

As mentioned previously the decision-making tree was implemented in Unity. Unity comes with a built-in C# and behavior tree framework which allows us to trigger certain intentions and control the behavior of the agents. Table 1 summarizes the characteristics of our framework.

5   User Studies and Evaluation

This paper presents crowd behavior during an active shooter event. We have presented how the agents behave during an active shooter in the model world and compare it with a real-world scenario. A presence questionnaire (PQ) was used based on Witmer et al. and Singer et al. [29] presence questionnaire in the user study to evaluate the effectiveness and engagement of our immersive active shooter environment. A limited user study was conducted for this evaluation. A total of 7 participants were chosen for this study which included 5 males and 2 females. Participants were asked to fill out a short survey at the end of the study. The participants were asked a series of 11 questions. The questions were based on a presence questionnaire (PQ) framework and are outlined below. Each question on the questionnaire was answered using a 7-item Likert scale. Tables 2 outline the questions asked, the most common score, and the average response score for each question:

Table 2. Presence Questionnaire (PQ) framework

QUESTION NUMBER	QUESTIONS	MOST COMMON SCORE	AVERAGE
1	How responsive were the agents when an active shooter was present?	6,7	6.4
2	How natural was the flow of agents prior to the shooter arriving on the scene?	5,6,7	6.0
3	How natural was the flow of agents after the shooter after the shooter arrived on the scene?	3,4,5	3.9
4	How much did the visual aspects of the simulation involve you?	5	5.0
5	How much did the auditory aspects of the crowd simulation environment involve you?	3,4,6	3.6
6	How well could you identify different audios?	2,4,5	3.7
7	Were you able to localize sounds in the environment?	1,3,7	3.3
8	Did you experience any delay when the "Q" key was pressed?	6,7	6.6
9	Were you able to anticipate what would happen prior to pressing the "Q" key on the keyboard?	4,5,7	5.6
10	How quickly did you adjust to the virtual environment experience?	5,7	6.0
11	How much did your experiences in the virtual environment seem consistent with your real-world experiences?	1,2,3,4	2.6

Figures 6 show the bar graph visualizing how the scores were spread between each of the questions asked in the survey. Based on the bar graph and Table 2 we can see that the mean score value for questions 1, 2, 4, 8, 9, and 10 is approximately 5.8, showing that most participants agreed that the agents in the system were responsive. The flow of agents was natural and was able to predict what the agent's response would be when an active shooter is present. The system experienced no delays from keyboard inputs. As we move onto questions 3, 5, 6, 7, and 11 we notice that the mean score value is around 3.6 showing that most participants didn't find the flow of agents natural when an active shooter was present. Some users couldn't identify and got immersed in the environment with different sound effects. Most users weren't able to localize the sounds in the environment. Lastly, the users didn't find the virtual environment to be coherent with real-world situations. When we implemented sound effects on the agents in Unity, we used a logarithmic scale as opposed to a linear scale, which is why most participants were not able to hear localized sounds in the environment. One of the reasons why we chose a logarithmic scale was because we wanted to make the environment feel more natural, as the sounds would dissipate over distance by using a logarithmic scale. With a linear scale, however, the sound effects are discrete and so they feel less natural. However, they are good at localizing sounds. When we implemented behavior trees into our system, we only added limited behaviors which included "run", "walk" and "idle" states when an active shooter was present. This is because the machine on which the AI behavior system was built wasn't powerful enough to create intelligent behavioral AI systems.

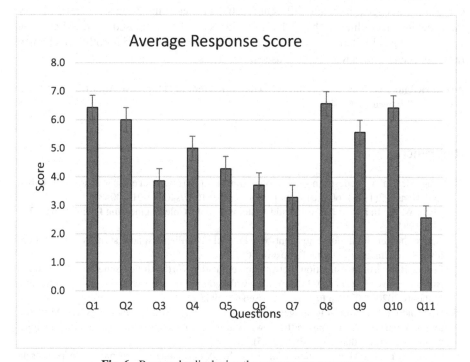

Fig. 6. Bar graphs displaying the average response scores

6   Conclusions

In conclusion, we have presented a virtual reality (VR) experimental setup where experiments for active shooter response can be conducted using computer-controlled (AI)

agents and user-controlled agents. The setup can simulate human behavior during an active shooter event in a campus setting. The techniques presented in this paper include the ability of agents to move from one goal post to another (pathfinding), a decision-making system, and intention states, providing an approach to creating a simple crowd behavior framework when an active shooter is present. In contrast to other frameworks, the decision-making model implemented in our system meets all the modern requirements for developers to create their custom behaviors (depending on the PC specifications) since we use behaviors trees to implement our AI in the agents. The system is developed with the intent of having flexibility and scalability of all the components implemented into the system. The behavior tree is modeled in a way that new behavior structures can be implemented easily for different agents. This VR experimental setup can be used as a teaching and educational tool for navigation and performing VR evacuation drills for active shooter response.

Future work will involve achieving more realistic behaviors for the active shooter by adding deep learning methods to the decision-making tree. It will require behaviors to be implemented using utility AI since the algorithm will be able to adjust their utility curves for each agent to create different reactions for each intention state and will vary the behaviors according to the global intention state. Our proposed crowd simulation system is not just limited to active shooter scenarios but can be used for other emergency response scenarios such as bomb blasts or fire drills.

Acknowledgments. This work is funded by the NSF award 2131116, NSF Award: 2026412, and in part by NSF award 1923986.

References

1. Tang, M., Hu, Y.: Pedestrian simulation in transit stations using agent-based analysis. Urban Rail Transit. 3(1), 54–60 (2017). https://doi.org/10.1007/s40864-017-0053-5
2. Chen, W.-K.: In Linear Networks and Systems, Brooks/Cole Engineering Division, pp. 123–135 (1983)
3. Active shooter simulations: an agent-based model of civilian response strategy, Dissertation, Iowa State University Digital Repository (2017)
4. Federal Bureau of Investigation. Active Shooter Incidents in the United States in 2020 | Federal Bureau of Investigation (2021). https://www.fbi.gov/file-repository/active-shooter-incidents-in-the-us-2020-070121.pdf/view. Accessed 9 Nov 2021
5. Hoogendoorn, S., van Wageningen-Kessels, F., Daamen, W., Duives, D., Sarvi, M.: Continuum theory for pedestrian traffic flow: local route choice modelling and its implications. Transp. Res. Procedia 7, 381–397 (2015)
6. Chen, X., Li, H., Miao, J., Jiang, S., Jiang, X.: A multi-agent-based model for pedestrian simulation in sub-way stations. Simul. Model. Pract. Theory 71, 134–148 (2017)
7. Manley, M., Kim, Y., Christensen, K., Chen, A.: Airport emergency evacuation planning: an agent-based simulation study of dirty bomb scenarios. IEEE Trans. Syst. Man Cybern. Syst. 46(10), 1390–1403 (2016)
8. Helbing, D., Molnár, P.: Social force model for pedestrian dynamics. Phys. Rev. E 51(5), 4282–4286 (1995)
9. Park, J., Rojas, F., Yang, H.: A collision avoidance behavior model for crowd simulation based on psycho-logical findings. Comput. Anim. Virtual Worlds 24(3–4), 173–183 (2013)

10. Singh, S., Lu, S., Kokar, M.M., Kogut, P.A.: Detection and classification of emergent behaviors using multi-agent simulation framework (WIP). Modeling and Simulation of Complexity in Intelligent, Adaptive and Autonomous Systems (MSCIAAS 2017) (2017)
11. MomenTUM v2 pedestrian simulator DE - Lehrstuhl für. https://www.cms.bgu.tum.de/de/17-research-projects/99-momentum-v2-pedestrian-simulator-de. Accessed 08 Nov 2021
12. Kielar, P.M., Biedermann, D.H., Borrmann, A., Kielar, P.M., Biedermann, D.H., Borrmann, A.: MomenTUMv2: A Modular, Extensible, and Generic Agent-Based Pedestrian Behavior Simulation Framework, MomenTUMv2, pp.1–34 (2016)
13. Sharma, S., Avatarsim: a multi-agent system for emergency evacuation simulation. J. Comput. Meth. Sci. Eng. 9(1, 2), pp. S13–S22, ISSN 1472–7978 (2009)
14. Sharma, S., Bodempudi, S.T., Scribner, D., Grazaitis, P.: Active Shooter response training environment for a building evacuation in a collaborative virtual environment. In: IS&T International Symposium on Electronic Imaging (EI 2020), in the Engineering Reality of Virtual Reality. Burlingame, California (2020). https://doi.org/10.2352/ISSN.2470-1173.2020.13.ERVR-223
15. Sharma, S., Bodempudi, S.T.: Immersive virtual reality training module for active shooter events. In: Proceedings of the IS&T International Symposium on Electronic Imaging (EI 2022), in the Engineering Reality of Virtual Reality. Burlingame, California (2022)
16. Sharma, S., Bodempudi, S.T., Reehl, A.: Virtual Reality Instructional (VRI) module for training and patient safety. In: IS&T International Symposium on Electronic Imaging (EI 2021), in the Engineering Reality of Virtual Reality, pp. 178-1–178-6(6) (2021). https://doi.org/10.2352/ISSN.2470-1173.2021.13.ERVR-178
17. Sharma, S., Bodempudi, S.T.: Situational Awareness of COVID Pandemic data using Virtual Reality, IS&T International Symposium on Electronic Imaging (EI 2021), in the Engineering Reality of Virtual Reality, pp. 177-1–177-6(6). Burlingame, California (2021). https://doi.org/10.2352/ISSN.2470-1173.2021.13.ERVR-177
18. Sharma, S., Otunba, S.: Virtual reality as a theme-based game tool for homeland security applications. In: Proceedings of ACM Military Modeling and Simulation Symposium (MMS11), pp. 61–65. Boston, MA, USA (2011)
19. Sharma, S., Otunba, S.: Collaborative virtual environment to study aircraft evacuation for training and education. In: Proceedings of IEEE, International Workshop on Collaboration in Virtual Environments (CoVE -2012), as part of The International Conference on Collaboration Technologies and Systems (CTS 2012), pp. 569–574. Denver, Colorado, USA (2012)
20. Sharma, S., Vadali, H.: Simulation and modeling of a virtual library for navigation and evacuation. In: MSV 2008 - The International Conference on Modeling, Simulation and Visualization Methods, Monte Carlo Resort, Las Vegas, Nevada, USA (2008)
21. Sharma, S., Jerripothula, S., Mackey, S., Soumare, O.: Immersive virtual reality environment of a subway evacuation on a cloud for disaster preparedness and response training. In: Proceedings of IEEE Symposium Series on Computational Intelligence (IEEE SSCI), pp. 1–6. Orlando, Florida, USA (2014). https://doi.org/10.1109/CIHLI.2014.7013380
22. Anylogic.com. AnyLogic: Simulation Modeling Soft-ware Tools & Solutions for Business (2021). https://www.anylogic.com/. Accessed 2 Jan 2022
23. Kielar, P.M., Borrmann, A.: Spice: a cognitive agent framework for computational crowd simulations in complex environments. Autonom. Agent. Multi-Agent Syst. 32(3), 387–416 (2018). https://doi.org/10.1007/s10458-018-9383-2
24. Curtis, S., Best, A., Manocha, D.: Menge: a modular framework for simulating crowd movement, Collective Dynamics, vol. 1 (2016)
25. Li, X., Gui, X.: Modelling autonomic and dynamic trust decision-making mechanism for large-scale open environments. Int. J. Comput. Appl. Technol. 36(3/4), 297 (2009)
26. Kallmann, M., Thalmann, D.: Modeling behaviors of interactive objects for real-time virtual environments. J. Vis. Lang. Comput. 13(2), 177–195 (2002)

27. Bryson, J.: Intelligence by design: Principles of modularity and coordination for engineering complex adaptive agents, Ph.D. dissertation. Department of Electrical Engineering and Computer Science, Massachusetts Institute of Technology, Cambridge, MA, USA (2001)
28. Cerny, M., Plch, T., Brom, C.: Beyond smart objects: Behavior-oriented programming for NPCS in large open worlds. In: Lengyel, E. (ed.) Game Engine Gems 3, pp. 267–280. Boca Raton, FL, USA: CRC Press (2016)
29. Witmer, B.G., Singer, M.J.: Measuring presence in virtual environments: a presence questionnaire. Pres. Teleoper. Virtual Environ. 7(3), 225–240 (1998). https://doi.org/10.1162/105 474698565686

The Need for Universal Design of eXtended Reality (XR) Technology in Primary and Secondary Education

Identifying Opportunities, Challenges, and Knowledge Gaps from the Literature

Joschua Thomas Simon-Liedtke[1]([⊠]) [iD] and Rigmor C. Baraas[2] [iD]

[1] Norsk Regnesentral, Gaustadalléen 23 A, 0373 Oslo, Norway
joschua@nr.no
[2] National Centre for Optics, Vision and Eye Care, Faculty of Health and Social Sciences, University of South-Eastern Norway, Hasbergvei 36, 3616 Kongsberg, Norway
rigmor.baraas@usn.no

Abstract. eXtended Reality (XR) provides new opportunities for immersive and engaging ways of learning in primary and secondary education. Educators and educational decision-makers, however, lack knowledge about the opportunities of this emerging technology. At the same time, XR technology lacks a fundamental universal design framework targeted at improving accessibility and usability for all, specifically for pupils with disabilities. In the following paper, we present the results from two selective and weighed literature reviews identifying: (1) opportunities, positive outcomes and challenges of using XR technology in primary and secondary education; (2) general advantages and limitations in terms of universal design, including barriers and possible solutions of XR technology for pupils with disabilities. The results show that utilization of XR technology in primary and secondary education is versatile, may positively influence learning outcomes in pupils, contributes to increase motivation, engagement, and interest. The challenges in implementing XR technology were mainly related to economic cost, health-related limitations, pedagogy, editorial limitations, and lack of universal design. Pupils with disabilities and varying degrees of abilities face challenges because there is lack of multimodality, practical issues when setting up or using devices, lack of interoperability and compatibility with assistive technology, financial costs, health-related issues, overreliance on gamification, and ethical considerations. In addition, most devices are designed for adults and not recommended to be used by children younger than 13 years of age. Future research needs to address development of guidelines including best-practice examples for increased accessibility and usability of XR technology, as well as advance the standardization and solidification of said guidelines into standards, regulations, and laws.

Keywords: XR · VR · AR · MR · Education · Universal design · Accessibility · Usability · Primary and secondary education

© Springer Nature Switzerland AG 2022
J. Y. C. Chen and G. Fragomeni (Eds.): HCII 2022, LNCS 13318, pp. 121–141, 2022.
https://doi.org/10.1007/978-3-031-06015-1_9

1   Introduction

Extended reality (XR) is an umbrella term that incorporates both virtual reality (VR), augmented reality (AR), and mixed reality (MR) [1]. Existing literature [2] highlights three main characteristics that enhance user experience making XR technology very suitable for primary and secondary education: (1) new ways of interaction, (2) high degree of immersion, and (3) information density of its content. Although multiple short-term studies involving ample types of XR-technology exist [3, 4], there are still significant gaps in the current research.

First, there is a general knowledge gap among educators and educational policymakers about the opportunities and challenges of this emerging technology in an educational setting. Even though many surveys about XR technology in education exist from a scientific or technological point of view, there are no comprehensive studies focusing on the interaction and correlation of educational curricula, technology, scientific methods, funding schemes, skill requirements, and universal design.

Second, there are gaps concerning the needs of pupils and teachers with cognitive, sensory, vocal, and physical disabilities and different degrees of cognitive and sensory abilities. Many aspects of XR technology, for example, are not accessible enough for users with common eye problems [5]. In general, the universal design of XR technology has not been sufficiently discussed, and there is a lack of guidelines, frameworks, and best-practice examples to address these problems [6, 7].

We attempted to close these gaps by conducting a selective and weighed literature review, in which we chose the most relevant literature of the past five years related to (1) the use of XR technology in primary and secondary education, and (2) universal design of XR technology including issues about accessibility and usability. We compiled a summary of the relevant research to date, identified new gaps, and highlighted opportunities for future research.

2   Methodology

The need for a literature review arose in conjunction with the development of an interview guide. The guide would be implemented for conducting group interviews with representatives from schools, municipalities, user organizations, and XR developers about the educational use of XR technology, and the universal design of the technology. We defined a search protocol based on the research by [8] and simplified it with suggestions by [9]. The protocol consisted of three steps: (1) planning the review, (2) conducting the review and selecting the articles, and (3) extracting and analyzing the data.

During the planning phase, we defined research questions, inclusion criteria, as well as exclusion criteria, tested and selected relevant keywords, set up relevance assessment parameters including necessary requirements, and agreed on relevant search engines. We defined the following research questions:

1. What is the state of XR technology usage in primary and secondary education?

    1.1. For which courses in primary and secondary education has XR technology, e.g., VR, MR, and AR, been used?

1.2. What devices are most used in primary and secondary education?

1.3. What scientific design patterns and methods are deployed to evaluate the interventions? What kind of data is collected and how? How many participants participate in the interventions?

1.4. What are the positive outcomes of using XR technology in primary and secondary education?

1.5. What are the challenges and limitations of using XR technology in primary and secondary education?

2. What is the state of universal design of XR technology in the literature?

2.1. How is universal design of XR technology, including its accessbility and usability, addressed in the literature? Who is promoting the universal design of XR technology?

2.2. Who is researching and promoting the univesal design of XR technology?

2.3. What disability groups are addressed in the literature?

2.4. What are the general advantages of XR technology for pupils with disabilities and different degrees of sensory, physical, and cognitive abilities?

2.5. What are the general challenges and limitations of XR technology for pupils with disabilities and different degrees of sensory, physical, and cognitive abilities?

2.6. What barriers of XR technology for pupils with disabilities and different degrees of sensory, physical, and cognitive abilities does the literature address?

2.7. What solutions for the previously mentioned barriers does the literature address? What general strategies for improved universal design of XR technology increase accessibility and usability for all, including people with disabilities?

We decided on both popular (Google) and scientific (Google Scholar) search portals. General inclusion criteria were literature from the past five years (2016–2021) including systematic literature reviews, state-of-the-art articles, opinion and position papers, doctoral theses, master theses, and gray literature. General exclusion criteria were commercial articles, advertisements, individual projects, and meta-reviews.

During the review and selection phase, we recorded the first fifty most relevant hits for each search string and compiled the results into a list containing the articles' title, year, and link. Then, we proceeded to read the abstracts of each article and checked whether the respective article passed the necessary requirements of the relevance assessment parameters defined in the protocol. Moreover, we skimmed the articles for compliance with the remaining relevance assessment parameters listed, awarding one point if the corresponding parameter was satisfactorily discussed. Then, we summed the awarded points for each article and sorted them in declining order, i.e., from highest to lowest score. Finally, we selected the articles with the highest scores.

We prepared and conducted two literature searches independently using two independent sets of search strings: (1.) A search about XR projects in primary and secondary education. The protocol parameters can be found in Appendix A. (2.) A search about accessibility, usability, and universal design of XR technology. The protocol parameters can be found in Appendix B. Originally, we targeted literature about the universal design of XR technology in primary and secondary education only. However, this resulted in a very limited number of papers. Thus, we decided on a more general approach for the universal design review.

3 Results

For the first search about XR projects in primary and secondary education, we conducted the first step of the literature search using Google Scholar as a search engine resulting in a list with 128 entries. In the second step, 53 of the articles passed the necessary requirements of the relevance parameters. In the third step, we applied the remaining relevance parameters and obtained 12 articles that had a score of 13 or higher. We eventually selected three articles with the highest scores of 15 (one article [10]) and 14 (two articles [2, 11]). One of the articles [2] was one of a three-part literature review series of which the other two [12, 13] ranked just one point below. One of the second-highest-ranking articles focused on MR including VR and AR while the other two articles focused on AR and VR individually. Thus, we chose to include the remaining two articles in the results as well resulting in a total of five articles [2, 10–13]. Thereafter, we identified educational courses, technology solutions, positive as well as negative effects of using XR technology in primary and secondary education, and reviewed scientific methods used to implement and evaluate XR-related projects in schools.

For the second search about accessibility, usability, and universal design of XR technology, we conducted the first step of the literature search using Google Scholar as a search engine, resulting in a list with 224 entries. In the second step, 129 of the articles passed the necessary requirements of the relevance parameters. In the third step, we applied the remaining relevance parameters and obtained 21 articles that had a score of 13 or higher. We eventually selected 14 articles: 3 articles having a score of 17 [14–16], 2 having a score of 16 [17, 18], 2 having a score of 15 [7, 19], and 7 having a score of 14 [6, 20–25]. Then, we summarized the general opportunities and limitations of XR technology for people with disabilities. Moreover, we extracted data about how UD is addressed in the literature and by whom. Eventually, we summarized barriers prevalent for people with disabilities and varying abilities categorized into cognitive, sensory (seeing-, hearing- and touch-related), vocal, and movement-related (both motor- and mobility-related) impairments as well as solutions for said barriers. Finally, we extracted general universal design strategies to make the technology more accessible and usable for everyone. In the following paragraphs, we will present our results according to each research question they relate to.

RQ1-1: For which courses in primary and secondary education has XR technology, e.g., VR, MR, and AR, been used?

VR technology has been used in, for example, environmental science, biology, geology, technology, mathematics, English language learning, and music [13].

AR has been used in Science, Technology, Engineering, and Mathematics (STEM), Humanities & Arts, Social sciences, Business & Law, Health & Welfare, Services & Others. AR is most often used in Science, Technology, Engineering, and Mathematics (STEM) subjects in primary and secondary education, specifically in formal science, natural science, physical science, and social science [12]. In primary education, formal and natural science are somewhat more predominant, whereas natural science and physical science are somewhat more predominant in secondary education [12]. Relevant science courses for AR have been, for example, mathematics, geometry, biology, ecology, physics, chemistry, geology, and computer science [11]. It has also been used in lab experiments and field trips [11]. In Humanities & Arts, AR has been used in language learning, visual art and painting appreciation, and culture and multiculturalism [11]. Less common were Social Sciences, Business & Law with library instruction, management and sales, and business, and Engineering, Manufacturing and Construction with automatics and robotics, laboratories, computer networks [11]. The least common use for AR is Health & Welfare and Services & Others [11].

MR has been used in formal science, e.g. mathematics, computer science, robotics, or information theory; in natural physical science, e.g. physics, chemistry, astronomy, biology, earth science like geography; and in social science, anthropology, archaeology, communication studies, economics, history, story-telling, or dramatic play [2].

RQ1-2: What devices are most used in primary and secondary education?

The investigated articles cover all types of XR, i.e. AR [2, 10–12], MR [2], and VR [13].

There are four main technologies for VR used in education including (1) mobile VR like Samsung Gear VR or Google Cardboard, (2) wearable 360° spherical video-based VR, (3) room-sized 3D displays, typically with 2D or 3D projections on the wall, called Cave Automatic Virtual Environments (CAVE), and (4) head-mounted displays (HMD), e.g. Oculus Rift, Oculus Quest II, or HTC Vive, as well as hand-held displays (tablets, smartphones) [13, 26, 27]. The first two categories are most deployed in the classrooms whereas tethered HMDs with hand controllers are least commonly deployed [13]. Interaction is mostly done either by custom hand controllers, head movement detection through sensors embedded in the headset or through observation [13].

Devices used for MR are projectors projecting the augmentations on real objects, HMDs, barcode readers, large displays, monitors alone, or a monitor on a robot [2]. Many studies use embodied/authentic simulation MR as well as marker-based AR [2]. The interaction was provided by tangibles, AR cards, or motion-sensing devices [2]. Devices for AR technology used are (1) handheld devices like tablets (most common in primary education), and smartphones (especially for pupils with autism and intellectual disabilities), (2) computers combined with a (web)camera (most common in secondary education), (3) motion-sensing input devices (e.g. Microsoft Kinect), (4) head-mounted displays (HMD), (5) devices or screens mounted on the head (especially for pupils with hearing and vision impairments and autism), (6) glasses like Google Glasses, (7) large-screen projectors where stereoscopic projections can be combined with tracking cameras [10–12, 28–31]. Handheld devices are most common since mobile phones are very popular, followed closely by a PC combined with a webcam [11]. The trend towards handheld devices seems to be increasing [11]. There are several AR tracking strategies including (1) marker-based strategies, in which a camera and some type of visual marker trigger an event in the reader (QR, black-and-white pattern) [12]; (2) location-based strategies, in which GPS, digital compass, velocity meter, or accelerometer provides data about the user's location [12], and (3) markerless strategies, in which sensors accurately detect the real-world environment [12]. The most common software strategies are markers followed by location-based strategies. [10]. Marker-based AR is the most common strategy as it is considered as being effective, stable, and supported by a plethora of existing libraries [11, 12]. Location-based where position and orientation data of the device is used is the second most common. [11, 12]. Markerless AR where no marker is necessary is least common [11].

RQ1-3: What scientific methods are deployed to evaluate the interventions? What kind of data is collected? How many participants participate in the interventions?

Both quantitative, qualitative, and quantitative and qualitative methods combined are used to collect data [12]. Research methods are experimental studies like experimental-comparative methods or quasi-experimental studies, pure experimental study, user experience testing, usability testing, qualitative methods, literature reviews, single-subject design, transversal research, and mixed methods [10, 12, 13]. Other methods are mixed methods of qualitative and quantitative methods like qualitative-exploratory-case study, quantitative explanatory and causal research, quantitative-descriptive research, qualitative-exploratory-pilot case study [10, 11]. The most common research designs are explorative research methods or experimental comparative methods [2].

Tools used are questionnaires, interviews, surveys, tests, case observations, focus groups, surveys, case studies, and writing essays [2, 10–12]. The data is mainly collected with questionnaires, followed by interviews [11]. Less used methods are case observations, focus groups, and writing essays [11]. The data collected was of quantitative, qualitative, and mixed nature [2, 13].

Most studies take place inside the classroom [13]. The sample size of the scientific interventions is medium, and most commonly between 30/40 to 80/200 participants [2, 12, 13]. Some studies are low-sized with 30 or fewer participants, and very few were large-sized with more than 40 participants [10, 11]. The interventions are mostly short-timed, i.e. less than 50 min [13]. The intervention series are predominantly short-term and only a few long-term [11].

RQ1-4: What are the positive outcomes of using XR technology in primary and secondary education?

The following positive outcomes of utilization of XR technology have been reported: First, XR can influence learning outcomes in pupils, such as increased performance, gains, and feeling of achievement [2, 10–13]. Moreover, XR contributes to improvements in pupils' social skills through collaboration, socialization, participation, and interaction [2, 10–13]. In some studies, improved language association has been recorded as well [12]. Third, XR technology has been associated with pupils' improved self-image, including increased confidence, self-efficacy, and self-learning [10, 13]. Fourth, XR technology facilitates emotional reactions including enjoyment, general satisfaction, enthusiasm, and positive perceptions and attitudes towards learning [2, 10–13]. Fifth, XR technology is often reported to contribute to improvements in cognitive skills such as attention, memory, creativity, problem-solving [2, 10–13]. Likewise, XR technology is reported to increase motivation, engagement, and interest in pupils [2, 10–13].

RQ1-5: What are the challenges and limitations of using XR technology in primary and secondary education?

The studies have shown considerable challenges in multiple areas related to economic cost, physical space, health, pedagogy, editorial limitations, and universal design. First, XR technology devices tend to be more expensive than traditional education material. At the same time, XR devices, especially for MR and VR, can impose considerable space requirements for example for lighting and cable management [2, 10, 13]. Second, XR technology can be quite complex to set up and demand considerable training, at the same time there is limited qualification among teachers to utilize this technology [2, 10, 12]. Third, there can be health-related limitations in the form of so-called cybersickness where users experience for example nausea, as well as cognitive overload due to the sheer amount of stimuli user experience [13]. Fourth, the portfolio of available content tailored to individual national, regional or local curricula is still very limited [2, 10, 12]. Moreover, current XR technology is often very inflexible and does not allow adaptation or manipulation from one subject to another subject [2, 10, 12]. Fifth, XR technology lacks considerable research related to its accessibility and usability for pupils with common eye problems, physical and mental disabilities, or special needs [10, 32]. There is no robust framework to target general questions about the universal design of this emerging technology [6]. Sixth, there are considerable scientific uncertainties in existing studies as these often focus heavily on the novelty factor and acute results, leaving large gaps when it comes to long-term effects [2, 10, 12]. At the same time, there are challenges around limited sample sizes excluding any pupil with special needs, limitations on use of data collections tools, and comparing results between different curriculum subjects [2, 10, 12].

RQ2-1: How is universal design of XR technology, including its accessibility and usability, addressed in the literature to date?

Some of the articles present anecdotal cases, projects, and examples of barriers that people with disabilities might encounter, as well as solutions, or provide a compilation of helpful resources [17, 21, 22]. One article provides a thorough survey of concrete barriers of XR technology for people with disabilities [15]. Universal design of XR technology is addressed by providing some very general and loose guidelines or recommendations for developers [18–20, 23]. One of the articles revisits accessibility guidelines from other ICT areas, like WCAG 2.0 for websites [23]. A few articles provide very concrete and more standardized guidelines and examples [14, 16, 24]. Other articles discuss questions around universal design on a more general level [6, 7, 25].

RQ2-2: Who is researching and promoting the universal design of XR technology?

There are initiatives, communities, and workshops as well as research organizations that address accessibility, usability, and universal design of XR technology [7, 14, 17, 18, 24]. XR Access, for example, is an initiative dedicated to the promotion of universal design of XR technology by providing relevant resources addressing the topic, as well as organizing symposia where representatives from the XR community discuss barriers, solutions, and general frameworks associated with the universal design of XR technology [33–35]. Moreover, there is one working group and initiative by the World Wide Web Consortium (W3C) listing user needs and requirements for people with disabilities, which is the one attempt dedicated to a somewhat standardized process to date [14, 24].

RQ2-3: What disability groups are addressed in the literature?

We could find the following disability categories addressed implicitly or explicitly in the literature:

1. Cognition: [6, 7, 14–22, 24, 25]
2. Senses

   a. Seeing: [6, 7, 14–22, 24, 25]
   b. Hearing: [6, 7, 14–22, 24, 25]
   c. Touch: [15, 16]

3. Voice: [7, 14–18, 20, 21]
4. Physical

   a. Mobility: [6, 7, 14–22, 24, 25]
   b. Motor: [6, 7, 14–22, 24, 25]

RQ2-4: What are the general advantages of XR technology for pupils with disabilities and different degrees of sensory, physical, and cognitive abilities?

XR technology can offer opportunities for virtual access and inclusion, compensations for disabilities, safe spaces, personalization, assistive technologies, and rehabilitation.

With XR technology, people with disabilities can experience inclusion and virtual access that would be inaccessible in the real world [15, 21]. Users can, for example, travel to places around the globe, at the same time as XR technology can offer new opportunities for remote working [15, 20]. XR technology can compensate for disabilities in the virtual world. In virtual worlds, people with disabilities can overcome visual, auditory, vocal, or physical limitations or gain extra abilities like flight or superhuman strength [15, 20, 22]. Virtual worlds can create empathy in people without disabilities by letting them experience the world through the eyes and body of a person with disability [21, 22]. There are, for example, simulations for blind, deaf, and wheelchair users [15]. XR technology can offer a safe space where people with disabilities can learn to cope with new sensory or physical disabilities, as well as people with autism, social anxieties, and other mental health challenges can experience comfort and safety [21, 22]. Virtual worlds can be personalized such that they accommodate for special needs of pupils, for example, by eliminating or reducing visual or hearing barriers and distractions [15, 22]. XR technology can be used as assistive technology for example by guiding visual tasks or providing captions for hard-of-hearing people [14, 21, 22]. XR can offer various opportunities for therapy and rehabilitation [20, 21]. In the virtual world, users can experience reduced social isolation, anxiety PTSD, or pain [15, 20, 21].

RQ2-5: What are the general challenges and limitations of XR technology for pupils with disabilities and different degrees of sensory, physical, and cognitive abilities?

General challenges are mostly related to the lack of multimodality, practical issues when setting up or using devices, compatibility with assistive technology, financial costs, health issues, overreliance on gamification, and ethical considerations. XR technology, and especially VR and MR, is a multimodal medium, i.e. it has the capability of engaging multiple senses and functionalities like vision, hearing, and touch as well as motion and haptic control [6, 18]. However, the focus on the visual presentation of many XR applications, and the lack of multimodality, e.g. conveying the same information in multiple modalities through, for example, visual, audio, or haptic cues, impose barriers to people with disabilities [6, 15]. Moreover, many applications only allow one type of control, but it can be important to accommodate for and around assistive technology, controllers, sensors, and tether cabling for users with special needs, especially, people with visual, auditive, and physical disabilities [6, 14, 15, 18]. What is more, there are practical challenges associated with the setup of XR devices. Some users, for example, the elderly or people with cognitive disabilities, might encounter difficulties when setting up or learning how to use virtual reality due to the unfamiliarity or novelty of the technology [20]. Many users with disabilities report a lack of options and flexibility of integration with other hardware like keyboards, buttons, or paddles, as well as customization options that could benefit their specific special needs [14, 15]. In many cases, XR technology is not compatible with assistive technology (AT) that people with visual, auditory, or physical disabilities use [14, 15]. In some cases, manufacturers have implemented manufacturer locks that limit compatible software to one or a few specific brands or manufacturers [14, 15]. Likewise, there are significant financial challenges to XR technology. The cost of VR and MR equipment is often too expensive, as well as mobile devices capable of AR are often not feasible where the budget is limited [15, 22].

Furthermore, there are a few significant health issues connected to XR technology. VR devices might cause motion sickness, and vertigo [14, 15]. Thus, most manufacturers do not recommend their products for kids under the age of 13 [36, 37]. Finally, there are general challenges of ethical considerations related to for example virtual violence, bullying, virtual sex, and participation in the virtual worlds [20].

RQ2-6: What barriers of XR technology for pupils with disabilities and different degrees of sensory, physical, and cognitive abilities does the literature address?

We will present the most common barriers for people with cognitive, visual, auditory, haptic, vocal, and physical disabilities.

Cognitive barriers are mostly rooted in differing mental capabilities, as well as bodily reactions to virtual stimuli. The literature lists, for example, cognitive barriers for users that have difficulties learning hardware in the form of new interfaces, input devices, or controls [20]. Other users with cognitive disabilities can encounter barriers in thinking, remembering, and concentrating especially where no breaks are allowed [15]. Moreover, sensory overload can exhaust users, and even cause seizures [15]. Lastly, some users can experience vertigo or motion sickness in the virtual world [20, 25].

The most common visual barriers are related to lack of multimodality, inaccessible elements of the user interface like menus, texts, or buttons, barriers due to color vision deficiencies, peripheral vision or decreased stereopsis, and hardware incompatibility with assistive devices. XR is to date a predominantly visual medium [22]. Thus, the negligence of an equally rich sound scape, and the lack of conveying visual cues and information to other senses like hearing or touch, e.g. multimodality, can decrease the experience for people with visual disabilities or make it completely inaccessible [14, 15, 20, 22]. Inaccessible user interfaces that do not provide labels or alt-texts for elements, and that do not allow resizing of text or choice of different color contrasts, can make menus and other important elements of the application inaccessible for people with visual disabilities [15, 20, 25]. Users with reduced or absent color vision or stereopsis, as well as users with peripheral vision can encounter significant barriers in the virtual world [15, 20]. Moreover, hardware incompatibility with assistive technology (ATs) like screen readers or magnifiers can impose significant barriers for people with low or missing vision that often rely on the use of these ATs when interacting with ICT applications and devices [14, 15, 20].

Most barriers for people with hearing disabilities are rooted in the lack of alternate modalities, hardware difficulties, insufficient sound design, and lack of communication alternatives. In some applications, there are no alternative modalities for visual cues or commentary, like the visual barriers described above [15]. Hardware interference with hearing aids or feedback can impose significant barriers for people with auditory disabilities [15, 20]. Insufficient sound design that does not allow localization of spatialized sound can make an XR application inaccessible [20]. Finally, the lack of communication alternatives like missing captions or sign language support can make communication in the virtual world impossible for people with auditory disabilities [15, 20].

Some users can have problems sensing haptic cues due to a lack of tactile touch or the capability to sense haptic sensations [15, 20].

People with vocal disabilities can encounter barriers where speech is used for interaction, but no alternative is offered [16].

Many people with physical disabilities can encounter barriers with XR devices that often require full-body interaction [21, 23]. More precisely, barriers for people with physical disabilities are often related to inaccessible controllers, energy and stamina requirements, and the inability to customize or personalize. Many papers point out the overuse of motion tracking solely based on non-disabled abilities and functions as one of the biggest barriers for people with physical disabilities [14, 15, 22]. Many XR controllers can be difficult or impractical to operate, especially where two hands are required [14, 15, 20, 21]. Likewise, many XR devices and controllers do not allow for personalization or customization accommodating for varying levels of reflexes, dexterity, range of motion, or finger strength [14, 15]. Moreover, many XR applications do not account for fatigue and pain, especially where they do not allow users to take pauses during the interaction [14, 15, 21]. Likewise, balancing in virtual reality can be challenging for people with physical disabilities [15]. Other barriers can be categorized according to different body parts. People with disabilities related to the head can encounter difficulties moving their heads to control or interact with a virtual world [15, 20]. Likewise wearing a VR or MR headset can be inaccessible for people with glasses, or when the headset is too heavy [15, 21]. People with disabilities connected to the arms and hands can have difficulties moving their arms or hands, as well as tracking hands for holding and griping [15]. People in wheelchairs can encounter barriers due to restricted movement and wire management that can get entangled in a power chair [15, 20]. Some XR applications do not accommodate for different heights of a user who is sitting in a wheelchair [14, 15, 20].

RQ2-7: What solutions for the barriers mentioned above does the literature address? What general strategies for improved universal design of XR technology increase accessibility and usability for all, including people with disabilities?

The literature addresses these barriers by proposing solutions implementation on the hardware/device level, as well as the software/application level.

Hardware/device solutions target especially input controllers as well as more flexible headsets. There are for example input controllers targeted at people with visual, auditory, or physical disabilities like white cane or braille displaying controllers, voice command, accessible input wheels, joysticks, mouses, or buttons [14–16, 18, 21–23]. Some papers present assistive technology for people with visual, auditory, vocal, and physical disabilities like screen readers, second screens, white cane controllers, or sound mixers [14, 15, 21, 22]. Additionally, software exists that targets people with visual disabilities that can be used as plugins with existing applications [5, 22].

Software/application solutions include the emphasis on in-game flexibility, personalization and customization, alternative communication means, improved multimodality, and increased accessibility of the user interfaces. Increased in-game flexibility can be obtained through the possibility of teleportation, observer-only mode, flexible time and reaction limits, focus indicators [14, 15, 20] as well as virtual aids that suggest corrections for errors, cues for depth-perception [14, 15, 20]. Personalization and customization should accommodate text size, color contrast, controller layout, height, and sound management [14, 20, 23]. Likewise, compatibility with assistive devices should be promoted [15]. Multimodality should accommodate for alternatives to visual or auditory information in form of text, descriptions, captions, vibrations, as well as complementing visual or auditory cues [14, 15, 18, 20, 21]. Especially, the focus on improved localized sound has been pointed out [15, 21]. Alternative communication means may include keyboard support, as well as speech-to-text, text-to-speech, and captions [14–16]. Finally, the importance of developing more accessible graphical user interfaces has been pointed out [15, 16, 21, 25].

As general solutions to increase the universal design of XR technology, the literature points out the need for research about its barriers and solutions, standardization, improvement of XR devices, and the inclusion of people with disabilities in the design and development process [6, 7, 14, 16, 23]. Research about barriers and solutions should include literature review and ethnographic studies [6, 7]. Especially the need for increasing accessibility and usability of XR devices and their controls has been pointed out [6, 7, 25]. The results of the previous two points should result in a standardized framework containing guidelines, checklists, and best-practice examples [7, 14]. An outline of such a framework exists already today [14]. Finally, users with disabilities should be included very early when designing and developing XR technology to increase the accessibility and usability of XR devices and applications [6, 7, 25].

4 Discussion

In the following sections, we will discuss the limitations of our chosen methodology, the results related to the educational use of XR technology, and the results related to its universal design.

To begin with, we chose a selective, weighed literature review rather than a systematic literature review because of time and resource constraints. Our first initial trial searches revealed that there were many papers and articles about individual projects. However, our focus was to get an overview of the state-of-the-art of educational use of XR technology and its degree of universal design. Thus, we limited our selection to those papers and articles that addressed all or most of the research questions defined above. Moreover, we weighed each paper according to whether relevant themes and topics were covered explicitly or merely coincidentally. For the education research that meant the inclusion of surveys that investigated both advantages and challenges, education subjects, methods, and technology in both primary and secondary education. Special points were attributed to papers that addressed accessibility, usability, and universal design explicitly. For the universal design search, that meant the inclusion of articles and papers that investigated concrete barriers for people with disabilities and their practical solutions, addressing the needs of multiple user groups, and discussing general frameworks for universal design of XR technology to increase its accessibility and usability for all. Points were deducted were only individual or few user groups, and where individual projects were addressed.

In general, our search revealed numerous articles about individual and singular projects. The educational search provided many scientific papers, whereas the universal design search revealed mostly popular, popular scientific, and gray literature as we will discuss below. Moreover, we discovered a plethora of existing systematic literature reviews of various focal points for the educational search. In contrast, we could not identify a significant amount of systematic literature reviews concerned with the universal design of XR technology or its accessibility or usability. Papers concerned with the UD of XR technology were almost exclusively opinion, concept, or scoping articles. Thus, our present paper is one of the first literature reviews covering these topics. However, there is a need for a more systematic review of the literature in the future.

Likewise, we decided on a general approach when extracting data from the articles as well due to our defined need of getting an overview. The papers related to the educational search, for example, contained a variety of data including individual projects as well as detailed descriptions of scientific methods and others. The universal design articles contained concrete examples of barriers for people with disabilities as well as singular projects providing solutions for these barriers. Since the main purpose of this selective and weighed literature was to inform an interview guide for group interviews with representatives from schools, municipalities, user organizations, and XR developers, we limited the extraction of data to the points described above. Thus, a future systematic literature review could cover more detailed data points like the categorization and systematization of barriers for people with disabilities and their possible solutions.

On the one hand, our selective and weighed literature review revealed the key opportunities, and challenges of XR technology in primary and secondary education.

One common thread that runs through many of the XR projects compiled in the surveys is the singular nature of the interventions with significant research gaps. Even though research exists about the advantages, and limitations of using XR technology in education, there is still a research gap related to the repeatability and objectivity of these results. Most notably, future research could benefit from increased standardization of research methods and increased visibility of concrete advantages and limitations of the technology. Moreover, projects involving XR technology in primary and secondary schools are often individual interventions separate from the regular curriculum focusing on one single subject and taking place with a limited group of subjects for a limited period.

At the same time, the literature shows that the application areas of XR technology are extremely versatile covering areas from STEM, Social Science, Language Education, to Arts. We argue, thus, that research of XR technology as a mediator in primary and secondary schools has a dire need for diversification, integration, and additional and alternative reuse for multiple subjects simultaneously.

First, diversification of research should address multiple types of intervention, data collection methods used, sample size, intervention length, and the inclusion of more diverse subjects for the interventions. Many of the surveys we reviewed, for example, pointed out the need for more participants and a prolonged time for the interventions. Moreover, there is a need for the inclusion of pupils with disabilities that have been underrepresented in the literature so far.

Second, the integration of research means both the integration across multiple subjects and the integration with existing, more traditional teaching aids. Amit the vast range of possibilities that XR technology can offer, and that already exist, there is little correlation and intersection between individual projects. Likewise, many XR projects exist in a sandbox without any explicit connection or interactive interfaces to other teaching aids like books, physical models, or software. To exploit the full potential of and increase acceptance for XR technology, however, it is necessary to find a common ground for the individual projects, provide possible interfaces to interact and exchange information between projects, and investigate and highlight the opportunities and intersections of XR technology and the school curriculum.

Third, the integration of XR technology directly leads to the increased reuse of XR that eventually will increase the feasibility and sustainability of its technology. One major challenge reported in the literature is the cost of the technology. Even though costs for XR devices and applications have significantly decreased in the past years, many schools still struggle with the procurement of a still relatively young and unknown technology. Education budgets on both the national and local level have traditionally been very limited, and many schools have down-prioritized a technology with limited use and unknown outcomes like XR technology in favor of essential services and personal costs. As XR technology becomes more versatile, diverse, and better integrated, however, we argue that XR devices and applications could become a viable supplement to traditional teaching aids in the future. In addition to pedagogical opportunities, there might be yet unknown synergies as well. The possibilities in remote education, for example, have not been investigated so far. Providing engaging teaching experience for pupils that live in remote places or that cannot participate because of other reasons - one might think of pupils that are in quarantine during a pandemic not unlike the one we have seen in recent years - might lead to innovative and more inclusive ways for education.

On the other hand, our selected and weighed literature review highlighted the need for focused efforts to increase accessibility and usability of XR technology towards a significantly more inclusive and extended universal design of this emerging technology.

Our search results reveal that scientific research within the field of universal design of the technology is still limited. Whereas we found an impressive amount of scientific research articles addressing interventions of XR technology in primary and secondary education, there was only a very limited number of scientific papers concerned with the accessibility, usability, and general universal design (UD) of the technology. The most common types of scientific articles somewhat related to UD of XR technology were indeed usability studies of existing applications and devices. Many of those studies, however, did neither explicitly mention the inclusion of people with disabilities or address their needs. Moreover, there were some individual studies and reports investigating stand-alone solutions for specific user groups like toolboxes for people with low vision or special input devices for people in wheelchairs [5, 38]. A common finding of scientific studies or industrial reports was that research was missing a general, overarching framework or initiative to put needs, barriers, and solutions into correlation to each other. To put the experiences of multiple groups in context to each other makes sense since many people with disabilities can have multiple disabilities at once [39, 40]. At the same time, improvements for one user group might create synergies for other user groups and the public as well, a phenomenon often referred to as the "curb-cut effect" in universal design research [41]. Improving multimodality in XR, e.g. the process of conveying information to multiple senses simultaneously, could improve accessibility and usability for multiple user groups significantly. For example, providing auditory or haptic alternatives for visual information introduced for blind and low-vision people can significantly augment the experience for other user groups as well. Optimizing the graphical user interfaces (GUI) to accommodate people with screen readers might help users with other assistive devices as well. A more accessible GUI that accommodates for customization of font size, font color, color contrast and background noise reduction can benefit elderly people as well. Subtitles introduced for deaf or hard-of-hearing people can benefit both people with cognitive disabilities, as well as people that are in a physical environment with loud background noises. There is a need for research that investigates these synergies as well as communicates them to the public.

As we pointed out above, there was a noticeable lack of scientific research addressing the universal design of XR technology in a unified model. However, we could find an adequate number of articles in popular, popular scientific, and gray literature. Scientific studies that *do* address the UD of XR technology almost exclusively emphasize the need for more UD research [5, 6].

At the same time, the need for UD has not been unnoticed in the industry and communities involved in the design and development of XR devices and applications. There are communities of designers and developers of both XR hardware and software dedicated to tearing down barriers while increasing improvement with the accessibility, usability, and universal design of the technology. These communities take form as initiatives both explicitly dedicated to the inclusion of XR technology and subgroups of general XR associations, and working groups organizing, and arranging workshops and conferences from which they publish reports [7, 17, 24, 33–35, 42].

Moreover, we can witness the beginning of a standardization process under the direction of the World Wide Web Consortium (W3C) that has been a pioneer within the standardization of accessibility of websites, an effort that has been enshrined into both national and international laws and directives [14, 43–47]. However, this standardization effort has merely begun and lacks a more general and unifying approach addressing among others user needs of and requirements for several groups of people with disabilities. Many barriers for people with disabilities, and possible solutions for those barriers, have been investigated in one significant report by Lucasfilm's ILMxLab and the Disability Visibility Project [15]. We could not, however, find an independent, equally comprehensive, and peer-reviewed report in the scientific literature that would test the repeatability of their research, confirm or refute their findings, and fill in the gaps that have been pointed out by the report. Research that investigates barriers for people with disabilities and their needs, as well as solutions is very much needed to establish, develop, and promote a robust universal design framework for XR technology.

As mentioned earlier, there are some papers and initiatives outlining the general concepts of a universal design framework for XR technology [6, 7, 14, 16]. Besides the comprehensive compilation of user needs and requirements including descriptions of possible barriers for people with disabilities as mentioned above, there is a lack of practical guidelines and call for actions supporting designers and developers of XR devices and applications. Such guidelines are well established in other areas of ICT like the Web Accessibility Guidelines (WCAG) administered by the W3C or guidelines for inclusive game design [43, 44, 48]. Such guidelines often follow a structure that explains common barriers for affected user groups, compiles solutions of those barriers and provides use cases and best-practice examples on how the solutions can practically be implemented. At the same time, guidelines like WCAG 2.0 and WCAG 2.1 and checklists derived from these guidelines can be used as reference by user organizations, municipalities, supervisory authorities to investigate whether an ICT device or application contains some of the barriers or conforms to the best-practice examples presented in the guidelines to eventually examine the degree of accessibility, usability and universal design of the device and application. It has been shown that a system of audit and certification based on standards and guidelines is the most common means by which universal design is enforced in other areas of ICT [49]. Thus, there is a need for developing the existing guidelines for practical use by designers and developers of XR devices and applications, as well as user organizations and authorities.

5 Future Work

Our selective and weighed literature review uncovered multiple opportunities for future research both scientific and practical, related to the use of XR technology in education as well as related to the universal design of the technology. There is a need for strengthening research on both the educational use of XR technology and its universal design. In general, there is a need for a more detailed, systematic literature review focusing on literature related to barriers of XR technology for people with disabilities, and questions around the accessibility, usability, and universal design of this emerging technology. Education research should focus on, for example, longitudinal studies, inclusion, and a combination of different and multiple research methods and data types increasing the sample size as well as including more pupils with disabilities. At the same time, future research should investigate the educational effects and impacts of using XR technology in the classroom as well as its integration with existing curricula and traditional teaching aids. Universal design research should focus on the identification, categorization, and systemization of barriers for people with different types of disabilities, as well as the development of solutions for these barriers. Moreover, future research should intensify the development of guidelines including best-practice examples for increased accessibility and usability of XR technology, as well as advance the standardization and solidification of said guidelines into standards, regulations, and laws. Lastly, there is a need for as strengthening, consolidating, and integrating national and international communities concerned with the universal design of XR technology, as well as raising awareness for, making visible, and promoting the need for universal design for people with disabilities and all people, to developers and designers of XR devices and applications, authorities, municipalities, educators, and the public.

6 Conclusion

This research shows that XR technology offers promising opportunities for primary and secondary education in most educational courses due to its representational fidelity and multimodality, as well as the possibility for a high degree of immersion, engagement, and interaction. Especially, the possibilities that come with the visualization of abstract concepts have been highlighted by many sources. At the same time, we reveal some significant opportunities for future research related to study design (the need for longitudinal studies, diversification of the scientific methodologies and the educational assessment), hardware development, cost reduction, as well as the need to improve teachers' digital skills, and finally the need to advance universal design of the technology. Further to this, our research reveals an urgent need for making XR technology more accessible and user-friendly to all people, including breaking down existing barriers experienced by people who have cognitive, sensory, and physical disabilities and varying cognitive and sensory abilities. Especially people with common eye problems, physical or cognitive impairments are partially or completely excluded from using XR technology today. Many sources emphasize the need of including representatives of these groups in the design process [5–7, 50]. Moreover, there is a need for a general discussion about the universal design of XR technology as a whole, resulting in guidelines, standards, or frameworks similar to those known from other areas of ICT like the Web Content Accessibility Guidelines (WCAG) for websites [23, 43, 44].

Acknowledgment. This work was partly supported by the UnIKT program of the Norwegian Directorate for Children, Youth, and Family Affairs.

Appendix A: Protocol Parameters for the Search About XR Technology in Primary and Secondary Education

Sources: We are including the first fifty hits of the search results in Google Scholar.

Inclusion Criteria: We are using the general inclusion criteria described above. More precisely, we are looking for systematic literature reviews, scoping reviews, or survey articles about XR in primary and secondary education ("grunnskoler") including literature about XR OR Extended Reality, VR OR Virtual Reality, AR OR Augmented Reality, MR OR Mixed Reality, AND primary schools, secondary schools, elementary schools, middle schools, junior high schools.

Exclusion Criteria: We are using the general exclusion criteria described above. We excluded all papers that did not focus mainly on the technology part of XR technology. Moreover, we excluded papers that had the main focus on the following topics: (Senior) High school, and Higher education.

Search strings (separated by ";"): ("extended reality" or "augmented reality" or "virtual reality") AND ("grunnskoler" OR "grunnskole" OR "grunnskolen"); ("extended reality" OR "augmented reality" OR "virtual reality") AND ("elementary schools" OR "elementary school") AND ("case study" OR "case studies") AND ("systematic literature review" OR "state-of-the-art"); ("extended reality" OR "augmented reality" OR "virtual reality") AND ("elementary school students") AND) AND ("education" AND "learning" AND "teaching") AND ("systematic literature review" AND "case studies"); ("elementary school students") AND ("extended reality" OR "augmented reality" OR "virtual reality") AND ("education" AND "learning" AND "teaching") AND ("systematic literature review" AND "case studies").

Relevance Assessment: We awarded 0 or 1 point to each paper in each of the following relevance assessment categories:

- Does the paper address mainly AR, VR, or both (i.e. MR or XR). When the article addressed both, two points were awarded. (Necessary requirement.)
- Is the article a scoping state-of-the-art article, scoping article, or systematic literature review? (Necessary requirement.)
- Does the article discuss mainly primary and lower secondary school education? (Necessary requirement.)
- Does the article have clearly defined research questions?
- How many individual cases does the article address? None, one or multiple?
- Are the educational courses mentioned? When the article addressed more than one project, two points were awarded.
- Is the technology, e.g. devices, software, hardware, mentioned in the article?
- Are the benefits of XR technology mentioned in the article? Are the challenges mentioned in the article?
- Are barriers for people with different needs mentioned in the article?
- Is anything related to UU, accessibility or usability mentioned in the article explicitly?
- Are teachers' skills mentioned in the article?
- Are there explanations on how the outcomes have been assessed in the article?

Appendix B: Protocol Parameters for the Search About Universal Design of XR Technology

Sources: We are including the first fifty search results in Google Scholar, and Google.

Inclusion Criteria: We are looking for systematic literature reviews, scoping reviews, or survey articles about barriers, accessibility, usability, and universal design of XR technology including literature about XR OR Extended Reality, VR OR Virtual Reality, AR OR Augmented Reality, MR OR Mixed Reality, AND Universal Design, Accessibility, Usability, Barriers, Disability, AND Education, Learning.

Exclusion Criteria: We are excluding all studies that only mention universal design, accessibility, and usability peripherally, as well as usability or accessibility studies for individual projects whose results cannot be generalized.

Search strings (separated by ";"): ("extended reality" OR "augmented reality" OR "virtual reality") AND ("accessibility" AND "usability" AND "universal design") AND ("systematic literature review" AND "state-of-the-art"); ("extended reality" OR "augmented reality" OR "virtual reality") AND ("universal design" AND accessibility AND barriers) AND (disability OR disabled OR impairment OR disorder); ("extended reality" OR "virtual reality" OR "augmented reality") AND (accessibility OR usability OR "universal design") AND education AND (disability OR disabled); General literature search: ("virtual reality" OR "augmented reality" OR immersive) AND ("accessibility" AND "usability") AND (challenge* AND oportunit* AND need* AND barrier*); ("extended reality" OR "virtual reality" OR "augmented reality") AND (accessibility OR usability OR "universal design") AND education AND (disability OR disabled); ("extended reality" OR "virtual reality" OR "augmented reality") AND (accessibility OR usability OR "universal design") AND education AND (disability OR disabled) AND (challenge* AND oportunit* AND need* AND barrier*) ("upper limb" OR "upper body") OR ("lower limbs" OR "lower body" OR "wheelchair") OR (voice AND muteness) OR (blind OR "low vision") OR (deaf OR "hard of hearing") OR (cognitive OR intellectual OR developmental OR emotional); accessibility AND ("virtual reality") AND disability AND barriers; (barriers OR challenges) AND (VR OR AR OR XR) AND accessibility AND disability.

Relevance Assessment: We awarded 0 or 1 point to each paper in each of the following relevance assessment categories:

- Does the paper address mainly AR, VR, or both (i.e. MR or XR). When the article addressed both, two points were awarded. (Necessary requirement.)
- Is the article a systematic literature review, scoping article, or concept/opinion article? Does the article represent comprehensive guidelines or a standard? (Necessary requirement.)
- Does the article address XR in education?
- Does the article address universal design?
- Does the article address the accessibility of the XR technology?
- Does the article address the usability of the XR technology?
- Does the article address the barriers of XR technology for people with disabilities?
- Does the article propose solutions to the previously mentioned barriers?
- Does the article address people with disabilities?
- Does The article address any of the following disabilities? Motor, Mobility, Voice, Senses (seeing), Senses (hearing), Senses (touch), Cognition

References

1. Andrews, C., Southworth, M.K., Silva, J.N.A., Silva, J.R.: Extended reality in medical practice. Curr. Treat. Options Cardiovasc. Med. **21**(4), 1–12 (2019). https://doi.org/10.1007/s11 936-019-0722-7

2. Pellas, N., Kazanidis, I., Palaigeorgiou, G.: A systematic literature review of mixed reality environments in K-12 education. Educ. Inf. Technol. **25**(4), 2481–2520 (2019). https://doi. org/10.1007/s10639-019-10076-4

3. Yavoruk, O.: The study of observation in physics classes through XR technologies. In: 2020 the 4th International Conference on Digital Technology in Education, pp. 58–62. Association for Computing Machinery, New York (2020)

4. Huang, Y., Richter, E., Kleickmann, T., Wiepke, A., Richter, D.: Classroom complexity affects student teachers' behavior in a VR classroom. Comput. Educ. **163**, 104100 (2021)

5. Zhao, Y., Cutrell, E., Holz, C., Morris, M.R., Ofek, E., Wilson, A.D.: SeeingVR: a set of tools to make virtual reality more accessible to people with low vision. In: Proceedings of the 2019 CHI Conference on Human Factors in Computing Systems, pp. 1–14. Association for Computing Machinery, New York (2019)

6. Mott, M., et al.: Accessible by design: an opportunity for virtual reality. In: 2019 IEEE International Symposium on Mixed and Augmented Reality Adjunct (ISMAR-Adjunct), pp. 451–454 (2019)

7. Elor, A., Ward, J.: Accessibility needs of extended reality hardware: a mixed academic-industry reflection. Interactions **28**, 42–46 (2021)

8. Kitchenham, B.: Guidelines for Performing Systematic Literature Reviews in Software Engineering (2007)

9. Tricco, A.C., et al.: A scoping review of rapid review methods. BMC Med. **13**, 1–15 (2015)

10. Quintero, J., Baldiris, S., Rubira, R., Cerón, J., Velez, G.: Augmented reality in educational inclusion. A systematic review on the last decade. Front. Psychol. **10**, 1835 (2019)

11. Bacca Acosta, J.L.: Framework for the design and development of motivational augmented reality learning experiences in vocational education and training (2017). https://dugi-doc.udg. edu/handle/10256/14459

12. Pellas, N., Fotaris, P., Kazanidis, I., Wells, D.: Augmenting the learning experience in primary and secondary school education: a systematic review of recent trends in augmented reality game-based learning. Virtual Reality **23**(4), 329–346 (2018). https://doi.org/10.1007/s10055-018-0347-2

13. Pellas, N., Mystakidis, S., Kazanidis, I.: Immersive virtual reality in K-12 and higher education: a systematic review of the last decade scientific literature. Virtual Reality **25**(3), 835–861 (2021). https://doi.org/10.1007/s10055-020-00489-9

14. XR Accessibility User Requirements. https://www.w3.org/TR/xaur/. Accessed 23 Sept 2021

15. Wong, A., Gillis, H., Peck, B.: VR accessibility: survey for people with disabilities (2017)

16. Harun: XRA's Developers Guide, Chapter Three: Accessibility & inclusive design in immersive experiences. https://xra.org/research/xra-developers-guide-accessibility-and-inclusive-design/. Accessed 30 Jan 2022

17. XR Access Initiative: XR Access – Resources. https://xraccess.org/resources/. Accessed 23 Sept 2021

18. McGrath: Universal Design for Learning - XR Accessibility. https://udl.berkeley.edu/access ibility/xr-accessibility. Accessed 23 Sept 2021

19. Formaker-Olivas, B.: Why VR/AR developers should prioritize accessibility in UX/UI design. https://medium.com/inborn-experience/why-ar-vr-developers-should-prioritize-acc essibility-in-ui-ux-design-66b97e73a3ac. Accessed 23 Sept 2021

20. Normand, A.: Accessibility of Virtual Reality Environments. https://www.unimelb.edu.au/ accessibility/guides/vr-old. Accessed 23 Sept 2021

21. VanFossen, L.: Accessibility, disabilities, and virtual reality solutions. https://educatorsinvr. com/2019/05/31/accessibility-disabilities-and-virtual-reality-solutions/. Accessed 23 Sept 2021

22. Gonzalez, M.: VR and AR can support students with special needs. https://www.thegenius. ca/vr-and-ar-can-support-students-with-special-needs/. Accessed 23 Sept 2021

23. Clark, J., Lischer-Katz, Z.: Barriers to Supporting Accessible VR in Academic Libraries (2020). https://doi.org/10.34944/dspace/6230
24. World Wide Web Consortium (W3C): Report of W3C workshop on web & virtual reality. https://www.w3.org/2016/06/vr-workshop/report.html. Accessed 23 Sept 2021
25. Evans, L.: Barriers to VR use in HE. In: Proceedings of the Virtual and Augmented Reality to Enhance Learning and Teaching in Higher Education Conference 2018, pp. 3–13 (2019)
26. Wolfartsberger, J.: Analyzing the potential of virtual reality for engineering design review. Autom. Constr. **104**, 27–37 (2019)
27. Southgate, E., et al.: Embedding immersive virtual reality in classrooms: ethical, organisational and educational lessons in bridging research and practice. Int. J. Child-Comput. Interact. **19**, 19–29 (2019)
28. Cascales-Martínez, A., Martínez-Segura, M.-J., Pérez-López, D., Contero, M.: Using an augmented reality enhanced tabletop system to promote learning of mathematics: a case study with students with special educational needs. Eurasia J. Math. Sci. Technol. Educ. **13**, 355–380 (2016)
29. Fernandez, A., Fernandez, P., López, G., Calderón, M., Guerrero, L.A.: Troyoculus: an augmented reality system to improve reading capabilities of night-blind people. In: Cleland, I., Guerrero, L., Bravo, J. (eds.) IWAAL 2015. LNCS, vol. 9455, pp. 16–28. Springer, Cham (2015). https://doi.org/10.1007/978-3-319-26410-3_3
30. Rauschnabel, P.A.: A conceptual uses & gratification framework on the use of augmented reality smart glasses. In: Jung, T., tom Dieck, M.C. (eds.) Augmented Reality and Virtual Reality. PI, pp. 211–227. Springer, Cham (2018). https://doi.org/10.1007/978-3-319-64027-3_15
31. Cai, S., Chiang, F.-K., Sun, Y., Lin, C., Lee, J.J.: Applications of augmented reality-based natural interactive learning in magnetic field instruction. Interact. Learn. Environ. **25**, 778–791 (2017)
32. Baraas, R.C., Imai, F., Yöntem, A.Ö., Hardeberg, J.Y.: Visual perception in AR/VR. Opt. Photonics News **32**, 34 (2021)
33. XR Access: 2019 XR Access Symposium Report. https://docs.google.com/document/d/131 eLNGES3_2M5_roJacWlLhX-nHZqghNhwUgBF5lJaE/edit. Accessed 24 Sept 2021
34. XR Access: 2020 XR Access Symposium Report. https://docs.google.com/document/d/1L0 grg1nR8S89OLtTQ9g7y1KvzgtpWwX21PcQHuRGXRo/edit. Accessed 24 Sept 2021
35. XR Access: 2021 XR Access Symposium Report. https://docs.google.com/document/d/10K_ 26fcpYopkaAo5KCZuOa9Ee0p3q-X-1U-ha5eKsi4/edit. Accessed 24 Sept 2021
36. Oculus: Oculus Sikkerhetssenter. https://www.oculus.com/safety-center/. Accessed 06 Nov 2021
37. Cooney, B.: Is VR Safe for Kids? https://www.bobcooney.com/is-vr-safe-for-kids/. Accessed 06 Nov 2021
38. WalkinVR: WalkinVR - Virtual Reality for People with Disabilities. https://www.walkinvrd river.com/. Accessed 10 Jan 2022
39. The US Census Bureau: Americans with Disabilities: 2010 (2012). https://www.census.gov/ library/publications/2012/demo/p70-131.html
40. The US Census Bureau: Americans with Disabilities: 2014 (2018). https://www.census.gov/ library/publications/2018/demo/p70-152.html
41. Heydarian, C.H.: The Curb-Cut Effect and its Interplay with Video Games (2020)
42. XR Association: Welcome to the XR Association. https://xra.org/. Accessed 19 Feb 2022
43. World Wide Web Consortium (W3C): Web Content Accessibility Guidelines (WCAG) 2.0. https://www.w3.org/TR/WCAG20/. Accessed Nov 2021
44. World Wide Web Consortium (W3C): Web Content Accessibility Guidelines (WCAG) 2.1. https://www.w3.org/TR/WCAG21/. Accessed Nov 2021

45. European Union (EU): Web Accessibility Directive (WAD) - Directive (EU) 2016/2102. https://eur-lex.europa.eu/eli/dir/2016/2102/oj
46. Kommunal- og moderniseringsdepartementet: Forskrift om universell utforming av informasjons- og kommunikasjonsteknologiske (IKT)-løsninger (FOR-2013-06-21-732). https://lovdata.no/dokument/SF/forskrift/2013-06-21-732
47. Kulturdepartementet: Lov om likestilling og forbud mot diskriminering (likestillings- og diskrimineringsloven, LOV-2017-06-16-51). https://lovdata.no/dokument/NL/lov/2017-06-16-51
48. Ellis, B., Ford-Williams, G., Graham, L., Grammenos, D., Hamilton, I., Ed Lee, J.M., Westin, T.: Game accessibility guidelines. http://gameaccessibilityguidelines.com/. Accessed 10 Dec 2021
49. Giannoumis, G.A.: Implementing Web Accessibility Policy. Case Studies of the United Kingdom, Norway, and the United States (2019)
50. Fuglerud, K.S., Sloan, D.: The link between inclusive design and innovation: some key elements. In: Kurosu, M. (ed.) HCI 2013. LNCS, vol. 8004, pp. 41–50. Springer, Heidelberg (2013). https://doi.org/10.1007/978-3-642-39232-0_5

Towards Improvement of UX Using Gamification for Public Artistic and Historical Artifacts in AR

Maurizio Vergari[1(✉)], Tanja Kojic[1], Katerina Georgieva Koleva[1],
Stefan Hillmann[1,2], Sebastian Möller[1,2], and Jan-Niklas Voigt-Antons[2,3]

[1] Quality and Usability Lab, Technische Universität Berlin, Berlin, Germany
maurizio.vergari@tu-berlin.de
[2] German Research Center for Artificial Intelligence (DFKI), Berlin, Germany
[3] Immersive Reality Lab, University of Applied Sciences Hamm-Lippstadt,
Lippstadt, Germany

Abstract. Recently, Augmented Reality (AR) applications have emerged as a powerful tool to empower users in touristic use cases, for example, by recreating digital representations of lost or difficult accessible artifacts. More emphasis has been put on researching possible solutions for tourism with AR technology. As part of such a research project, an AR touristic experience was designed to enhance historical artifacts, promote surroundings exploration, and study how to improve the User Experience (UX). This resulted in developing an engaging and interactive cross-platform AR mobile application. The final application includes multiple gamified reward systems, such as collecting points for each artistic/historical spot visited. Users' available time while visiting or exploring was also considered in the design of the experience, so the option to choose between complete and short routes was offered. Following the intended route was supported by instructing the users to collect a sequence of AR coins placed based on GPS functionalities. Despite some limitations, especially given by the GPS feature used to support route navigation, the analysis showed that the developed AR application was evaluated as very good in terms of usability score. This technical limitation was more evident in users that played the experience with old-generation smartphones. The assessment of the developed application has concluded that the attention paid to features, content, and duration of the activity has a positive impact, succeeding both in terms of product results and users' satisfaction.

Keywords: User experience · Augmented Reality · Gamification · Tourism

1 Introduction

Over the last decade, the overall interest in Augmented Reality (AR) technology has significantly increased [1]. Such facts led to major improvements in its use

© Springer Nature Switzerland AG 2022
J. Y. C. Chen and G. Fragomeni (Eds.): HCII 2022, LNCS 13318, pp. 142–152, 2022.
https://doi.org/10.1007/978-3-031-06015-1_10

and development, especially in the gaming industry. More recently, AR applications have also emerged as a powerful tool to empower users in touristic use cases. The potential for mixing AR technology with tourism comes from the possibility of AR altering tourists' perceptions of their physical environment and providing additional touristic experiences and chances for engagement. Therefore more emphasis has been put on researching possible solutions for tourism with AR technology. However, this broad field needs to be researched for more specific scenarios. Specifically, as tourism is most of the time done to have fun, learn and explore, the combination of gamification elements and tourism applications presents itself as very interesting to provide users with better experiences. That is because there is room to test different kinds of elements, ranging from user interfaces to interaction paradigms, looking for best practices and approaches. Making tourism a more entertaining experience is the goal of such research, and through innovative approaches, traditional artifacts can be rediscovered and enhanced.

2   Related Work

2.1   AR and Tourism

AR has been employed in various industries over the years, including medical, manufacturing, rehabilitation, to provide new methods to experience and interact with the environment. There are numerous examples of AR in tourism settings, as proven by [8], which examines the use of XR technology in depth in fields like retail, tourism, hotel, restaurants, and destinations. Many studies also emphasize the benefits of utilizing this technology, considering its limitations and how eager individuals are to switch from a more common type of experience to one that combines reality and virtuality.

Some people may be intrigued by it, while others may prefer a more traditional approach. People who are more familiar with new technology are more willing to try it and are more concerned about the quality of the system. In contrast, those who have never tried it or have little to no understanding are more concerned about the quality of the materials [4]. For example, Cranmer et al. [5], showed that the exploration of the perceived value of AR for the tourism industry from the perspective of tourism experts brought to an extension of the list of value dimensions that AR can bring to touristic scenarios.

Bekele et al. [2] evaluated augmented, virtual, and mixed reality from a cultural heritage perspective and came up with a reasonable model. Technical issues like tracking and registration, virtual world modeling, presentation, input devices, interaction interfaces, and systems were addressed. However, their review also divides the various XR application zones in cultural heritage, including teaching, exhibition improvement, exploration, reconstruction, and virtual museums. According to the developers, a final decision on enabling technology should be based on the experience that an application is anticipated to provide. Although augmented, virtual, and mixed reality can all be utilized to achieve the same goals, the results suggest that augmented reality is the best option for exhibition improvement. Most AR applications are designed to improve exhibitions, followed by reconstruction and exploration. The use of markerless, sensor-based, and marker-based approaches in hybrid tracking is prevalent.

Moreover, outdoor applications are more suited to a reconstruction method since reconstructed historical images can be superimposed over the real world. Furthermore, outdoor sites that have been damaged or worn away are frequently given a reconstruction theme. Visual and audio content is frequently displayed on mobile screens. However, some systems also use custom-built HMDs, and combinations of different types of presentation devices to display real-virtual content. Handheld mobile devices, phones, and tablets can all be used to create augmented reality. However, head-mounted display technologies that fit over the eyes are becoming more popular. Due to the usage of a headset that provides a 3D viewpoint, holographic AR, also known as Mixed Reality, enables a more immersive AR experience.

2.2   Gamification

Gamification can be defined as "the use of game design elements in non-game contexts" [6]. An example of gamification application to AR scenarios can be found in work by Paliokas et al. [9], who proposed the use of additional game and educational elements in an AR application in order to enhance the overall visitors' experience. Xu et al. identified extrinsic and intrinsic game design elements that contribute to meaningful gamification in tourism applications. Such elements include badges, rewards, points, relation, autonomy, and competence [10].

3   Methods

3.1   Application Design Setup

The developed application included different aspects that needed to be designed. Specifically, the main components can be categorized in designing the: Navigational Routes, User Interface, User Experience and Gamification aspects.

Navigational Routes. The navigational routes were mainly designed using Google Maps support[1]. The first step while defining them was finding suitable points of interest around the area, which was a university campus for the scope of this project. The most important task while designing the routes was to identify interesting statues, landmarks and art installations (artifacts) placed in the vicinity of the campus. A total of 22 distinct points of interest were selected. All of them are structured to include an ID, a set of coordinates, a short description, a longer detailed description and a set of multiple-choice questions.

---

[1] https://maps.google.com/.

Furthermore, each was categorized by its artistic or historical nature. Out of the 22 total points of interest, 12 were in the art category, 13 in the historical one and 4 in both. When displaying the routes in the app, the points of interest in the art category were represented in red (Fig. 1, left), while the historical one was in yellow (Fig. 1, right). Only points of interest of the same category are shown along the path. In addition, the walking distance between them was minimized as much as possible. Both complete routes resulted almost three-kilometre long and consisted of 12–13 points of interest, which were estimated to be completed in less than 40 min at a normal pace.

Fig. 1. Artistic route (left) and historical route (right).

The shorter routes were designed as a quicker version of the complete ones. As simple alternatives, they keep the main characteristics of the longer routes. This means that the points of interest are again divided into the same two categories, art, and history, each corresponding to one shorter route. The main different aspect is that the shorter routes contain a significantly reduced amount of points of interest. More precisely, both historical and artistic shorter routes contain 7 points of interest. The main reason behind their development was the ongoing worldwide Covid-19 pandemic. Regarding this aspect, the starting point, which was previously situated indoors, was moved to a closer outdoor environment. Furthermore, among the non-trivial ones, all points of interest that were situated inside buildings or inner yards are not included in this version of the routes. This way, the shorter routes are safer because they contain only outdoor points of interest that do not require the players to walk through any closed space. Further reasons that were taken into account while creating the shorter routes were: possible lack of time or low mobility of certain users. Therefore, accessibility, distance, and time were key factors in their development. All these details aim at making the app more accessible, appealing, and more suitable for a wide variety of users.

User Interface. A meaningful color scheme for the application was selected as a first step of the User Interface (UI) design. In this specific application, the color red was the predominant one, as it is the primary color in the university logo (TU Berlin), and also because it represents a feeling of excitement, generating enthusiasm in the users [7].

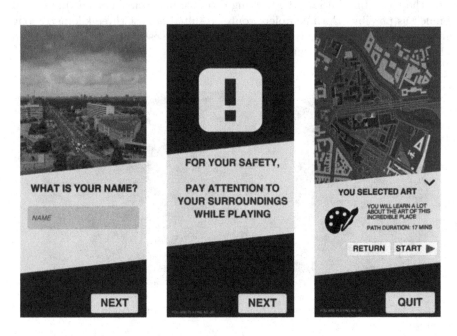

Fig. 2. Screenshots of the user interface.

Figure 2 shows exemplary screenshots of the implemented user interface. After clicking a start button, the user is asked to type in the name the application is supposed to use for them, and choose the preferred path. Also, the user will be prompted with a warning message informing them to pay attention to the surroundings while using the app. In the subsequent screen, the chosen path is shown on a map together with the estimated duration. A return button is provided to revert their path choice if necessary. Of course, a start button and a quit button are also provided. The menu can be collapsed and expanded to view the route map in full-screen. When a path is chosen, the app transitions to AR mode, where a timer for the duration of the path and a counter for the collected coins is provided. In case of disorientation, a button for an AR mini-map was provided while exploring the place. Upon pressing a big red-marked coin, which indicates a point of interest, a bar with the name and a small picture of the monument shows up on the top of the screen. The user can either read more about the artifact or directly begin a quiz. The "read more" button leads to a screen with additional information for the point of interest, which is decorated with a half-transparent black gradient so the user can view the point of interest through their device while reading. The quiz interface is designed similarly with half-transparent black panels that change their colors to green or red to indicate whether the answer to the question is correct or not.

3.2 User Experience and Gamification

With the aim of studying how certain elements can impact the User Experience in AR through gamification, specifically for tourism scenarios, the decision to create an interactive game using AR was made. Before developing the game, a target audience was determined. This case was based on users' profiles of current students, potential students, and employees who were more likely to interact with the campus. One of the main points is understanding the context in which the application will be used and the role that such applications play in daily situations. For the experience is also important to explore how the user should interact with typical AR Elements of such kind of application. By placing coins in the path between the points of interest, which the user has to collect to obtain points and guide them to the next monument, the user can interact more with the game and its features. That way, the app can stand out from a simple GPS game with just endpoints. The use of coins supports the idea of a gamified sight-seeing app, as coins have been used in many games to mark a route that needs to be covered. As a result, it is usually intuitively possible for the users to play the game. This is expected to improve the user experience. Besides the simple golden coin, two more coins were also generated. These have been provided with the symbol for the artistic or historical route and appear at the point of interest (see Fig. 3). It means that the two "special" coins symbolize the reaching of the new point of interest and that the information and quiz unit will open.

Fig. 3. Different coins as symbols for routes (historical-left and artistic-right) and navigational paths (middle).

In order to create an app that can provide an enjoyable experience, it was decided only to show information that is necessary, not to exaggerate the size of the information texts of the points of interest. An AR mini-map was added so that the user can know the path to the next point of interest and play with the AR elements simultaneously, thus developing a greater interaction with the game. A timer was also added so the user could know how long it took them to finish the game without needing to memorize when they started playing. The coin counter motivated the user to interact with the AR objects and collect as many coins as possible. Players are rewarded additional coins for every correct answer during the quiz to further enhance this feature. Figure 4 show a preview of application content when users are in front of a specific point of interest.

Fig. 4. Coin for artistic point of interest (left), information on the point of interest (middle), mini-map (right).

Since quality can only be measured by perceiving and judging users, an app evaluation with potential users to gather new ideas, criticism and see how they perform using the game, was conducted.

3.3   Test Setup

The user tests were executed on the University Charlottenburg Campus of TU Berlin. The experiment always started in front of the main building and was planned to be around 45 min long. The scenario tested was as follows: an individual tries the artistic route of the app for the first time. Before the actual test, every user was given a task description and some basic knowledge about the project - collecting coins, opening the mini-map, or seeing the information about an artifact. As the test began, the user was handed the test device, and the instructor followed the participant silently and interfered just if the user had a question. After completing the route, the user was asked to fill out an online questionnaire. The questionnaire was divided into five sections: Technical and General, Interface and Usability, Content, Duration, and a Free section, followed by some demographic questions. The standard System Usability Scale (SUS) [3] questionnaire was used to measure the usability of the final application. The General and Technical questions were required to be answered by the 5-point customer satisfaction scale or "Yes", "No", "I don't know". Questions were designed to assess UI (e.g., if colors and images were nice), content (e.g., how informative the content was), and duration evaluation aspects.

3.4 Participants

Sixteen participants took part in the study with the age between 20 and 25 years. Participants for the study were mainly recruited using word-of-mouth among representatives of the target group. They were asked to select available slots, and they were matched with a moderator. 75% of the people were students or employees of the university campus; hence they could orientate themselves around it quite well. The study was conducted outside in compliance with Covid-19 hygiene measures. All participants provided written informed consent before participating in the experiment.

4 Results

4.1 Navigation System

Results report that six users were somewhat unsatisfied, and two very unsatisfied with the navigation system, which translates into a 50% rate of dissatisfaction with the implemented navigation system. It has been noticed that different results were obtained depending on the used device. In fact, it has been noticed that older smartphones were more inaccurate in getting GPS data.

Regarding the overall design of the application, about 70% are somewhat satisfied or very satisfied with the overall design. When asked how satisfied the users are with the AR aspect, for example, the precision and size of the coins, six people rated their satisfaction as neutral, which is almost 40%, and the rest of the users have very different opinions regarding the AR aspect.

Finally, they were asked how satisfied they were with the functionalities of the application. More than 60% are somewhat satisfied or very satisfied with the functionalities. Four are neutral, and three are somewhat unsatisfied or very unsatisfied. We can see here that the functionalities of the application are good, but there is still some room for improvement.

After obtaining these results, it was possible to create a heatmap with all the questions and answers. In Fig. 5, it is possible to see that excluding the GPS and the AR aspect, all the other technical aspects of the app satisfy the users' expectations or desires. Compared with the others, the AR aspect cannot meet the users' expectations, but it was not rated as bad. The GPS is the worst-rated technical aspect.

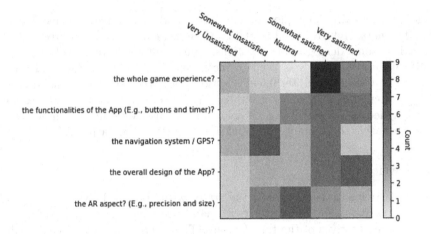

Fig. 5. Heatmap of the technical aspects ratings.

4.2 System Usability

The System Usability Score was calculated for each participant. The mean score for the 16 participants has been calculated to be 76. The score indicates that the application usability is above average (>68), which indicates good usability of the system [3].

4.3 Gamification Approach

Duration. Two participants did not finish the game. Those who could not play until the end had severe problems with the GPS. They could not find any more coins and consequently had to quit the game. Among those who managed to finish the game, the amount of time needed to play the game until the end was quite different. In fact, 50% of all the users needed between 26 and 33 min. The mean time in minutes is approximately 31 min. Excluding the one person who took 81 min to complete the route, it took to all the other users between 18 and 42 min. It depends on how fast one walks, how much one wants to read, and how fast one needs to answer the questions. The users were asked if the duration of the game was too short or too long. As a result, nobody thought that the time needed to finish the game was too long or too short. They also had to rate their satisfaction regarding the time taken to finish the game. Different as previously expected, nobody rated their satisfaction as somewhat unsatisfied or very unsatisfied. The majority of the users are somewhat satisfied or very satisfied with their time to finish the game.

Application Content. The users were first asked to rate (1-little informative, 5-highly informative) how informative the game was. That resulted in a mean value of 3.5, with a standard deviation of approximately 1.2. Users were asked their opinion regarding the difficulty of the questions (1-very easy, 5-very difficult). Results show that the questions in the game are perceived as really easy and understandable by the participants with a mean value of 1.5, and a standard deviation of 0.63. Lastly, when the users were asked their opinion on how interesting the game content was (1-very boring , 5-very interesting) this resulted in a mean value of 3.75 and a standard deviation of 0.86.

5 Discussion and Conclusion

For this paper, an AR application was developed with the aim to study possible improvements to the UX using Gamification for public artistic and historical artifacts in AR. Based on a user research study, participants have reported that navigation systems play an important role in the user experience. In fact, without precise location information, the users were dissatisfied. This problem, as mentioned, was more evident in older devices, suggesting that as long as location detection systems keep getting better, the negative effect detected will be reduced. As long as there are still people using older phones which provide lower accuracy when it comes to GPS, developers have to consider at least the possibility of unstable position information.

Regarding the overall application, results indicate that the app features designed and implemented led to a positive impression of the users. Nevertheless, once again, the device plays a role. The AR elements were more often misplaced when older devices were used (e.g., coins were placed too high). Most probably, this was a combination of wrong space tracking due to old camera sensors. Hence, the recommendation is once again to use up-to-date devices for the best experience. The features included in the application were perceived positively by the users. This is justified by the good SUS score and also by the overall positive scores obtained on the gamification approach dimensions.

Concerning the gamification aspects, results showed that in terms of duration of the experience and application content, the users were quite happy. The duration was appropriate for the kind of experience, suggesting that there would be room also to add additional points of interest to such experiences. Moreover, it is still too early to assess how informative the game is. Further user testings with a larger sample can also support results in this regard. Results show also that the questions asked were very easy and understandable. That is because the point of this application was not to overload the users with information but rather convey simple and immediate content to make them feel engaged while learning the key information about an artifact.

A limitation of this study lies in the number of participants. In fact, a larger sample would have led to more meaningful results. Also, the use of different devices might have altered the experience, so it is recommended to be consistent in device choice and to pick top-notch ones.

Eventually, the presented results can pave the way towards improving the user experience of touristic augmented reality applications. In order to achieve such a goal, some aspects like GPS, UI navigational directions, embedded tutorials, and AR mini-map require great improvements in future stages.

Acknowledgements. This work would not have been possible without the effort of Alexandra Sipos, Christoph Penno, Eduardo Luiz Rhein, Jonathan Wendler, Katerina Georgieva Koleva, Sandra Phuong Nhi Vu, and Nicole Stefanie Bertges, who took part in the design and development of the shown digital tourism application. This work was partly funded by the Federal Ministry of Education and Research (BMBF) and the state of Berlin under the Excellence Strategy of the Federal Government and the Länder.

References

1. Alsop, T.: Mobile augmented reality (ar) market size 2025, September 2021. https://www.statista.com/statistics/282453/mobile-augmented-reality-market-size/

2. Bekele, M.K., Pierdicca, R., Frontoni, E., Malinverni, E.S., Gain, J.: A survey of augmented, virtual, and mixed reality for cultural heritage. J. Comput. Cult. Heritage (JOCCH) **11**(2), 1–36 (2018)

3. Brooke, J., et al.: Sus-a quick and dirty usability scale. Usability Eval. ind. **189**(194), 4–7 (1996)

4. Bulchand-Gidumal, J., William, E.: Tourists and augmented and virtual reality experiences. In: Xiang, Z., Fuchs, M., Gretzel, U., Höpken, W. (eds.) Handbook of e-Tourism, pp. 1–20. Springer, Cham (2020). https://doi.org/10.1007/978-3-030-05324-6_60-1

5. Cranmer, E.E., tom Dieck, M.C., Fountoulaki, P.: Exploring the value of augmented reality for tourism. Tour. Manage. Perspect. **35**, 100672 (2020)

6. Deterding, S., Sicart, M., Nacke, L., O'Hara, K., Dixon, D.: Gamification. using game-design elements in non-gaming contexts. In: CHI 2011 Extended Abstracts on Human Factors in Computing Systems, pp. 2425–2428 (2011)

7. Labrecque, L.I., Milne, G.R.: Exciting red and competent blue: the importance of color in marketing. J. Acad. Mark. Sci. **40**(5), 711–727 (2012). https://doi.org/10.1007/s11747-010-0245-y

8. Loureiro, S.M.C., Guerreiro, J., Ali, F.: 20 years of research on virtual reality and augmented reality in tourism context: a text-mining approach. Tour. Manage. **77**, 104028 (2020)

9. Paliokas, I., et al.: A gamified augmented reality application for digital heritage and tourism. Appl. Sci. **10**(21), 7868 (2020)

10. Xu, F., Buhalis, D., Weber, J.: Serious games and the gamification of tourism. Tour. Manage. **60**, 244–256 (2017)

Intertwining History and Places: The Design of TongSEE Location-Based Augmented Reality Application for History Learning

Wenjia Wang, Yate Ge, Hang Yu, Xu Lu, XueChen Li, Yao Cheng, and Xiaohua Sun[✉]

College of Design and Innovation, Tongji University, Shanghai, China
{wangwenjia,geyate,2133662,1950703,2133662,xsun}@tongji.edu.cn

Abstract. Visualizing the past and engaging learners in real-world learning contexts is important for history learning. Location-based Augmented reality (AR) technologies offer new possibilities for supporting place-based learning, by tracking users' position and superimposing layers of visual information on the real world. This paper presents a location-based AR application TongSEE that enables users to learn history in authentic context. We describe the design approaches of the interface, physical interaction, and contextual guidance of the application. Twenty participants were evaluated using the application. The results show that, in general, TongSEE is a promising educational tool that helps learners better understand the history and increase their interest in history learning. Our study contributes insights into how location-based AR technologies could be designed to support place-based learning and users' perspective on this learning method.

Keywords: Location-based augmented reality · Mobile application · History learning

1 Introduction

Combining the digital world with the physical one seamlessly, augmented reality (AR) creates a reality that is enhanced and augmented [1,2]. According to Hsin-KaiWu, AR can be defined as a technology that incorporates three basic features: a combination of real and virtual worlds, real-time interaction, and accurate 3D registration of virtual and real objects [3]. The use of such a technology brings new possibilities for teaching and learning and has increasingly drawn attention from educators and researchers worldwide. The coexistence of virtual objects and real environments makes it possible to juxtapose human senses (visual, aural, and touch) with "invisible" objects only seen in the virtual world [4], allows learners to visualize complex spatial relationships and abstract concepts [5,6], and offers first-hand experience, thereby increasing the learning motivation and

© Springer Nature Switzerland AG 2022
J. Y. C. Chen and G. Fragomeni (Eds.): HCII 2022, LNCS 13318, pp. 153–169, 2022.
https://doi.org/10.1007/978-3-031-06015-1_11

providing positive reinforcement for learners during authentic learning activities [7,8].

These educational benefits have made AR learning practiced in many disciplines, among which history is an important area [9,10]. Visualizing the past is critical in history education [10]. Using virtual objects (e.g., pictures, videos, animation, and 3D models), AR could restore historical scenes or reconstruct historical buildings which have lost some of their original design, thus bringing history to life and enabling learners to gain more accurate knowledge on the topic [11]. learners could also virtually manipulate various learning objects and handle the information in a novel and interactive way, which helps remove "boring" in history education and facilitates learning interest and motivation [10,12].

For history education, another important aspect is "place-aware." Historical events always take place in certain places, and many historic buildings, artifacts, and monuments are bound to geographic places in the real world. Place-based learning could leverage tangibility and authenticity of the real world environment: history is not just texts and pictures in textbooks, but what actually happened, shaped today's life, and left some marks in the real world. Learners may feel more grounded in "reality" when learning in authentic contexts [13]. As mobile devices, such as phones and tablets, have been getting ubiquitous as platforms, AR no longer requires specialized equipment in a fixed place. Mobile AR can take any situation, location, environment, or experience to a whole new level of meaning and understanding [14]. Utilizing location-registered technology (e.g., Global Positioning System [GPS]), location-based AR could track the user's locations as they physically move throughout the real world and provide virtual content in corresponding locations. Place-based learning using this technology can raise users' context-sensitivity [15], foster enjoyment [16], and may help learners give new meaning to their familiar locations [17]. However, In previous researches, AR was often used as teaching aids for history learning in classrooms or museums. Few studies focus on place-based history learning using location-based AR technologies. The interface and interaction design of location-based AR applications also need further research.

Hence, in this paper, we aim to present a location-based AR application, TongSEE, which supports place-based history learning. Our study contributes insights into how location-based AR applications could be designed to contextualize history learning and how learners felt about this kind of history learning method. In the following sections, we started with an overview of AR in history education and location-based AR technologies for learning (Sect. 2). The design approaches and development methods of the application were introduced in Sect. 3. Then, we had it evaluated by twenty learners (Sect. 4) and analyzed the results in terms of users' interest, feedback of interface and interaction, and the system's usability and learnability (Sect. 5). We further discussed the results and indicated our future work (Sect. 6 and Sect. 7).

2   Related Works

2.1   AR for History Learning

AR technologies enable the integration of real-world experiences with digital content, making it possible to visualize "invisible" abstract history into visible and clarity. One example would be the House of Olbrich performed by Keil et al. [18] on visualizing the history of architecture that had lost some of their original design. The mobile AR application created by Keil et al. allowed the user to take a photograph of the house in its current state and have it augmented with a 3D model constructed from the original drawings. More detailed textual information and featured media content could also be augmented using further interaction. The application leads users' attention to the impressive historical architecture and lets them know the details about the architecture and corresponding area. Another research performed by I. Utami et al. [11] implemented a marker-based AR program for students to learn ancient Indonesian history. Using the phone's camera to scan the marker image cards and then the 3D object of heritage will appear. The result of comparing the students' scores before and after using AR showed that as history learning media, AR could increase students' knowledge and learning achievement. The author argued that this due to AR could clarify abstract concepts by giving real examples and has implicit user control of the point of view and interactivity so that it can add clarity to history.

An additional benefit of AR for history learning is providing an immersive learning environment. Being in the realistic and immersive perspective provides the user with a sense of historical empathy that cannot be achieved from a classroom with a textbook. This topic was explored by Blanco-Fernández et al. [19] on their research for engaging groups of people into immersive experiences to improve their learning about historical battles and wars. In the study, users would use an AR application to reenact a battle as a major historical figure and make decisions over the battle. AR technologies were used to enhance the immersion, such as providing 360° views of historical scenarios or by linking 3D contents with the QR markers laid on the physical environment. These types of immersive educational experiences allow the students to understand actions and decisions in the battle in a more contextualized way, therefore providing a sense of empathy and/or sympathy with historical figures.

History education is often perceived as a boring subject [20], and the most important factor in students' engagement is teaching aids [21]. As mentioned above, AR for educational tasks provides virtual content, immersive learning environment, and playful interaction, thus having the potential to motivate learners on history learning beyond what traditional learning would be capable of. The research of B. Schiavi et al. [22] showed that using AR as a tool for understanding history allows students to better work in autonomy, as they can progress at their speed and investigate the elements that interest them. Therefore, students showed greater learning enthusiasm and motivation using AR than classical teaching methods. This was also proved by M. Garcia [10] in his research focusing on providing users immersive storytelling experience for history learning. In the mobile AR application presented by M. Garcia, the historical narrative was employed as a storytelling technique to portray historical events using animated scenes with photorealistic 3D models. The study's findings showed that consistent and immersive visual storytelling experience provided by AR could increase student motivation, change the attitude towards the lesson, and foster enjoyment in history learning.

2.2 Location-Based AR for Learning

Location-based AR technologies could track users' actual geological location through mobile devices and geological positioning systems, providing relevant information as they arrive at specific locations [23]. Using these technologies for educational purpose could encourage learners "in authentic exploration in the real world" through interactions with the physical environment. Therefore, location-based learning using AR brings a sense of authenticity to learners [13], which helps them gain more accurate and concrete knowledge in domains and promotes an understanding of complex and abstract concepts [24,25]. Learners have better learning outcomes when physically visiting the location with AR application than learning in the laboratory environment. Because location-based AR allows learners to observe and experience comparisons between real sites and virtual information [16]. Compared to virtual environments, location-based AR depends not only on the virtual interface and content but also on the locality and context of the AR activity [26]. The research of Georgiou and Kyza [27] indicated that these factors make the AR environment more immersive and help learners become more focused and engage deeply with the learning content [27,28]. Additionally, the research of Harley et al. [16] showed that location-based AR mobile learning provides learners more positive emotions, such as enjoyment, engagement, and a sense of control and value.

3   TongSEE

3.1   Overview

TongSEE is a location-based AR application enabling students to visualize the past and learn the history of Tongji University, a comprehensive university with a history of over a hundred years in China. The capability of TongSEE is dependent on GPS and space mapping using the devices' camera thus can track the user's position and overlying target media in the corresponding places. The system displays a simulated map that correlates different places according to their geographic coordinates. The learners can select desired destinations to view general information, such as the history and importance of that place, including how to travel to that place. In the beta vision, TongSEE contains six places on the Tongji University campus, including (1) Siping Gate; (2) Student Movement Memorial Park; (3) Alumni Home; (4) Wenyuan Building; (5) Sanhaowu Park; and (6) Guoli Monument.

3.2   Design Approaches

Information Displaying and Interface Design. In TongSEE, we used visual and aural media to augment historical information in the real world. As shown in Fig. 1, three types of virtual material were designed and implemented to visualize the past. We reconstructed 3D models of historic buildings based on the original drawings and photographs. These 3D models were sized to match the real historic buildings and were rendered with high-quality textures, which help to increase learners' sense of authenticity when they are learning in an AR environment. 3D animations were created to show some historical events, for example, overlaying flame animations on a building in the real world to represent the historical event in which the building has burned down. In addition, virtual information cards consisting of text, pictures, and videos were used to present more detailed historical information. Furthermore, we recorded brief audio for every six places about the history associated with the place. When learners walk to the place, the system automatically plays the audio, giving them a quick overview of the history and the essential features.

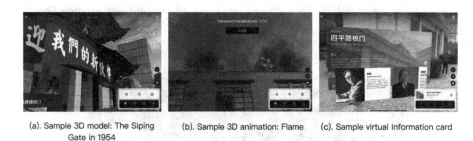

(a). Sample 3D model: The Siping Gate in 1954   (b). Sample 3D animation: Flame   (c). Sample virtual information card

Fig. 1. Three types of virtual material

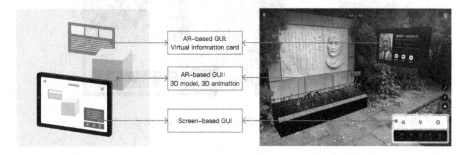

Fig. 2. Two types of GUI in TongSEE

The interface in TongSEE shows a full-screen camera feed and overlays virtual objects on that feed when locations are recognized. We designed two types of Graphic User Interface (GUI) (Fig. 2) : (1) Screen-based GUI, which is rendered fixed at the top layer. It contains global functions of the application (e.g., simulated map), general historical information, and guidance; (2) AR-based GUI, which exists in the 3D virtual world and is augmented to corresponding positions in the real- world. The coordinates of virtual objects are unique and fixed and cannot be changed by learners. To interact with AR-based GUI, we support a set of basic interactions in touch-based environments. Learners can tap the virtual cards to show more information and move their fingers up and down, left and right on the touchscreen to rotate 3D models. When learners double-tap the object, it reverts to its initial orientation. Furthermore, to increase the immersion of the AR learning environment and create a historical atmosphere, filters were used in TongSEE as post-processing of the camera feed (Fig. 3). By adjusting the hue and reducing the color saturation, the interface looks like an old movie, making the learners feel like they are actually back in the past. The further away from today, the higher the filter parameters until the image becomes completely black and white. Conversely, the closer the time is to the present, the closer the image is to realistic colors. In addition, we have added ambient sounds (background noise, such as loud streets or gunfire) to provide historical context and help learners more immersed in the AR learning environment.

Fig. 3. Camera filters used in TongSEE

Physical Interaction. Thanks to Location-based AR technologies, TongSEE allows learners explore freely out of the classroom thus providing more spaces for physical interaction compared to marked-based AR. Therefore, in TongSEE, we leveraged learners' moving ability in the physical world, and designed the moving path for them in every place. This enables learners better interact with the physical world: they are encouraged to stay, move around, observe and use the space. It also provides authentic context helping learners better understand history. The moving path was designed by following three steps: (1) Research the history represented by the place and determine the Point of interest (POI) that overlaying historical information; (2) Cope with the constraints of the actual environment (e.g. spatial layout, road conditions) and ensure that POI are in safe locations, away from dangerous areas such as roads. Then design a moving path connecting all POI; (3) Place virtual triggers on the path to guide the user through each POI. By detecting the coincidence of the coordinates of the learners' mobile device with the trigger in the virtual world, different virtual features were activated in POI location. For example, the Siping Gate has been rebuilt many times and its appearance has varied at different times in history. We designed a moving path with 4 POI crossing the front of the gate and each POI represents a year in history (Fig. 4). When learners reach a POI, a 3D gate model reconstructed from its original appearance at that time will appear, as well as other historical information (e.g., architects, construction process, historical events at that time) presented in the form of virtual information cards.

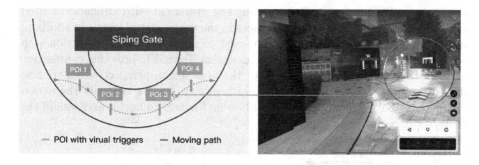

Fig. 4. Sample moving path at the Siping Gate

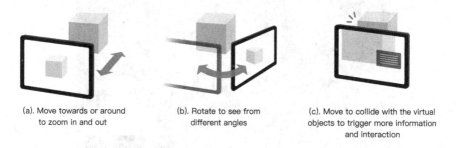

(a). Move towards or around to zoom in and out

(b). Rotate to see from different angles

(c). Move to collide with the virtual objects to trigger more information and interaction

Fig. 5. Physical interactions in TongSEE

In addition, as illustrated in Fig. 5, learners can physically move towards or around to zoom in and out of the virtual objects or rotate to see them from a different angle. Some virtual objects were designed as colliders, requiring learners to bring their mobile devices close until collide with the virtual objects to trigger more information and interaction.

Contextual Guidance. Learning in AR environments requires learners to accomplish some complex tasks, such as spatial navigation, collaboration, problem solving and technology manipulation [29]. It could be a challenge for learners, especially for younger learners and novices [2]. Therefore, additional guidance should be provided to guide learners' action, help them interpret the clues in the devices and embedded in the real world environment, and navigate between fancy and reality [2,30]. In TongSEE, we designed guidance both on the logical level: "What the learners should do next", and on the spatial level: "What the learners should go next", to help learners find the target place and interact smoothly in a large space. Furthermore, to increase immersive learning experience, the guidance should be contextual, that is intertwining the environmental and semantic characteristics of the place. We used 3D models with animation as guidance to support learning process. As shown in Fig. 6, in Sanhaowu Park, a virtual cat was selected as guidance because one of the important features of the park is that there are many cats living there. The visual cat with animation moved around and led learners to different places in the park (spatial level). In addition, screen-based textual instructions were used to guide learners' interaction step by step (logical level). Contextual guidance in TongSEE provides consistency between the virtual and real worlds for the first-person-perspective experience, thus increasing the learner's sense of authenticity. It acts not only the action instructions, but also as learning aids allowing learners to better understand the characteristics of the local places.

Fig. 6. Contextual guidance in TongSEE

3.3   System Development

The 3D models (e.g., building, figures, 3D guidance) with textures were made in Cinema 4D and the 2D GUI components were designed in Figma. Then these virtual assets were exported into Unity3D (version 2019.4.18f1). Inside Unity3D, an AR Software Development Kit (SDK) for mobile devices called Immersal has been added. It enables the precise positioning in large the physical world by using GPS and recognizing point clouds and textured meshes of the mapped spaces in real-time. Once the location is recognized inside the system a coordinate system is built up and associated to the target location. The coordinate system is then used as a reference to set the virtual assets positions and orientations thus creating location-based AR experience. We first used Immersal Mapper APP to map the real world locations using phones' camera. The maps are constructed and hosted on Immersal's Cloud Service. Then we exported the map file with. bytes extension into Unity3D and enter Developer Token to access cloud services. After that, we placed virtual assets in the corresponding positions of the map (Fig. 7), and coded interaction of users using C# in Unity3D. The application can run both on Android and iOS devices.

Fig. 7. Place virtual assets in maps created by immersal in Unity3D

4   Evaluation

The goal of the evaluation is to invite users to use the TongSEE application following a pre-defned sequence of tasks, and evaluation the users' interest, interface and interaction experience, and system usability and learnability.

4.1   Participant

We invited twenty students (6 female; 14 male) from Tongji University volunteered to participate. Participants were between 21 and 30 years old (M = 24.45;

SD = 2.38), and were labelled as P1–P20, respectively. Most participants (80%) have the experience of leaning history of Tongji University through different ways (participant lectures, read books or documents, visit museum, and view videos or films), while 20% of the participants had no such experience. For the experience of AR, 12 participants have no or barely no experience of using mobile AR, and 8 participants have used or experienced some mobile AR applications, such as IKEA and Pokémon Go.

4.2   Measures and Materials

The evaluation was conducted on the Tongji University campus and participants were asked to learn and explore history using TongSEE. The TongSEE mobile application was installed to an 11 inch iPad, and acquired access to the device's camera, GPS, and Wi-Fi to make the AR features works properly. In addition, earphones were connected so that participants can hear the audio in the application. Two self-report measures were used during the evaluation process. Before the learning session, participants answered a 4-item pre-test questionnaire about demographic issues, and their experiences of leaning history and using AR. After the learning session, participants were asked to completed a post-test questionnaire that had 20 questions which were divided into three following aspects: (1) Users' interest, 5 questions about participants' interest and motivation of learning history using TongSEE; (2) interface and interaction experience, 4 questions about participants perspective of interface and interaction in the application; and (3) System usability and learnability, using the System Usability Scale (SUS) [31] to rate the usability and learnability of the system. At the end of the evaluation, a semi-structured interview was conducted to obtain participants' subjective perceptions of the TongSEE application. All the participants signed an informed consent, which explained the possible risks of the mobile AR outdoor, and gave us permissions to use the audio recordings. The test followed a standard ethical procedure of the research institute.

4.3   Evaluation Procedure

The evaluation took approximately 35 min. Participants first completed a consent form and the pre-test questionnaire. Then participants were asked to learn and explore history in six places on campus using TongSEE (Fig. 8) following three steps: (1) Navigate to one place and point the iPad's camera to the place, until the GPS and point cloud alignment to display AR features; (2) Through the iPad's camera, explore the surroundings and learn the historical information; (3) Mark the place after learning in application and navigate to the next place, until complete test in six places. During the learning session, participants were encouraged to "think aloud" to share their views on interaction, virtual information, likes and dislikes, and difficulties and problems they encountered. A researcher followed the participants, recorded what participants said and provided guidance when necessary. After the test, every participant rated TongSEE using post-test questionnaire. They also participated in a 15-minute semi-structured interview and were asked to explain more and discuss about their self-report results.

Fig. 8. User testing

5   Results

5.1   Users' Interest

As stated in the previous study related to users' perspective about a location-based AR application for learning [16], participants highlighted an expressive level of interest when using TongSEE. Table 1 shows percentage, means and standard deviations for each item about users' interest. The average score was at 4.00 (SD = .88). Therefore, it can be concluded that the level of users' interest of the system was at a "good" level. Most participants (75%) felt fun and more involved when using TongSEE in their leaning process. In addition, 85% of participants stated that they think the application would encourage more people to learn history. TongSEE provided visible and clarity historical knowledge through multiple kinds of visual material. According to the results, the application allows participants to understand complex history better and faster (70%). In addition, regarding the interest of installing TongSEE on their personal mobile devices, the majority of participants (65%) confirmed their desire to install it. Among the 7 participants who did not express interest in installing, 4 mentioned that large memory of the application as the main factor influencing their decision.

Table 1. Percentage, means and standard deviations for each item about users' interest. 1 means strongly disagree, 5 means strongly agree

Item	Percentage of rating					$\bar{X}$(SD)
	1	2	3	4	5	
I felt fun when learning history using the application	5%	5%	15%	35%	40%	4.00 (1.10)
I felt more involved when using the application	0%	0%	25%	45%	30%	4.05 (0.74)
The application allows me to understand history better and faster	0%	5%	25%	65%	5%	3.75 (0.70)
I think the application encouragesmore people to learn history	0%	5%	10%	20%	65%	4.45 (0.86)
I would like to install the application on my own mobile devices	0%	15%	20%	40%	25%	3.75 (1.00)
Average	**1%**	**6%**	**19%**	**40%**	**34%**	**4.00 (0.88)**

Table 2. Types of information that participants most and least focus on

Information	Percentage of the most focused	Percentage of the least focused
Screen-based GUI	15%	30%
AR-based GUI (3D models and 3D animation)	70%	5%
AR-based (Virtual cards)	0%	20%
Audio	15%	45%

5.2   Interface and Interaction

TongSEE provides users with historical information in visual and auditory modalities, integrates it with the surroundings, and allows learning history in an interactive way. According to the results, 60% of participants stated that TongSEE provides more information than the other traditional ways of learning history. Table 2 shows which types of information participants most and least focused on. The majority of participants (70%) most focused on the AR-based 3D visual material (3D models and 3D animation). On the contrary, audio was considered information that did not consistently attract attention by 45% of participants, followed by Screen-based GUI (30%). In addition, when asked about "TongSEE was well designed to integrate visual content with the real environment," most participants (85%) agreed with the statement. Main interaction factors mentioned by participants are "Overlaying interactive historical information at corresponding places (P1, P3–6, P8, P17–18), " "Providing contextual guidance (P1, P4, P7, P17–18)," and "Allowing explore freely in the real world with the moving path (P3, P9–10, P16, P18–19)."

5.3 Usability and Learnability

The overall SUS scores given by the 20 participants are presented in Fig. 9 (M = 66.4, SD = 14.1). According to the research of Bangor et al. [32] the overall SUS score no fewer than 50.9 is considered as "ok," no fewer than 71.4 is "good", no fewer than 85.5 is "excellent", and no fewer than 90.9 is "best imaginable." One participant (P18) rated TongSEE as "best imaginable." One (P17) rated it as "excellent." Six (P1, P4–P5, P8, P12, P20) rated it "good." Eight (P3, P6–P7, P9–P11, P13, P15) rated it as "ok," and four participants (C10) rated it below "ok." The average overall SUS score of TongSEE falls between "ok" and "good," indicating the usability and learnability of the application need to be improved. As validated by Lewis and Sauro [33], the SUS has two factors - Usability (8 items) and Learnability (2 items - specifically, Items 4 and 10). The average usability score is 64.7 (SD = 14.0), and the learnability score is 73.9 (SD = 17.3), suggesting TongSEE is satisfactory for learnability but has some usability issues that need improvement.

We further compared the evaluation of usability and learnability of participants with different levels of experience using AR. Figure 10 shows the overall SUS scores of participants with no experience of using AR and experienced users. The average overall SUS score of inexperienced participants is 60.8 (SD = 13.1),

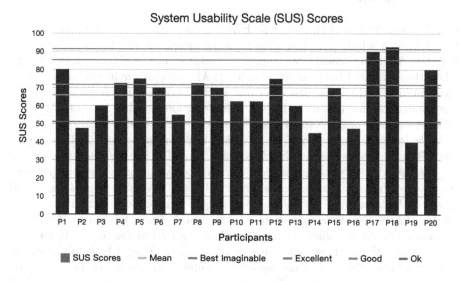

Fig. 9. The SUS scores given by the 20 participants

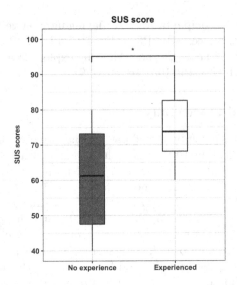

Fig. 10. The SUS scores of participants with different levels of experience using AR

lower than experienced participants with 75.3 (SD = 11.6). The Independent-Samples t-test shows that on usability and learnability of TongSEE, there is a significant difference for the previous experience of using AR (F = .725, p = .025 <.05).

6 Discussion

Our findings indicated that TongSEE is a promising educational tool for history learning, which is in line with existing reviews of the literature suggesting that AR environments can support users learning [9,34]. Learners felt fun when they explored freely in an immersive AR learning environment and were more motivated to learn history. Compared to traditional teaching methods, the application provides more historical information visually. As P3 mentioned, *"The restoration of the historical site using virtual 3D models makes me able to describe better its characteristics-e.g., color, size, and structure."* Different from the AR applications used in the classroom, TongSEE intertwines the places in the real world with virtual historical information, which provides another perspective for the user to understand history. P17 said, *"When compared the virtual historical building and what it looks like today, I became more aware of what has happened here and its impact on today."* P19 said, *"the application allowed me to gain a new understanding of nearby places that I was familiar with but had not noticed."* However, as mentioned by P6 and P12, TongSEE mainly presents historical knowledge (e.g., time, location, results of historical events, and original appearance of historic buildings). However, the reasons why these historical events occurred and the process were not clearly converted to the learners (*P6:*

"The application provided much information about the "result" of history, but little about the why and how."). This may result in partial and deficient understanding of history.

The evaluation of the interface illustrated that when using TongSEE, learners paid most attention to the 3D components of the AR-based GUI (e.g., 3D models and 3D animations), as these objects present the information virtually and intuitively, thus attracting learners' attention quickly. Virtual cards consisting of text, pictures, and video were less focused by learners. Due to the rendering resolution of AR and environmental factors (such as strong sunshine), these virtual cards sometimes can not be displayed clearly. Furthermore, in an AR learning environment, learners may feel overwhelmed due to a large amount of information they encounter and the complex tasks they have to accomplish [35]. Participants stated that they felt it difficult to focus their attention on information-intensive content like the virtual cards. It should be noted that nearly half of the learners paid little attention to the audio in the application, possibly due to the learner's limited perception and the noisy outdoor environment.

According to the SUS score, the usability of TongSEE is at "ok" level and needs to be improved. Learners reported several technical issues that affect usability, such as positioning errors, oscillation of the virtual objects, and lag issues. Some learners also required a tutorial in the application to help them know how to interact with the virtual objects. Comparing the SUS scores of experienced and inexperienced learners, we found that experienced learners thought the application was more usable and learnable than novices. Because their previous experience of using AR helped them master and apply some essential skills in an AR learning environment, such as technology manipulation, spatial navigation, interaction, and problem-solving. Lacking these essential skills could be a challenge for novices learning using AR.

7 Conclusion

In this paper, a location-based AR application TongSEE that enables users to learn history in an AR learning environment in an authentic context was designed, implemented, and evaluated. We visualized the history using various types of virtual material and intertwined it with places in the real world. We also created the ways for learners to interact in the large space physically and provided them with contextual guidance for their actions. From the evaluation results with 20 participants, we found that TongSEE helps increase learners' interest and motivation and allows them to understand history better and faster. Although usability and learnability of the application still need to be improved, especially for novices using AR. Overall, Our findings confirmed location-based AR's potential for history learning and highlighted the values of combining places with history. In our future work, we would like to continue the development of the application while researching the design of interface and interaction in location-based AR applications. Over the long term, a database containing various types of virtual assets will be available, enabling educators, researchers, and learners to add content to the AR learning environment.

References

1. Bronack, S.C.: The role of immersive media in online education. J. Cont. High. Educ. **59**(2), 113–117 (2011)
2. Klopfer, E., Squire, K.: Environmental detectives: the development of an augmented reality platform for environmental simulations. Educ. Technol. Res. Dev. **56**(2), 203–228 (2008)
3. Wu, H.K., Lee, W.Y., Chang, H.Y., Liang, J.C.: Current status, opportunities and challenges of augmented reality in education. Comput. Educ. **62**(2), 41–49 (2013)
4. Azuma, R.T.: A survey of augmented reality. Presence Teleoperat. Virtual Environ. **6**(4), 355–385 (1997)
5. Arvanitis, T.N., Petrou, A., Knight, J.F., Savas, S., Gargalakos, S.S.M., Gialouri, E.: Human factors and qualitative pedagogical evaluation of a mobile augmented reality system for science education used by learners with physical disabilities. Pers. Ubiquit. Comput. **13**(3), 243–250 (2009)
6. Kaufmann, H., Steinbügl, K., Dünser, A., Glück, J.: General training of spatial abilities by geometry education in augmented reality. Cyberpsychol. Behav. (2005)
7. Kai-Yi, C., Ching-Sheng, W., Yen-Lin, C.: Effects of an augmented reality-based mobile system on students' learning achievements and motivation for a liberal arts course. Interact. Learn. Environ. **27**, 1–15 (2018)
8. Khan, T., Johnston, K., Ophoff, J.: The impact of an augmented reality application on learning motivation of students. Adv. Hum. Comput. Interact. **2019** (2019)
9. Hedberg, H., Nouri, J., Hansen, P., Rahmani, R.: A systematic review of learning through mobile augmented reality. Int. J. Interact. Mob. Technol. (iJIM) **8** (2018)
10. Garcia, M.B.: Augmented reality in history education: an immersive storytelling of American Colonisation period in the Philippines. Int. J. Learn. Technol. **15**(3), 234–254 (2020)
11. Utami, I., Lutfi, I., Jati, S., Efendi, M.Y.: Effectivity of augmented reality as media for history learning. Int. J. Emerg. Technol. Learn. **14**(16), 83 (2019)
12. Spierling, U., Winzer, P., Massarczyk, E.: Experiencing the presence of historical stories with location-based augmented reality. In: Nunes, N., Oakley, I., Nisi, V. (eds.) ICIDS 2017. LNCS, vol. 10690, pp. 49–62. Springer, Cham (2017). https://doi.org/10.1007/978-3-319-71027-3_5
13. Rosenbaum, E., Klopfer, E., Perry, J.: On location learning: authentic applied science with networked augmented realities. J. Sci. Educ. Technol. **16**(1), 31–45 (2007)
14. Sungkur, R.K., Panchoo, A., Bhoyroo, N.K.: Augmented reality, the future of contextual mobile learning. Interact. Technol. Smart Educ. **13**(2), 123–146 (2016)
15. Squire, K., Klopfer, E.: Augmented reality simulations on handheld computers. j. Learn. Sci. **16**(3), 371–413 (2007)
16. Harley, J.M., Poitras, E.G., Jarrell, A., Duffy, M.C., Lajoie, S.P.: Comparing virtual and location-based augmented reality mobile learning: emotions and learning outcomes. Educ. Technol. Res. Dev. **64**(3), 359–388 (2016). https://doi.org/10.1007/s11423-015-9420-7
17. Klopfer, E., Sheldon, J.: Augmenting your own reality: student authoring of science-based augmented reality games. New Direct. Youth Dev. **2010**(128), 85–94 (2010)

18. Keil, J., Zollner, M., Becker, M., Wientapper, F., Engelke, T., Wuest, H.: The House of Olbrich-an augmented reality tour through architectural history. In: 2011 IEEE International Symposium on Mixed and Augmented Reality-Arts, Media, and Humanities, pp. 15–18. IEEE (2011). https://doi.org/10.1109/ISMAR-AMH. 2011.6093651

19. Blanco-Fernández, Y., López-Nores, M., Pazos-Arias, J.J., Gil-Solla, A., Ramos-Cabrer, M., García-Duque, J.: Reenact: a step forward in immersive learning about human history by augmented reality, role playing and social networking. Exp. Syst. Appl. **41**(10), 4811–4828 (2014)

20. John, F.: Engaging students in learning history. Can. Soc. Stud. **52**(2) (2005)

21. Al-Shara, I.: Learning and teaching between enjoyment and boredom as realized by the students: a survey from the educational field. Eur. Sci. J. **11**(19) (2015)

22. Schiavi, B., Gechter, F., Gechter, C., Rizzo, A.: Teach me a story: an augmented reality application for teaching history in middle school. In: 2018 IEEE Conference on Virtual Reality and 3D User Interfaces (VR), pp. 679–680. IEEE (2018). https://doi.org/10.1109/VR.2018.8446412

23. Selwyn, N.: Augmented Learning: Research and Design of Mobile Educational Games. MIT Press, Cambridge (2010)

24. Kerawalla, L., Luckin, R., Seljeflot, S., Woolard, A.: Making it real": exploring the potential of augmented reality for teaching primary school science. Virtual Reality **10**(3), 163–174 (2006)

25. Selwyn, N.: Immersive Interfaces For Engagement And Learning. Science **323**(5910), 966–969 (2009)

26. Kim, M.J.: A framework for context immersion in mobile augmented reality. Autom. Constru. **33**, 79–85 (2013)

27. Georgiou, Y., Kyza, E.A.: A design-based approach to augmented reality location-based activities: investigating immersion in relation to student learning. In: Proceedings of the 16th World Conference on Mobile and Contextual Learning, pp. 1–8 (2017). https://doi.org/10.1145/3136907.3136926

28. Cabiria, J.: Augmenting engagement: augmented reality in education. In: Increasing Student Engagement and Retention Using Immersive Interfaces: Virtual Worlds, Gaming, and Simulation. Emerald Group Publishing Limited (2012)

29. Dunleavy, M., Dede, C., Mitchell, R.: Affordances and limitations of immersive participatory augmented reality simulations for teaching and learning. J. Sci. Educ. Technol. **18**(1), 7–22 (2009)

30. Squire, K.D., Jan, M.: Mad city mystery: developing scientific argumentation skills with a place-based augmented reality game on handheld computers. J. Sci. Educ. Technol. **16**(1), 5–29 (2007)

31. Brooke, J.: SUS: a "quick and dirty" usability. Usabil. Eval. Ind. **189**(3) (1996)

32. Bangor, A., Kortum, P., Miller, J.: Determining what individual SUS scores mean: adding an adjective rating scale. J. Usabil. Stud. **4**(3), 114–123 (2009)

33. Lewis, J.R., Sauro, J.: The factor structure of the system usability scale. In: Kurosu, M. (ed.) HCD 2009. LNCS, vol. 5619, pp. 94–103. Springer, Heidelberg (2009). https://doi.org/10.1007/978-3-642-02806-9_12

34. Cheng, K.H., Tsai, C.C.: Affordances of augmented reality in science learning: suggestions for future research. J. Sci. Educ. Technol. **22**(4), 449–462 (2013)

35. Chang, Y.L., Hou, H.T., Pan, C.Y., Sung, Y.T., Chang, K.E.: Apply an augmented reality in a mobile guidance to increase sense of place for heritage places. J. Educ. Technol. Soc. **18**(2), 166–178 (2015)

VAMR in Aviation

Practice Makes Perfect or Does It? Practice Effect in Flying HUD Localizer-Guided Low Visibility Takeoffs

Inchul Choi[1] ⓘ, Daniela Kratchounova[2](✉) ⓘ, Theodore Mofle[1] ⓘ,
Jeremy Hesselroth[3], Scott Stevenson[3], and Mark Humphreys[1]

[1] Cherokee Nation 3S, Catoosa, OK, USA
{Inchul.CTR.Choi,Theodore.C-CTR.Mofle}@faa.gov
[2] Federal Aviation Administration Civil Aerospace Medical Institute, Oklahoma City, OK, USA
Daniela.Kratchounova@faa.gov
[3] Federal Aviation Administration Flight Technologies and Procedures Division,
Oklahoma City, OK, USA
{Jeremy.J.Hesselroth,Scott.Stevenson}@faa.gov

Abstract. This research highlighted an interesting aspect of the relationship between practice, flight technical error (FTE), workload, and safety margin. The results showed that with practice, the FTE values were not affected and no practice effect was observed. However, practice did affect the reported perceived workload levels, where the NASA-TLX ratings significantly decreased as the research study progressed. Based on these results, we proposed that the observed significant decrease in the subjective measure of crew workload could result in an increased safety margin even though the objective measure of performance remained relatively unchanged. Specifically, the subjective assessment of workload level could be characteristic of the pilot's assessment of the size of safety margin across different operational conditions where the perception of reduced workload levels could be considered as a form of cognitive capacity "capital." We assert that practice affords an added sense of optimized levels of workload and increased confidence. With that, it could virtually increase the size of safety margin.

Keywords: Practice effect · Flight technical error · Crew workload · Head-up display (HUD) · Safety margin

1 Introduction

Our previous research efforts [1–3] examined flight technical error (FTE) and subjective crew workload [NASA Task Load Index (NASA-TLX)] during low visibility takeoffs using heads-up display (HUD) with localizer guidance. The main focus was on the differential contributions of guidance type, runway visual range (RVR), and lighting conditions (day/night). Although pilot participants were deemed proficient in using a HUD, they reported different levels of previous experiences in flying HUD localizer-guided takeoff. Notionally, varying distribution of previous HUD experience could affect future pilot performance and perceived workload.

© Springer Nature Switzerland AG 2022
J. Y. C. Chen and G. Fragomeni (Eds.): HCII 2022, LNCS 13318, pp. 173–182, 2022.
https://doi.org/10.1007/978-3-031-06015-1_12

Herein, we focused on trends in the FTE and NASA-TLX data and the potential practice effect by examining the 96 takeoff scenarios per crew completed during the original research. Pilots were grouped according to their previous HUD localizer-guided takeoff experience. The results showed that with practice, the FTE values were *not* affected. More specifically, pilots performed well within the acceptable FTE values throughout the study and no practice effect was observed. Remarkably, practice *did* affect the reported perceived workload levels, where NASA-TLX ratings significantly decreased as the research study progressed.

2   Background

According to the Free Dictionary by Farlex [4], the old proverb "Practice makes perfect" began as "Use makes mastery." In the English language, it dates back to the 15th century. However, conceivably it was a version of an older Latin proverb. While it exists in many languages and most people would likely agree with it; an English author once wrote [5, p. 11], "There is a limit to what can be done by taking pains. Practice never makes perfect. It improves up to a point." Reliance on what would be considered as "common sense" or "common knowledge" such as the notion that the more one does something, the better one becomes at it; rather than on a careful consideration of empirical findings, can be both deceptive and counterproductive.

For instance, research exploring the distribution of practice effect has been conducted for over a century now. Yet, several gaps remain in the research literature, which limit our ability to make concrete conclusions regarding this effect. In addition, many studies have failed to identify the distribution of practice effect, raising the possibility of boundary conditions within which this effect operates. Past research has generally been unsuccessful in considering or attempting to understand what factors either (a) optimize or amplify this effect or (b) limit, repudiate, or even reverse this effect under different task types, different inter-trial intervals, and different means of measuring performance [6]. Furthermore, it is important to note that most of the research on practice effect has been conducted in the domain of training, instruction and education. Nonetheless, these findings could have potentially important implications for domains well outside the aforesaid such as aviation; especially because research studies addressing practice effect and its distribution in aviation are notably absent.

Here, we examine the connection between the apparent lack of practice effect in the FTE data, the reported decreasing levels of crew workload over the course of the study, and the resulting potential improvement in safety margin. In our previous research [7] we upheld the notion that in aviation, there is a constantly fluctuating margin between two distinct boundaries. First, a lower boundary that could represent a pilot/crew's workload level resulting from performing normal pilot tasks and responses to hazards presented by actual conditions. Second, an upper boundary representing a pilot/crew's total capacity to positively respond to hazards and safely manage tasks under those conditions. For example, as the distance between the two boundaries decreases, the safety margin decreases, leaving less spare capacity for the pilot to resolve hazards or successfully complete required tasks; and vice versa.

The results of this follow-on study highlighted an interesting aspect of the relationship between practice, FTE, and perceived workload. Based on that, we proposed that the observed significant decrease in the subjective measure of crew workload could result in an increased safety margin even though the objective measure of performance remained relatively unchanged.

3 Method

3.1 Participants

Twenty-four pilot crews (48 pilots) consented to participate in this research: 12 airline crews and 12 business jet crews, who were deemed proficient[1] in using a HUD. This research was approved by the Civil Airspace Medical Institute (CAMI) Institutional Review Board (IRB). Before taking part in the research study, all participants were briefed on the general purpose of the study, signed an informed consent form, and filled out a demographics questionnaire. A key question about the participants' demographics information pertained to previous experience using HUD localizer guidance symbology in either a simulated or actual environment.

3.2 Procedures

In two consecutive days, crews performed a total of 96 takeoff scenarios: 60 normal and 36 abnormal operational conditions. For normal operations, wind speeds ranging between 3 knots (calm) and 22 knots[2] and varying wind directions were randomly assigned to scenarios. For abnormal operations (failure cases), winds ranged between 3 knots (calm) and 15 knots. All tailwinds were limited to 10 knots (Boeing 737-800NG Airplane Flight Manual Limitation). All experimental trials were conducted on a CAT I runway at the Memphis International Airport, using the Rockwell Collins Head-up Guidance System (HGS) model 6700, installed in the FAA's Boeing 737-800NG Level D simulator. Unique trial sequences were generated and pseudo-randomized for individual crews to avoid learning and order effects. Each pilot was able to fly from both left and right seat by changing seats after each 16-run session.

3.3 Independent Variables

In the original research, three independent variables were examined including type of guidance, RVR, and lighting conditions (day/night) [3]. Here, two independent variables were examined to investigate the effects of previous experience and practice on pilot performance and crew workload: previous HUD localizer-guided takeoff experience and run number (covariate).

To report the results of this study, two important and distinctly different terms were used: scenario number and run number. Scenario number directly identified the experimental condition (e.g., scenario #1 presented the same experimental conditions to all crews). Run number referred to the order in which each scenario appeared within the unique sequence per crew. That is, scenario numbers 1 to 96 were semi-randomized to create a unique sequence of 96 runs for each crew.

---

[1] See [3] for proficiency criteria and assessment.

[2] AC 120-28D-Criteria for Approval of Category III Weather Minima for Takeoff, Landing, and Rollout.

3.4 Dependent Variables

For each trial, FTE score was calculated by a root-mean-square-error (RMSE) of deviations from centerline [3]. After completing each run, both the Pilot Flying (PF) and the Pilot Monitoring (PM) completed the NASA-TLX workload questionnaire [8]. In this study, only the PF total weighted NASA-TLX ratings were calculated and used for statistical analyses [9].

Thirty-six of the 96 scenarios represented baseline normal operational conditions and were performed *without* HUD localizer guidance and were excluded from the analyses for a like-to-like comparison when exploring the effects of previous HUD localizer-guided takeoff experience.

4   Results

4.1   Previous HUD Localizer-Guided Takeoff Experience

Based on the demographics data, 18 pilot participants did not have HUD localizer-guided takeoff experience prior to attending the study while 30 pilots reported previous experience. The total weighted NASA-TLX ratings were analyzed using a *t*-test (see Fig. 1). The results indicated that pilots without previous localizer-guided takeoff experience rated their workload significantly higher than those pilots with previous experience, $t(1047.805) = 2.368, p = 0.018$.

However, the FTE scores of pilots without HUD localizer-guided takeoff experience were not significantly different from those with previous experience, $t(900.407) = 1.653$, $p = 0.099$ (see Fig. 2). Scenario number was used to graph the NASA-TLX ratings and FTE scores in this section[3]. By using scenario number, operation types, RVR, lighting conditions, as well as wind speeds could be kept the same to make it possible to visualize *only* differences based on previous HUD localizer-guided takeoff experience. As a whole, pilots with no previous experience rated their workload higher (Fig. 1). However, the general patterns were the same across the experimental conditions. On Fig. 1 and Fig. 2, FTE scores and total weighted NASA-TLX ratings in normal operations are shown on the left side of the vertical line, while those in abnormal operations on the right side of the line.

4.2   Practice Effect

To identify a potential practice effect in the FTE scores as well as the effect of practice on the NASA-TLX ratings, the data were ordered by run number. This approach provided a way to visualize any potential trends in the data over the course of the study. Total weighted NASA-TLX ratings of both pilot groups, those without previous HUD localizer-guided takeoff experience ($\beta_{standardized} = -0.152, t(538) = -3.575, p < .001$, 95% CI [−0.176, −0.051]; $R^2_{adj} = 0.021, F(1, 538) = 12.778, p < 0.001$) and those with previous experience ($\beta_{standardized} = -0.236, t(898) = -7.274, p < 0.001$, 95%

---

[3] Scenario numbers from 1 to 18 and from 31 to 48 were omitted in figures because those scenarios were not using HUD localizer-guidance.

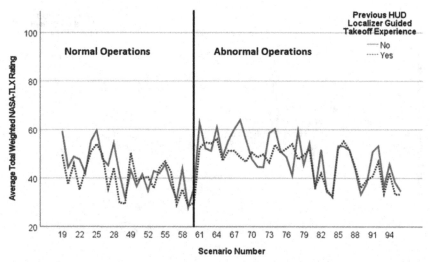

Fig. 1. Average total weighted NASA-TLX ratings by scenario number and previous HUD localizer-guided takeoff experience.

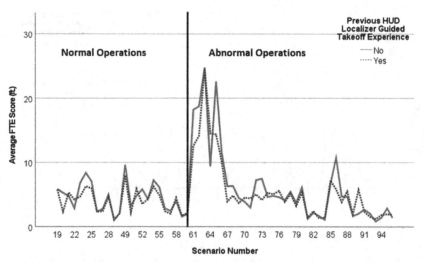

Fig. 2. Average FTE score by scenario number and previous HUD localizer-guided takeoff experience.

CI $[-0.204, -0.117]$; $R^2_{adj} = 0.055$, $F(1, 898) = 52.905$, $p < 0.001$) significantly decreased (Fig. 3). Furthermore, the regression coefficient of the NASA-TLX data representing the group with previous HUD localizer-guided takeoff experience was smaller (i.e., a larger decrease) than the group without previous experience.

On the contrary, regression coefficients of the FTE scores were not significant for both pilot groups. On Fig. 3 and Fig. 4, the two solid lines visualize the trends of FTE and total weighted NASA-TLX ratings over the course of study.

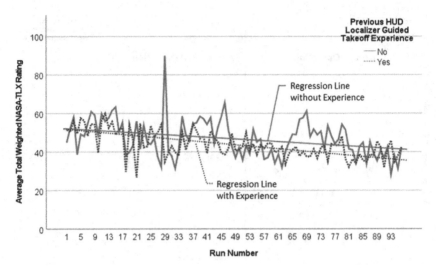

Fig. 3. Average total weighted NASA-TLX rating by run number and previous HUD localizer-guided takeoff experience.

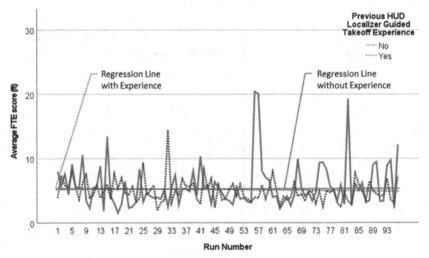

Fig. 4. Average FTE score by run number and previous HUD localizer-guided takeoff experience.

5   Discussion

5.1   Crew Workload

The NASA-TLX workload ratings are based on self-reported subjective perception of workload [8]. Notionally, pilots' assessment of workload may be influenced by previous operational experience and training. Therefore, pilots with more previous experience in low visibility conditions may perceive workload differently than less experienced pilots given the same conditions. In day-to-day flight operations, actual weather conditions are seldom as low as most of the conditions used in this study. In addition, in a simulator or research environment, pilots may not know what to expect; therefore, they are initially operating at a heightened alertness. It is possible that the exposure to low visibility takeoff conditions in this study initially exceeded the entire sum of the pilots' actual prior operational experience with low visibility takeoffs. Consequently, during the early data collection runs, pilots may have naturally perceived the workload to be elevated. However, as they gained experience they may have become more comfortable with operating under those conditions, causing their perception of workload to be lower even for the same weather conditions.

Additionally, to certain crews, the concept of using the HUD localizer guidance may have been somewhat challenging initially, thus they perceived their workload as higher. After a number of runs using this type of takeoff guidance, pilots became more comfortable with using it. This could be attributed to an increased comfort with operating the simulator, an increased ease in assessing abnormal situations, and/or an increase in the pilots' overall level of confidence in dealing with future events after successfully handling previous events.

5.2   Flight Technical Error (FTE)

In contrast to the workload ratings, which were based on a self-reported subjective perception, the FTE scores were based on objective metric of deviation from runway centerline. In general, during takeoff, pilots attempt to maintain centerline for overall safety and in the event an engine is lost. The centerline stripes, centerline lighting, and (in this research study) the HUD centerline symbology were all highly compelling visual cues utilized to achieve this goal. In low visibility conditions, with the associated reduction of visual cues (e.g., distant centerline stripes and centerline lights), pilots may not be comfortable being even slightly off the centerline. A common pilot mindset is that during takeoff 'the aircraft is either on centerline or correcting towards it.'

In comparison, under some landing conditions, pilots may accept being slightly off centerline and nevertheless allowing no such deviation during the takeoff roll. To illustrate the difference further, when landing, pilots may prioritize being wings level with the nose pointed straight down the runway and aiming to land within the first third of the runway length. Namely, while accepting a landing a few feet off centerline, the primary focus is on where to land along the runway length. In assessing the risk, pilots take into consideration that it is safer to accept this slight deviation from centerline rather than to land long (touching down at a point where the aircraft cannot be stopped before running off the end of the runway) or to dip a wing for a last second centerline correction.

Some aspects of this research may have revealed several boundary conditions associated with the observed lack of practice effect in the FTE data. These include temporal factors (e.g., task duration), human factors (e.g., reaction/response times), and technological factors (e.g., HUD symbology). First, as a whole, takeoff is a relatively short maneuver; therefore, the ability to focus intensely for this short period would be easily achievable. The "go/no-go" decision of the PF and the observations and callouts of the PM are standardized and highly practiced across professional pilot crews.

Second, during the takeoff, acceleration to the "decision speed" (V_1) and continuing to liftoff is a critical phase of flight where pilots have already completed a pre-takeoff briefing for very specific events in which they will reject or continue the takeoff. Consequently, what they are focused on may exclude potential "distractions" until a safe altitude is reached. The PF would typically be monitoring adherence to runway centerline whether that be visually, or per this study, visually and with reference to the HUD localizer guidance and listening to callouts from the PM.

Furthermore, there are natural limits to human response time to detect a tracking error, and introduce a correction; as well as inherent design limits to the technology used. As such, the combined (a) limited external visual cues, (b) available HUD symbology guidance, and (c) human performance limits may have positively affected pilots' performance to be at its effective maximum throughout the study.

Third, it is also plausible that experience and previous training (not necessarily with using a HUD or HUD with localizer guidance) may have played a role in the lack of practice effect in the FTE data. The takeoff is a maneuver crews have performed literally thousands of times with no or minimal deviation from the "norm" [10]. A relatively short study (only a couple of days long) may not have been long enough to demonstrate any improvement in performance because pilots are already performing near the best of their abilities given the years of flying and thousands of takeoffs performed and practiced in training. Furthermore, the highly experienced and qualified pilots who participated in this study may have been operating near, or at, a 'performance ceiling'. This ceiling could potentially be attributed to piloting skills and proficiency that experienced pilots possess. For example, the average total flight hours of the pilots who participated in this research was ~14,000 h. Likewise, engine failures during the takeoff roll are usually a part of initial and recurrent training syllabi. As such, pilots are very well aware of any lateral deviation during the takeoff roll, and will make an immediate correction to centerline as soon as a lateral deviation is recognized.

During the original research, for any given set of weather conditions and HUD guidance used, pilots could only see a fixed number of outside visual references under those conditions. The HUD provided consistent rate of movement of the guidance cue and localizer line symbology; therefore, providing a powerful aid to the pilots and allowing them to maintain a high level of performance throughout the study. More specifically, the fact that no significant differences were present in the FTE data between pilots with and without previous experience was a testament to the utility, usability, and versatility of the HUD Localizer symbology used in the original research.

In summary, it is conceivable that pilots were less comfortable with the early experimental study runs while at the same time their actual FTE performance was close to an optimal level from the first run.

5.3 Safety Margin

The notion of margin of safety is fundamental to the notion of aviation itself and it applies to many areas of flight operations including flight environment (e.g., weather), ground infrastructure (e.g., runway markings and lighting), etc. Numerous factors affect the size of safety margin in this context. Furthermore, they may do so dynamically, in the different phases of flight, and across varying operational and environmental conditions. Theoretically, its size could be defined as the "distance" between a crew workload profile, and a potential incident or accident boundary in a given flight situation. The probability of safety margin reduction as a function of some type of hazard, or a combination of hazards, is referred to as risk. The way people recognize risk is fundamentally subjective and reflects their: (a) previous experience with a particular hazard; (b) perception of the potential, direct or indirect, negative consequences and how imminent these consequences are; (c) sense of control over the situation; and (d) individual biases toward competency and control [7].

Hart [9] emphasized the concept of workload as "the human cost (e.g., fatigue, stress, illness, and accidents) of maintaining performance" [p. 904]. The results of this and our previous research [7] suggest that the subjective assessment of workload level could be characteristic of the pilot's perception of the size of safety margin across different operational conditions. More specifically, while the FTE might remain stable, the perception of reduced workload levels could be considered as a form of cognitive capacity "capital" that virtually increases the size of safety margin. In other words, if the task at hand requires less of an effort, that capital can be put towards several other potential commodities, such as increased situational awareness, improved Crew Resource Management (CRM), and the ability to handle any ensuing malfunctions or non-normal situations. It is not always the initial malfunction that serves as the proximate cause of an aviation violation, mishap, or an accident. It may be the case that the initial malfunction utilizes the entire safety margin, with the aircrew able to appropriately handle that single malfunction, but leaving no remaining safety margin to handle anything else. This lack of available safety margin could result in anything from missed radio calls and poor communication between aircrew members to incorrectly handling subsequent malfunctions or not noticing cockpit warning alerts.

6 Conclusion

In summary, based on the results from this and our previous research [1–3, 7], we assert that when pilot performance is already at, or close to, what is considered to be "perfect"; practice *keeps* it perfect. Namely, practice affords an added sense of optimized levels of workload and increased confidence. With that, it could virtually increase the size of safety margin.

Acknowledgements. This project was funded by the FAA NextGen Human Factors Division (ANG-C1) in support of the FAA Office of Aviation Safety, Low Visibility Operations Unit, Flight Technologies & Procedures Division, Flight Operations Group (AFS-410). This paper and the research behind it would not have been possible without the exceptional support of Larry Miller who served as a research pilot for the original study and data collection. His enthusiasm, outstanding work ethics, knowledge, and exacting attention to detail have been an inspiration for us all.

References

1. Kratchounova, D., Humphreys, M., Miller, L., Mofle, T., Choi, I., Nesmith, B.L.: Crew workload considerations in using HUD localizer takeoff guidance in lieu of currently required infrastructure. In: Chen, J.Y.C., Fragomeni, G. (eds.) HCII 2020. LNCS, vol. 12190, pp. 507–521. Springer, Cham (2020). https://doi.org/10.1007/978-3-030-49695-1_34

2. Kratchounova, D., Miller, L., Choi, I., Mofle, T., Humphreys, M., Nesmith, B.L.: Flight technical error in using head-up display (HUD) with localizer guidance in lieu of required infrastructure for takeoff. In: 2020 AIAA/IEEE 39th Digital Avionics Systems Conference (DASC), pp. 1–6. IEEE, October 2020

3. Kratchounova, D., Miller, L., Choi, I., Humphreys, M., Mofle, T.C., Nesmith, B.L.: Human factors considerations in using HUD localizer takeoff guidance in lieu of currently required infrastructure. In: DOT/FAA/AM-2007, Oklahoma City, OK (2020)

4. Idioms and Phrases. https://idioms.thefreedictionary.com

5. The Vulgar Voice (1902). http://archive.spectator.co.uk/article/10th-may-1902/11/the-vulgar-voice

6. Donovan, J.J., Radosevich, D.J.: A meta-analytic review of the distribution of practice effect: now you see it, now you don't. J. Appl. Psychol. **84**, 795–805 (1999). https://doi.org/10.1037/0021-9010.84.5.795

7. Kratchounova, D., et al.: No one is superman: 3-D safety margin profiles when using head-up display (HUD) for takeoff in low visibility and high crosswind conditions. In: Chen, J.Y.C., Fragomeni, G. (eds.) HCII 2021. LNCS, vol. 12770, pp. 336–352. Springer, Cham (2021). https://doi.org/10.1007/978-3-030-77599-5_24

8. Hart, S.G., Staveland, L.E.: Development of NASA-TLX (task load index): results of empirical and theoretical research. Adv. Psychol. **52**, 139–183 (1988). https://doi.org/10.1016/S0166-4115(08)62386-9

9. Hart, S.G.: NASA-task load index (NASA-TLX); 20 years later. Proc. Hum. Factors Ergon. Soc. 904–908 (2006). https://doi.org/10.1177/154193120605000909

10. Federal Aviation Administration: 120-28D criteria for approval of category III weather minima for takeoff, landing, and rollout. AC 120-28D, Washington D.C., U.S. Department of Transportation (1999)

Identification of Expert Tower Controller Visual Scanning Patterns in Support of the Development of Automated Training Tools

Jerry Crutchfield[1](✉), Ziho Kang[2], Ricardo Palma Fraga[2], and Junehyung Lee[2]

[1] Civil Aerospace Medical Institute, Federal Aviation Administration, Oklahoma City, OK, USA
jerry.crutchfield@faa.gov

[2] School of Industrial and Systems Engineering, University of Oklahoma, Norman, OK, USA

Abstract. Researchers from the Federal Aviation Administration's (FAA) Civil Aerospace Medical Institute and from the University of Oklahoma's School of Industrial and Systems Engineering are studying the characteristics of expert tower controller visual scanning behavior in support of the FAA's exploration of ways to enhance controller training. Training enhancements potentially include the use of advanced simulation tools (such as virtual reality systems) to teach controller trainees critical scanning skill(s). We collected eye-tracking data from controller subject matter experts while they controlled simulated air traffic scenarios in a high fidelity tower cab simulator. In this paper, we describe the methodology used to collect and analyze the data as well as summarize the results of the analyses. These results may inform the design of scanning training tools. Furthermore, we summarize lessons learned from our use of simulation and our methods of collecting performance measures that may be useful for those developing scanning training tools that will also use simulation. Our findings suggest that training tools should continue to train what is taught in today's curriculum regarding scanning, to frequently scan "hot spots" such as both ends of an active runway, and to prioritize traffic at the airfield before traffic occurring farther out. Our findings also suggest that controllers could be taught to use different scanning patterns based on the ATC task they are currently carrying out and to use these patterns consistently.

Keywords: Air traffic control · Aviation · Eye-tracking · Simulation · Training · Virtual reality

1 Introduction

On behalf of the FAA's Human Performance Team, researchers at the University of Oklahoma (OU) and the Federal Aviation Administration's (FAA) Civil Aerospace Medical Institute (CAMI) continue to conduct studies, to explore the use of simulation based tools to enhance controller training. One recent objective of these studies is to characterize the visual scanning behavior of expert Air Traffic Control Tower (ATCT) controllers. Experts' visual scanning characteristics can inform instructional content and the design of tools meant for use in teaching critical visual scanning skills to novices. Air traffic

J. Y. C. Chen and G. Fragomeni (Eds.): HCII 2022, LNCS 13318, pp. 183–195, 2022.
https://doi.org/10.1007/978-3-031-06015-1_13

controllers must continually and systematically scan their environment to gather vital information that enables them to maintain the safe and expeditious movement of air traffic. In the airport tower environment, the visual field that controllers must scan includes an out-the-window (OTW) view of runways and operating areas on the airport surface as well as the airspace that surrounds the airport.

Our initial study efforts began with a review of the literature and of the FAA's training curriculum for visual scanning in the tower environment. Most of the existing research attempted to quantify controller heads-up vs heads-down time [1–3]. One report was a task analyses that associated the need for scanning with particular controller tasks [4]. Other research looked at OTW information requirements [5, 6]. The review of curriculum material included interviews with FAA Academy instructors. What we learned is that controller training course material instructs novice controllers to make frequent visual scans of pertinent information sources and to make sure that those scans include certain critical hot spots in the airport movement areas on the surface and in airspace near the airport. Critical hotspots are locations, visible out the tower window, where aircraft paths most frequently cross and where errors or off-nominal events can have severe consequences. The instructors who we interviewed also added that novices are often taught to use certain rules of thumb, although these rules may vary depending upon when and where the training occurs and which instructor leads their training.

Next, we convened a working group of FAA human factors specialists and pilot and controller Subject Matter Experts (SME). The working group produced a list of scanning best practices and a recommendation that research be done to examine the possibility of training tower controllers to use specific scanning patterns in much the same way that a pilot is taught to scan on the flight deck. Before we can evaluate the effectiveness of such training, we need to identify the specific scanning patterns that are suitable to be taught. Based on the working group's recommendation, we began to focus research on detecting and identifying scanning patterns. An additional challenge is that the type of visual environment necessary to teach a tower scanning pattern and the inability of instructors to accurately observe a trainee's scanning behavior directly, suggest the possibility that a specialized training tool will need to be developed. Virtual Reality (VR) systems are one type of specialized tool that might meet the scanning training needs and thus be a candidate for future evaluation [7, 8].

We speculated that analysis of eye-movement behavior of expert controllers, as recorded using eye-tracking technology while the controllers controlled high fidelity simulations of air traffic, would be an effective approach to identify suitable scanning patterns to be used in training novice controllers. Similar techniques have been used in other studies conducted primarily as a way to evaluate new systems and look for ways to improve controller efficiency [9–11].

In the remainder of this paper, we describe how we used an immersive ATCT simulation and head mounted system to collect eye-tracking data from controller subject matter experts. We discuss the usefulness of eye-tracking data to characterize general visual scanning behavior and the scanning patterns used by expert controllers. We also summarize results and recommendations that could inform the development of tower scanning training tools, such as those that might use head mounted VR.

2 Method

2.1 Participants

Participants were 15 retired controllers who were working as FAA Academy instructors. The participants' experience in ATCT operations ranged from 10 to 42 years and the average was 26.33 years. Due to technical difficulties with the simulator, we excluded the data from one participant.

2.2 Materials

We used an Adacel Tower Simulation System to provide a simulated air traffic control tower environment and air traffic scenarios. The system provided the participants with simulated radar and ground surveillance displays as well as an OTW view (see Fig. 1). The OTW view was presented on twelve 55″ high definition monitors in portrait orientation subtending approximately 270° around the participant. The simulator projected a 360° view from the simulated tower onto the twelve monitors. Participants were also provided with two digital timers and pieces of paper providing flight progress strip information in a format commonly used in the Academy simulators. Participants took the role of the Local control position while another tower controller SME, employed as a study confederate, took the role of the Ground control position. Pilot communications were represented by the Adacel software and by a remote simulated pilot operator. Use of the Adacel software automated the pilot voices providing a level of consistency with regard to when aircraft would call into the scenario. The remote simulated pilot operator served as a backup to the automation, stepping in to adjust the aircraft's response whenever they recognized that the automation misinterpreted voice clearances delivered by the participant.

Fig. 1. CAMI's air traffic control advanced research tower simulator.

The airport configuration used in this experiment comprises three runways: a set of parallel runways and one runway that crossed the set of parallels. The airport configuration was the same as that used at the FAA Academy. Researchers scripted thirteen air traffic scenarios at this airport that ranged in length from 22 to 38 min. Weather was always simulated as clear and the scenarios always occurred during daylight.

A single scenario was used to familiarize participants with this simulator. It also served to allow the participants time to become accustomed to wearing the eye-tracking glasses while controlling simulated traffic.

Seven scenarios were scripted to enable the analysis of scanning behavior for specific controller tasks (arrivals and departures) and for different runway configurations (single runway, two crossing runways, and two parallel runways). These scenarios were: Single Runway Arrivals, Single Runway Departures, Single Runway Mixed, Crossing Runway Departures, Crossing Runway Arrivals, Parallel Runway Arrivals and Parallel Runways Mixed. Another single scenario was created for use as a Baseline to elicit natural eye-movement behavior during nominal air traffic conditions. This scenario represented the use of all three runways for both arrivals and departures.

Four scenarios were designed to measure scanning performance. These were scripted to include the occurrence of six off nominal air traffic events. All of these events, if occurring in the real world, would require the controller to respond according to a given procedure. The events were included to allow researchers to track which controllers detected the events and how long it took them to detect the events. Off-nominal events included: a smoking aircraft engine, the appearance of a flock of birds, a lawnmower crossing a runway exit without authorization, an aircraft attempting to land on an incorrect runway, an aircraft attempting to taxi to the wrong runway and an aborted takeoff.

Materials used included an over-the-shoulder controller performance rating form. This form was a modified version of form 3120-25 used in the field and at the Academy to score controller performance. The form was modified to include a broader range of scoring categories. This form included 24 items (tasks) categorized into 6 sections (i.e., Separation, Coordination, Control Judgment, Methods & Procedures, Equipment, and Communication). Tasks were included on the form if they involved scanning. If our scenarios and procedures did not lead to participants performing a given task, it was not included on the form. The OTS rating scale ranged from 0 to 4 for *'Unsatisfactory'*, *'Needs Improvement'*, *'Meets Expectations/Satisfactory'*, *'Exceeds Expectations'*, and *'Outstanding'*.

Participants were asked about the use, in the field, of certain scanning techniques. Certain scan patterns may be task specific. Participants were asked what types of events occur while controlling air traffic that may prompt a particular scan.

While participants controlled the simulated traffic, they wore head-mounted eye-tracking glasses (see Fig. 2). These glasses were part of the Tobii Pro 2 eye-tracking system. They comprise a set of frames with magnets to hold in prescription lenses, 4 infrared lights per lens to illuminate the wearer's pupil, 2 cameras per lens to capture the wearer's pupil, and a scene view camera mounted at the temple. The recording device also communicated wirelessly with a computer running Tobii Pro 2 software in a location in the lab apart from the simulator. Researchers are able to watch what the participant is seeing after a small lag time, on a monitor at this computer's location.

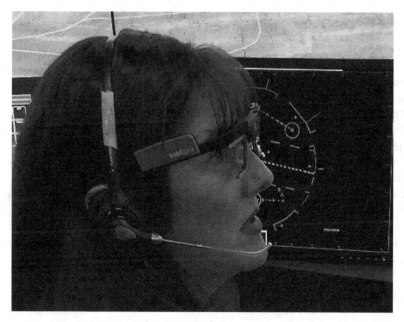

Fig. 2. Researcher wearing the Tobii Pro 2 eye-tracking frames.

2.3 Procedure

Participants ran scenarios across two consecutive days. If the participant was wearing glasses, the researcher and participant would engage in an exercise to determine the strength of the participants' prescription by using a Snellen Eye Chart. The researcher then would place lenses of comparable prescription into the eye-tracking frames and perform the calibration procedure. Calibration required the participant to spend a few seconds looking at each of two black dots taped to the lab room wall while a researcher checked the Tobii display to make sure the participant's pupils and eye-glints were sufficiently visible to the Tobii cameras. The participant was then seated and to receive a brief about air traffic control related details such as runway configuration from the Ground Controller.

All participants ran all the scenarios in the same sequence across the two days. Instructions on the second day merely reiterated what the participant heard on the first day. The order of the scenarios was as follows:

Day 1:

- Familiarization
- Single Runway Arrivals
- Single Runway Departures
- Single Runway Mix
- Crossing Runways Departures
- Crossing Runways Arrivals

- Parallel Runways Mix

Day 2:

- Parallel Runways Arrivals
- Baseline
- Off Nominal 1 (flock of birds and rogue lawn mower)
- Off Nominal 2 (aircraft nose past the hold line, aircraft smoking engine, and deviation upon departure)
- Off Nominal 3 (rogue truck, and an aircraft that lines up to land on the wrong surface)
- Off Nominal 4 (interrupted take off, people on the runway, and aircraft taxis to wrong runway)

After the participant finished the last scenario, they completed the post experimental questionnaire.

3 Summary of Results

3.1 Expert Controller Scanning Characteristics

We found the application of immersive simulation and eye-tracking technology to be a useful way to obtain the data needed to characterize controller scanning behavior. Our eye-tracking analyses focused primarily on fixations and involved the use of Areas of Interest (AOI) and transition matrices. A fixation occurs any time a participant's gaze stayed at one location for at least 60 ms. An AOI is a location, in the potential field of view of the participant that is of interest from the standpoint of a research question. Transition matrices are matrices listing the AOIs across both column and row headings, that show in each cell how many times the participant's eye fixation moved from the AOI listed in the row to the AOI listed in the column. For a more detailed description of how fixations were classified and assigned to AOI, we refer the reader to [12].

The use of fixation counts and fixation duration allowed us to confirm that controllers frequently scan hotspots in their area of responsibility and that the hotspots matched those identified in the scanning training curriculum. Eye-tracking researchers often use heat maps to depict the relative number of fixations occurring at locations on a scene view picture. As can be seen on the heat map in Fig. 3 hotspots included both ends of an active runway and places where traffic crosses the runway.

The AOI defined for this study are shown in Fig. 4 AOI were situation displays and parts of the OTW view that can serve distinct operational functions. We designated the AOI with generic names such that they would correspond in function to similar locations at other airports. The Tobii eye-tracking system automates the task of correlating the scene video captured from the eye-tracking frames worn by the participants, while controlling traffic, with a reference picture taken of the tower cab simulator. Besides surveillance displays and the OTW view, participants can also fixate on flight progress strips, digital timers, the ground controller's face, the counter top, their own hands or any other object visible in the lab from where the participant is sitting.

Approach end and
runway exits

Runway crossings and
departure end

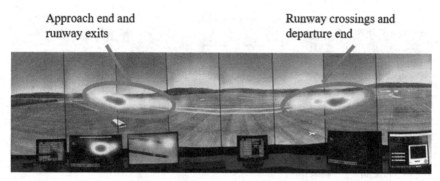

Fig. 3. Heat map indicating Hotspots frequently scanned by participants over 25 min scenario. Red indicates where participants were fixating the most with yellow indicating an intermediate number of fixations and green the least number of fixations. (Color figure online)

The use of transition matrices allowed us to determine what rules of thumb or general scanning techniques, were used by participants when they controlled simulated traffic. We analyzed the data to determine if the instructors were naturally using certain rules of thumb identified by the working group. One rule of thumb taught at the Academy, referred to here as Airfield-Out, states that one should prioritize looking at the airfield over looking further out into the airspace. Data regarding fixations at AOI associated with the airfield were aggregated as were AOI associated with areas considered "out". Airfield AOI included the ground surveillance display as well as the out the window view of the airport surface. AOI classified as associated with "out" included the radar display as well as airspace above the airport surface. We found that participants spent roughly twice as much time looking at AOI associated with Airfield than looking at AOI associated with Out. We examined the use of other rules of thumb as well. For more on those analyses we refer the reader to [13].

3.2 Associating Scanning Behavior with Performance

We collected two types of performance ratings during this study. One was an over the shoulder (OTS) rating technique and the other was performance at detecting off-nominal events. Three controller SMEs reviewed the video recording data from the fifteen participants, as they ran the Baseline scenario to provide group OTS ratings for each participant. To get the maximum number of points for a task, a participant had to be rated *'Outstanding'* at that task during the scenario. Some tasks were considered more critical than other tasks by SMEs and therefore worth more potential points. OTS task items for Separation were weighted by 16, Coordination (10) Control judgment (5), Methods & Procedures (5), and Communication (1) to provide an OTS score. OTS scores ranged from 61 to 162. Participants needed to score a 74 or above for their performance to be considered satisfactory. Subsequently, we dropped two participants from further analysis because those participants scored below Satisfactory in the Needs Improvement range.

The number of off-nominal events detected and time to detect the events were derived for the remaining participants. We found the time to detect events by using eye-tracking

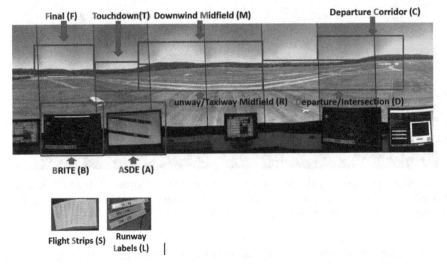

Fig. 4. Scene view picture overlaid with the Areas of Interest (AOIs) we defined.

video recordings, starting at the time the participants verbally responded to an event and viewing backward until the initiation of the participant's last fixation on the presentation of a target associated with the event. Then we subtracted the time of event onset from the time of fixation initiation. We provide a list of the events and the average time it took participants to detect them in Table 1.

We grouped the participants into low and high performing groups using the OTS ratings and again using their detection performance scores. We compared frequency of fixations at AOI of the high and low scoring groups. Regardless of the performance measure used, we found no significant differences between the two groups with regard to the use of any of the rules of thumb.

3.3   Identification of Scanning Patterns

Analyses of AOI and fixation transitions between the AOI also allowed us to identify specific visual scanning patterns used by participants as they controlled traffic. We conducted analyses to determine if individual controllers consistently repeated scanning patterns between AOI during scenarios and whether multiple controllers shared any of these scanning patterns in common. We assumed that if scanning patterns reoccurred across high performing participants, then these patterns would be clear candidates for patterns that should be taught to novice controllers. Questionnaire data we collected suggested that controllers might use different patterns when they carry out different ATC tasks. Therefore, we decided to focus our search for patterns on eye-movements that occurred within 30 s of four common ATC clearance types. The four clearances were Cleared for Takeoff, Cleared to Land, Line Up and Wait, and Hold Short. We examined eye-movements for ten instances of each clearance type for four participants selected both for their performance ratings and the quality of the gaze sample collected.

Table 1. Time to detect off-nominal events

Off-nominal events	Average detection time [MM:SS]	Number of times detected	ATC detection description
Smoking engine on approach	1:58	12	Asked aircraft if needed assistance; cleared aircraft to land
Line up to land on wrong runway	1:59	11	Repeated RWY instructions and emphasized over the numbers; Left base or Left downwind to correct aircraft
Noncompliant ground vehicle	0:33	10	Asked Ground if talking to vehicle; and or pointed at truck
Flock of birds	0:42	12	Cautioned aircraft; announced flock of birds; and or pointed to birds
Aborted takeoff	0:14	12	Asked aircraft intentions; instructed to exit taxiway and or hold short
Taxi to wrong runway	3:24	11	Instructed aircraft for movement and to contact Ground

Researchers at Oklahoma University painstakingly compared sequences of AOI to find reoccurring transitions. They visualized the results by superimposing them on top of scene view pictures with demarcated AOI. We present an example of this in Fig. 5 for the Cleared to Land clearance. We found that participants used different patterns before issuing each of the four selected clearances, but that eye-movement sequences did reoccur for participants within each clearance.

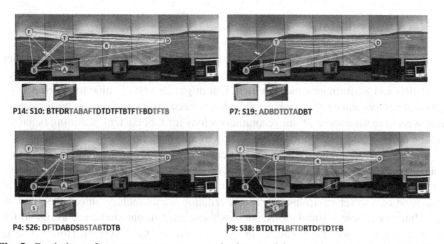

P14: S10: BTFDRTABAFTDTDTFTBTFTFBDTFTB   P7: S19: ADBDTDTADBT

P4: S26: DFTDABDSBSTABTDTB   P9: S38: BTDLTFLBFTDRTDFTDTFB

Fig. 5. Depictions of eye-movement sequences for four participants 30 s prior to issuing the Clear to Land clearance.

Researchers at OU also conducted a network analysis to see how similar patterns were across the ten instances and across the four different participants. We provide an example network for the Cleared to Land clearance in Fig. 6. Although there were some scanning sequence similarities between participants, there were more similarities within a given participant's scanning sequences.

C14: **Blue**   C7: **Yellow** C4: **Cyan**   C9: **Red**
(C14 is controller 14. S1~S10 are the 10 samples from controller 14.)

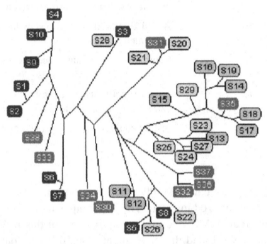

Fig. 6. Network analysis of eye-movement sequences prior to ten instances of the Cleared to Land clearance for four participants (indicated by the four different colors). (Color figure online)

4 Recommendations

We conducted our study to inform the content of tools designed to teach tower controller scanning skills. Additionally, there were lessons learned during our use of immersive simulation and performance measurement that might also be of value to developers of tools that will present a simulation to students and need to measure student performance. Here we summarize some of our recommendations for tool content, scanning behavior that the tools should teach, and for measuring trainee performance.

It is possible for a tool to teach the principles of scanning without a live simulation of an airport environment. We assume, however, that for a tool to enable trainees to have practice in the use of these principles it will require an interactive and operationally valid simulation of a tower environment. This simulation would include an out-the-window view. Immersive tower simulations, such as those used in our study, are available for use in training at most FAA Towers in the National Airspace System. However, it is possible that a scanning training tool will use a head mounted VR simulation of a tower cab instead. Advantages of VR systems include the smaller physical footprint of such a head mounted system versus the multiple large screens used in today's simulators, as well as being potentially powerful tools for evaluation of trainee scanning in real or near real time. Regardless of the platform, our results suggest that it is important to include representations of surveillance displays (such as radar and ground surveillance displays), flight progress strips, and an out-the-window view. The out-the-widow view should include all the hot spots and AOI that participants fixated during our study. It would also be helpful to include operational examples of why the hot spots are critical to scan frequently. For example, the airport represented should include crossing runways or necessitate the use of runway crossings that allow for traffic conflicts. Areas depicted should at least include the airspace of the Final, the touchdown and departure ends of the runway, the runway midfield, and runway exits and crossings.

A successful training tool would teach the trainees to use the general scanning behaviors of expert controllers. These general scanning behaviors include scanning both inside and outside the tower cab, and fixating most often on hotspots particularly those on the airport surface, prior to scanning the surrounding airspace. The tool should train to give the appropriate amount of emphasis to scanning the airfield over scanning airspace further out from the runways as well. The tool should teach trainees the need to use different scanning patterns in the performance of different ATC tasks. These patterns should efficiently provide the information that each ATC task requires for successful completion. Finally, the tool should encourage the trainees to practice using these scan patterns consistently.

We used eye-tracker recordings together with custom behavior rating forms as a way of ranking the performance of our participants. A similar approach may be useful for training tools that use VR. Some VR systems allow observers not wearing the head mounted displays to see what the person using them sees and where they are looking. A system like this would theoretically allow an instructor to directly observe if a trainee is scanning the AOI they should be scanning for a given task. Furthermore, some VR systems incorporate the use of gaze control and are thus theoretically capable of capturing and recording when users look at certain areas in the virtual environment automatically. This could aid the scoring process by enabling the system to create an objective performance score the instructor can use along with other scores to evaluate a trainee's progress. In the same manner we used off-nominal event detection, VR simulation scenarios could include off-nominal air traffic events and measure the time it takes trainees to respond to the events as well.

Our analyses were successful at identifying patterns and we found that each controller is likely to have patterns that they use consistently. We also found that different controllers used different sets of patterns. It was not possible, however, to link particular scanning patterns to performance. Therefore, a question remains as to whether novice controllers should be taught specific patterns and if so, which one pattern, per controller task, represents the optimal pattern trainees should be taught to use. Our results identified a number of representative scanning patterns but they also provided a useful characterization of expert scanning behavior. Based on those general scanning characteristics, a viable alternative to teaching a single set of patterns, might be developed. This alternative would be to teach trainees to develop and consistently use their own scanning patterns. Furthermore, instructors would provide trainees with the necessary knowledge and tools, including example patterns from those collected in this study, to develop their own effective patterns.

5 Discussion

We found collecting eye-tracking data from controller SMEs, as they control high fidelity simulations of air traffic, to be an effective way to learn about expert controller scanning behavior. A better understanding of controller visual scanning is needed to inform the development of enhanced controller training tools. To date we have used objective data to validate and quantify the behavior taught in current training curriculum including the frequent visual coverage of safety critical hot spots and the airfield-out rule of thumb. We have added to our knowledge of scanning by also determining that controllers use different scanning patterns for different ATC tasks and they tend to use the same scanning patterns repeatedly. We also discovered that different controllers use different scanning patterns. Although this finding is not surprising, it presents a challenge to the prospect of selecting a single set of patterns to teach novices to use particularly given that our performance measures have not been powerful enough to detect differences between the performances of highly experienced air traffic controllers. In this paper we summarized some of these findings and included lessons learned using immersive simulation and eye-tracking technology that might also prove valuable toward the simulation training tool development effort. For example, the SMEs that conducted our OTS performance rating found the ability to discern where participants being evaluated are looking to be useful for the evaluation of scanning behavior. As VR systems also provide this capability it may be a feature worth considering when selecting among tools.

Researchers from OU and CAMI have also been looking at scanning behavior in a radar control environment [14]. We are currently starting a study to evaluate the effectiveness of a prototype training tool for teaching trainees to use the scanning patterns of expert en route controllers. Simulation of a radar display is in many ways less complex than simulation of a tower cab environment. Nevertheless, we believe the results of this study provide useful information about how scanning patterns can be effectively trained, in the tower environment as well.

Our research has gone on to collect eye-tracking data from current front line tower controllers as they controlled air traffic simulations of the airport tower at which they currently worked. We are analyzing this eye-tracking data in the same way as described above to inform about general scanning behavior and to identify similarities across scanning patterns that are used. There may be many important reasons for controllers to develop different scanning patterns. Although we attempt to make our findings generic by categorizing the AOI into information sources that are found at all airports, there are differences between airport control towers that may impact scanning needs. Furthermore, individual differences in the cognitive abilities of controllers, such as working memory span, may lead individual controllers to adjust their span to leverage or moderate their cognitive abilities accordingly. We plan to continue our studies together with controllers and ATC instructors to determine what enhanced scanning training elements would be most effective.

Acknowledgements. This research was supported and funded by the FAA NextGen Organization's Human Factors Division, ANG-C1. The FAA Technical Sponsor was the Air Traffic Organization's Safety and Technical Training Service Unit's Policy and Performance Division, Safety Performance Group, Human Performance Team (AJI-342).

References

1. Hilburn, B.: Head down time in aerodrome operations: a scope study. EUROCONTROL. Center for Human Performance Research, Brétigny-sur-Orge (2004)
2. Pinska, E.: Warsaw tower observations. Experimental Centre Note No. 02/07. EUROCONTROL, Brétigny-sur-Orge (2007)
3. Pinska, E., Tijus, C.: Augmented reality technology for control tower analysis of applicability based on the field study. In: Proceedings of the 1st CEAS European Air and Space Conference, pp. 573–580 (2007)
4. Federal Aviation Administration: FAA Air Traffic Control Operations Concepts Volume 7: ATCT Tower Controllers (DOT/FAA/AP-87-0). http://www.dtic.mil/dtic/tr/fulltext/u2/a21 0455.pdf
5. Durso, F.T., Johnson, B.R., Crutchfield, J.M.: Dimensions of air traffic control tower information needs: from information requests to display design. J. Exp. Psychol. Appl. **16**(3), 219–237 (2010)
6. Ellis, S.R., Liston, D.B.: Static and motion-based visual features used by airport tower controllers: some implications for the design of remote or virtual towers. NASA/TM—2011–216427. National Aeronautics and Space Administration, Moffett Field, California (2011)
7. Abich, J., Parker, J., Murphy, J.S., Eudy, M.: A review of the evidence for training effectiveness with virtual reality technology. Virtual Reality **25**(4), 919–933 (2021). https://doi.org/10.1007/s10055-020-00498-8
8. Kaplan, A.D., Cruit, J., Endsley, M., Beers, S.M., Sawyer, B., Hancock, P.A.: The effects of virtual reality, augmented reality, and mixed reality as training enhancement methods: a meta-analysis. Hum. Factors **63**(4), 706–726 (2020)
9. Li, W.C., Kearney, P., Braithwaite, G., Lin, J.J.H.: How much is too much on monitoring tasks? Visual scan patterns of single air traffic controller performing multiple remote tower operations. Int. J. Ind. Ergon. **67**, 135–144 (2018)
10. Manske, P.G., Schier, S.L.: Visual scanning in an air traffic control tower – a simulation study. In: 6th International Conference on Applied Human Factors and Ergonomics (AHFE 2015) and the Affiliated Conferences, AHFE 2015, vol. 3, pp. 3274–3279. Elsevier (2015)
11. Svensson, Å.: Air traffic controllers' work-pattern during air traffic control tower simulations: a eye-tracking study of air traffic controllers' eye-movements during arrivals. Linköping University Examiner. https://doi.org/10.1108/02686900410549457
12. Kang, Z., Crutchfield, J., Palma Fraga, R., Mandal, S.: Spatial-temporal cluster approach to discover visual scanning behaviors in virtual reality. In: Proceedings of the 21st International Symposium on Aviation Psychology, Corvallis, OR (2021)
13. Crutchfield, J., Kang, Z., Palma Fraga, R., Mandal, S.: Applying eye-tracking technology to explore the visual scanning practices of air traffic control tower controllers. In: Proceedings of the 21st International Symposium on Aviation Psychology, Corvallis, OR (2021)
14. Palma Fraga, R., Kang, Z., Crutchfield, J., Mandal, S.: Visual search and conflict mitigation strategies used by expert en route air traffic controllers. Aerospace **8**(7), 170 (2021)

A Civil Aircraft Cockpit Control Device Design Using Mixed Reality Device

Wei Guo[1($\boxtimes$)], Xiaoli Wang[1], Zhi Deng[1], and Hongpeng Li[2]

[1] COMAC Beijing Aircraft Technology Research Institute, Beijing, China
{guowei2,dengzhi2}@comac.cc
[2] Beijing Hongyu Feituo Technology Co., Ltd., Beijing, China

Abstract. Mixed Reality are considered enabling technologies for the Industry 4.0 paradigm. In this paper, the cockpit control device design and evaluation system based on mixed reality technology is established, which is suitable for rapid iteration in the initial stage of civil aircraft design. It can provide aircraft designers with a more efficient and realistic design environment. It also provides a user evaluation environment, allowing pilots to participate in the cockpit design at an early stage of the design. According to the operation task and operation pattern classifying of common control equipment in the cockpit, also determines the control unit from the industrial model to virtual reality model of the conversion process. The conversion process of the control device from industrial model to virtual reality model is determined. The paper also puts forward the design mode of double coordinate system based on design eye reference point and controller panel, which is suitable for the design process of civil aircraft cockpit. For the system, we also conducted a preliminary user research and analysis. The experimental and analysis results are used for the subsequent system design and upgrading. It provides useful guidance for the design of human-computer interaction interface in mixed reality environment.

Keywords: Cockpit control devices · Mixed reality · Civil aircraft

1 Introduction

As a complex human-computer interaction system, civil aircraft cockpit design is a long design process that requires repeated iterations, revisions and evaluations. According to the principles of human-centred design (HCD) ISO 9241-210 (2010) [1] and participatory design of interactive systems, it is crucial to involve end-users and other stakeholders in the design and evaluation of technological products. In the design process of the civil aircraft cockpit, by constructing virtual prototypes and engineering prototypes, users, that is, pilots, can participate in the design process as early as possible. The virtual prototype is a computer simulation of a physical product [2]. Engineering prototype refers to the prototype manufactured for verification test in the process of engineering development [3]. Both can be analyzed, tested and evaluated of human factors from all aspects of the program during the early stages of cockpit development.

© Springer Nature Switzerland AG 2022
J. Y. C. Chen and G. Fragomeni (Eds.): HCII 2022, LNCS 13318, pp. 196–207, 2022.
https://doi.org/10.1007/978-3-031-06015-1_14

The International Ergonomics Association has a standardized definition of human factor. "This is the scientific discipline concerned with the understanding of interactions among humans and other elements of a system, and the profession that applies theory, principles, data and methods to design in order to optimize human well-being and overall system performance" [4]. By providing an effective human-in-the-loop task assessment environment for designers and pilots, it can accelerate the design optimization process, reduce the cost of later design changes, and optimize the pilot's convenience of operation, so as to improve the overall cockpit operating efficiency.

The evaluation method of the desktop simulation is based on virtual prototype and digitized virtual human. First of all, the digitization of the geometric characteristics of the human body is realized through the digitized virtual human modeling technology. Secondly, using the technique of virtual driving and tracking to improve the Human Body Molding Technology [5]. The small sized inertial tracking measurement system or optical tracking measurement system is used to collect the pilot's motion data and attitude data. Thirdly, standardize the collected pilot data, and then transfer it to the virtual prototype of cockpit to reconstruct the model. Finally, the designer matches the relative position of the digitized virtual human and the digital cockpit to complete the accessibility evaluation and operation task evaluation under different conditions in the desktop virtual environment. Digital human models can be used for proactive analysis of human factors in design [6]. Although the desktop simulation method can help designers complete the layout design of cockpit, it cannot provide a man-machine interaction environment for designers to evaluate the interaction logic of man-machine interface. At the same time, desktop simulation cannot be used to evaluate the pilot's information processing mechanism. Designers cannot optimize the interactive design and error prevention design of cockpit man-machine interface according to the simulation results.

Physical prototypes such as engineering prototypes build a high fidelity interactive environment to support pilots to complete task-based human-system interaction evaluation. Some researchers have also added human physiological monitoring equipment, such as eye trackers [7] and electrocardiographs [8, 9], to the engineering prototype to study the pilot's mental workload during flight [10]. However, the physical prototype is expensive and time-consuming, which is not suitable for the early rapid iteration of cockpit design. In addition, due to the rapid development of civil aircraft onboard system technology and cockpit interaction technology, it is impossible to evaluate the availability of advanced interaction technology using relatively fixed physical prototypes.

Both prototypes are indispensable in the civil aircraft design process. However, none of them can realize the participatory design of the cockpit in the pre research stage. The evolution of virtual reality systems offers designers new options. In 1993, Kalawsky defined virtual reality (VR) technologies in order to provide human beings with the means of manipulation and sensory modalities [11]. It means that humans are able to manipulate objects (e.g. turn a steering wheel) and get sensory feedback (e.g. visual or auditory) [12].

From the mature development of virtual reality (VR) technology, augmented reality (AR) has been born, and the continuous improvement of technology and hardware has created the emergence of mixed reality (MR). Whatever which stage the three types of technology development may be, its core principles are based on the simulation, interaction and integration of the digital world and the real world. Because the mixed reality is based on the natural perception of human beings, it is essentially a what you see is what you get human-machine interaction interface [13].

Mixed reality systems combine real and virtual environments in a single interactive display [14]. Mixed reality has been widely applied in education, military, medical, entertainment, industry, construction and transportation fields, especially in industry. Mixed Reality are considered enabling technologies for the Industry 4.0 paradigm. Mixed Reality applications are also growing in popularity in aerospace field. With the commercialization of Mixed Reality, we expect this technology to be applied in R&D and design. With Head-Mounted Displays (HMD), finger tracking solutions and other interaction tools available, you can build a complete virtual reality interactive solution [15].

2   System Design

2.1   Classification of Cockpit Control Devices

The cockpit control device is a central component of the civil aircraft used by pilots to control aircraft. It is an important part of aircraft cockpit man-machine interface design. The controller needs to consider the rationality of the control layout position, the convenience of operation, the consistency of logic, the comfort of lighting and the visibility of indication in the design process. There are more than 300 controllers on various control panels in the cockpit of common trunk airliners (excluding keyboard) [16]. The difficulty for designers is how to reasonably distribute and arrange these control devices in an effective space without appearing crowded. In addition, the logic consistency of the control device is also the core of the control switch design. Logical consistency mainly means that the pilot can easily make judgments and choices based on certain principles during the flight process, so it will not cause flight accidents due to human error. Especially in the cockpit environment with static and dark design concept, the lighting design of the push button annunciator and the direction design of the toggle switches are the elements that can best reflect the consistency of control logic.

We have counted and classified the control devices and switching components used in the cockpit of civil aircraft in service. According to the type of control panel integrated switch, it can be divided into the following five types.

1. Push Button (PB)

The PB used in the cockpit is generally momentary type. The momentary PB has a single pole and is initially in an off state. When the operator presses the push button switch, it changes to on.

2. Push Button Annunciator (PBA)

PBA is LED illuminated push button switches. The PBA includes two types: alternate and momentary. The PBA mainly has two kinds of display logic. First, the push switch with light does not work when it is not pressed, and the corresponding system works when it is pressed. This logic can feed back the system operation status to the pilot in real time. Second, when each system works normally, the man-machine control interface does not prompt or display the working state of the system. When there is any prompt tone or light on the PBA, it means that the system has failed. At this time, the pilot needs to operate the illuminated PBA to remove the fault.

3. Toggle switches

Toggle switches shall be used for applications in which two or three selection positions are required. When the system has special requirements, the designer will add a switch guard or use the cat-eye handle.

4. Rotary Switches and Encoders.

Rotary switches include three types of multi-position rotary switches, single-deck potentiometers and double-deck potentiometers. Multi-position switches are selected when system control requires several discrete selection positions, such as system of main and standby switching or manual and automatic mode selection. Designers will select single deck potentiometers to realize continuous adjustment of the system, such as aircraft heading adjustment. Double-deck potentiometers is generally used for continuous adjustment of two related attributes. The purpose is to facilitate the pilot's operation, strengthen the memory of switch position and optimize the cockpit layout. When the system needs special requirements, some rotary switches and encoders also have selection ability by pressing. For example, altitude knob of the automatic flight system control panel (AFS CP). The outer knob has two positions: 100 and 1000, to set the target altitude increments of 100ft or 1000ft. When the inter knob turned, sets the target altitude. When pulled, activates the target altitude.

5. User-defined.

User-defined switches, such as landing gear control lever, flap/slat control lever, engine fuel cut-off switch etc., and their selections shall be in accordance with the applicable requirements of the systems.

The implementation methods of control devices in virtual environment are distinguished according to the task types and evaluation contents of control devices. The first four categories are realized by virtual reality, and all the design and evaluation are completed in the virtual reality environment. For the user-defined controller, virtual reality is used in the early design to evaluate the shape and function. In the later stage, the controller entity is constructed by using 3D printing. The combination of entity and virtual reality model forms a Mixed reality environment, which is used to evaluate the controller position, operation load, operation accuracy and so on.

2.2 Model Construction

CATIA software is the control device model design tool of choice for designers and suppliers in the aerospace industry. CATIA displays the superiority in dealing with shape design. The model built by CATIA is a Non-Uniform Rational B-Splines (NURBS) model. NURBS model needs tessellation to enter the mixed reality development engine, that is, converted to polygon model. In the conversion process, in order to maintain the accurate shape, a large number of faces will be generated, so it is necessary to reduce the face of the model. In addition to using the existing tessellation software, we also to re topology the existing polygon model. Physically-Based Rendering (PBR) process is adopted to realize the basecolor, metallic, roughness and normal of materials. The controller light is constructed by using emissive map. After the model is built, it is imported into Unreal Engine 4 (UE4) [17] in the form of FBX file, in order to improve their degree of verisimilitude and absorbing feel (Fig. 1).

Fig. 1. Comparison before and after model treatment

2.3 Coordinate System Selection

Its core goal is to ensure the pilot's vision in the process of civil aircraft cockpit design. The design eye position, also known as eye datum or design eye reference point (DERP) is used to size the cockpit windows and define the location of all the controls, displays and instruments [18]. In the process of system design, design eye reference point is used as the coordinate origin. Its advantage is that it conforms to the positioning habits of traditional aviation designers and is convenient for designers to use. And, it is in line with the characteristics of accessing the virtual reality world of the head mounted display (HMD).

Based on DERP as the coordinate origin, we constructed the dual coordinate system of XYZ rectangular coordinates and spherical coordinate system. In addition, a plane rectangular coordinate system based on the plane of the controller panel is also provided as an auxiliary coordinate system. Thus, the controller realizes the design based on double coordinate system.

We define the DERP of the left pilot (the main pilot), as the origin of the coordinate system. Visual front, that is, the heading direction is the positive direction of the x-axis, the left side is the y-axis, and the positive direction of the z-axis is vertical upward. In this work, following the mathematics convention [19], the symbols for the radial, azimuth, and zenith angle coordinates are taken as r, θ, and ϕ, respectively. Define θ to be the azimuthal angle in the xy-plane from the x-axis with $0 \leq \theta < 2\pi$, ϕ to be the polar angle (also known as the zenith angle and colatitude) from the positive z-axis with $0 \leq \theta < 2\pi$, and r to be distance (radius) from the center point of controller interaction surface to the origin. In addition, we also provide a method to convert the cockpit origin coordinate system into the whole aircraft coordinate system.

The auxiliary coordinate system is established based on the controller plane. The control panels are all located in the first quadrant of the auxiliary coordinate system.

Provide the designer with the relative position of the plane geometric center of the controller in this coordinate system.

With the aid of multiple coordinate system, it is convenient for designers to determine the position of the controller and judge various constraints of the position of the controller. For example, the accessibility of the operating device is judged by the r value. The designer judges the viewing angle of the identification text on the operating device by the θ, and ϕ value to determine the visibility of the control device.

2.4 Implementation Scheme

We refer to different visualization solutions and mixed reality spatial positioning solutions [20–22]. The scheme adopted by the standard is based on virtual reality equipment and hand tracking and positioning equipment. The use of hand tracking and positioning equipment enables users to observe their hands in the virtual scene, so as to complete the manipulation of the equipment. At the same time, the virtual reality equipment is used to calibrate the physical environment equipment, and the spatial coordinate transformation of the virtual model equipment is carried out in the virtual scene to realize the combination of virtual and real. We also establish a communication mechanism for the system to drive and trigger the model elements in the virtual reality environment by external signals.

3 Test

3.1 Conditions of Subjects

10 subjects are involved in the test aging from 27 to 36 years old, of which 7 males and 3 females. All subjects were divided into two groups. 5 subjects in group A had previous experience of using head-mounted display (HMD) devices for gaming or research, 5 in group B had no experience of VR/MR applications. There are 3 subjects in each group who understand the design process of the cockpit control device. Other subjects had flight simulation experience.

3.2 Test Equipment and Environment

We used HTC's Vive Pro Eye and integrated a Leap Motion Controller on the headset. In this setup, the position and orientation of the headset in the virtual scene are controlled through the SteamVR Tracking system. After the virtual reality equipment is calibrated, the hand tracking equipment needs to be calibrated with the target equipment. In order to fully match the physical environment with the virtual scene, we build a 1:1 accurate 3D model based on the existing sidestick.

3.3 Test Design

Test mainly focuses on the availability of the cockpit control device design and evaluation system in mixed reality. The two independent variables of the experiment are Group and

Design. The experiment requires the subjects to complete two tasks in a mixed reality environment. First, operate PBA and knob to complete temperature regulation. The second item is to complete the sidestick control test.

Specific implementations of the test are as follows:

1. Check the of PBA in the control panel.
2. Press to turn off the "off" light on the PBA (see Fig. 2 and Fig. 3).
3. Turn the knob to adjust to the specified temperature.
4. Find and hold the sidestick (see Fig. 4).
5. Complete push and pull rod operation according to instructions (corresponding to aircraft pitching operation).
6. Complete left and right lever operation according to instructions (corresponding to aircraft roll operation).
7. End the experiment.

Fig. 2. The "off" light on PBA is on

Fig. 3. The "off" light on PBA is off

Fig. 4. Sidestick.

3.4 Design Feedback

Questionnaires were used as data collection method in this semi-structured experiment. Participant demographics and consent forms were collected first. The subjects were given a questionnaire asking for their feedback on design at the end of the experiment. We use scores on a Likert scale from 1 (poor) to 5 (excellent) on the following a questionnaire.

The setting of questionnaire is shown in Table 1.

Table 1. Questionnaire

Num.	Question	Survey Scale: 1 = Poor 2 = Fair 3 = Good 4 = Very Good 5 = Excellent				
Q1	How well were you adapt to the virtual environment?	1	2	3	4	5
Q2	How well does the behavior in the virtual environment match your expected behavior?	1	2	3	4	5
Q3	How satisfied are you with the design and feedback of PBA pressing operation? environment?	1	2	3	4	5

(*continued*)

Table 1. (*continued*)

Num.	Question	Survey Scale: 1 = Poor 2 = Fair 3 = Good 4 = Very Good 5 = Excellent				
Q4	How satisfied are you with the design and feedback of knob rotation operation?	1	2	3	4	5
Q5	How naturally you hold the sidestick?	1	2	3	4	5
Q6	How satisfied are you with the control feedback of the sidestick?	1	2	3	4	5
Q7	How much fluency do you feel about the system?	1	2	3	4	5
Q8	Besides this have you other suggestions?					

4 Results and Discussion

4.1 Statistical Methods

To analyze questionnaire responses, we used the independent-Sample T test and independent-Sample T test. Analysis was conducted using SPSS software. We report p-values for two-tailed tests. We report p-values below .05 as demonstrations of significance. Sample size was limited due in the particularity of the subjects' experience requirements.

In statistics, we classified the subjects. Statistics shall be carried out according to the following four categories.

- A: Subjects had previous experience of using HMD devices for gaming or research.
- B: Subjects had no experience of VR/MR applications.
- F: Subjects had rich flight experience or simulated flight experience.
- D: Subjects had previous experience of cockpit control device design.

4.2 Result Analysis

Q1 and Q2 mainly focus on the adaptability and operation ability of the subjects in the virtual environment. [Q1: A vs B, Sig. = 0.252, p = 0.096; Q2: A vs B, Sig. = 1.000, p < 0.05]. For the question about adaptability, a significant difference was no found between the A and B groups. For the question about operation ability, the group A was significantly larger than that reported by group B. The adaptability of virtual reality environment itself has low requirements for the experience of operators, but if operators are required to complete the specified operation tasks, they need to be trained in advance.

For the Q5, a significant difference was no found between the F and D groups. [Q5: F vs D, Sig. = 6.14, p < 0.05]. Designer (Mean value = 4.33) as significantly lower than that reported by group F (Mean value = 3.25). The main reason for this difference is that the sidestick is the most important control device to control the aircraft, so the pilot has very high requirements for the accuracy and texture of the sidestick. Designers pay more attention to the function realization of the sidestick.

For the question about press (Q3) operation and rotation operation (Q4), feedback of pressing operation significantly larger than that reported by rotation operation. [Q3 vs Q4, Q3 (mean value) = 4.1, Q4 (mean value) = 3.6, t = 3, p < 0.05]. The interactive design of rotation operation is more challenging than pressing operation in virtual reality environment. The system changes the angle of the knob by capturing the subtle position and angle changes of the tested fingers. The accuracy of the hand tracking and positioning equipment should be improved to improve the user experience. In addition, the operator will determine the type of knob through the shape of the cockpit knob. Users cannot perceive the shape of the knob through touch, which is also the reason for the low evaluation score.

A significant difference was no found between the operational feedback with and without entities [Q3 vs Q6, t = 0.429, p = 0.678; Q4 vs Q6, t = −1.50, p = 0.168]. This shows that it is acceptable for the subjects to adopt different implementation methods of VR and MR in the system.

4.3 Discussion

All subjects responded to the question about system aspects needing improvement. According to the communication with subjects and the answers to open-ended questions, the following experiences are summarized and put forward:

1. It is acceptable to complete the design and evaluation of knob, PBA and other control devices based on virtual environment. The evaluation content should not only be limited to the size, color, position and visibility of the control device, but also be more comprehensive, which can increase the design of control stroke and control type.
2. The feedback of controllers' design should improve the performance of tasks. Approximately half of subjects referred to haptic feedback.
3. The design interface and evaluation interface should be independent of each other. There are differences in concerns between designers and evaluators (flight cadets). Designers focus on the expression of design elements, while pilots pay more attention to the fidelity of the model and the response of control devices. Two subjects indicated that visual was not realistic enough.

5 Conclusions

This paper preliminarily puts forward the implementation scheme and test case of a civil aircraft cockpit control device design and evaluation system based on Mixed reality. The virtual cockpit design and evaluation environment is constructed based on UE4, and the transformation method from aviation industry model to virtual reality model is proposed. In addition, a dual coordinate system positioning method based on the spherical coordinate system of the DERP and the plane rectangular auxiliary coordinate system of the control panel is constructed. The communication between controller logic model and virtual reality model is realized, and the external trigger mechanism of virtual reality model feedback is established.

Through the test, it is clear that the design and evaluation method of virtual reality environment evaluation, simple feedback operating devices, such as pressing, rotating and complex operating devices, adopts the combination of virtual and real.

During the writing of the paper, we have begun to continuously develop and improve the system according to the opinions of the appraisers. Mainly around the following three aspects.

1. Add tactile feedback to the control device. For example, active tactile feedback mechanisms such as tactile feedback gloves are added.
2. Further improve the operation accuracy of control devices in the virtual environment and improve the overall manipulation experience of evaluators.
3. Develop the display interface in the cockpit, and the subsequent system will add the design and evaluation of the display interface (including touch screen).

References

1. EN ISO 9241-210:2010-10
2. Wang, G.G.: Definition and review of virtual prototyping. J. Comput. Inf. Sci. Eng. **2**(3), 232–236 (2002)
3. Joyce, R., Robinson, S.K.: Evaluation of a virtual reality environment for cockpit design. In: Proceedings of the Human Factors and Ergonomics Society Annual Meeting, vol. 63, no. 1, pp. 2328–2332 (2019)
4. IEA. Definition and Domains of Ergonomics (2000)
5. Yang, L.Q.: Summarization of human body molding technology development for man-machine engineering field. J. Acad. Armored Force Eng. **20**(2), 59–63 (2006)
6. Chaffin, D.B.: Improving digital human modelling for proactive ergonomics in design. Ergonomics **48**(5), 478–491 (2005). https://doi.org/10.1080/00140130400029191
7. Mohan, D.B., Jeevitha, S., Prabhakar, G., Saluja, K.S., Biswas, P.: Estimating pilots' cognitive load from ocular parameters through simulation and in-flight studies. J. Eye Mov. Res. **12**(3) (2019)
8. Ramacci, C.A., Ottalevi, A., Modugno, G., Meineri, G., Berti, R.: [Behavior of central critical fusion frequency of the retina and various cardiocirculatory parameters (ECG, humeral arterial pressure and heart rate) in military jet pilots before and after operational flight]. Riv. Med. Aeronaut. Spaz. **47**(1–4), 55–64 (1982)
9. Mohino-Herranz, I., Gil-Pita, R., Ferreira, J., Rosa-Zurera, M., Seoane, F.: Assessment of mental, emotional and physical stress through analysis of physiological signals using smartphones. Sensors **15**(10), 25607–25627 (2015)
10. Gentili, R.J., Rietschel, J.C., Jaquess, K.J., Lo, L.C., Hatfield, B.D.: Brain biomarkers based assessment of cognitive workload in pilots under various task demands. In: Conference on Proceedings of IEEE Engineering in Medicine and Biology Society (2014)
11. Kalawsky, R.S., Wesley, A.: The Science of Virtual Reality and Virtual Environments. Addison Wesley Longman Publishing Co., Inc., Boston (1993)
12. Aromaa, S., Väänänen, K.: Suitability of virtual prototypes to support human factors/ergonomics evaluation during the design. Appl. Ergon. **56**, 11–18 (2016)

13. Chen, B., Qin, X.: Composition of virtual-real worlds and intelligence integration of human-computer in mixed reality. Sci. China (Inf. Sci) **46**(12), 11 (2016)
14. Borst, C., Volz, R.: Evaluation of a haptic mixed reality system for interactions with a virtual control panel. Presence **14**(6), 677–696 (2005)
15. Lee, L.H., Hui, P.: Interaction methods for smart glasses: a survey. IEEE Access **6**, 28712–28732 (2018)
16. Tian, G.: Research on the human factors Design principle of A380 aircraft based on Reverse engineering methods Civil Aviation Flight University of China (2013)
17. https://www.unrealengine.com/zh-CN/
18. Wang, Y., Guo, X., Liu, Q., Xiao, H., Bai, Y.: Three-dimensional measurement applied in design eye point of aircraft cockpits. Aerosp. Med. Hum. Perform. **89**(4), 371–376 (2018)
19. https://mathworld.wolfram.com/SphericalCoordinates.html
20. Caputo, A., Jacota, S., Krayevskyy, S., Pesavento, M., Giachetti, A.: XR-Cockpit: a comparison of VR and AR solutions on an interactive training station. In: ETFA 2020: IEEE International Conference on Emerging Technologies and Factory Automation, ETFA 2020 (2020)
21. Hattori, K., Hirai, T.: Inside-out tracking controller for VR/AR HMD using image recognition with smartphones. In: SIGGRAPH 2020: Special Interest Group on Computer Graphics and Interactive Techniques Conference (2020)
22. Kress, B.C., Cummings, W.J.: 11-1: invited paper: towards the ultimate mixed reality experience: HoloLens display architecture choices. In: SID Symposium Digest of Technical Papers, vol. 48, no. 1 (2017)

Comparing the Effect of Airflow Direction on Simulator Sickness and User Comfort in a High-Fidelity Driving Simulator

Elizaveta Igoshina[1,2,3], Frank A. Russo[1,2,3], Bruce Haycock[1,3], and Behrang Keshavarz[1,2(✉)]

[1] KITE-Toronto Rehabilitation Institute, UHN, Toronto, ON M5G 2A2, Canada
behrang.keshavarz@uhn.ca
[2] Ryerson University, Toronto, ON M5B 2K3, Canada
[3] University of Toronto, Toronto, ON L5L 1C6, Canada

Abstract. Minimizing simulator sickness is crucial for ensuring the well-being of users and for guaranteeing the integrity of driving performance data. Here, we compared the effect of direct and indirect airflow as potential countermeasures against simulator sickness in a high-fidelity driving simulator, further exploring the relationship between airflow, body temperature, and subjective comfort. Twenty-three healthy adults completed a 25 km simulated drive (incl. 1.7 km practice) while their simulator sickness level was monitored. To study the effects of airflow direction on simulator sickness, the car's vents were positioned to either generate airflow directly to the driver's torso and head (*direct airflow condition*) or towards the vehicle's ceiling avoiding any contact with the driver (*indirect airflow condition*). Results suggested that simulator sickness did not differ between the two airflow conditions. Body temperature was lower in the indirect compared to the direct airflow condition, but no significant correlations with simulator sickness were observed. Overall, participants reported a higher level of comfort when airflow was directed to the car's ceiling, suggesting that indirect airflow may be the favoured setting for driving simulation studies.

Keywords: Motion sickness · Driving simulation · Airflow · Temperature

1 Background

Driving simulators have become a valuable asset for research, rehabilitation, and training purposes. However, they are also known to persistently cause simulator sickness [1–4], a phenomenon similar to traditional motion sickness [5–7]. Signs and symptoms of simulator sickness include, but are not limited to, (cold) sweating, pallor, disorientation, dizziness, eyestrain, and nausea [2, 4, 8]. Simulator sickness increases user discomfort and often results in users prematurely terminating a driving simulation session. In addition, the presence of simulator sickness may bias driving performance results and alter intended outcomes [9, 10], demonstrating the need for novel solutions that can successfully preventing or minimize simulator sickness.

© Springer Nature Switzerland AG 2022
J. Y. C. Chen and G. Fragomeni (Eds.): HCII 2022, LNCS 13318, pp. 208–220, 2022.
https://doi.org/10.1007/978-3-031-06015-1_15

Several theories try to explain the underlying causes of simulator sickness (see [8, 11] for overviews), with the sensory conflict theory being arguably most frequently cited. According to this theory, a mismatch of information received from the visual, vestibular, and proprioceptive senses can generate simulator sickness [5, 12]. In a fixed-base simulator, for instance, the eyes convey the sensation of self-motion (or vection, [13, 14]), whereas the vestibular and proprioceptive senses signal stasis. If this situation is new to the user and the individual has not yet adapted to the novel, simulated environment, simulator sickness may occur [12]. From an evolutionary perspective, it has been argued that this sensory conflict is reminiscent of an intoxication of the body, triggering biological defense mechanisms that aim to slow down the spread of the toxin and ultimately expel it from the body, which may explain the nature of the observed symptoms of simulator sickness (e.g., increased stomach activity with nausea/vomiting) [15].

A variety of non-pharmacological strategies for reducing simulator sickness have been previously proposed, including music [16, 17], postural restraint [18, 19], or vibrations [20, 21]. Although some of these treatments delivered promising results, none of these methods were able to fully reduce simulator sickness, highlighting the need for further improved countermeasures. In a recent study [22], providing constant airflow to passive observers of a motion sickness-inducing video has been shown to successfully reduce the severity of motion sickness by almost 50%. However, two important questions remain unanswered. First, it needs to be determined whether airflow is also effective in reducing simulator sickness in more complex situations that actively engage participants, such as being involved in a simulated driving task. Second, the underlying mechanisms of how airflow reduces simulator sickness remain unclear and may involve the role of body temperature [23–25]. It has been anecdotally reported that individuals experiencing simulator/motion sickness often report an increased feeling of warmth and seek ways to cool themselves. Interestingly, it has also been documented that core body temperature actually decreases during motion sickness [26, 27], resulting in hypothermia, which might be the result of the body's attempt to deal with the initial feeling of warmth experienced at the early stages of motion sickness. Providing airflow may either expedite this cooling process and/or prevent feeling hot in the first place, which may alleviate simulator sickness.

The primary goal of the present study was to further examine airflow as a potential countermeasure against simulator sickness in a high-fidelity driving simulator by addressing two research questions. First, we aimed to determine whether airflow directed towards the driver's torso and face is more effective in reducing simulator sickness than airflow directed to the ceiling of the car avoiding any contact with the driver's skin. We hypothesized that airflow contacting the driver's skin is more effective in reducing simulator sickness as it cools the skin and may counteract the initial feeling of warmth accompanying simulator sickness onset. Second, we wanted to enhance our knowledge of how body temperature and the associated level of comfort change as a consequence of simulator sickness. Based on previous research [26, 27], we hypothesized that participants experiencing simulator sickness would show a decrease in body temperature compared to those who with no simulator sickness.

2 Method

2.1 Participants

Twenty-three[1] healthy participants (13 female, 10 male; mean age of 24 years) were engaged in a simulated driving task. All participants were healthy, younger adults with no self-reported recent history of stroke or brain injury, epilepsy or seizures, active vestibular disorder(s), acute psychiatric disorder(s), or dementia or mild cognitive impairment. They were told to refrain from drinking alcohol 24 h before the study and from consuming marijuana 72 h before the study. All participants fluently spoke English, had normal or corrected-to-normal vision (visual acuity measured via a Snellen Chart Eye test and a dynamic visual acuity test), and a valid Canadian driver's license with 2 or more years of driving experience. All participants gave written informed consent prior to the study which was approved by the Research Ethics Boards of the University Health Network and Ryerson University. Participants were recruited from the KITE-Toronto Rehabilitation Institute, Ryerson University, and the broader community. Participants were compensated with a 15$ gift card as a token of appreciation for their time commitment to the study. Participants were free to withdraw their participation at any time during the experiment without penalty.

2.2 Study Design

A one-factorial, between-subjects design including the factor airflow condition (direct, indirect) was chosen. Accordingly, participants were randomly assigned to one of two experimental conditions. For one group (n = 11), the car's vents were directed towards the driver's head and torso to provide the sensation of airflow on the parts of uncovered skin of their face and torso (*direct airflow condition*). For the other group (n = 12), the car's vents were pointed towards the cars' ceiling avoiding contact with the participants' skin (*indirect airflow condition*). In both experimental groups, airflow remained turned on continuously throughout the drive to ensure constant ambient room temperature of the car (approx. 22 °C)[2]. To avoid differences in temperature perception due to clothing, all participants were asked to dress in a single layer with short sleeves such as a t-shirt.

2.3 Stimuli and Apparatus

This study was conducted at the KITE-Toronto Rehabilitation Institute, University Health Network, using DriverLab, the most-advanced driving simulator in Canada located at KITE (Fig. 1). DriverLab is a dome-shaped VR laboratory equipped with

---

[1] Note that data collection had to be terminated prematurely due to the COVID-19 pandemic and associated disruptions in research at KITE-UHN, resulting in a smaller sample size than originally anticipated. No sex-related difference showed in any of the simulator sickness measures and, given the small sample size, are not further reported here.

[2] Ambient temperature inside the car was recorded during the drive using a thermistor sensor placed in the back of the driver's seat. Due to recording issues, ambient room temperature data could not be recorded for 7 participants, we therefore do not include this measure in the data analysis.

a full-sized passenger car (Audi A3) that has most of its original components (e.g., steering wheel, gas/brake pedals, seats, and dashboard). Twelve projectors created a seamless, 360° visual field that offered an immersive VR experience. A turntable provided full physical rotations of the car about the yaw axis during turning maneuvers or when changing lanes. No other motion cues were present.

Fig. 1. Picture of *DriverLab* showing the passenger car mounted on the turntable and surrounded by a seamless, curved projection screen.

Participants completed a 25 km long simulated drive (23.3 km experimental, 1.7 km practice drive) including equidistant city, highway, and rural sections. The drive was designed using AVSimulation SCANeRStudio and resembled a typical Canadian environment and landscape, mimicking a drive from a busy downtown location to a rural community. A variety of events such as overtaking a slow-moving vehicle or reacting to pedestrians suddenly crossing the street were included to captured driving-related measures[3]. Participants drove during simulated daytime with clear weather conditions and the weather changed to simulated nighttime and rain for the last section of the part of the drive. Participants were asked to drive as they would normally do while obeying traffic rules. There was no break in-between the practice and experimental drive.

2.4 Dependent Measures

Simulator Sickness Measures. Simulator sickness was measured using the Fast Motion Sickness Scale (FMS) [28] and the Simulator Sickness Questionnaire (SSQ) [29]. The FMS is a subjective rating scale ranging from 0 (*no sickness*) to 20 (*severe sickness*) and was assessed during the simulated driving session every minute to obtains real-time changes in simulator sickness severity. The peak FMS score (i.e., the highest FMS score reported during the simulated drive) was used to estimate participants' level of simulator sickness experienced during the driving session. The SSQ is a standardized questionnaire that consists of 16 items capturing a broad range of symptoms scored on a 4-point scale ranging from 0 (*not at all*) to 3 (*severe*). Three sub-scores (nausea,

---

[3] Note that driving performance metrics were collected but are not of relevance in the context of the present publication. These results will be reported elsewhere.

oculomotor, disorientation) and a total score can be derived. Both the FMS and SSQ are common measurement tools that have been widely used in simulator sickness studies. The peak FMS score and the SSQ scores have been shown to correlate strongly with each other [28].

Objective Temperature Measures. Participants' body temperature was measured using a touchless infrared forehead thermometer before and after the driving task. Five temperature readings were recorded one minute apart starting 5 min prior to the simulated drive, and five temperature readings were recorded one minute apart immediately following the simulated drive. For data analysis, the average temperatures from the five temperature readings before and after the driving session were calculated. In addition, participants' facial skin temperature was recorded throughout the driving session using a thermistor attached to the left temple of the participant's head.

Subjective Temperature and Comfort Ratings. Subjective ratings on perceived body/room temperature and associated comfort level were collected before and after experimentation using a customized Subjective Temperature Questionnaire (STQ). The STQ consisted of four questions that measured participants' subjective perception of their body temperature and the room temperature ($-4 = $ *very cold*; $0 = $ *neutral*; $+4 = $ *very hot*) and the perceived comfort level associated with their body and room temperature ($-3 = $ *very uncomfortable*; $0 = $ *neutral*; $+3 = $ *very comfortable*).

2.5 Procedure

Participants were first screened for their eligibility to participate in this study and then provided written consent. Prior to the drive, while seated inside the driving simulator, participants completed the STQ and the SSQ and their body temperature readings were collected from the forehead. A short practice drive allowed participants to familiarize themselves with the car's operation and get used to the study setup. Participants then completed the experimental driving session, where they were prompted to report their FMS score every minute. In addition, participants were instructed to report their FMS score if there was a change in their FMS score between prompts. The experiment was terminated either after completion of the simulated drive or if participants reported a score of 10 on the FMS scale to prevent severe sickness and to minimize the risk for potential after-effects. Immediately after the drive, participants filled out the STQ and the SSQ and their body temperature was measured at their forehead again. Participants remained under the experimenter's care until any simulator sickness symptoms had subsided and they felt fine to leave the laboratory.

2.6 Data Analysis

To investigate the effects of airflow on simulator sickness, a one-way MANOVA including the between-subjects factor airflow condition (direct, indirect) was conducted for all simulator sickness measures (peak FMS score and all SSQ scores). Pearson correlations were calculated to explore the relationship between changes in facial skin/body temperature (i.e., difference in temperature post- vs. pre-drive) and simulator sickness measures.

To further analyze the effect of airflow on temperature measures (facial skin/body temperature, SQT), mixed factorial ANOVAs including the within-subjects factors time (pre-drive, post-drive) and the between-subjects factor airflow condition (direct, indirect) were calculated for each variable. For all statistical analysis, a priori significance level was set to alpha = .05. The software packages R and SPSS were used for data analysis.

3 Results

3.1 Airflow and Simulator Sickness

Three of the 23 participants (13%) aborted the experiment prior to completing the drive due to increased discomfort but were not excluded from the data analyses. Average scores for the SSQ subscales nausea, oculomotor, disorientation, and the SSQ total score as well as the peak FMS score separated by airflow condition are shown in Fig. 2. The MANOVA revealed no significant main effect of airflow condition, $F(5,17) = 1.52, p = .235$.

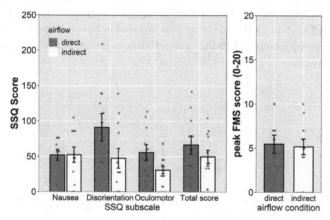

Fig. 2. SSQ scores (left) and peak FMS scores (right) separated by airflow condition. Error bars represent ± SEM, grey dots indicate individual scores.

3.2 Simulator Sickness and Objective Temperature Measures

To assess present associations between simulator sickness and facial skin/body temperature, Pearson correlations were calculated between all simulator sickness measures and changes in facial skin temperature and body temperature measures (i.e., difference in temperature post-drive compared to pre-drive; see Table 1). Results showed no significant correlations between facial skin temperature or body temperature changes with any of the simulator sickness measures.

Table 1. Pearson correlation coefficients for all simulator sickness measures and changes in facial skin/body temperature

Temperature	Simulator sickness measure				
	Peak FMS	SSQ N	SSQ O	SSQ D	SSQ TS
Facial skin	−.307	.141	.047	−.056	−.041
Body	−.154	−.027	.148	.163	−.078

Note: N = nausea, O = oculomotor, D = disorientation, TS = total score

The mean body temperature and facial skin temperature scores separated by airflow condition and time (pre-drive, post-drive) are given in Fig. 3. For body temperature, the mixed-factorial ANOVA revealed a significant main effect of time, $F(1,19) = 10.16$, $p = .005$, $\eta_p^2 = .349$, indicating that all participants had significantly decreased body temperature from pre to post-drive. A significant interaction between time and condition showed as well, $F(1,19) = 5.69$, $p = .028$, $\eta_p^2 = .23$, with post hoc tests (Bonferroni corrected) suggesting a significant drop in body temperature post-drive in the indirect airflow group, $t(10) = 3.625$, $p = .004$, but not in the direct airflow group (see Fig. 3). For facial skin temperature, a main effect of airflow condition was found, $F(1,17) = 14.80$, $p = .013$, $\eta_p^2 = .309$, indicating that facial skin temperature was lower in the direct airflow group compared to the indirect airflow group. No other main effect of interaction showed.

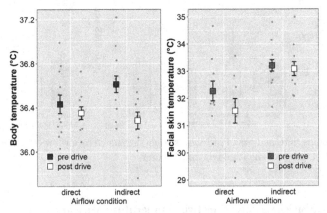

Fig. 3. Mean body temperature (left) and mean facial skin temperature (right) separated by airflow condition and time. Error bars represent ± SEM, grey dots indicate individual scores.

3.3 Simulator Sickness and Subjective Temperature and Comfort Ratings

Figure 4 shows the subjective ratings for body and room temperature before and after the driving task with respect to the different airflow conditions. For subjective body temperature ratings, the mixed-factorial ANOVA showed a significant main effect of airflow condition, $F(1,21) = 10.63$, $p = .004$, $\eta_p^2 = .336$, suggesting that body temperature was overall perceived as cooler in the direct airflow condition compared to the indirect airflow condition. Additionally, a significant interaction between time and airflow condition was found, $F(1,21) = 8.87$, $p = .007$, $\eta_p^2 = .297$. Post hoc tests (Bonferroni corrected) revealed a significant decrease in subjective body temperature from pre to post-drive in the direct airflow condition, $t(10) = 2.78$, $p = .019$, but not in the indirect airflow condition, $t(11) = -1.17$, $p = .266$. These results indicate that participants in the direct airflow condition felt significantly cooler post-drive when compared to participants in the indirect airflow condition who experienced no significant changes in subjective temperature perception.

For subjective room temperature ratings, the mixed-factorial ANOVA revealed a main effect of time, $F(1,21) = 17.76$, $p < .001$, $\eta_p^2 = .458$, indicating that the room temperature was overall rated as cooler post-drive compared to pre-drive. No other significant effect showed.

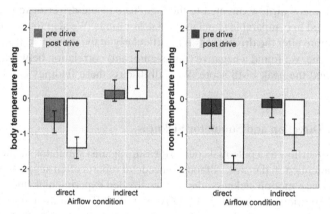

Fig. 4. Subjective body temperature (left) and room temperature (right) ratings compared pre and post drive, separated by airflow condition (direct, indirect). Error bars represent ± SEM.

Figure 5 shows the subjective ratings for body and room temperature comfort before and after the driving task with respect to the different airflow conditions. The mixed-factorial ANOVAs revealed a main effect of time for body temperature comfort, $F(1,21) = 15.93$, $p = .001$, $\eta_p^2 = .431$, and room temperature comfort ratings, $F(1,21) = 15.47$, $p < .001$, $\eta_p^2 = .424$, indicating a reduction in comfort ratings post-drive compared to pre-drive. No other effect was significant.

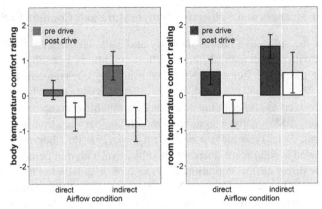

Fig. 5. Subjective body comfort (left) and room comfort (right) ratings compared pre and post drive, separated by airflow condition (direct, indirect). Error bars represent ± SEM.

4 Discussion

The present study investigated the role of airflow direction on simulator sickness and its relationship to body and facial skin temperature. Our findings suggested that both airflow conditions – airflow directed to the torso/face of the driver or to the ceiling of the car – resulted in comparable simulator sickness ratings. We also found a decrease in body temperature after the driving session, particularly in the indirect airflow condition. At the same time, we found a negative (non-significant) correlation between facial skin temperature and the peak FMS score. We will discuss these findings in the following sections.

4.1 Airflow Direction and Simulator Sickness

The efficacy of airflow as a potential countermeasure against simulator sickness has only gained little attention in the past. Although anecdotal reports often suggest that fresh air might help to ease motion sickness, the only controlled experimental study directlyaddressing this question was presented by D'Amour et al. [22]. In their study, D'Amour and colleagues found a significant reduction in simulator sickness when airflow was provided compared to a condition where airflow was absent. However, we did not find a difference between the two airflow conditions with regards to simulator sickness in the present study, contradicting our initial hypothesis. One explanation for this null finding could be that the intensity of airflow directed to driver's torso/face might have been too strong. The vent settings were set to maximum, and this may have caused irritation and discomfort for those in the direct airflow condition. This assumption is supported by the fact that participants in the direct airflow condition tended to report higher SSQ oculomotor and disorientation scores compared to those in the indirect airflow condition (although this result was not statistically significant). Future studies may vary the intensity or airflow to explore optimal airflow settings for reducing simulator sickness.

Additionally, the simulator sickness scores reported in D'Amour et al.'s [22] airflow condition were very similar to the simulator sickness scores observed in the present study (i.e., average peak FMS scores around 5). Considering that simulator sickness was higher in the no-airflow condition in D'Amour et al. [22] (i.e., FMS score of 10), it is possible that both direct and indirect airflow conditions were equally effective in potentially reducing simulator sickness. However, as the current study did not include a control condition with no airflow (see Limitations for more details), this assumption remains speculative and needs to be further investigated in future studies.

4.2 Facial Skin Temperature, Body Temperature, and Simulator Sickness

The relationship between facial skin/body temperature, subjectively perceived body temperature, and simulator sickness has only gained little attention in the past [23–25, 30]. With regards to body temperature, the few studies that have directly investigated thermoregulation in relation to motion sickness found that core body temperature typically decreases when experiencing motion sickness [26, 27, 31]. This thermoregulatory process could represent the body's attempt to counteract the subjective feeling of warmth/heat that often accompanies the onset of simulator sickness. In the present study, we also found an overall decrease in body temperature after the driving session; however, this drop was only observed in the indirect but not in the direct airflow condition. The reason for this finding remains speculative, but it seems possible that airflow directed at the participants' torso and face successfully prevented participants from feeling warm/hot in the first place, and, consequently, there was no need for the body to initiate a thermoregulatory process. In the indirect airflow condition, however, participants may have felt warm/hot, triggering a thermoregulatory response. Support for this interpretation is given by the subjective temperature ratings, where participants in the indirect airflow condition rated their body temperature as significantly warmer compared to those in the direct airflow condition after the driving session. Although our results suggest that airflow directed to the torso and face may prevent excessive feelings of heat/warmth and attenuate a decrease in body temperature, this cooling effect did not affect the level of simulators sickness. Similarly, we did not find any meaningful correlations between body temperature and the severity of simulator sickness, which may support the fact that a drop in body temperature does not necessarily reflect an increase in simulator sickness severity.

With regards to facial skin temperature, we found a moderate, negative (but non-significant) correlation with the peak FMS score, where lower facial skin temperatures were associated with higher simulator sickness ratings. This decrease in facial skin temperature could be caused by (cold) sweating, which is known to be one of the cardinal symptoms of simulator sickness and may have resulted in lower facial skin temperatures as simulator sickness increased. However, this interpretation remains speculative, as this correlation was not observed across all simulator sickness measures and participants' actual sweating response (e.g., electrodermal activity) was not recorded.

4.3 Limitations and Future Directions

One of the limitations of the present study is that the sample size was smaller than initially anticipated, yielding a lower power than planned and required to find medium-to-large effects. Thus, it is possible that more and/or greater effects could emerge with an increased sample size.

Additionally, we stopped the driving session once a moderate level of simulator sickness (FMS score of 10) was reached. This was done to prevent participants from experiencing severe simulator sickness but may have also impacted our ability to observe a more accurate relationship between body temperature and simulator sickness. For instance, it could be argued that thermoregulatory changes are more pronounced in case of strong/severe simulator sickness. Future research investigating the efficacy of airflow as a countermeasure against simulator sickness could consider increasing the study termination to an ethically reasonable threshold (e.g., FMS score of 15).

Another limitation of the present study is that we could not include a control condition without any airflow at all. This was not possible given the design of the driving simulator, where the car's interior temperature is solely regulated via the car's vents. Shutting off the vents would have resulted in a notable increase in the car's interior temperature, which would have posed a confounding factor. Due to this caveat, we were only able to compare direct vs. indirect airflow conditions, but we cannot draw conclusions on the general efficacy of airflow per se.

Lastly, we were able to record facial skin temperature readings in real-time during the driving session, but only recorded body temperature before and after the driving session. Thus, we cannot fully recreate the time course of body temperature changes during the driving session. Future research could apply methods for continuous collection of body temperature measures that are unimpacted by environmental factors throughout the experimental session.

5 Conclusion

Our results indicated that the direction of airflow (i.e., directed to the driver's torso/face or to the car's ceiling) did not affect the level of simulator sickness overall. However, participants tended to report slightly more oculomotor issues and disorientation as well as lower room temperature comfort ratings when airflow was directed to their face compared to when airflow was directed to the car's ceiling. This suggests that the use of indirect airflow might be the preferrable of the two airflow settings for driving simulation studies.

Acknowledgments. We thank Susan Gorski and Robert Shewaga for technical support as well as Niki Akbarian and Karinna Pe for their help with data collection. This work was supported by the Natural Sciences and Engineering Council (NSERC) of Canada (Discovery Grant, RGPIN-2017-04387). The funding source had no direct involvement in any research activities related to this study.

References

1. Classen, S., Bewernitz, M., Shechtman, O.: Driving simulator sickness: an evidence-based review of the literature. Am. J. Occup. Ther. **65**, 179–188 (2011). https://doi.org/10.5014/ajot.2011.000802

2. Johnson, D.M.: Introduction to and review of simulator sickness research. Rotary-Wing Aviation Research Unit, U.S. Army Research Institute for the Behavioral and Social Sciences (2005)

3. Mourant, R.R., Thattacherry, T.R.: Simulator sickness in a virtual environments driving simulator. In: Proceedings of the Human Factors and Ergonomics Society Annual Meeting, vol. 44, pp. 534–537 (2000). https://doi.org/10.1177/154193120004400513

4. Kennedy, R.S., Hettinger, L.J., Lilienthal, M.G.: Simulator sickness. In: Crampton, G.H. (ed.) Motion and Space Sickness, Boca Raton, FL (1990)

5. Reason, J.T., Brand, J.J.: Motion sickness. Academic Press, London; New York (1975)

6. Cha, Y.-H., et al.: Motion sickness diagnostic criteria: consensus document of the classification committee of the Bárány society. J. Vestib. Res. (2021). https://doi.org/10.3233/VES-200005

7. Keshavarz, B., Golding, J.F.: Motion sickness: current concepts and management. Curr. Opin. Neurol. **35**, 107–112 (2022). https://doi.org/10.1097/WCO.0000000000001018

8. Keshavarz, B., Hecht, H., Lawson, B.D.: Visually induced motion sickness: characteristics, causes, and countermeasures. In: Hale, K.S., Stanney, K.M. (eds.) Handbook of Virtual Environments: Design, Implementation, and Applications, pp. 648–697. CRC Press, Boca Raton (2014)

9. Brooks, J.O., et al.: Simulator sickness during driving simulation studies. Accid. Anal. Prev. **42**, 788–796 (2010). https://doi.org/10.1016/j.aap.2009.04.013

10. Domeyer, J.E., Cassavaugh, N.D., Backs, R.W.: The use of adaptation to reduce simulator sickness in driving assessment and research. Accid. Anal. Prev. **53**, 127–132 (2013). https://doi.org/10.1016/j.aap.2012.12.039

11. Rebenitsch, L., Owen, C.: Review on cybersickness in applications and visual displays. Virtual Reality **20**(2), 101–125 (2016). https://doi.org/10.1007/s10055-016-0285-9

12. Reason, J.T.: Motion sickness adaptation: a neural mismatch model. J. Roy. Soc Med. **71**, 819–829 (1978)

13. Palmisano, S., Allison, R.S., Schira, M.M., Barry, R.J.: Future challenges for vection research: definitions, functional significance, measures, and neural bases. Front. Psychol. **6**, 193 (2015). https://doi.org/10.3389/fpsyg.2015.00193

14. Berti, S., Keshavarz, B.: Neuropsychological approaches to visually-induced vection: an overview and evaluation of neuroimaging and neurophysiological studies. Multisens. Res. **34**, 153–186 (2020). https://doi.org/10.1163/22134808-bja10035

15. Treisman, M.: Motion sickness: an evolutionary hypothesis. Science **197**, 493–495 (1977). https://doi.org/10.1126/science.301659

16. Yen Pik Sang, F.D., Golding, J.F., Gresty, M.A.: Suppression of sickness by controlled breathing during mildly nauseogenic motion. Aviat. Space Environ. Med. **74**, 998–1002 (2003)

17. Peck, K., Russo, F., Campos, J.L., Keshavarz, B.: Examining potential effects of arousal, valence, and likability of music on visually induced motion sickness. Exp. Brain Res. **238**(10), 2347–2358 (2020). https://doi.org/10.1007/s00221-020-05871-2

18. Bonnet, C.T., Faugloire, E., Riley, M.A., Bardy, B.G., Stoffregen, T.A.: Self-induced motion sickness and body movement during passive restraint. Ecol. Psychol. **20**, 121–145 (2008). https://doi.org/10.1080/10407410801949289

19. Chang, C.-H., Pan, W.-W., Chen, F.-C., Stoffregen, T.A.: Console video games, postural activity, and motion sickness during passive restraint. Exp. Brain Res. **229**, 235–242 (2013). https://doi.org/10.1007/s00221-013-3609-y

20. Weech, S., Moon, J., Troje, N.F.: Influence of bone-conducted vibration on simulator sickness in virtual reality. PLoS ONE **13**, e0194137 (2018). https://doi.org/10.1371/journal.pone.019 4137

21. Bos, J.E.: Less sickness with more motion and/or mental distraction. J. Vestib. Res. **25**, 23–33 (2015). https://doi.org/10.3233/VES-150541

22. D'Amour, S., Bos, J.E., Keshavarz, B.: The efficacy of airflow and seat vibration on reducing visually induced motion sickness. Exp. Brain Res. **235**(9), 2811–2820 (2017). https://doi.org/10.1007/s00221-017-5009-1

23. Nalivaiko, E.: Thermoregulation and nausea. Handb Clin Neurol. **156**, 445–456 (2018). https://doi.org/10.1016/B978-0-444-63912-7.00027-8

24. Nalivaiko, E., Rudd, J.A., So, R.H.: Motion sickness, nausea and thermoregulation: the "toxic" hypothesis. Temperature (Austin). **1**, 164–171 (2014). https://doi.org/10.4161/23328940.2014.982047

25. Graybiel, A., Lackner, J.R.: Evaluation of the relationship between motion sickness symptomatology and blood pressure, heart rate, and body temperature. Aviat Space Environ Med. **51**, 211–214 (1980)

26. Nobel, G., Tribukait, A., Mekjavic, I.B., Eiken, O.: Effects of motion sickness on thermoregulatory responses in a thermoneutral air environment. Eur. J. Appl. Physiol. **112**, 1717–1723 (2012). https://doi.org/10.1007/s00421-011-2142-6

27. Nobel, G., Eiken, O., Tribukait, A., Kölegård, R., Mekjavic, I.B.: Motion sickness increases the risk of accidental hypothermia. Eur. J. Appl. Physiol. **98**, 48–55 (2006). https://doi.org/10.1007/s00421-006-0217-6

28. Keshavarz, B., Hecht, H.: Validating an efficient method to quantify motion sickness. Hum. Factors **53**, 415–426 (2011). https://doi.org/10.1177/0018720811403736

29. Kennedy, R.S., Lane, N.E., Berbaum, K.S., Lilienthal, M.G.: Simulator sickness questionnaire: an enhanced method for quantifying simulator sickness. Int. J. Aviat. Psychol. **3**, 203–220 (1993). https://doi.org/10.1207/s15327108ijap0303_3

30. Money, K.E.: Motion sickness. Physiol. Rev. **50**, 1–39 (1970). https://doi.org/10.1152/physrev.1970.50.1.1

31. Mekjavic, I.B., Tipton, M.J., Gennser, M., Eiken, O.: Motion sickness potentiates core cooling during immersion in humans. J. Physiol. **535**, 619–623 (2001). https://doi.org/10.1111/j.1469-7793.2001.00619.x

Preliminary Findings: Application of Maintenance Instructions Displayed in Augmented Reality

Kylie Key[1][✉], Maggie Ma[2], Chris Towne[2], Inchul Choi[3] , Peter T. Hu[3] ,
Steven C. Franzman[2], David R. Aguilar[2], David J. Schroeder[3], and Katrina Avers[1]

[1] Civil Aerospace Medical Institute, Federal Aviation Administration, Oklahoma City, OK
73125, USA
Kylie.N.Key@faa.gov
[2] The Boeing Company, Seal Beach, CA 90740, USA
[3] Cherokee Nation Support, Service and Solutions, Oklahoma City, OK 73125, USA

Abstract. This paper explores the use of Augmented Reality (AR) in aviation maintenance and describes a new research study conducted in partnership with a manufacturer and a Part 121 operator. The study aims to understand the applicability of displaying maintenance instructions on a head-worn AR device. In the current study, four aviation maintenance technicians interacted with novel AR technology while performing a landing gear lubrication task. Participants reported generally positive perceptions of usability and user experience. However, some ergonomic/comfort and safety concerns were identified, along with considerations and practical applications for the AR technology. These preliminary findings illustrate the possible utility of AR in aviation maintenance, but further work is needed.

Keywords: Aviation maintenance · Augmented reality · HoloLens

1 Introduction

It is well known that conventional (e.g., paper-based or digitized) maintenance instructions can be challenging to use. In aviation, the leading cause of maintenance-related aircraft accidents is procedural errors/deviations from approved maintenance procedures [2, 4, 8, 11, 14, 17, 19, 22, 23].[1] One commonly cited issue is how understandable and accessible the content is for Aircraft Maintenance Technicians (AMTs) [1]. AMTs can get lost in the large number of safety messages (warnings/cautions), linked-references and other details, and can miss important safety-critical information. A written instruction or illustration may be missing in the manual, or may be inaccurate/out of date. The introduction of electronic devices such as tablets in the maintenance environment allows for process-oriented applications that ensure the information is available in a way that more readily supports maintenance activities [7, 26, 27, 30].

---

[1] Note: rates vary depending on factors such as the database, aircraft type, years of study, etc.

J. Y. C. Chen and G. Fragomeni (Eds.): HCII 2022, LNCS 13318, pp. 221–232, 2022.
https://doi.org/10.1007/978-3-031-06015-1_16

AR has been identified as a potential technology for displaying maintenance instructions (see [20] for a review). One benefit of AR over other presentation methods is that information (e.g., images, text, animation) is overlaid atop real-world sensory input. In practice, the augmented information can be shown via head-worn displays similar to a pair of sunglasses or via portable devices (tablets, smartphones). Instead of fusing information onto a video feed (and thus requiring the user to look at a computer screen), AR head-worn devices can fuse information directly onto the user's field of view; this makes it easy for users to switch between physical and digital worlds.

When applied to aviation maintenance, AR gives users real time access to procedures, 3D visualization of airframe and components, and interconnectivity of maintenance information systems. It allows the instant visualization of critical data, reduces the quantity of text content, and enables easy status tracking and completion verification.

2 Background

Previous research demonstrates potential benefits, but also some potential challenges with utilizing AR in industrial settings. Integration of AR technology into the working environment has been shown to improve efficiency [13, 24, 28], user satisfaction, and to reduce workload [9]. These applications of AR are promising; however, these studies were either conducted in laboratory environments or industrial settings other than aircraft maintenance. Subsequent investigations applying AR to aviation maintenance have found similar benefits such as a reduction in preparatory and repair time [15] and reduced learning curve for beginners [18].

Laboratory investigations using head-worn AR displays of maintenance instructions have shown decreased task completion time and workload [5] and an improvement in task performance [12], compared to paper-based methods. Notably, participants in these studies also identified usability and comfortability limitations of the head-worn display (e.g., weight, limited window of view, eyestrain; see [5, 16]). However, as these studies were conducted in laboratory settings, open questions remain about whether head-worn devices can be integrated into complex, operational environments. Previous studies of AR in aviation maintenance did not superimpose 3D models directly atop the user's field of view as they completed the task, and doing so may confer more advantages compared to other display methods.

To the best of our knowledge, the current study is among the first to investigate the application of head-worn AR instructions specifically for AMTs operating in an operational aviation maintenance environment.

3 Research Purpose

The purpose of the current collaborative research study was to further investigate and characterize the applicability of AR head-worn displays providing maintenance instructions in operational aviation maintenance settings. A secondary goal was to identify any barriers before the technology can be broadly adopted. The research questions examined:

- Are users satisfied with the AR device?
- Is the AR head-worn device comfortable to wear in the aviation maintenance environment?
- Are there any perceived safety concerns with using AR?
- What changes (if any) to the AR design are needed to integrate this technology in the aviation maintenance environment?

4 Method

4.1 Participants

In a preliminary study, participants were $n = 4$ AMTs working at a large Part 121 air carrier in the United States. All spoke English as a first language and had normal or corrected-to-normal vision. Participants had worked as a professional AMT for 1–5 years ($n = 3$) or 6–10 years ($n = 1$) and held credentials that included Mechanic Certificate with Airframe and Powerplant Privileges.

Participating AMTs had varying levels of task experience with the B777 lubrication task (ranged from completing < 5 times to > 20 times) and recency (ranged from completion within the last week to more than a year ago).

4.2 The Maintenance Task

The maintenance task modeled for the study was the lubrication of the main landing gear (MLG) on B777-200 aircraft (see Fig. 1). This task is routinely scheduled per the Maintenance Planning Data (MPD) with a defined frequency. The associated task card is typically provided with pages of instructions including the lubrication fitting locations (a total of more than 160 lubrication points per MLG), types of grease, and subsequent multiple diagrams that pictorially identify where the lubrication fittings are located on the MLG. Each MLG side (left and right) takes about 4 h to complete on the B777-200.

To perform this task, a pair of AMTs work their way across the MLG to systematically lubricate each fitting one by one, using the required type of grease, and then checking off each fitting as completed. One AMT operates the lubricant guns to physically lubricate (i.e., primary role), and the other follows the instruction, refers to diagrams, assists with tools and equipment (e.g., lifts/ladders), handles the paperwork, and tracks task progress (i.e., assisting role). Task completion and accuracy are usually verified by a visual check for fresh grease on the fitting itself.

This task has been identified as particularly error-prone given the number of fittings and multitude of locations (e.g., some fittings are hidden behind structures, are in hard-to-reach locations, or are buried underneath old dirty clumps of lubricant). It is common for AMTs to miss certain locations due to a lack of means or accuracy in tracking completed fitting locations. The missed locations can be in plain sight or hidden behind other MLG components. In addition to missing lubrication points, other common errors for this servicing task include using the wrong type of grease, under lubrication, and excessive lubrication (e.g., too much grease that may catch dust).

Fig. 1. An AMT demonstrates the lubrication task while wearing the AR head-worn device (a 1st Generation of Microsoft HoloLens is featured in this photo).

5 Materials

5.1 The AR Instructions

The AR display highlighted the lubrication fitting locations and made task information readily available to the AMTs including: 3D holographic MLG model, work card information and steps, number of fittings, type of lubricant to use, and cautions and warnings.

The 3D holographic model, superimposed on the actual 777 MLG, highlights all of the fitting locations via fly around or fly through technology, which is expected to be a major improvement over the 2D graphics where hidden locations are described via flagnotes (i.e., not actually shown in the 2D graphics). In the AR display, fittings were also depicted in different colors to reflect their status, with completed fittings displayed in green, versus to-be-lubricated fittings in red.

5.2 HoloLens 2

The aviation maintenance environment is noisy and AMTs need their hands free to complete tasks, which may last several hours. The Microsoft HoloLens 2 offers extended-use features and improved user experience compared to other and earlier generation of head-worn devices (e.g., HoloLens 1). Interaction with HoloLens 2 incorporates touching, grasping, and moving holograms, and voice commands work through incorporated microphones with natural language speech processing. The user can move freely without wires or external packs to get in their way; an onboard battery lasts 3–4 h for active use or longer with a backup portable charger. Therefore, the HoloLens 2 was selected for displaying AR work instructions.

6 Protocol

Participants conducted a MLG lubrication task during their shift and were assigned to conduct the task using the HoloLens 2. The maintenance site was prepared with all required equipment, tools, and consumables before each experimental session. Participants completed a portion of the task while wearing HoloLens 2, and then reported their subjective perceptions of the technology in a post-task questionnaire administered via an iPad.

To determine the applicability of AR instructions in the aviation maintenance environment, variables of interest were collected: usability, user satisfaction, ergonomics and comfortability of wearing the device, and perceived workplace safety concerns related to wearing AR. Ratings were made on a 5-point agreement Likert scale[2]. Participant demographics, experience with the task, technology familiarity and acceptance were also measured because these variables may shape users' perceptions of the technology.

7 Results

The survey items were categorized into six topical subscales, and the aggregated responses are graphically presented below. Open-ended feedback is reported where relevant.

There are limitations to consider when interpreting the results of this study. First, the study utilized a small sample of maintenance technicians due to complications associated with the COVID-19 pandemic. Additionally, the AR application was examined for a single task on a single aircraft type. These limitations threaten the generalizability of the results, as elaborated in the Discussion section.

7.1 Technology Familiarity and Acceptance

As shown in Fig. 2, the four study participants consider themselves to be early adopters of technology; however, they reported relatively less experience with the Microsoft HoloLens device.

7.2 Usability

Participants reported high system usability, as shown in Fig. 3. They reported feeling confident using the application; the 3D model and work instructions were well integrated; the application was easy to use; and they would like to use the application frequently. Participants disagreed that the system was unnecessarily complex or that there was too much inconsistency compared to the real world. Responses were neutral regarding need for technical support to be able to use the device.

---

[2] The response options were: Strongly disagree (1); Somewhat disagree (2); Neither disagree or agree (3); Somewhat agree (4); Strongly agree (5).

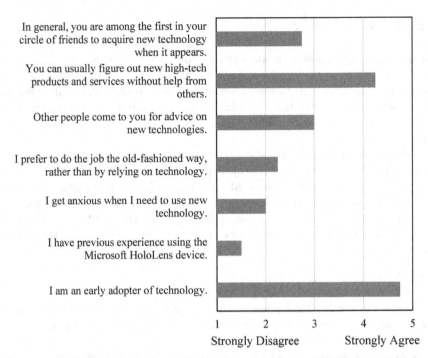

Fig. 2. Participant agreement responses to technology acceptance and familiarity question items.

7.3 User Satisfaction

As shown in Fig. 4, participants were generally satisfied with the AR application. They reported high agreement that they are confident finding information; that they intend to be a heavy user of the technology; and that they all strongly agree that they intend to check the system's announcements/notifications/alerts/messages. Participants somewhat agreed that they were positive toward the application and that using it to perform my task is a good idea.

When asked what they liked best about the application, the four participants responded:

- "Ease of use"
- "The details of the gear components"
- "Being able to see points without having to struggle to look for them"
- "Imagery"

7.4 Ergonomics and Comfort

Given the novelty of head-worn AR devices in the aviation maintenance environment, participants were asked if they experienced any discomfort using the HoloLens to perform the task. One participant commented, "Tight around the head. Feels heavier after a while." Participants provided no additional feedback regarding ergonomics and comfort.

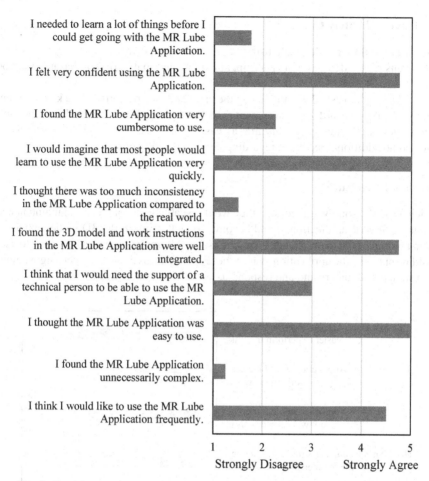

Fig. 3. Participant agreement responses to system usability scale question items [6].

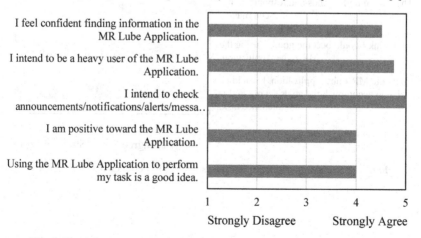

Fig. 4. Participant agreement responses to User Satisfaction question items.

7.5 Perceived Safety Concerns

When asked if they feel less safe using the HoloLens to perform the task, three of four participants responded yes. One participant commented that, "trip/slip hazards may be harder to see."

Similarly, when asked whether using the application to perform the task creates any workplace safety hazard, one participant responded yes and that, "With the application running you might not notice hazards as easily when walking around." Participants provided no additional feedback regarding perceived safety concerns.

7.6 User Experience

Participants all strongly agreed that: they would be able to accomplish the maintenance task using the AR application; could become good at using it; the 3D model enhances understanding of the maintenance instructions; the AR application was very easy to use; would want to use the application every time. Feedback was neutral concerning whether the system could understand and respond to users' commands. See Fig. 5.

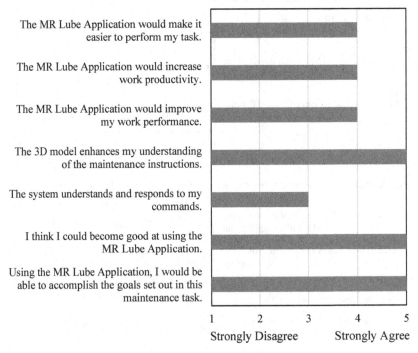

Fig. 5. Participant agreement responses to User Experience question items.

When asked to describe how the application compares to traditional work instruction (either paper or iPad), the four participants responded:

- "I would consider it an enhancement to paper"
- "Much easier and cleaner"
- "Good for people who are visual learners"
- "Better"

When asked if there is anything that would improve the application, participants commented: "Training"; "Different colors for different lubricant"; and "Zoom feature".

When asked whether they would recommend work instructions delivered on the HoloLens to a colleague, two participants said yes, one did not respond, and one said, "50/50". The latter is the same participant who commented on the weight of the device and safety concerns, which may explain the reluctance to recommend the technology to others.

Finally, users reported that the AR application changes their work behaviors. Two of four participants indicated the application changes the way they move around the MLG when completing the task, with one participant stating "more cautious with my steps." Participants indicated the application changes the workflow sequence and the way they account for lubrication fitting completion compared to their normal method (but did not provide sufficient detail about how).

8 Discussion

This preliminary study is among the first to explore the applicability of AR work instructions displayed via a head-worn device in an operational aviation maintenance environment. Certified AMTs interacted with the technology while completing a portion of a MLG lubrication task, and then reported on their subjective experience. Participants were favorable towards the AR application in terms of system usability and user satisfaction, and agreed that the AR application was better than paper-based instructions. However, they reported some concerns with ergonomics and comfort (e.g., device weight), and with workplace safety (e.g., increased risk of trip/fall hazards). Participants also suggested improvements to training and the AR display (e.g., zoom feature; color-code the grease type needed for each lubrication point). These results are in line with research on AR in other industrial settings [5, 16].

8.1 Limitations

Although the results suggest that AR work instructions displayed on head-worn devices may be beneficial applicable in the aviation maintenance environment, there are limitations to note. First, the study utilized a small sample due to complications associated with the COVID-19 pandemic such as travel restrictions and a significant reduction in the availability of aircraft for routine maintenance. A clear recommendation is that future research should capture a larger, representative sample of AMTs.

Another limitation concerns the generalizability of the results, as the current study investigated a single aircraft task. The results cannot answer if AR can be applicable to all aspects of maintenance, or whether it is more appropriate for some task types than others. Previous research in other industrial settings has determined that AR is differentially beneficial depending on factors such as task complexity and expertise. These studies measured task completion time or efficiency, finding that AR may reduce task completion time when the task is complex [13, 28] or when the user is a beginner [18]. There is need for additional research on what maintenance task types may benefit from AR instruction, and which users (e.g., beginners versus experts) may benefit the most. This is an under-investigated area, though the question is relevant for training schools as well as for the development and display of real-time work instructions.

8.2 Practical Applications and Considerations

The information collected during this study can be used in several ways including: further develop AR applications, scope operational maintenance use cases, and inform the overall applicability and human factors considerations for the use of AR applications in the maintenance environment.

Advances in technologies such as AR create unique opportunities for improved training. Such new technologies allow for hands-on practical exercises to supplement classroom training, and may be more cost-effective than conventional methods due to a reduction in training time [3, 16, 21]. AR can also be applied to teaching and competency assessment [24, 29].

Another potential application of AR is improving compliance with work procedures. Technicians may perform steps incorrectly, skip steps in procedures, or perform steps in the wrong sequence when sequence of steps matters. It is possible that AR can mitigate top factors contributing to technicians' failure to follow procedures like task interruption, distraction, complacency due to familiarity, and possibly limited knowledge/expertise. One study showed that AR reduced task completion time and errors in a complex automotive maintenance task - assembling a motor vehicle combustion chamber [13] (see also [12]).

Another opportunity for using AR is for remote assistance and inspection. A 2018 study showed that an immersive, virtual reality environment can be helpful for completing inspection tasks [10]. This capability may be particularly useful during the COVID-19 pandemic, which is forcing organizations to find new ways of doing business while social distancing.

Although these AR applications are promising, consideration should be given to barriers to integrating AR into the operational aviation environment. First, there is a need to consider return-on-investment (ROI) given the initial investment cost of technology that would be required. Specifically, the AR software must be developed for each task and aircraft type, and there is also a cost of the hardware (e.g., head-worn devices). Data management can also be costly, as maintenance data and aircraft engineering data need to be in a readily consumable format by the new AR technologies. All said, total costs can add up quickly.

Furthermore, human factors and ergonomics regarding new technologies should be considered. Some users have experienced disorientation, eye strain, or motion sickness when using AR [5, 12]. AMTs also may have different preferences or acceptance with respect to new technologies. For instance, AMTs may resist the technology because AR may limit the somatosensory feedback and cognitive reference that familiar behaviors such as touching and writing on a piece of paper allows a seasoned maintainer.

Thus, further work is needed to resolve potential roadblocks to the implementation of AR to ensure that the applications are dedicated to tasks in a way that maximizes safety and compliance while crediting differences in work preferences and styles.

References

1. Avers, K.E., Johnson, W.B., Banks, J.O., Nei, D.: Prioritizing Mx human factors challenges and solutions. In: Workshop Proceedings (Report No. DOT/FAA/AM-11/11). Federal Aviation Administration Office of Aerospace Medicine, Washington, DC (2011)
2. Baron, R.I.: An exploration of deviations in aircraft maintenance procedures. Int. J. Appl. Aviat. Stud. 9(1), 197–206 (2009)
3. Bowling, S.R., Khasawneh, M.T., Kaewkuekool, S., Jiang, X., Gramopadhye, A.K.: Evaluating the effects of virtual training in an aircraft maintenance task. Int. J. Aviat. Psychol. 18(1), 104–116 (2008). https://doi.org/10.1080/10508410701749506
4. Boyd, D., Stolzer, A.: Causes and trends in mx-related accidents in FAA-certified single engine piston aircraft. J. Aviat. Technol. Eng. 5(1), 17–24 (2015)
5. Braly, A.M., Nuernberger, B., Kim, S.Y.: Augmented reality improves procedural work on an International Space Station science instrument. Hum. Factors 61(6), 866–878 (2019). https://doi.org/10.1177/0018720818824464
6. Brooke, J.: SUS: a quick and dirty usability scale. Usabil. Eval. Indust. 189(194), 4–7 (1996)
7. Buderath, M., McDonald, N., Grommes, P., Morrison, R.: The operational impact to the maintainer (ground crew support and human factors). In: IET Seminar on Aircraft Health Management and New Operational and Enterprise Solutions, London (2008). https://doi.org/10.1049/ic:20080633
8. Civil Aviation Authority: CAP 1036 - Global fatal accident review 2002 to 2011. United Kingdom (2013)
9. De Crescenzio, F., Fantini, M., Persiani, F., Di Stefano, L., Azzari, P., Salti, S.: Augmented reality for aircraft maintenance training and operations support. IEEE Comput. Graphics Appl. 31(1), 96–101 (2011). https://doi.org/10.1049/ic:20080633
10. Eschen, H., Kötter, T., Rodeck, R., Harnisch, M., Schüppstuhl, T.: Augmented and virtual reality for inspection and maintenance processes in the aviation industry. Proc. Manuf. 19, 156–163 (2018). https://doi.org/10.1016/j.promfg.2018.01.022
11. Goldman, S.M., Fiedler, E.R., King, R.E.: General aviation maintenance-related accidents: a review of ten years of NTSB data (Report No. DOT/FAA/AM-02/23). Federal Aviation Administration, Office of Aerospace Medicine (2002)
12. Hebert, T.R.: The impacts of using augmented reality to support aircraft maintenance. Master's thesis, Air Force Institute of Technology, Wright-Patterson Air Force Base, Ohio (2019)
13. Henderson, S.J., Feiner, S.K.: Augmented reality in the psychomotor phase of a procedural task. In: 2011 10th IEEE International Symposium on Mixed and Augmented Reality, Basel, Switzerland (2011). https://doi.org/10.1109/ISMAR.2011.6092386
14. Hobbs, A., Williamson, A.: Aircraft maintenance survey results. Australian Transport Safety Bureau (2000)
15. Jo, G-S., et al.: A unified framework for augmented reality and knowledge-based systems in maintaining aircraft. In: Proceedings of the Twenty-Sixth Annual Conference on Innovative Applications of Artificial Intelligence, pp. 2990–2997 (2014)

16. Keesling, R.B.: Exploratory analysis of the potential use of augmented reality in aircraft maintenance. Theses and Dissertations, Air Force Institute of Technology, 2305 (2019)

17. Langer, M., Braithwaite, G.R.: The development and deployment of a maintenance operations safety survey. Hum. Factors **58**(7), 986–1006 (2016). https://doi.org/10.1177/001872081665 6085

18. Loizeau, Q., Danglade, F., Ababsa, F., Merienne, F.: Methodology for the field evaluation of the impact of augmented reality tools for maintenance workers in the aeronautic industry. Front. Virtual Real. **1**, 603189 (2021). https://doi.org/10.3389/frvir.2020.603189

19. Marais, K.B., Robichaud, M.R.: Analysis of trends in aviation maintenance risk: an empirical approach. Reliab. Eng. Syst. Saf. **106**, 104–118 (2012)

20. Palmarini, R., Erkoyuncu, J.A., Roy, R.: An innovative process to select augmented reality (AR) technology for maintenance. Proc. CIRP **59**, 23–28 (2017). https://doi.org/10.1016/j.procir.2016.10.001

21. Pozzi, J.: Will Virtual Reality Shape the Future of MRO Training? (2016). http://www.mro-network.com/

22. Rankin, W.: Failure to follow procedures: airline engineering and maintenance safety. In: Flightglobal and Flight International in Partnership with the Flight Safety Foundation Airline Engineering and Maintenance Safety, London, England (2013)

23. Schmidt, J., Lawson, D., Figlock, R.: Human Factors Analysis and Classification System-Maintenance Extension (HFACS-ME) Review of Select NTSB Maintenance Mishaps: An Update (2012). https://www.faa.gov/about/initiatives/Mx_hf/library/documents/media/hfacs/ntsb_hfacs-me_updated_study_report.pdf

24. Tang, A., Owen, C., Biocca, F., Mou, W.: Comparative effectiveness of augmented reality in object assembly. In: Proceedings of the SIGCHI Conference on Human Factors in Computing Systems, pp. 73–80 (2003). https://doi.org/10.1145/642611.642626

25. Tang, K.S., Cheng, D.L., Mi, E., Greenberg, P.: Augmented reality in medical education: a systematic review. Canadian Med. Educ. J. **11**(1), e81–e96 (2020)

26. Taylor, M.: TATEM: technologies and techniques for new maintenance concepts. Published Summary. http://cordis.europa.eu/publication/rcn/11816_en.html

27. Ward, M., Gaynor, D., Nuget, T., Morrison, R.: HILAS maintenance solutions: challenges and potentials for the aircraft maintenance industry. In: 2008 IET Seminar on Aircraft Health Management for New Operational and Enterprise Solutions, London. (2008). https://doi.org/10.1049/ic:20080643

28. Wiedenmaier, S., Oehme, O., Schmidt, L., Luczak, H.: Augmented reality (AR) for assembly processes design and experimental evaluation. Int. J. Human Comput. Interact. **16**(3), 497–514 (2003). https://doi.org/10.1207/S15327590IJHC1603_7

29. Williams, M.A., McVeigh, J., Handa, A.I., Lee, R.: Augmented reality in surgical training: a systematic review. Postgraduate Med. J. **96**(1139), 537–542 (2020)

30. Worsfold, M., Asseman, P.: TATEM's contribution to a future health managed enterprise (overview, context and emerging operational needs). In: IET Seminar on AHM for New Operational Enterprise Solutions. IET, Savoy Place, London, UK (2008). https://doi.org/10.1049/ic:20080631

Human Factors Considerations for Head-Worn Displays in Civil Aviation

David C. Newton[⊠] [ID]

FAA Civil Aerospace Medical Institute, Oklahoma City, OK 73169, USA
David.C.Newton@faa.gov

Abstract. Head-worn displays (HWDs) superimpose primary flight information that is traditionally presented on head-down displays on the pilot's natural, far-field vision. When compared to traditional head-down instrumentation, the HWD advantages include (a) reduced head-down time, (b) fewer instances of refocusing eyes between cockpit instruments and the far-field view, (c) information presentation that conforms to the natural world, and (d) freedom of head movements while still viewing symbology. Because HWD imagery and real-world information are superimposed, HWD design should strike a balance between effort required to scan various information sources and amount of visual clutter added to the pilot's forward field of view. When this balance is achieved, HWDs can facilitate efficient use of pilot attentional resources, manifesting as increased flight path tracking accuracy and improved detection of expected traffic when compared to traditional head-down presentation of flight information. Whether virtual information is presented to just one eye or to both eyes carries important implications for pilot performance and flight safety. Previous research indicates that monocular presentation can have a negative impact on target detection and tracking performance when compared to binocular presentation, implicating binocular rivalry. This raises the question of whether the binocular rivalry is impacting pilots' ability to focus attention on HWD imagery, switch attention between HWD imagery and far-field scenery, and integrate information that appears in HWD imagery with the far-field scenery.

Keywords: Aviation · Head-worn displays · Binocular rivalry

1 Introduction

Civil aviation pilots need to see where they are going and keep track of important flight information in order to safely fly. One of the challenges with these activities is that pilots need to scan a variety of displays and information sources while also maintaining sufficient visual contact with the out-the-window scenery. In a traditional flight deck with only head-down instrumentation, doing so requires significant visual scanning and strategic allocation of attention to displays that are located throughout the flight deck, as well as to far-field information through the windshield. This process presents a challenge because it requires significant time and effort to attend to this information. One way to mitigate this challenge is to reduce the distance between all

© Springer Nature Switzerland AG 2022
J. Y. C. Chen and G. Fragomeni (Eds.): HCII 2022, LNCS 13318, pp. 233–250, 2022.
https://doi.org/10.1007/978-3-031-06015-1_17

of these sources of information by virtually superimposing primary flight information onto the outside world using a virtual image display system. These systems present information about the aircraft's altitude, attitude, and position relative to the earth's terrain and landmarks onto a clear, transparent screen that allows the pilot to maintain visual contact with the outside world while also viewing primary flight information. The head-worn display (HWD) is one system that is designed to accomplish this. In the civil aviation flight deck, HWD technology is novel. HWDs are beneficial in that they reduce the need for head-down transitions and reduce the amount of visual travel between information sources needed to acquire flight information.

The HWD is viewed as a natural evolution of the traditional head-up display (HUD), which has been an integral part of the civil aviation flight deck since the mid-1990's (Weintraub and Endsing 1992). HWDs represent a form of augmented-reality given that they supplement the pilot's natural vision with information that otherwise is not immediately available when looking out the window. There are four key benefits associated with using a HWD compared to the traditional head-down presentation of flight information, as well as HUD presentation of that information: (a) reduced visual travel, (b) minimal eye accomodation, (c) wider field of view, and (d) unlimited field of regard. The benefit of superimposing virtual information on out-the-window scenery is that there is minimal time and effort required to scan all of the various sources of visual information. This is possible due to the transparent nature of the combiner screen, which reflects light from the virtual image projector toward the pilot's eye or eyes. This benefit is also shared with the HUD (Wickens and Yeh 1997).

Similar to the benefit of reduced visual travel when compared to traditional head-down instrumentation, HWDs offer the benefit of presenting primary flight information at a virtual distance of optical infinity, effectively the same distance at which out-the-window information appears (Wickens and Yeh 1997). This minimizes the need for the eye lenses to change their focus between the two information sources. This saves significant time and effort compared to traditional head-down instrumentation (Weintraub et al. 1985). To accomplish this, HWD optics are collimated; that is, the focal distance is set at near optical infinity by projecting the image in a way that causes the rays of light from the image source to be parallel to one another (Velger 1998).

One fundamental difference between the HUD and the HWD is that the HWD can afford a wider field of view. This is because the image generation and optical hardware is positioned closer to the user's eyes. This is accomplished by using smaller, lighter-weight display hardware than what is typically found in a HUD. Minimal size and weight of the HWD image generation hardware are of primary importance in order to minimize the user's physical fatigue and discomfort (Lindholm et al. 2001) The first HWDs in aviation implemented miniature monochrome CRT monitors (Velger 1998). As display technology has progressed, the size and weight of the image generation hardware have reduced further, accompanied by an increase in image resolution and luminance contrast. Modern HWDs typically employ liquid crystal on silicon (LCoS) displays, which have a high luminance output, low weight, compact size, and high resolution.

A final benefit of the HWD over the HUD is that the display is head-slaved; this makes it possible for imagery to be presented to the wearer even if their head is turned. This is accomplished using head-tracking sensors that track the user's head position relative to the position of the aircraft and geographical landmarks. For pilots, an expanded field of regard can have significant benefits in terms of awareness of terrain and obstacles. This is particularly the case in rotary wing applications, where the pilot may need to make lateral movements, which require scanning the area immediately to the left or right of the aircraft (e.g., see Beringer and Dreschler 2013). Unlimited field of regard HWDs for pilots afford more accurate path tracking performance and improved detection of incursions while taxiing (Arthur III et al. 2007).

2 Information Presented on HWDs

In aviation applications, HWDs can present information to the pilot that aids their awareness of (a) the aircraft's attitude, location, and trajectory, (b) the status and modes of the various aircraft systems, and (c) the location of important landmarks in the environment, such as runways and other aircraft. Imagery presented using a HWD can take several different forms, including system information presented alphanumerically, spatial information presented symbolically, and real-time video imagery taken from onboard sensors or databases (Weintraub and Endsing 1992). During flight, information about the aircraft's attitude, altitude, speed, and heading is displayed (Patterson et al. 2007). During critical phases of flight such as takeoff and landing, the HWD presents symbolic information to aid the pilot in executing the steps necessary to safely complete those operations, such as runway edge lines, flare cues, localizer guidance, and flight path guidance. To aid awareness of the surrounding terrain and obstacles during low-visibility operations, the HWD can present imagery from an enhanced flight vision system (EFVS), synthetic vision system (SVS), or combined vision system (CVS; Beringer 2020). Additionally, an HWD could present information to facilitate navigation during ground operations (Arthur et al. 2007).

3 HWD Configurations

While all HWDs benefit from the characteristics described previously, there are multiple types of HWD optical configurations. Each of these configurations has its own set of benefits and drawbacks that impact how the user perceives and interacts with their. There are three primary optical configurations of HWDs: monocular, biocular, and binocular environment (Yeh and Wickens 1997). In monocular HWDs, the image is projected to only one eye, whereas the other eye sees only real-world information from the outside world. The benefits to a monocular system are the small size and shape, as well as reduced weight, of the physical components. This may make monocular systems less physically fatiguing to wear for long periods of time. However, monocular systems can introduce problems with binocular rivalry, where visual perception alternates between the information in each eye. Because only one eye receives information from the HWD, this can result in suppression of the presented imagery and subsequent loss of awareness of information presented on the HWD (Melzer 2001).

In biocular HWDs, the image from a single video channel is projected to each eye. This results in the exact same image being presented to both eyes simultaneously. One advantage of biocular systems is they can be relatively inexpensive to produce given that there is only a single image source. However, the added complexity of images presented to both eyes introduce the risk of problems arising out of image misalignment. If the images in each eye are not exactly aligned—both spatially and temporally—the user can experience eyestrain, headaches, blurring, and double vision (Melzer and Mofitt 1996). In binocular HWDs, an image is presented to both eyes simultaneously, however—unlike biocular HWDs—a separate, unique image is presented to each eye using distinct image sources. This configuration can support apparent depth of imagery by conveying binocular disparity depth cues (Yeh and Wickens 1997).

For each of these optical configurations, a fundamental aspect of the design is ensuring that the optics are calibrated to the user's interpupillary distance and eye relief. According to Drascic and Milgram (1996), many perceptual issues of augmented reality devices such as HWDs arise from errors in eye relief and interpupillary distance calibration. In order for the virtual image to be properly scaled in space, the parameters that determine the correct geometric characteristics of the viewer, virtual image, and real world must be accurately specified. Perceptual distortions due to calibration errors can have deleterious effects on performance. For example, if the display is not designed to exactly match the interpupillary distance of the user, the spatial relationships between the virtual images and the real world will appear distorted.

4 Conformal and Non-conformal Imagery

Superimposing virtual information over real-world information is beneficial in that it reduces the amount of visual travel needed to acquire flight information, however it comes at a cost of increased visual clutter (Wickens 2021). One way to reduce visual clutter in this setting is to present virtual information so that it is coupled with natural visual information in the far field, also known as conformal imagery. Imagery that is presented in a conformal manner is typically earth referenced, such as the horizon line and heading. This information is anchored to natural visual cues and should compensate for changes in the aircraft's position and the pilot's head position. To make this possible, the HWD must be able to track the pilot's head position and compare it to geographical reference points. For the imagery to be world-stabilized, its positioning must change with changes in head position to match the shift in real-world visual information that naturally occurs with head movement (Rash 1998).

In some cases, there may be information in the imagery that is fixed in the pilot's head frame. This information has a fixed position in the HWD and is unaffected by aircraft position, attitude and HWD line-of-sight. Non-conformal information in HWD imagery typically has no relation to the aircraft's position in space relative to the earth. For example, textual flight guidance mode annunciations might be fixed in position on the HWD display, along with airspeed, altitude, and certain navigational information (Rash 1998). The primary reason for presenting non-conformal imagery in a HWD is to reduce the amount of visual scanning needed to scan the information, relative to the traditional head-down presentation of this information (Yeh and Wickens 1997). A head-tracking function continuously monitors the dynamic relationship between the pilot's head, aircraft, and the earth (Velger 1998). In addition to correctly positioning displayed information, the HWD must also have a means to avoid visual interference with the pilot's internal view of flight deck instruments, indications and controls. For example, the HWD might use the head-tracking function to detect that the pilot's line of sight is below the windshield, and remove any information from the display that would interfere with the internal cockpit view.

5 Perceptual Factors

5.1 Dark Focus and Dark Vergence

To perceive objects in space in sharp focus, the human eye must adjust its optical power by changing the shape of the lens so the light rays are projected toward the retina in parallel. This process is known as eye accommodation. Along with accommodation, lateral movement of the eyes in opposite directions occurs to maintain binocular fixation on a single stimulus. This process is known as vergence. In most settings, accommodation and vergence are fast and reliable (Toates 1972). However, when the environment is dark or is devoid of defined features or stimuli, the eye lenses tend to relax and drift toward their resting state of accommodation, which is a distance of approximately one meter from the observer (Hennessy et al. 1976). Along with accommodation drifting toward dark focus, eye vergence drifts toward a state of dark vergence as well. The vergence angle in degraded stimulus conditions matches the focal distance achieved with resting focal distance (Patterson et al. 2006). The practical implication of this phenomenon is that when HWD focal distances are farther than the user's dark focus and dark vergence distance, there is a risk of blurred, out-of-focus imagery, as well as double vision, especially during low illumination (Patterson et al. 2006). In these cases, the pilot's ability to comprehend the imagery and successfully use it to fly the aircraft is compromised (Velger 1998). Insuring that the virtual image brightness is appropriately matched to the ambient brightness of real, far-field information is one method for mitigating this risk (Patterson et al. 2006).

5.2 Perceptual Constancy

The misperception of size, depth, and motion characteristics of virtual imagery and real-world information may be a consequence of accommodation and vergence drifting toward a resting state in degraded stimulus conditions. This occurs because of a discrepancy between the characteristics of the real, physical objects in the environment (i.e., patterns of light projected into the eye from the HWD) and the perceived characteristics of those objects or stimuli as realized through processing of sensory information that occurs throughout the visual pathway of the central nervous system. Problems with HWD use could arise when the user misperceives their distance from the HWD imagery (e.g., see Patterson et al. 2006). This misperception negatively affects the process of size-distance scaling, which is one of the bases for estimating the distance and location of objects in visual space (Gallagher and Hoefling 2013). Therefore, if the HWD user's accommodation and vergence drift toward resting state, there is a possibility that they will misperceive the distance and location of objects in their visual field and compromise their ability to maintain an ideal flight path (Patterson and Martin 1992).

5.3   Eye Accommodation to Virtual and Real-World Information

Because HWDs superimpose near-field virtual imagery onto far-field visual information, such as the runway environment and terrain, and because the human eye cannot
keep near-field and far-field visual information in sharp focus simultaneously, HWD
design must take into account the distance the imagery appears to be from the user. In
most aviation applications, HWD virtual imagery is presented at optical infinity. This
is achieved by collimating the image; that is, the light rays that produce the image are
projected parallel to one another (Velger 1998). The goal of this is to make the virtual
image appear to be at the same distance from the user as natural scenery that appears
out the window. The primary reason for this is it minimizes the amount of time it takes
for the user's eye accommodation to adjust between the virtual and real-world visual
information, facilitating the switching of attention from the near-field virtual imagery
and the far-field natural scenery (Velger 1998). Collimating the virtual image also elim-
inates any motion parallax. Motion parallax, which is the relative movement of images
across the visual field resulting from lateral movement of the observer's head, conveys
information about those objects' depth (Rogers and Graham 1979). This presents two
problems: First, conveying this information artificially could conflict with contextual
depth information, such as relative size and linear perspective. Second, any motion parallax would cause issues of misalignment and non-conformality of the imagery relative
to the natural scenery upon which it is superimposed (Velger 1998).

The logic behind collimated imagery is that eye lens accommodation will need minimal adjustment to change focus from the imagery to the real world, or vice versa, making it easier for the pilot to switch attention. However, according to previous research,
eye accommodation does not switch precisely between the two sources of information, which can result in illusions of size and distance of objects (Iaveccia et al. 1988).
Roscoe and his colleagues (1979a, 1979b) initially investigated this phenomenon in a
series of experiments in which pilots making landing approaches viewed virtual and
synthetically-projected out-the-window scenery. During approach, pilots under these
conditions misestimated the size and distance of the runway, perceiving it to be smaller
and farther away compared to when viewed directly, and resulting in pilots approaching
too high and flaring too soon.

Despite this finding, the practical significance of this finding has been debated.
Roscoe's (1987) publication, which described the problems of misaccommodation that
occur with HUDs and HWDs, as well as the subsequent misperceptions of size and
distance of real-world information, received responses that contested the practical significance of these concerns. The rebuttals to Roscoe's publication (i.e., Newman 1987;
Silverstein and Wilbert 1987; Weintraub 1987) argue that many of the drawbacks of
these virtual image displays can be counteracted by pilot training and that the benefits of
these systems outweigh their drawbacks. They argue that the improvements to flight path
tracking and reduction in visual search offers benefits beyond any drawbacks associated
with misperceptions of size and distance. Importantly, these researchers do not argue
that these misperceptions do not occur.

5.4 Vergence-Accommodation Mismatch

When viewing virtual stereoscopic imagery, such as when using a binocular HWD, the eyes accommodate to the virtual distance to which the imagery is projected. However, the vergence angle to which the eyes must adjust in order to view the imagery is often not aligned with the accommodative distance (Patterson et al. 2006). This phenomenon is known as the vergence-accommodation mismatch (Wann et al. 1995). The optical characteristics of binocular HWDs can result in a vergence accommodation mismatch and subsequent problems that arise out of the inherent coupling of vergence and accommodation for depth perception.

The vergence-accommodation mismatch can result in a variety of issues for HWD users. When using HWDs for an extended period of time, vergence-accommodation mismatch can cause the user to experience eyestrain and visual discomfort and can cause the virtual imagery to appear out of focus (Patterson et al. 2006). This can arise out of the strong link between vergence and accommodation, whereby eye accommodation is partially influenced by the degree of eye vergence. This can result in the eyes accommodating to a distance that is different from the focal distance of the virtual imagery.

5.5 Binocular Rivalry

Under normal viewing conditions, both eyes receive information from the same region of visual space; as such, perception arises from a fusion between each signal presented to the two eyes. Usually, the only difference between the information presented to each eye arises from binocular disparity; that is, the difference in an image due to the horizontal separation of the eyes (Howard and Rogers 1995). In cases where the two eyes are presented with separate, unique images, such as when using a monocular HWD, binocular rivalry can occur. When this happens, the observer does not experience a stable, fused percept; rather, they experience an alternation between the stimuli presented to each eye (Blake 2001; Patterson et al. 2007). The eye whose stimulus is perceived at a given moment in time is referred to as the "dominant eye", whereas the eye whose stimulus does not reach visual awareness at this point in time is referred to as the "suppressed eye" (Blake 2001).

Binocular rivalry has been a continuous subject of research for several centuries, with the first known reference to the phenomenon coming from the Italian scholar, Giambattista della Porta (1593, as cited by Wade 1996). Della Porta observed that by putting one book in front of each eye with a partition between the books, he was able to read from only one book at a time. Sir Charles Wheatstone (1838) is credited with conducting the first systematic study of binocular rivalry using his mirror stereoscope. During this study, Wheatstone observed a breakdown in perceptual cooperation between the two eyes when the two eyes viewed different stimuli. In the preceding years, this phenomenon garnered the attention of Hermann von Helmholtz, William James, and Sir Charles Sherrington, all of whom studied the phenomenon. In the years since, hundreds of empirical papers have been published on binocular rivalry.

Binocular rivalry has been a prominent concern with HWDs in aviation since they were first implemented in the US Army's AH-64 Apache helicopter in the mid-1980s.

The HWD system in the AH-64, known as the Integrated Helmet and Display Sighting System (IHADSS), incorporated a monocular display that presented primary flight information, weapon information, and night vision imagery via forward-looking infrared (FLIR) sensors. Early in its use, pilots complained of degraded visual cues, eyestrain, and visual illusions while using the IHADSS (Hiatt et al. 2008). A common theme among pilots who used the IHADSS is alternating perception between the eye viewing the HWD imagery and the eye with only natural visual cues available. Pilots reported that they were unable to effectively control their allocation of attention to information from one eye or the other, and often had to resort to work-arounds, such as closing one eye (Hiatt et al. 2008).

Binocular rivalry during monocular HWD use can affect pilot reaction time to basic visual stimuli, which may subsequently impact higher-order aspects of pilot performance. This delayed reaction time is due to the visual suppression that occurs during binocular rivalry, where there is a general loss of sensitivity to visual information performance (Patterson et al. 2007). Suppression during binocular rivalry impacts the ability to detect a variety of changes in visual stimuli, including changes is orientation, color, position, and brightness (Blake and Fox 1974). One aspect of modern HWDs is that the combiner is transparent; that is, the observer is able to see far-field visual information through the virtual imagery. This characteristic is an important consideration when applying the classical literature on binocular rivalry to HWDs because this literature nearly exclusively involves opaque monocular displays, stereoscopes, or other apparatuses that result in fully dichoptic viewing.

Transparent HWDs, on the other hand, result in partially-dichoptic viewing, which brings into question the relevance of the classical binocular rivalry literature to modern HWDs. To this point, Laramee and Ware (2001) conducted a study to determine the effects of binocular rivalry on reaction time while using either a binocular or monocular HWD. A fundamental component of their experiment was the comparison between opaque and transparent HWDs, as well as a comparison between static and dynamic background stimuli. The purpose of this comparison was to gauge whether there were attention-capture effects of dynamic far-field visual information when attempting to attend to near-field virtual imagery. In this study, observers completed a question-answer task that required attending to text in the HWD imagery. The results showed that observers' reaction times when answering the questions was significantly longer with a monocular HWD than with a binocular HWD, and dynamic background imagery was associated with a further increase in reaction times.

These findings indicate that focusing attention on near field HWD imagery may be impeded by binocular rivalry while using a monocular HWD. Additionally, the attention-capturing nature of moving stimuli in either the near or far domain may further impede attention switching, particularly when using a transparent monocular HWD. In the context of binocular rivalry, these findings indicate that the impact of binocular rivalry on switching attention between competing visual stimuli is just as much of a concern under partially-dichoptic viewing conditions as it is during fully-dichoptic viewing conditions. In the context of HWDs for aviation applications, these findings suggest that binocular rivalry is indeed a concern despite the fact that aviation HWDs incorporate a transparent, rather than opaque, combiner.

Understanding the relationship between attention and binocular rivalry has been a research interest for nearly two centuries. Helmholtz (1925) emphasized the role of attention in binocular rivalry after observing that he was able to bias dominance toward one of two rival stimuli by focusing attention on that stimulus and employing top-down attentive strategies, such as counting aspects of the stimulus, to maintain attention. Inevitably, however, dominance toward that stimulus succumbed to suppression after a period of time. These observations led Helmholtz to formulate an attention-based hypothesis of rivalry, which was based on the idea that eye dominance during binocular rivalry is controlled to a degree by voluntary, goal-directed attention as well as involuntary, stimulus-directed attention.

Empirical literature on this subject corroborates Helmholtz's findings, indicating that a degree of volitional control over binocular rivalry is possible. Lack (1978) investigated whether it is possible to control the rate of switching between stimuli during dichoptic viewing and found that his subjects were easily able to speed, as well as slow, the rate that perception alternated between each eye, suggesting that it is possible to switch attention between rival stimuli during dichoptic viewing with relative ease. It is important to make the distinction, however, that while observers have some control over which of two stimuli are perceived, this does not necessarily mean that observers can alternate perception between eyes. Past research indicates that, aside from relying on oculomotor work-arounds (e.g., blinking or closing one eye), observers seem unable to voluntarily switch perception between the left and right eyes.

5.6 Eye Dominance

With a monocular HWD, where only a single eye views the virtual imagery, the question of whether it matters which eye views the virtual imagery is important. In general, there is a tendency for binocular rivalry to be biased such that perception is based more on the retinal image of one eye than that of the other (Patterson et al. 2007). Initially, this eye dominance was thought to be a result of body lateralization, such as hand dominance (Borrelli et al. 2017). However, the empirical literature on the subject points to no correlation between eye dominance and other types of dominance in the body (Bourassa 1996). Rather, eye dominance appears to be a multifactorial concept, with different types of dominance. The majority of individuals are right-eye dominant and therefore tend to rely more on information from the right eye when performing visually-guided actions (Rash et al. 1990).

There is conflicting evidence on whether eye dominance affects dominance during binocular rivalry and suppression under dichoptic viewing conditions. On one hand, past research has shown that there is little to no correlation between sighting tests of eye dominance and eye dominance during binocular rivalry (Washburn et al. 1934). This suggests that the cognitive and perceptual processes behind sighting dominance and binocular rivalry dominance may have little to no relationship. For example, sighting dominance may be influenced by perceived visual direction whereas dominance during binocular rivalry may be influenced by inhibitory processes (Patterson et al. 2007). On the other hand, there is evidence indicating that sighting eye dominance does affect dominance during binocular rivalry, resulting in the imagery presented to the dominant eye being seen more frequently than imagery presented to the non-dominant eye (Collins and Blackwell 1974). Rash et al. (1990) corroborated this by suggesting that a pilot's ability to attend to one or the other eye while using a monocular HWD is affected by sighting eye dominance. Eye dominance in the context of HWDs is an important consideration when comparing monocular to binocular HWDs. The conflicting evidence on whether eye dominance affects attention under dichoptic viewing conditions warrants further investigation, considering that the possibility of eye dominance hindering attentional switching could affect a pilot's ability to effectively attend to real-world and HWD information.

5.7 Binocular Overlap

Binocular overlap refers to the proportion of the field of view that is shared by both eyes in biocular and binocular HWDs. Full binocular overlap involves both eyes receiving the same image fully overlapped with one another (Melzer and Moffitt 1989). Partial binocular overlap, however, is characterized by each eye receiving a unique image where a portion of each image is identical (i.e., the binocular region). Constraints in HWD size, hardware, and optics geometry sometimes make it impractical for the HWD to present visual information with 100% binocular overlap. Instead of constricting the overall field of view of the HWD, the alternative is to reduce the amount of binocular overlap while maintaining a high overall field of view (Velger 1998).

Research involving displays with partial binocular overlap indicate that performance on visual search tasks tend to be poorer when overlap is less than 100% (Edgar et al. 1991). This poorer performance could be attributed to perceptual conflicts, such as luning, which refers to the perceived darkening of the monocular regions of the visual field compared to the binocular region (Velger 1998). Melzer and Moffitt (1989) suggest that luning is attributed to binocular rivalry, where perception alternates between the left and right monocular regions of the virtual image, making the edges of the binocular region of that image more apparent. Previous research has shown that luning can be minimized by using a convergent display system, where the right eye views the area to the right of the binocular region and the left eye views the area to the left of the binocular region, as well as by reducing the display luminance near the edges of the binocular region (Patterson et al. 2007).

6 Attention

A foundational characteristic of human cognition is the limited capacity for processing information; humans cannot attend to everything in the environment at once and therefore must flexibly allocate attention based on task demands and immediate goals (Strayer and Drews 2007). Among the variety of aspects of attention involved in aviation, selective attention and divided attention are the primary means by which pilots receive and process information relevant for safe flight. Selective attention is involved when an operator is processing only that information which is relevant for the current task and filtering out all other information (Johnston and Dark 1986). Divided attention is involved when an operator is processing information needed for carrying out two or more concurrent tasks or activities at the same time (Strayer and Drews 2007).

To aviate effectively, pilots must allocate attention between information in the near domain, which consists of instruments on the head-down instrument panel and virtual head-up imagery, and the far domain, which consists of the external environment, such as terrain, obstacles, and airports. In addition to the primary task of aviating, pilots must perform the duties of communicating (e.g., with the first officer and air-traffic control) and navigating (e.g., reaching waypoints in 3D space and avoiding bad weather; Wickens 2007). These tasks often compete with one another for the pilot's attention, so they must choose which to perform if the tasks cannot be performed simultaneously. Pilots' selection of which activity to attend to is driven by the salience of information, relative effort required for the activity, the degree of expectancy of the activity, and the relative value in performing the activity (Wickens et al. 2004).

Attention allocation processes in the flight deck can largely be categorized into two groups: goal directed and stimulus directed. That is, pilots' allocation of visual attention can be driven by the goals that are relevant to the current task (e.g., attending to the airspeed indicator when the goal is to determine the current altitude) or by the nature of the visual stimuli present in the visual field (Yantis 1993). When attention is goal directed, it involves top-down information processing, which is driven by prior knowledge, experience, and contextual information. Top-down processing also involves the ability to correctly deduce what a stimulus or event is, even in the absence of clear characteristics necessary to identify it using bottom-up processing (Wickens et al. 2004). When attention is stimulus driven, it involves bottom-up processing, which is driven by characteristics of stimuli in the environment. For example, sudden-onset stimuli (e.g., flashing lights) and movement are likely to attract attention (Yantis and Jonides 1990). The latter process is known as stimulus-driven attentional capture. Stimulus-driven attentional capture can be a powerful mechanism in the context of HWD use. On one hand, it can be utilized to draw the pilot's attention toward a process that requires their immediate attention (e.g., flashing light to indicate a warning or alert). On the other hand, if utilized inappropriately, it can draw the pilot's attention away from the primary task and hinder their performance.

A variety of HWD design characteristics can influence the degree to which attentional capture can occur. These characteristics include symbology format, field of view, expectancy, and eye accommodation (Prinzel and Risser 2004). Regarding symbology format, previous research has shown that when symbology is conformal pilots are better able to allocate their attentional resources, thereby reducing the time it takes for pilots to determine if it is safe to land after breaking out from low clouds (Wickens and Long 1995). At the same time, conformal symbology may present a hindrance to the attentional capture mechanisms that aid pilots in detecting unexpected events in the environment. Fadden et al. (2001) found that conformal HUD symbology resulted in improved flight path tracking and detection of expected events. However, conformal symbology contributed to poorer detection of unexpected events in the environment when compared to non-conformal symbology, indicating that the HUD can induce cognitive tunneling and attenuate the attentional capture effects of an unexpected event, such as a runway incursion.

The superimposition of information that traditionally appears within the flight deck instrumentation onto the external environment when using a virtual image display, such as a HUD or HWD, changes the attention allocation process compared to flying aircraft with only traditional head-down instrumentation. With these displays, tasks can require the pilot to (a) focus attention exclusively on near domain information, such as when attempting to maintain a specific airspeed or rate of descent; (b) focus attention exclusively on far domain information, such as when attempting to scan the runway environment for potential threats to safe landing; or (c) integrate related information between the two domains, such as when using the flight director on the HUD or HWD and the runway lighting infrastructure during landing to align the aircraft with the runway (Wickens and Long 1995). Additionally, attention allocation between the near and far domains when using a virtual image display can alternate between three primary states. First, attention may be divided between information in both the near and far domains such as when information in both domains is easily integrated, but also when the demands involved with processing that information is low. Second, attention may be focused on one domain while information in the other domain is disregarded. Third, attention may be switched between the two domains, such as when the pilot must discontinue processing information in the primary flight display and begin scanning the runway environment to ensure that it is safe to land (Weintraub et al. 1984; Wickens and Long 1995).

The addition of a virtual image display in the flight deck, including the HUD and HWD, also changes the nature of the attention allocation process compared to traditional head-down instruments by optimizing the process of extracting information from the primary flight symbology and aspects of the external environment relevant to flight. By superimposing the imagery, there is a reduced need to scan the instruments on the conventional head-down instrument panel (Martin-Emerson and Wickens 1997). The idea behind this it is that improving the spatial layout of the instrumentation will facilitate the pilot's ability to process near and far domain information in parallel. Studies that investigate the utility of the HUD in facilitating parallel processing show that the HUD affords an advantage over traditional head-down instruments, which manifests primarily as improved flight path tracking (Lauber et al. 1982; Shelden et al. 1997) and increased performance in detecting obstacles in the external environment when those obstacles are expected by the pilot (Fadden et al. 1998).

A potential pitfall of this increased information presentation ability, however, is increased visual clutter. The second design characteristic of the HWD that is relevant for pilot information processing is the presentation of imagery to a single eye when using a monocular HWD. Previous studies have indicated that perception and attention during normal, binocularly-fused viewing may be different than during with dichoptic viewing, which is inherent to monocular HWDs. Kimchi et al. (1995) conducted an experiment to determine if individuals could voluntarily direct attention to stimuli presented to only a single eye. Participants performed a target detection task that involved selectively attending to information in one or the other eye. The results of the experiment indicated that providing the participants with advanced knowledge on which eye would receive the target stimulus did not improve performance over not providing such information. Their findings suggest that humans are not able to voluntarily direct attention toward one or the other eye.

6.1 Attentional Tunneling

To fly safely and effectively, a pilot should be able to control the locus of their attention, focusing, switching, and dividing it among all of the various sources of information. However, in some cases, this strategic control breaks down and the pilot attends to a particular source of information for too long while neglecting other important sources of information. This phenomenon, termed "attentional tunneling", is defined by Wickens (2005) as "the allocation of attention to a particular channel of information, diagnostic hypothesis or task goal, for a duration longer than optimal, given the expected costs of neglecting events on other channels, failing to consider other hypotheses, or failing to perform other tasks" (p. 812). A strong case can be made that nearly all controlled-flight into terrain (CFIT) accidents are attributed to attentional tunneling (Shappell and Wiegmann 2003).

Previous research has found that pilots can experience attentional tunneling when viewing virtual head-up imagery. In this context, attentional tunneling is characterized by a reduced performance in detecting and responding to unexpected events, such as runway incursions and conformity errors in the primary flight symbology, and is attributed to a breakdown in the process of switching attention from primary flight symbology in the near domain to the runway environment in the far domain (Larish and Wickens 1991). Attention tunneling has been well documented in the empirical aviation literature and has been implicated as one of the primary causes of breakdowns in pilot task management (Wickens 2005). Head-up imagery is well documented as being a contributor to attentional tunneling during flight. A now classic report by Fischer and Haines (1980) was among the first to document the drawbacks of head-up presentation of flight information, finding that pilots flying with a HUD were less likely to detect unexpected runway incursions than those flying without a HUD, despite the fact that flying with a HUD significantly increased the amount of time pilots spent looking out the window with the runway in foveal vision. The findings of this study have been replicated multiple times using both low- and high-fidelity simulations and more robust sample sizes, further demonstrating the prevalence of this phenomenon, and linking (e.g., Fadden et al. 2001; Hofer et al. 2000; Wickens and Long 1995). Failure to detect unexpected events in the runway environment with a HUD or HWD is attributed to the compellingness of these displays, which in turn makes attentional tunneling during their use more likely. Wickens and Yeh (2018) define compellingness as a property of a display that attracts attention at the expense of less attention being allocated to other displays or tasks.

While the research on how HUD use impacts pilot attention is comprehensive, there is a relative scarcity of research examining this construct as it relates to HWD use, particularly how it is related to the various optical configurations of the HWD. As discussed previously, there may be an attentional component involved with maintaining dominance during binocular rivalry. As such, when viewing primary flight symbology with only a single eye through a monocular HWD, a greater degree of attentional control may be required to (a) focus attention on the symbology or on far domain information, (b) integrate information from the near and far domains and process them in parallel, and (c) switch attention from one domain to the other. This may result in a greater likelihood of attentional tunneling occurring when using a monocular HWD compared to when using a binocular HWD.

7 Summary and Future Research

The research discussed in this review covers a wide spectrum of information on the human factors of HWD use in aviation. This research reveals that a variety of perceptual and cognitive factors are at play during HWD use, and the optical configuration of the HWD can influence these factors. A primary takeaway from the literature is that binocular rivalry during dichoptic and partially-dichoptic viewing may present a challenge to pilots when attempting to focus attention, switch attention between imagery and real-world information, and integrate imagery with real-world information when using a monocular HWD. As discussed in previous literature, binocular rivalry may impact a pilot's ability to effectively switch attention between the HWD imagery and the real world, as the interference caused by continuous alternations of dominance and suppression during binocular rivalry may impede the process of deliberately switching attention between two competing stimuli. This may be particularly detrimental if critical information is presented to only the non-dominant eye. If the pilot is not able to switch attention at critical points, such as during landing, performance may be impacted. Furthermore, the process of maintaining focused attention on one stimulus, such as when tracking the primary flight symbology to maintain a specific airspeed, heading, and descent rate, may be negatively affected by the continuous alternation between suppression and dominance of competing stimuli that is inherent to dichoptic viewing conditions. This process may be further hindered when such information is presented only to the non-dominant eye. As such, future research should addresses the impact of binocular rivalry and eye dominance on pilot performance with monocular HWDs and investigate whether these phenomena degrade performance compared to when using a binocular HWD, as well as compared to the traditional HUD.

Future research should address the question of whether partially-dichoptic viewing with a monocular HWD places different demands on pilots' attentional resources than normal viewing with a binocular HWD or HUD. These demands should be assessed in instances where pilots must focus attention on the display for extended periods of time. Lower-visibility approaches (i.e., 1200 ft. RVR and below) require prolonged focusing on near-domain information throughout the approach and landing. If flight technical error is greater during these approaches with a monocular HWD than it is with a binocular HWD, it would indicate that the process of continuously focusing attention on one of two competing visual stimuli places more demands on attentional resources compared to when performing the same activity with normal, fused, binocular vision. The demands on pilots' attentional resources should also be assessed in instances where pilots must switch attention from one information source to another (i.e., from the virtual imagery to natural visual information, such as during low-visibility approaches where there is a need to transition to natural visual cues during an approach in low-visibility conditions.

It is also important to take into account the varying levels of workload and operational conditions that pilots experience during flight. Previous research indicates that high levels of workload can result in attentional tunneling, where focused attention on one aspect of a multidimensional task can hinder the ability to attend to other aspects of the task. To extend this, future research should address whether pilots can effectively manage attention allocation between HWD imagery and real-world information during high-workload phases of flight (i.e., approach and landing) and whether the HWD optical configuration impacts this process. In addition to varying levels of workload, pilots can also experience varying operational conditions, such as reduced visibility and high winds. As such, future research should address how varying visibility levels impact pilot performance with HWDs. Because reduced visibility reduces the salience of far domain information, such as runway markings and runway incursions, such conditions may impact a pilot's ability to effectively allocate attention between HWD imagery and real-world information. The attentional capture mechanisms that aid in attentional switching, such as the appearance of runway lighting systems and their movement in the visual field, may not be as affective in low-visibility conditions and therefore make it more difficult for pilots to switch attention from HWD imagery to the real world when approaching a runway during landing.

References

Arthur III, J.J., et al.: Design and testing of an unlimited field-of-regard synthetic vision head-worn display for commercial aircraft surface operations. In: Enhanced and Synthetic Vision 2007, vol. 6559, p. 65590E. International Society for Optics and Photonics, April 2007

Beringer, D.B.: Synthetic vision applied to general aviation: an evaluation of pilot performance and preferences when using head-up, head-down, and head-mounted synthetic vision displays for SA CAT I approaches in flat terrain and missed approaches in challenging terrain (report no. DOT/FAA/AM-20/02). Office of Aerospace Medicine, Washington, D.C. (2020)

Beringer, D.B., Drechsler, G.: Enhancing helicopter-pilot obstacle avoidance using a binocular head-mounted display. In: Proceedings of the 2013 International Symposium on Aviation Psychology, pp. 500–505 (2013)

Blake, R.: A primer on binocular rivalry, including current controversies. Brain Mind **2**, 5–38 (2001). https://doi.org/10.1023/A:1017925416289

Blake, R., Fox, R.: Binocular rivalry suppression: insensitive to spatial frequency and orientation change. Vis. Res. **14**(8), 687–692 (1974)

Borrelli, A., Hon, G., Zik, Y. (eds.): The Optics of Giambattista Della Porta (ca. 1535–1615): A Reassessment. Springer, Cham (2017). https://doi.org/10.1007/978-3-319-50215-1

Bourassa, D.C.: Handedness and eye-dominance: a meta-analysis of their relationship. Laterality **1**(1), 5–34 (1996)

Collins, J., Blackwell, L.: Effects of eye dominance and retinal distance on binocular rivalry. Percept. Mot. Skills **39**(2), 747–754 (1974)

Drascic, D., Milgram, P.: Perceptual issues in augmented reality. In: Stereoscopic Displays and Virtual Reality Systems III, vol. 2653, pp. 123–134. International Society for Optics and Photonics, April 1996

Edgar, G.K., Carr, K.T., Page, J., Clarke, A.L.: The effects upon visual performance of varying binocular overlap. British Aerospace Systems PLC, Bristol (1991)

Fadden, S., Ververs, P.M., Wickens, C.D.: Pathway HUDS: are they viable? Hum. Factors **43**(2), 173–193 (2001)

Fadden, S., Ververs, P.M., Wickens, C.D.: Costs and benefits of head-up display use: a meta-analytic approach. In: Proceedings of the Human Factors and Ergonomics Society Annual Meeting, vol. 42, no. 1, pp. 16–20, October 1998

Fischer, E., Haines, R.F.: Cognitive issues in head-up displays (NASA technical paper 1711). NASA, Moffett Field (1980)

Gallagher, S.P., Hoefling, C.L.: A size–distance scaling demonstration based on the Holway-Boring experiment. Teach. Psychol. **40**(3), 212–216 (2013) von Helmholtz, H.: Treatise on Physiological Optics. Dover, New York (1925)

Hennessy, R.T., Iida, T., Shiina, K., Leibowitz, H.W.: The effect of pupil size on accommodation. Vis. Res. 16(6), 587–589 (1976)

Hiatt, K.L., Rash, C.E., Heinecke, K.: Visual issues associated with the use of the integrated helmet and display sighting system (IHADSS) in the apache helicopter: three decades in review. In: Brown, R.W., Marasco, P.L., Harding, T.H., Jennings, S.A. (eds.) Proceedings of SPIE: Head-and Helmet-Mounted Displays XIII: Design and Applications (2008)

Hofer, E.F., Braune, R.J., Boucek, G.P., Pfaff, T.A.: Attention switching between near and far domains: an exploratory study of pilots' attention switching with head-up and head-down tactical displays in simulated flight operations (report no. D6–36668). The Boeing Commercial Airplane Co., Seattle (2000)

Howard, I.P., Rogers, B.J.: Binocular Vision and Stereopsis. Oxford University, Oxford (1995)

Iaveccia, J.H., Iaveccia, H.P., Roscoe, S.N.: Eye accommodation to head-up virtual images. Hum. Factors 30(6), 689–702 (1988)

Johnston, W.A., Dark, V.J.: Selective attention. Ann. Rev. Psychol. 37(1), 43–75 (1986)

Kimchi, R., Trainin, O., Gopher, D.: Can attention be directed voluntarily to an eye? Acta Physiol. 89(3), 229–238 (1995)

Lack, L.C.: Selective Attention and the Control of Binocular Rivalry. Mouton, Paris (1978)

Laramee, R.S., Ware, C.: Visual interference with a transparent head mounted display. In: CHI 2001 Extended Abstracts on Human Factors in Computing Systems, pp. 323–324, March 2001

Larish, I., Wickens, C.D.: Divided attention with superimposed and separated imagery: implications for head-up displays (no. 91-4/NASA HUD 91-1). University of Illinois, Aviation Research Laboratory, Savoy (1991)

Lauber, J.K., Bray, R.S., Harrison, R.L., Hemingway, J.C., Scott, B.C.: An operational evaluation of head-up displays for civil transport aircraft (NASA technical paper 1815). NASA Ames Research Center, Moffett Field (1982)

Lindholm, J., Pierce, B., Scharine, A.: Liquid-crystal displays and moving-image quality. In: Proceedings of the 2001 Interservice/Industry Training, Simulation, and Education Conference, pp. 1–9. National Training Systems Association, Arlington (2001)

Martin-Emerson, R., Wickens, C.D.: Superimposition, symbology, visual attention, and the head-up display. Hum. Factors 39(4), 581–601 (1997)

Melzer, J.E., Moffitt, K.: Head-Mounted Displays: Designing for the User. McGraw-Hill Professional, New York (1996)

Melzer, J.E.: Head-mounted displays. In: Spitzer, C., Ferrell, U., Ferrell, T. (eds.) Digital Avionics Handbook. CRC Press, Boca Raton (2001)

Melzer, J.E., Moffitt, K.: Partial binocular-overlap in helmet-mounted displays. In: Display System Optics II, vol. 1117, pp. 56–62. International Society for Optics and Photonics, Bellingham, March 1989

Newman, R.L.: Response to roscoe, "the trouble with HUDs and HMDs." Hum. Factors Soc. Bull. 30(10), 3–5 (1987)

Patterson, R., Martin, W.L.: Human stereopsis. Hum. Factors 34(6), 669–692 (1992)

Patterson, R., Winterbottom, M.D., Pierce, B.J.: Perceptual issues in the use of head-mounted visual displays. Hum. Factors 48(3), 555–573 (2006)

Patterson, R., Winterbottom, M., Pierce, B., Fox, R.: Binocular rivalry and head-worn displays. Hum. Factors 49(6), 1083–1096 (2007)

Prinzel III, L.J., Risser, M.: Head-up displays and attention capture (report no. NASA/TM-2004-213000). Langley Research Center, Hampton (2004)

Rash, C.E.: Helmet Mounted Displays. Design Issues for Rotary-Wing Aircraft (1998). http://www.usaarl.army.mil/hmdbook/cp_0002_contents.htm

Rash, C.E., Verona, R.W., Crowley, J.S.: Human factors and safety considerations of night-vision systems flight using thermal imaging systems. In: Helmet-Mounted Displays II, vol. 1290, pp. 142–164, October 1990

Roscoe, S.N.: When the day is done and the shadows fall, we miss the airport most of all. Hum. Factors **21**, 721-731 (1979a)

Roscoe, S.N.: Ground-referenced visual orientation with imaging displays: final report (report no. Eng Psy-79-4/AFOSR-79-4). University of Illinois, Department of Psychology, Champaign (1979b)

Roscoe, S.N.: The trouble with HUDs and HMDs. Hum. Factors Soc. Bull. **30**(7), 1–3 (1987)

Shappell, S.A., Wiegmann, D.A.: A human error analysis of general aviation controlled flight into terrain accidents occurring between 1990–1998 (report no. DOT/FAA/AM-03/4). Office of Aerospace Medicine, Washington, D.C. (2003)

Shelden, S.G., Foyle, D.C., McCann, R.S.: Effects of scene-linked symbology on flight performance. In: Proceedings of the Human Factors and Ergonomics Society Annual Meeting, vol. 41, no. 1, pp. 294–298 (1997)

Silverstein, L., Wilbert, J.: Responses to roscoe, "the trouble with HUDs and HMDs." Hum. Factors Soc. Bull. **30**(10), 5–6 (1987)

Strayer, D.L., Drews, F.A.: Attention. In: Durso, F. (ed.) Handbook of Applied Cognition, 2nd edn. Wiley, West Sussex (2007)

Velger, M.: Helmet-Mounted Displays and Sights. Artech House, Boston (1998)

Wann, J.P., Rushton, S., Mon-Williams, M.: Natural problems for stereoscopic depth perception in virtual environments. Vis. Res. **35**(19), 2731–2736 (1995)

Wade, N.J.: Descriptions of visual phenomena from Aristotle to Wheatstone. Perception **25**(10), 1137–1175 (1996)

Washburn, M.F., Faison, C., Scott, R.: A comparison between the Miles ABC method and retinal rivalry as tests of ocular dominance. Am. J. Psychol. **46**(4), 633–636 (1934)

Weintraub, D.J., Endsing, M.: Human factors issues in head-up display design: the book of HUD (report no. SOAR 92-2). University of Dayton Research Institute, Dayton (1992)

Weintraub, D.J.: HUDs, HMDs, and common sense: polishing virtual images. Hum. Factors Soc. Bull. **30**(10), 1–3 (1987)

Weintraub, D.J., Haines, R.F., Randle, R.J.: The utility of head-up displays: eye-focus vs decision times. In: Proceedings of the Human Factors Society Annual Meeting, vol. 28, no. 6, pp. 529–533 (1984)

Weintraub, D.J., Haines, R.F., Randle, R.J.: Head-up display (HUD) utility, II: runway to HUD transitions monitoring eye focus and decision times. In: Proceedings of the Human Factors Society Annual Meeting, vol. 29, no. 6, pp. 615–619, October 1985

Wheatstone, C.: Contributions to the physiology of vision—part the first. On some remarkable, and hitherto unobserved, phænomena of binocular vision. Philos. Trans. Roy. Soc. Lond. **128**, 371–394 (1838)

Wickens, C.D.: Attentional tunneling and task management. In: 2005 International Symposium on Aviation Psychology, pp. 812–817 (2005)

Wickens, C.D.: Aviation. In: Durso, F. (ed.) Handbook of Applied Cognition, 2nd edn. Wiley, West Sussex (2007)

Wickens, C.: Attention: theory, principles, models and applications. Int. J. Hum.-Comput. Interact. **37**(5), 403–417 (2021)

Wickens, C.D., Lee, J., Liu, Y., Gordon-Becker, S.: An Introduction to Human Factors Engineering. Pearson Education, Inc., Upper Saddle River (2004)

Wickens, C.D., Long, J.: Object versus space-based models of visual attention: Implications for the design of head-up displays. J. Exp. Psychol. Appl. **1**(3), 179–193 (1995)

Wickens, C.D., Yeh, M.: Display compellingness: a literature review (report no. DOT/FAA/AM-19/13). Office of Aerospace Medicine, Washington, D.C. (2018)

Yantis, S.: Stimulus-driven attentional capture. Curr. Dir. Psychol. Sci. **2**(5), 156–161 (1993)

Yantis, S., Jonides, J.: Abrupt visual onsets and selective attention: voluntary versus automatic allocation. J. Exp. Psychol. Hum. Percept. Perform. **16**(1), 121 (1990)

Yeh, M., Wickens, C.D.: Performance issues in helmet mounted displays (report no. ARL-97-9/ARMY-FED-LAB-97-1). Aviation Research Laboratory, Savoy (1997)

Estimating Cognitive Load and Cybersickness of Pilots in VR Simulations via Unobtrusive Physiological Sensors

G. S. Rajshekar Reddy[1]([✉]), Cara A. Spencer[1], Kevin Durkee[2], Brennan Cox[3], Olivia Fox Cotton[2], Sheila Galbreath[2], Sarah Meyer[2], Michael Natali[3], Todd Seech[3], Gabriella Severe-Valsaint[4], Gavin Zimmerman[1], and Leanne Hirshfield[1]

[1] Institute of Cognitive Science, University of Colorado, Boulder, CO, USA
{rajshekar.gudasubhash,cara.spencer,gavin.zimmerman,
leanne.hirshfield}@colorado.edu
[2] Aptima, Inc., Dayton, OH, USA
{kdurkee,ofox,sgalbreath,smeyer}@aptima.com
[3] U.S. Navy, Wright-Patterson Air Force Base, Dayton, OH, USA
michael.w.natali.mil@us.navy.mil, todd.seech1@navy.mil
[4] Naval Air Warfare Center Training Systems Division, Orlando, FL, USA
gabriella.severe-valsaint.civ@us.navy.mil

Abstract. Predicting real-time estimates of cognitive load in pilots assists intelligent flight systems in alleviating high workloads, thereby averting accidents and directly impacting safety in aviation. Virtual Reality (VR) flight simulations provide an immersive stage to evaluate physiological measures and identify their cognitive correlates. In this work, unobtrusive sensors such as eye-tracking, pupillometry, and photoplethysmography (PPG) record physiological data while six participants perform six flying tasks of varying complexity in VR. The extracted feature sets such as pupil diameter change, number of fixations and saccades, and heart rate variability (HRV) are compared to the Pilot Inceptor Workload (PIW) measures, specifically duty cycle and aggressiveness. The PIW, number of saccades, and the self-reported workload measures were significantly affected by the tasks. However, the number of saccades measure demonstrated a significant negative correlation with the PIW's measures, contradicting prior work. The remaining feature sets, including the pupil diameter change and the number of fixations, display a nearly identical trend to the PIW measure, though no significance was detected.

Keywords: Cognitive load · Cybersickness · Virtual reality · Aviation

1 Introduction

Modern-day aviation involves interfacing with incredibly complex technologies, and simulations help train pilots to operate these complex technologies efficiently.

© Springer Nature Switzerland AG 2022
J. Y. C. Chen and G. Fragomeni (Eds.): HCII 2022, LNCS 13318, pp. 251–269, 2022.
https://doi.org/10.1007/978-3-031-06015-1_18

For decades, flight simulators have been used in commercial pilot training and military aviation. Nevertheless, there are several significant challenges with traditional flight simulators: (i) the high costs to acquire, operate and maintain, (ii) large space requirements, and (iii) their limited capabilities that are specific to a particular aircraft.

These challenges make them a liability and hamstring the user in ways that VR training does not. VR has presented itself as a promising modality to offer a more immersive and adaptable simulation experience at a fraction of the cost of traditional flight simulators. VR flight training tools provide the opportunity to evaluate aviation systems and human performance through various new and informative approaches that improve upon the science of training effectiveness and human system integration.

Furthermore, piloting fighter aircraft and performing mid-air maneuvers under high G's are complex multi-tasking and cognitively demanding activities requiring working memory to satisfy task demands [30]. Simulating such resource-intensive VR scenarios and accurately predicting the pilots' cognitive state is of crucial importance for many reasons: (i) using VR can save money, time, and machinery (ii) provide pilots with enhanced learning experiences, (iii) provide instructors with guidance and evaluation metrics to best help students, (iv) and lead to the prevention of declines in performance through training flight assistance systems.

With physiological sensors integrated into VR Head-mounted Displays (HMDs) such as eye tracking and PPG, it is now possible to objectively estimate the users' mental workload in real-time. These unobtrusive and non-invasive measures are of particular value in complex environments, such as the cockpit, because they typically do not increase cognitive load and do not require shifting attention from the complex task at hand. In addition, obtrusive sensors may hinder the user's performance and delay critical reaction times which are crucial in aviation.

Eventually, the data from these measures can be used to construct a machine learning classifier such that flight systems are better informed when to assist the pilot, ultimately paving the way to safer aviation.

However, a significant downside to using immersive simulators is cybersickness caused by the visual-vestibular conflict. Users tend to feel nauseous, dizzy, and generally disoriented when they experience moving visual stimuli while the vestibular system in the inner ear cannot sense actual motion [32]. Real-time biomarkers such as electrodermal activity, respiration, PPG, and eye movement characteristics provide the necessary physiological measures closely related to cybersickness [9,28]. Identifying the precise correlations of these measures would enable future VR systems to mitigate cybersickness symptoms in real-time and consequently improve the VR experience.

Considering all these benefits of real-time prediction of the pilot's cognitive load and cybersickness, we undertook a study to examine the respective correlates and extend previous work by validating the feasibility of using unobtrusive physiological sensors in VR. We built a testbed to induce cognitive load and cybersickness using the Prepar3D [34] flight simulator, which entails performing six flying tasks of various complexity in succession. Specifically, the tasks involve flying an aircraft through virtual gates while executing maneuvers in between. Participants comprise university students who operate a trainer aircraft using a Hands-on Throttle-and-Stick (HOTAS). While the participants perform the task, a suite of physiological sensors capture various data metrics like pupil diameter change, number of fixations and saccades, and HRV; and are described further in Sect. 3.2. We then investigate the correlations of these metrics to the PIW's [18] parameters, namely duty cycle and aggressiveness, which serve as a reliable ground truth estimate of task complexity, and hence workload.

The key contributions of this paper are:

- Validating the use of unobtrusive physiological sensors in VR to estimate cognitive load in flight training scenarios.
- Examining correlations between behavioral and physiological parameters, thus corroborating prior work indicating that pupil dilation and fixations are a reliable workload indicator while also contradicting prior work by demonstrating saccades to be negatively correlated with workload.
- Designing and constructing a VR flight simulation testbed that induces cognitive load and cybersickness through a series of six flying tasks of varying complexity.

In the subsequent sections, we discuss other prior work in estimating a pilot's cognitive load, followed by a thorough description of the study undertaken in Sect. 3. Sections 4 and 5 report the results from the study and their interpretations. We then conclude and outline directions for future work.

2   Background

Mental overload plays a significant role in aviation safety and must be mitigated. It can be assessed through various means such as self-reported measures like the NASA-Task Load Index (TLX) [20] and the Bedford Workload Scale [46], or physiological measures. However, self-reported measures are limiting as humans may not always accurately document their physiological state. For instance, a study showed that motorists were inaccurate in their self-reported vigilance measures compared to the objective physiological measures [48]. In addition to being a real-time estimate, researchers have proved that physiological measures are more sensitive and have employed various physiological-based indices to estimate cognitive states; Lohani et al. [35] provide a detailed review of the measures used, including heart rate and HRV, blood pressure, skin conductance, and pupillometry, among others.

Grant and others [15] introduced a research tool, TOME, to collate and examine real-time neurophysiological data and predict workload. The TOME server analyzes the sensor streams and generates alerts, including the inferred cognitive states of the user. They validated their tool through a flight-sim study where workload is assessed through a suite of sensors measuring blood flow in the frontal cortex (fNIRS), respiration rate, heart rate, galvanic skin response, and pupil dilation. The tasks involved flying a plane while maintaining specific altitude levels under varying weather conditions. They found that pupil dilation correlated highly with task difficulty and was the strongest workload indicator.

In their study, Huttunen et al. [25] estimate cognitive load by observing prosodic features in the pilots' speech. They recorded fifteen military pilots' speech patterns and utterances while they performed a simulated combat flight. The tasks required participants to perform tactical maneuvers, beyond-visual-range interceptions, and so on while serving as a leader of a pair of F/A-18 jets. They showed that the mean fundamental frequency and vocal intensity increased as a function of cognitive load, establishing speech prosody as a viable indicator of cognitive state.

Babu [2] investigated the correlation between PIW against three factors of a pilot's workload: flying quality, secondary task difficulty, and the closing-opposing boundary size levels. The investigation involved a simulator study and an in-flight study, where military pilots performed a pitch-tracking task of a moving target. All the three factors listed above had significant effects on the duty cycle and aggressiveness, the two variables representing PIW. It was also revealed that PIW highly correlated with the Workload Buildup Flight Test Technique, which is based on the Boundary Avoidance Theory [16,17], thereby establishing PIW as a reliable ground truth measure of pilot workload.

Heart rate and HRV are common measurements for flight simulator studies due to their sensitivity to autonomic driven states, especially sympathetic arousal which prepares the central nervous system for activation [45,49]. Villafaina et al. [58] monitored HRV as an indicator of autonomic responses induced by combat flight maneuvers and when combined with the Electroencephalography (EEG) recordings, they were able to discriminate which maneuvers required more attention and which were more mentally demanding. Itoh et al. [26], with similar measures to the current study, used HRV and subjective rankings to determine that mental demand was not different between piloting plane models in their simulators. Mohanavelu et al. [39], employed visibility manipulations and secondary tasks to examine cognitive workload and using an array of HRV metrics with subjective measures, they were able to determine which condition elicited higher cognitive workload.

Chen and Epps [6] look at eye activity to measure cognitive load changes and improve patient care in a healthcare setting. A series of arithmetic-based tasks indicated that pupil features were the most robust discriminator of cognitive load followed by cumulative blinks. They further revealed that saccade amplitude also increased with increased task difficulty. Krejtz et al. [29] analyze whether microsaccades and pupil diameter can serve as a reliable discriminant of cognitive load. Microsaccades are involuntary jerk-like eye movements that typically happen during prolonged fixations [61]. Their study involving three difficulty levels of mental calculation tasks revealed a significant effect of the three tasks on the microsaccade magnitude, but only a marginal main effect on the microsaccade rate. Detecting microsaccades requires a high-frequency eye tracker, and since we are limited by 120 Hz eye tracker in the VR HMD, we do not investigate it in this study.

The role of ocular parameters in estimating a pilot's cognitive load was investigated by Babu et al. [3]. Specifically, they analyze pupil dilation and eye movements such as fixations, saccades, and saccadic intrusions of military pilots during different flight phases and maneuvers. It was found that all parameters were significantly different for the three task difficulty levels. Moreover, the number of fixations and saccades strongly correlated with variations of PIW in the second and third tasks. They further undertook an in-flight study that revealed that the fixation rate was higher during take-off and landing than while cruising. However, our study contradicts this work regarding saccades being a positive workload indicator.

Hebbar et al. [21] explored the correlations between performance-based metrics and physiological measures like EEG and ocular parameters in pilots. Their flight-simulation study involved tasks with three difficulty conditions, the final one requiring participants to perform a secondary selection task on a multi-function display while maintaining their altitude within a range of 1000 ft. They found that the tasks significantly impacted the EEG signal in the low-beta and theta bands. They also found a significant impact on ocular parameters such as the Nearest Neighbour Index (NNI), which represents the distribution pattern of fixations, and the L1 Norm of Spectrum (L1NS) derived from the pupil dilation signal. Moreover, they established a significant correlation between L1NS and NNI and observed positive correlations between duty cycle and EEG and between duty cycle and the ocular parameters.

In summary, several studies have shown that physiological indicators, in particular ocular and heart rate parameters have been proven to be a valuable and pragmatic indicator of task complexity and consequently, cognitive state. However, most of the above studies use obtrusive sensors that may hamper task performance and slow critical reaction times. Our study focuses on examining whether unobtrusive sensors in VR can be used to estimate workload and cybersickness reliably.

3 Methodology

3.1 Experiment Setting

This study aims to induce cognitive load and cybersickness through a series of six flying tasks of various complexity. The weather conditions were kept constant during all the tasks and were simulated to be bright, clear, sunny, and with no wind. The tasks involve flying a Boeing T-45C jet through six virtual gates placed at regular intervals and are described in further detail in Table 1. A vertical inside loop maneuver is "when the pilot pulls the plane up into the vertical, continues around until they are heading back in the same direction, like making a 360° turn", and a barrel roll maneuver is "a combination of a loop and a roll. The flight path during a barrel roll has the shape of a horizontal corkscrew" [60].

The simulation is built entirely in Lockheed Martin's Prepar3D [34] flight simulator, which allows precise customization and provides Steam VR [57] support. Moreover, Prepar3D allows for creating scenarios where developers can

Table 1. Description of the flying tasks

Task no.	Task name	Task description
1	Flying straight	Requires flying in a straight line path while making sure to pass virtual gates at regular intervals
2	Minor turns	Requires performing minor turns between gates. A virtual arrow points to the next gate
3	180-degree turns	Requires performing 180-degree turns between gates. A virtual arrow points to the next gate but requires participants to look over their shoulders to notice the gate
4	Loop maneuver	Requires performing 180-degree turns between gates and executing a total of 5 vertical inside loop maneuvers upon hearing an audio prompt
5	Barrel roll maneuver	Requires performing 180-degree turns between gates and executing a total of 5 barrel roll maneuvers upon hearing an audio prompt
6	Nearsight/Farsight focusing	Requires performing 180-degree turns between gates and reporting the flight's current airspeed, altitude, and heading upon hearing an audio prompt. Participants are instructed to read this information off of the head-up display

customize the flight simulation's environment and provide additional guidance to users through user interface elements, sound, object visibility, and more. It also enables logging flight data through additional scripting. Upon completing each task, participants fill out two questionnaires, pertaining to their workload and cybersickness. These questionnaires were administered within the VR environment by placing a 2D plane showing survey items in a 3D space. Participants were able to use the HOTAS controls to toggle through and select survey items.

The HP Reverb G2 Omnicept Edition headset [24] is utilized in this study as it packs a suite of unobtrusive physiological sensors, namely, Eye-tracking, Pupillometry, and a PPG sensor. The headset bears a resolution of 2160×2160 per eye, a 90 Hz refresh rate display, and a field of view of $114°$. Participants control the aircraft by operating a Thrustmaster Warthog HOTAS [55] and the Thrustmaster Pedals [56] to manipulate the rudder. Figure 1(a) shows the user flying the jet in VR and Fig. 1(b) depicts a screen capture of the testbed in Prepar3D.

3.2   Measured Feature Sets

The cognitive load of a pilot can be assessed through various techniques and is classified into three categories: (i) Objective, (ii) Subjective, and (iii) Physiological [5,53]. Our study employs measures from all three categories and are described below.

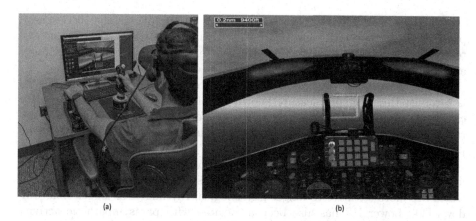

Fig. 1. (a) A user flying the Boeing T-45C jet using a HOTAS, and (b) a screen capture of the testbed in Prepar3D.

Pilot Inceptor Workload. PIW is the workload expended to control the aircraft through the primary flight controls [18]. It is characterized by two individual measures: duty cycle and aggressiveness, which are closely associated with the pilot's appreciation of their workload [41].

   Duty Cycle: Duty cycle is defined as "the percentage of time the pilot changes his input on the inceptor" [19].

   Aggressiveness: Aggressiveness is defined as "the root-mean-squared per-second average of the inceptor position rate of change with respect to time" [18,19].

Here, inceptor refers to the flight stick used in the study. These behavioral metrics are analyzed to identify their correlations to cognitive load and cybersickness, and they serve as a ground truth measure of task complexity. Prepar3D outputs the stick deflection measure in the X and Y axis, from which duty cycle and aggressiveness are computed as follows [41]:

$$\text{Duty cycle} = 100\% * \frac{1}{t_n - t_2} \sum_{i=2}^{n} x_i$$

$$\text{Here, } x_i = \begin{cases} 0, & \text{if } \frac{\delta_i - \delta_{i-1}}{t_i - t_{i-1}} < noise\ threshold\ and\ |\delta_i| < \delta_{max} \\ 1, & \text{otherwise} \end{cases}$$

$$\text{Aggressiveness} = \sqrt{\frac{1}{n-1} \sum_{i=2}^{n} \left(\frac{\delta_i - \delta_{i-1}}{t_i - t_{i-1}}\right)^2}$$

where δ_i refers to the discrete value of the stick deflection, t_i refers to the discrete value of time, and n is the number of discrete data points.

Heart Rate and Heart Rate Variability. Omnicept, via the PPG sensor, provides Heart Rate (HR) and Heart Rate Variability (HRV), which are consistently used in workload research due to their sensitivity to autonomic responses and the relationship to cognitive functions [37,49].

Root Mean Square of Successive Differences (RMSSD): The RMSSD is a robust time-domain measure known to reflect vagal nerve mediated HRV changes (i.e. autonomic nervous system influences) and is not sensitive to respiration mediated HRV changes like other measures, such as HR Max - HR Min [38,50,51,59].

High Frequency (HF): HF is the appropriate frequency-domain measure for the time windows chosen for this study as compared to lower frequencies which are more sensitive to longer physiological rhythms over longer time windows [40]. Lower HF has also been associated with parasympathetic activity driven by stress, panic, anxiety and worry, as well as inflexibility to changing environmental demands, and is connected to attentional and emotional self-regulatory systems [12,49,54].

Eye Tracking and Pupillometry. Eye-tracking offers the most dependable and non-invasive estimate of cognitive load [8]. The Omnicept system enables access to various eye-tracking metrics, although this study utilizes only the pupil dilation data and the combined eye-gaze vectors.

Pupil Diameter Change: Pupil dilation activity is a physiological signal directly linked to the peripheral nervous system [6]. Regardless, changes in pupil dilation are susceptible to changes in ambient light intensity [4] and off-axis distortion [36], and the changes that are related to cognitive activities are relatively small [6]. Hence, pupil dilation should be measured with respect to an average dilation measure during a baseline trial. In that regard, a baseline average was calculated during the period the participants read the study instructions in VR.

The pupil dilation signal is passed through 4 Hz Butterworth low-pass filter to remove artifacts and high-frequency noise. The left and right eye pupil diameters are averaged to further reduce noise in the signal. The baseline average is then subtracted from this signal to get the pupil diameter change measure.

Number of Fixations and Saccades: Fixations are a type of eye movement wherein the eye focuses on a central foveal vision such that the visual system can gather information about the object in focus. Saccades are a type of eye movement used to move the central focus rapidly from one point to another. Fixations and saccades are linked to cognitive activity as they are encoded by neural signals from cortical and subcortical systems [6]. Fixations and saccades are extracted from the combined gaze vector data through the Velocity-Threshold Identification (I-VT) algorithm [42,47], which classifies gaze vectors into either a fixation or a saccade depending on their point-to-point angular velocities. The angular velocity threshold used in this study is 30 degrees per second and was chosen based on the study by Olsen and Matos [43].

Omnicept's Cognitive Load Measure. The Omnicept system also entails a machine learning model, which takes as input all of the Omnicept's physiological measures and outputs a real-time cognitive load metric, ranging from 0 to 1. Their model was trained based on a dataset including behavioral and physiological indicators while users performed mentally demanding tasks in VR. HP details this system in their white paper [52].

Self-reported Measures. The self-report measures administered in VR after each task were designed to assess participants' mental workload and cybersickness. These surveys included the mental demand sub-item from the NASA-TLX [20] questionnaire, which prompts them to rate how mentally demanding the task was on a scale of one to ten, and the Virtual Reality Sickness Questionnaire (VRSQ) [27] which asks participants to rate on a 4-point Likert scale any VR symptoms they experienced, including General discomfort, Fatigue, Eyestrain, Difficulty focusing, Headache, Fullness of the head, Blurred vision, Dizziness, and Vertigo.

Moreover, participants also completed a Motion Sickness Susceptibility Questionnaire (MSSQ) [14] prior to the study, asking them to rate how nauseated or sick they felt during various scenarios in the past, on a 4-point Likert scale, and the Motion Sickness Assessment Questionnaire (MSAQ) [13] after the study, where they rate their experience on different criteria related to motion sickness on a 9-point Likert scale. The scores from these two questionnaires can be examined to determine if VR induces cybersickness in participants who have increased susceptibility to motion sickness and in what effect.

3.3   Study Design

This study used only one independent variable: the flying tasks with six levels of complexity. The study used a wholly within-subjects design, with each participant performing all six flying tasks in succession. A total of 6 participants comprising students from a university in the western United States, of which all 6 were males and with ages ranging from 23 to 26 (M = 24.7, SD = 1.2), took part in the study. Out of the 6 participants, only 1 participant had prior experience with VR. All participants had experience playing video games and averaged 2.9 h (SD = 1.8) of video games played in a week.

Participants first provide informed consent to participate in the study, complete a demographics questionnaire, followed by the MSSQ assessment. Following this, they were debriefed on the tasks they had to perform and were shown video tutorials on how to perform a loop and a barrel roll maneuver. They were also trained on using the HOTAS to operate the aircraft. Participants are informed to pass through the gates as efficiently as possible and interpret missing a gate as a flight safety violation. They complete a tutorial round to become familiar with the simulator and controls. The tutorial is similar to task 1, although participants were allowed to practice maneuvers between gates. The participants were allowed to take breaks between tasks as and when required. To acquire accurate eye-gaze data, an eye calibration was performed using HP's Eye Calibration software [22], each time the headset was taken off and worn again.

Between each task, participants fill out two questionnaires in VR. The first one is the VRSQ for self-reporting cybersickness. The second questionnaire is a sub-item from NASA-TLX for self-reporting workload. After completing the study, participants fill out the MSAQ and are also advised to list any comments they might have related to the study.

4   Results

We examined the responses of the feature sets listed in Sect. 3.2 to the six flying tasks. The data were averaged over a 30-s window, starting when a participant crossed a gate and was averaged across five gates. This window was specifically chosen considering that much of the effort applied during the tasks was during this period as participants had to orient themselves to the next gate, perform loops or barrel rolls, and so on. Figure 3 illustrates the comparison of the mean measures for all tasks, while the error bars depict the 95% confidence interval of these means. We tested for normality using the Shapiro-Wilk tests for all feature sets. The results were not significant, indicating that the feature sets did not deviate from normality. Considering the different task conditions as the independent variable, we performed a one-way repeated measures ANOVA followed by Bonferroni post hoc tests of the feature sets to test for significance. Due to a technical difficulty described in Sect. 5.2, heart rate data could not be collected for three of the six participants and is not investigated further.

The results show that the duty cycle ($F(5, 25) = 4.27$, $p < .01$, $r = .46$) and aggressiveness ($F(5, 25) = 7.55$, $p < .001$, $r = .6$) were significantly affected by the tasks, with Mauchly's test indicating that the assumption of sphericity had been met for both duty Cycle ($\chi^2(14) = 26.78$, $p > .05$) and aggressiveness ($\chi^2(14) = 11.29$, $p > .1$). Plotting aggressiveness versus duty cycle is commonly known as the PIW plot, and its general layout [18] is shown in Fig. 2(a). High aggressiveness and low duty cycle represent occasional fast inputs (upper-left corner), low aggressiveness and high duty cycle represent constant slow inputs (bottom-right corner), and high aggressiveness and high duty cycle represent constant fast inputs (upper-right corner) and are where the pilot gain is the highest. Figure 2(b) illustrates the PIW plot for the six tasks undertaken in our study.

Moreover, it was found that the tasks significantly affected the subjective NASA-TLX ratings ($F(5, 25) = 9.0$, $p < .001$, $r = .64$) and the Omnicept's cognitive load measure, ($F(5, 25) = 12.31$, $p < .001$, $r = .71$). The effect size indicated that the effect of tasks on the Omnicept's cognitive load measure was substantial. There was no significant affect of the tasks on the number of fixations ($F(5, 25) = 2.14$, $p = .094$, $r = .30$), the pupil diameter change ($F(5, 25) = 2.16$, $p = .092$, $r = .30$) and the VRSQ scores ($F(5, 25) = 1.37$, $p = .27$, $r = .21$). Meanwhile, the number of saccades measure was significantly affected by the tasks ($F(1.51, 7.58) = 5.13$, $p < .05$, $r = .50$) while having violated the sphericity assumption indicated by Mauchly's test ($\chi^2(14) = 29.14$, $p <$ .05); therefore the degrees of freedom were corrected using Greenhouse-Geisser estimates of sphericity ($\epsilon = .30$).

Bonferroni post hoc tests revealed a significant difference in the duty cycle only between tasks 1 and 2 (CI.95 $= -16.68$ (lower) -4.0 (upper), $p < .01$). No other comparisons were significant (all $ps > .05$). For aggressiveness, Bonferroni post hoc tests revealed a significant difference between tasks 1 and 2 (CI.95 $= -.13$ (lower) $-.001$ (upper), $p < .05$), tasks 1 and 3 (CI.95 $= -.15$ (lower) $-.004$ (upper), $p < .05$), and tasks 1 and 5 (CI.95 $= -.14$ (lower) $-.011$ (upper), $p < .05$). The post hoc tests for Omnicept's cognitive load measure and the number of saccades measure did not reveal any significant differences.

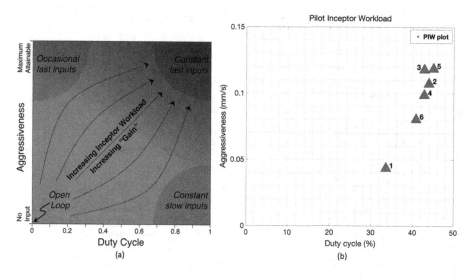

Fig. 2. (a) General layout of a Pilot Inceptor Workload (PIW) plot [18], and (b) PIW plots of the six flying tasks, averaged across all participants.

Additionally, we carried out a Pearson's correlation between the feature sets, listed in Sect. 3.2, the results of which are presented as a correlation matrix in Fig. 4 with the highlighted cells denoting a significant correlation. A strong positive correlation was observed between the ground truth measures: duty cycle and aggressiveness ($\rho = .80$, $p < .001$). Aggressiveness also exhibited a significant positive correlation with Omnicept's cognitive load measure ($\rho = .35$, $p < .05$) and the NASA TLX rating ($\rho = .43$, $p = .01$). Contrary to expectations, the number of saccades measure demonstrated a statistically significant negative correlation with duty Cycle ($\rho = -.52$, $p = .001$), aggressiveness ($\rho = -.45$, $p < .01$), and Omnicept's cognitive load measure ($\rho = -.64$, $p < .001$).

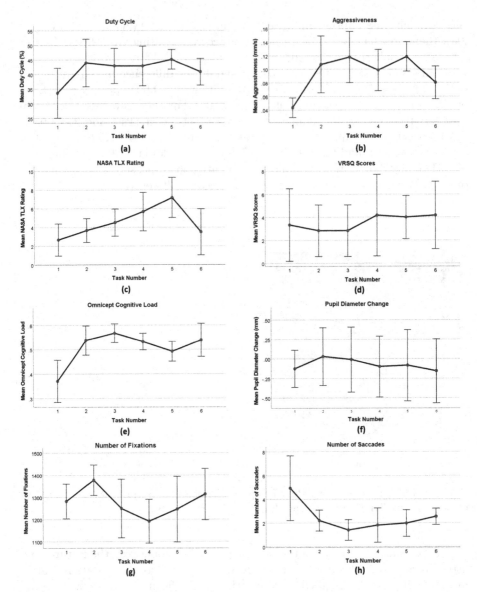

Fig. 3. Comparison of the measured feature sets: (a) Duty cycle, (b) Aggressiveness, (c) NASA TLX, (d) VRSQ scores, (e) Omnicept cognitive load, (f) Pupil diameter change, (g) Number of Fixations, and (h) Number of saccades to the six flying tasks, averaged across all six participants. Error bars represent 95% confidence intervals.

		Number of Fixations	Number of Saccades	Duty Cycle	Aggressiveness	Pupil Diameter Change	Omnicept Cognitive Load	NASA TLX Rating
Number of Fixations	Pearson Correlation	1						
	Sig. (2-tailed)							
Number of Saccades	Pearson Correlation	.341*	1					
	Sig. (2-tailed)	.042						
Duty Cycle	Pearson Correlation	.203	-.522**	1				
	Sig. (2-tailed)	.236	.001					
Aggressiveness	Pearson Correlation	.134	-.448**	.802**	1			
	Sig. (2-tailed)	.435	.006	<.001				
Pupil Diameter Change	Pearson Correlation	-.051	-.019	-.161	.071	1		
	Sig. (2-tailed)	.768	.914	.348	.681			
Omnicept Cognitive Load	Pearson Correlation	-.200	-.644**	.270	.352*	-.191	1	
	Sig. (2-tailed)	.241	<.001	.111	.035	.265		
NASA TLX Rating	Pearson Correlation	-.151	-.186	.235	.426**	-.108	.211	1
	Sig. (2-tailed)	.379	.278	.168	.010	.529	.218	

Fig. 4. Pearson correlation matrix of the feature sets, with significant correlations highlighted and starred (* corresponds to significance at the 0.05 level and ** corresponds to significance at the 0.01 level).

Lastly, we investigated the correlation between the MSSQ and the MSAQ scores to understand whether prior susceptibility to motion sickness influenced cybersickness. The results show no correlation between the two measures ($\rho = .008$, $p = .99$). Figure 5 portrays this correlation via a scatter plot of the scores provided by the six participants.

5 Discussion

5.1 Experimental Findings

The main results of this study were that the PIW measures and some of the physiological measures (number of saccades measure and Omnicept's cognitive load measure) were significantly affected by the tasks having varying levels of complexity. The PIW plots in Fig. 2(b), when compared to the general layout of a PIW plot in Fig. 2(a), provide an exceptional overview of the complexity involved in the six tasks used in this study. A higher duty cycle implies that more time was required to bring the aircraft under control, whereas higher aggressiveness refers to random quick movements of the aircraft's control inceptor. In our study, the tasks 180-degree Turns and the Barrel Roll Maneuver induce the highest pilot gain. The results also show that aggressiveness had a large effect size, which further strengthens our argument to use it as a ground truth measure.

Moreover, It can be inferred from Fig. 3 that except for the number of saccades, all other feature sets display an almost similar trend across the six tasks;

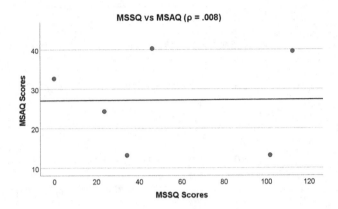

Fig. 5. A scatter plot depicting the correlation between the MSSQ and the MSAQ scores.

participants found tasks to be increasing in complexity until task 3. Furthermore, they found the Barrel Roll Maneuver to be the most cognitively demanding task according to their NASA-TLX ratings, which are also corroborated by the uptick in the physiological responses and the PIW measures.

However, the Loop Maneuver task (task 4) shows a drop in all measures except the number of saccades which exhibit a negative correlation. The Loop Maneuver task was the most challenging for participants since if not done correctly, the aircraft would stall (as it requires flying against gravity before flying towards it) and stumble into an uncontrolled spiral, at which point the task had to be restarted. This was the case with five out of six participants from our observations. We infer that this could have led to practice effects among the participants, and hence the decline in the measures. Another reason could be a compensatory mechanism invoked by increased novelty, complexity, or difficulty of the task [31,62], hence exhibiting a lower physiological response. Another alternative possibility is that pausing and restarting the task skewed the dependent measures being collected, and we note that future work should be done to further explore these measurements.

The lower aggressiveness can be attributed to participants being more steady with the flight stick during the loop, which is necessary for a more even and precise circle. Similarly, as participants held the stick at a stable position, this period was not accounted for in the duty cycle calculations and is a limitation of the equation. The duty cycle formula does account for situations where the stick is in its maximum position with the reasoning that pilots would move it further if possible. However, in our study, participants rarely used the stick in its maximum position as this would cause high G's on the pilot, and the simulation would blackout until the stick was restored to a suitable position.

Meanwhile, the number of fixations measure displayed similar variations as the duty cycle measure, consistent with previous findings [1,3,7,10,11], although except for task 6. The task required participants to fixate on the head-up display

(HUD) to report the flight's information, and they often complained about the information being hard to read due to the low contrast between the sky and the numbers displayed on the transparent HUD. Our reasoning for the increase in fixations in this task is that participants had to strenuously focus on the HUD to report accurate information.

Though past research has shown that the number of saccades and saccade rates are positively correlated with cognitive load [3,7,44], we cannot corroborate their findings as we encounter a statistically significant negative correlation between the PIW and Omnicept's cognitive load measures. The mean number of saccades also exhibits an uptick in task 4, opposing all other physiological and PIW measures. The effect size also indicates that the number of saccades had a large effect. The argument of whether saccades are a dependable positive indicator of mental effort needs to be re-evaluated.

The mean pupil diameter change measure shows a similar trend to the duty cycle measure, albeit having larger variability. This trend agrees with past work establishing pupil diameter change as a reliable workload indicator [6,15,29]. Regardless, no significant correlation was detected between the pupil diameter change measure and the PIW measures. The Omnicept cognitive load measure, on the other hand, exhibited a large effect size ($r = .71$) and demonstrated a significant correlation with the aggressiveness measure, although not a strong one. We conjecture that it may serve as a reliable workload estimate, though it should not be the only estimate.

Lastly, the VRSQ scores display a nearly similar trend to the number of saccades measure, which would mean that saccades could be a positive indicator of cybersickness and should be explored further. Comparing MSSQ and MSAQ scores showed no correlation between them, hinting that prior susceptibility to motion sickness may not influence VR cybersickness. However, no significance was detected in this correlation, and the sample size was limited to only six - one of the participants also claimed to feel nauseous but was unsure if it was from the simulation or food poisoning; hence necessitating further research.

5.2   Study Limitations

Although we demonstrated a significant negative correlation of saccades with cognitive load, saccades are swift movements of the eye to shift the central foveal vision, and detecting them accurately requires an eye tracker with a high sampling rate ($\approx$1000 Hz) [33]. A limitation in our study is the low sampling rate (120 Hz) of the in-built eye tracker [23], which may impact its ability to detect saccades. Nonetheless, there does not yet exist a VR HMD with an eye-tracking frequency greater 200 Hz. Babu et al. [3], however, used the Tobii Pro Glasses 2 with 100 Hz sampling frequency to establish a positive trend between the number of saccades and workload. Additionally, the I-VT algorithm used to classify eye movements in this study, by its nature, is more targeted towards classifying fixations than saccades [42].

Furthermore, we experienced a failure to capture the heart rate data for all participants, had a limited sample size, and our simulation testbed contained an issue for Task 4. Due to an unknown reason, heart rate data was only captured for three of the six participants. Upon further inspection of the three data files, one was unusable due to severe noise in the signal, so these data were not included in this study. After some troubleshooting, we found that the noise was likely due to the tightness of the headset, but we could not find a reason for the complete failure to capture. Our sample was limited mostly in part to a small subject pool available at the time of data collection. The issue with Task 4 was an uncontrollable spiraling and required restart triggered by a failed attempt at the loop. The testbed is being investigated to find a solution that prevents these outcomes for future testbed usage.

6   Conclusion and Future Work

In the present study, we validated the use of unobtrusive sensors in estimating cognitive load through VR simulations. Our study supports previous findings demonstrating that ocular parameters such as pupil diameter change and the number of fixations pose a sensitive and reliable discriminant of task complexity in regards to cognitive load. We also contradict prior research by demonstrating a significant negative correlation between the number of saccades and cognitive load. In further research, it would be useful to conduct the study with a more representative sample such as military pilots. Using virtual gates during maneuvers would assist participants in performing them more accurately and diligently. Consequently, future research should also examine fixations and saccades through other less explored classification algorithms such as the Dispersion-Threshold Identification algorithm [47], which classifies fixations and saccades based on their clusterization.

Acknowledgements. We would like to acknowledge the U.S. Navy for supporting this research via contract number N68335-18-C0133.

References

1. Arjun, S., Rajshekar Reddy, G., Mukhopadhyay, A., Vinod, S., Biswas, P.: Evaluating visual variables in a virtual reality environment. In: 34th British HCI Conference 34, pp. 11–22 (2021)
2. Babu, M.D.: Investigation of pilot inceptor workload and workload buildup technique through simulator and in-flight studies. Int. J. Aerosp. Psychol. **32**(2–3), 65–94 (2022)
3. Babu, M.D., JeevithaShree, D., Prabhakar, G., Saluja, K.P.S., Pashilkar, A., Biswas, P.: Estimating pilots' cognitive load from ocular parameters through simulation and in-flight studies. J. Eye Mov. Res. **12**(3) (2019)
4. Beatty, J., Lucero-Wagoner, B., et al.: The pupillary system. In: Handbook of Psychophysiology, 2nd edn, pp. 142–162 (2000)
5. Casner, S.M., Gore, B.F.: Measuring and evaluating workload: a primer. NASA Technical Memorandum, NASA–TM 2010-216395 (2010)
6. Chen, S., Epps, J.: Automatic classification of eye activity for cognitive load measurement with emotion interference. Comput. Methods Programs Biomed. **110**(2), 111–124 (2013)

7. Coral, M.P.: Analyzing cognitive workload through eye-related measurements: a meta-analysis. Ph.D. thesis, Wright State University (2016)

8. Cowley, B.U., et al.: The psychophysiology primer: a guide to methods and a broad review with a focus on human-computer interaction. Found. Trends Hum. Comput. Interact. **9**(3–4), 151–308 (2016)

9. Davis, S., Nesbitt, K., Nalivaiko, E.: A systematic review of cybersickness. In: Proceedings of the 2014 Conference on Interactive Entertainment, IE 2014, pp. 1–9. Association for Computing Machinery, New York (2014). https://doi.org/10.1145/2677758.2677780

10. Di Nocera, F., Camilli, M., Terenzi, M.: Using the distribution of eye fixations to assess pilots' mental workload. In: Proceedings of the Human Factors and Ergonomics Society Annual Meeting, vol. 50, pp. 63–65. SAGE Publications, Los Angeles (2006)

11. Feng, C., Wanyan, X., Yang, K., Zhuang, D., Wu, X.: A comprehensive prediction and evaluation method of pilot workload. Technol. Health Care **26**(S1), 65–78 (2018)

12. Forte, G., Favieri, F., Casagrande, M.: Heart rate variability and cognitive function: a systematic review. Front. Neurosci. **13**, 710 (2019)

13. Gianaros, P.J., Muth, E.R., Mordkoff, J.T., Levine, M.E., Stern, R.M.: A questionnaire for the assessment of the multiple dimensions of motion sickness. Aviat. Space Environ. Med. **72**(2), 115 (2001)

14. Golding, J.F.: Motion sickness susceptibility questionnaire revised and its relationship to other forms of sickness. Brain Res. Bull. **47**(5), 507–516 (1998)

15. Grant, T., Dhruv, K., Eloy, L., Hayne, L., Durkee, K., Hirshfield, L.: A neurophysiological sensor suite for real-time prediction of pilot workload in operational settings. In: Stephanidis, C., et al. (eds.) HCII 2020. LNCS, vol. 12425, pp. 60–77. Springer, Cham (2020). https://doi.org/10.1007/978-3-030-60128-7_5

16. Gray, W.: Boundary-escape tracking: a new conception of hazardous PIO. Technical report, Air Force Flight Test Center, Edwards AFB, CA (2004)

17. Gray, W.: Boundary avoidance tracking: a new pilot tracking model. In: AIAA Atmospheric Flight Mechanics Conference and Exhibit, p. 5810 (2005)

18. Gray, W.: A generalized handling qualities flight test technique utilizing boundary avoidance tracking. In: 2008 US Air Force T&E Days, p. 1648. Aerospace Research Central (2008)

19. Gray, W.: A boundary avoidance tracking flight test technique for performance and workload assessment. In: Proceedings of the 38th Symposium of Society of Experimental Test Pilots, San Diego (2007)

20. Hart, S.G., Staveland, L.E.: Development of NASA-TLX (task load index): results of empirical and theoretical research. Adv. Psychol. **52**, 139–183 (1988)

21. Hebbar, P.A., Bhattacharya, K., Prabhakar, G., Pashilkar, A.A., Biswas, P.: Correlation between physiological and performance-based metrics to estimate pilots' cognitive workload. Front. Psychol. **12**, 954 (2021)

22. HP Development Company: Eye Tracking Calibration (2022). https://developers.hp.com/omnicept/eye-tracking-calibration. Accessed 23 Feb 2022

23. HP Development Company: Fundamentals (2022). https://developers.hp.com/omnicept/docs/fundamentals?language=es-un. Accessed 23 Feb 2022

24. HP Development Company: HP Reverb G2 Omnicept Edition (2022). https://www.hp.com/us-en/vr/reverb-g2-vr-headset-omnicept-edition.html. Accessed 23 Feb 2022

25. Huttunen, K., Keränen, H., Väyrynen, E., Pääkkönen, R., Leino, T.: Effect of cognitive load on speech prosody in aviation: evidence from military simulator flights. Appl. Ergon. **42**(2), 348–357 (2011)

26. Itoh, Y., Hayashi, Y., Tsukui, I., Saito, S.: The ergonomic evaluation of eye movement and mental workload in aircraft pilots. Ergonomics **33**(6), 719–732 (1990)

27. Kim, H.K., Park, J., Choi, Y., Choe, M.: Virtual reality sickness questionnaire (VRSQ): motion sickness measurement index in a virtual reality environment. Appl. Ergon. **69**, 66–73 (2018)

28. Kim, Y.Y., Kim, H.J., Kim, E.N., Ko, H.D., Kim, H.T.: Characteristic changes in the physiological components of cybersickness. Psychophysiology **42**(5), 616–625 (2005)

29. Krejtz, K., Duchowski, A.T., Niedzielska, A., Biele, C., Krejtz, I.: Eye tracking cognitive load using pupil diameter and microsaccades with fixed gaze. PLoS ONE **13**(9), e0203629 (2018)

30. Lancaster, J.A., Casali, J.G.: Investigating pilot performance using mixed-modality simulated data link. Hum. Factors **50**(2), 183–193 (2008)

31. Latham, G.P., Seijts, G., Crim, D.: The effects of learning goal difficulty level and cognitive ability on performance. Can. J. Behav. Sci. **40**(4), 220 (2008)

32. LaViola, J.J.: A discussion of cybersickness in virtual environments. SIGCHI Bull. **32**(1), 47–56 (2000). https://doi.org/10.1145/333329.333344

33. Leube, A., Rifai, K., Rifai, K.: Sampling rate influences saccade detection in mobile eye tracking of a reading task. J. Eye Mov. Res. **10**(3) (2017)

34. Lockheed Martin Corporation: Lockheed Martin Prepar3D (2022). https://www.prepar3d.com. Accessed 23 Feb 2022

35. Lohani, M., Payne, B.R., Strayer, D.L.: A review of psychophysiological measures to assess cognitive states in real-world driving. Front. Hum. Neurosci. **13**, 57 (2019)

36. Mathur, A., Gehrmann, J., Atchison, D.A.: Pupil shape as viewed along the horizontal visual field. J. Vis. **13**(6), 3–3 (2013)

37. McCraty, R., Shaffer, F.: Heart rate variability: new perspectives on physiological mechanisms, assessment of self-regulatory capacity, and health risk. Glob. Adv. Health Med. **4**(1), 46–61 (2015)

38. Mehler, B., Reimer, B., Wang, Y.: A comparison of heart rate and heart rate variability indices in distinguishing single-task driving and driving under secondary cognitive workload. In: Proceedings of the Sixth International Driving Symposium on Human Factors in Driver Assessment, Training and Vehicle Design, pp. 590–597 (2011)

39. Mohanavelu, K., et al.: Cognitive workload analysis of fighter aircraft pilots in flight simulator environment. Defence Sci. J. **70**(2), 131–139 (2020)

40. Mulder, L.J.M.: Assessment of cardiovascular reactivity by means of spectral analysis. Ph.D. thesis, Rijksuniversiteit (1988)

41. Niewind, I.: Pilot gain and the workload buildup flight test technique: about the influence of natural pilot gain on the achievable pilot gain range. Institute report IB 111-2012/69. German Aerospace Centre (2012)

42. Olsen, A.: The Tobii I-VT fixation filter. Tobii Technology, p. 21 (2012)

43. Olsen, A., Matos, R.: Identifying parameter values for an I-VT fixation filter suitable for handling data sampled with various sampling frequencies. In: Proceedings of the Symposium on Eye Tracking Research and Applications, ETRA 2012, pp. 317–320. Association for Computing Machinery, New York (2012). https://doi.org/10.1145/2168556.2168625

44. Prabhakar, G., Mukhopadhyay, A., Murthy, L., Modiksha, M., Sachin, D., Biswas, P.: Cognitive load estimation using ocular parameters in automotive. Transp. Eng. **2**, 100008 (2020)

45. Roscoe, A.H.: Assessing pilot workload. Why measure heart rate, HRV and respiration? Biol. Psychol. **34**(2–3), 259–287 (1992)

46. Roscoe, A.H., Ellis, G.A.: A subjective rating scale for assessing pilot workload in flight: a decade of practical use. Technical report, Royal Aerospace Establishment Farnborough, United Kingdom (1990)

47. Salvucci, D.D., Goldberg, J.H.: Identifying fixations and saccades in eye-tracking protocols. In: Proceedings of the 2000 Symposium on Eye Tracking Research & Applications, pp. 71–78 (2000)

48. Schmidt, E.A., Schrauf, M., Simon, M., Fritzsche, M., Buchner, A., Kincses, W.E.: Drivers' misjudgement of vigilance state during prolonged monotonous daytime driving. Accid. Anal. Prev. **41**(5), 1087–1093 (2009)

49. Shaffer, F., Ginsberg, J.P.: An overview of heart rate variability metrics and norms. Front. Public Health **5**, 258 (2017)

50. Shaffer, F., McCraty, R., Zerr, C.L.: A healthy heart is not a metronome: an integrative review of the heart's anatomy and heart rate variability. Front. Psychol. **5**, 1040 (2014)

51. Shakouri, M., Ikuma, L.H., Aghazadeh, F., Nahmens, I.: Analysis of the sensitivity of heart rate variability and subjective workload measures in a driving simulator: the case of highway work zones. Int. J. Ind. Ergon. **66**, 136–145 (2018)

52. Siegel, E., et al.: HP Omnicept cognitive load database (HPO-CLD)-developing a multimodal inference engine for detecting real-time mental workload in VR. Technical report, HP Labs, Palo Alto (2021). https://developers.hp.com/omnicept

53. Spyker, D., Stackhouse, S., Khalafalla, A., McLane, R.: Development of techniques for measuring pilot workload. Technical report, NASA (1971)

54. Thayer, J.F., Lane, R.D.: Claude Bernard and the heart-brain connection: further elaboration of a model of neurovisceral integration. Neurosci. Biobehav. Rev. **33**(2), 81–88 (2009)

55. Thrustmaster: HOTAS WARTHOG (2022). https://www.thrustmaster.com/products/hotas-warthog/. Accessed 23 Feb 2022

56. Thrustmaster: T.Flight Rudder Pedals (2022). https://www.thrustmaster.com/en-us/products/t-flight-rudder-pedals/. Accessed 23 Feb 2022

57. Valve Corporation: SteamVR on Steam (2022). https://store.steampowered.com/app/250820/SteamVR/. Accessed 23 Feb 2022

58. Villafaina, S., Fuentes-García, J.P., Gusi, N., Tornero-Aguilera, J.F., Clemente-Suárez, V.J.: Psychophysiological response of military pilots in different combat flight maneuvers in a flight simulator. Physiol. Behav. **238**, 113483 (2021)

59. Wang, Z., Yang, L., Ding, J.: Application of heart rate variability in evaluation of mental workload. Zhonghua lao dong wei sheng zhi ye bing za zhi= Zhonghua laodong weisheng zhiyebing zazhi= Chin. J. Ind. Hyg. Occup. Dis. **23**(3), 182–184 (2005)

60. Wikipedia contributors: Aerobatic maneuver – Wikipedia, the free encyclopedia (2021). https://en.wikipedia.org/w/index.php?title=Aerobatic_maneuver&oldid=1044302151. Accessed 23 Feb 2022

61. Wikipedia contributors: Microsaccade – Wikipedia, the free encyclopedia (2022). https://en.wikipedia.org/w/index.php?title=Microsaccade&oldid=1064617483. Accessed 23 Feb 2022

62. Wong, L., et al.: Performance on the robotics on-board trainer (ROBoT-r) spaceflight simulation during acute sleep deprivation. Front. Neurosci. **14**, 697 (2020)

Critical Review of Extended Reality Applications in Aviation

Brett Torrence[✉] and Jeffrey Dressel

Civil Aerospace Medical Institute, Oklahoma City, OK 73169, USA
{brett.s.torrence,jeffrey.dressel}@faa.gov

Abstract. In recent years, the growing availability of extended reality (XR) technology through mobile, tablet, headset, and wearable devices has led to increased research and development on XR applications in aviation. XR has the potential to enrich the task and training environment of pilots, air traffic controllers, maintenance technicians, and flight crews by augmenting elements of the physical world, enabling remote task support, and providing immersive, controllable environments for safety-critical training. This technology can also improve human factors experiments as it allows for the emulation of environments and systems in various areas of aviation. As this technology develops and new trends emerge, understanding the current state of research can illuminate best practices, limitations, and key considerations to support the application of XR. The purpose of this paper is to provide a critical review of XR applications within the field of aviation through two means: a scientometric analysis and qualitative review of recent scientific studies. Common trends, themes, and applications are identified in the existing literature providing a snapshot of the research at this time. Implications of these findings for future research directions and applications within aviation are discussed.

Keywords: Aviation · Extended Reality · Augmented Reality · Virtual Reality · Mixed Reality · Scientometrics

1 Introduction

The application of Extended Reality (XR) technology in aviation is not new with its history tracing back to the first uses of head-mounted displays (HMD) and head-up displays (HUD) to augment flight data and support pilot navigation in the 1950s and 1960s [1]. However, the rapid advancement of XR technologies and the increasing availability of low cost, off-the-shelf devices has made XR the subject of much interest in aviation research and development. The increased access to XR via mobile devices, tablets, and affordable head-worn devices has enabled research to investigate the utility of such technologies in areas such as maintenance support, flight crew training, pilot training, control tower operations, and ergonomic assessment. Similar growth in XR can be found in related research fields such as human factors, psychology, engineering, human-computer interaction, and medicine [2].

© Springer Nature Switzerland AG 2022
J. Y. C. Chen and G. Fragomeni (Eds.): HCII 2022, LNCS 13318, pp. 270–288, 2022.
https://doi.org/10.1007/978-3-031-06015-1_19

The concepts used to describe augmented, virtual, and mixed reality environments has expanded over the years, somewhat in correspondence with the progression of system capabilities and use [3, 4]. In general, XR refers to any combination of real and virtual elements in an environment and ranges from the overlaying of graphics on a physical object to an immersive, three-dimensional virtual environment [5]. XR has emerged as a collective term to describe immersive environments, such as Augmented Reality (AR), Mixed Reality (MR), and Virtual Reality (VR). As such, XR is a multi-dimensional concept that captures the different type of experiences offered by AR, MR, and VR. Generally, AR and MR are viewed synonymously in the literature with AR being technology that blends computer-generated content with the real world and enables interaction between the digital content and physical environment. MR, on the other hand, takes a step beyond AR allowing the user to interact with the virtual information [6]. VR uses software to create a fully synthetic virtual world [4].

XR applications have the potential to shape significantly the task and training environments of aviation professionals, including pilots, air traffic controllers, maintenance technicians, flight crews, and air accident investigators. The increasing attention given to XR in the field of aviation can be attributed to the number of proposed benefits offered by this technology. For example, Palmarini et al. [7] report that the aviation industry is one of the biggest users of AR for maintenance purposes as this technology can improve safety, reduce human error, and align better with the complex technology used on aircraft and aviation systems. XR devices have been proposed as cognitive support systems for maintenance and inspection [8]; tools for evaluating the ergonomics in system maintainability [9]; and improving pilot and controller visualization in low visibility conditions [10]. Similarly, XR might be effective for training purposes as it provides a more immersive environment than traditional non-immersive methods (e.g., computer desktop) and can prompt realistic behaviors and interactions, increase feelings of presence, and provide quality training for high-risk, off-nominal events [11, 12].

1.1 Purpose

As the use of XR in aviation grows and research continues to investigate the utility of such applications for improving safety, efficiency, and human performance, understanding the current state of the research can serve to inform future research and guide the application of XR throughout aviation. In this paper, a critical review of the scientific literature is provided to highlight the prevalence of XR technologies (AR, MR, VR) in aviation, including typical use cases and applications, current empirical evidence for the use of XR, and best practices and considerations. This critical review is accomplished through a scientometric analysis of the published literature (e.g., keywords, citations) and a qualitative review of selected articles. Since confusion exists among XR technologies, this paper will provide a set of common definitions for XR terms and briefly describe a conceptual framework of XR to create shared understanding of the topic prior to the review of the literature.

2 XR Definitions, Framework, and Characteristics

2.1 Definitions

In the XR literature, AR, MR, and VR (in particular AR and MR) are used somewhat interchangeably leading to a lack of conceptual clarity [2, 5, 6]. For example, AR and MR have been treated as synonyms, combinations, or subsets of one another [4]. The difficulty in defining these concepts is because XR is often defined in terms of its technology (e.g., hardware) and/or its psychological characteristics (e.g., level of immersion). While the goal of the paper is not to establish strict definitions within research on XR in aviation, commonly used definitions will be presented here to establish a common shared understanding of these concepts. Importantly, as XR technologies, and the immersive experiences they provide, continue to develop, so too will the definitions used to capture these concepts.

XR is an umbrella term encompassing the entire range of augmented and virtual realities provided by immersive technologies such as AR, MR, and VR [13]. AR is the combination of real and virtual objects where virtual objects are added to a real-world environment [1]. AR systems enhance the real world by allowing virtual content and real-world objects to coexist in a single display or common environment [14]. AR also enables some real-time interaction between the real and virtual objects [2]. There is less consensus regarding MR as it can be viewed as an extension of AR or an umbrella term similar to XR (i.e., any blend of real and virtual objects). Brown [6] states that MR "has all of the attributes of AR" and adds additional technological features such as holographic images, spatial sound, and geo-mapping. The level of interaction between real and virtual objects is also argued to differentiate MR from AR. MR enables greater interaction between virtual and real objects than AR and accounts for factors such as obstacles and boundaries in the visual display [5, 15]. Finally, VR is defined as a synthetic and artificial environment that simulates a user's presence within the virtual setting [14]. VR typically offers users the ability to directly participate in and manipulate objects in the virtual environment. VR is characterized by feelings of immersion and presence as users are "transported" away from one's physical environment [6].

2.2 Framework of XR Technologies

The most popular framework within the XR literature to describe different augmented and virtual technologies is the reality-virtuality continuum proposed by Milgram and Kishino [16]. The reality-virtuality continuum was developed to facilitate a better understanding of how virtual technologies are related and describe the level of reality and virtuality they display. This continuum describes environments ranging from a real environment to a fully-virtual environment with different combinations of real and virtual realities falling between those endpoints. VR is defined at the far end of the continuum with everything else representing MR (and AR being a subset of the MR space) [16]. Specifically, MR includes environments where the real world is augmented with virtual objects (i.e., AR) as well as environments where reality or physical objects are added to a virtual environment.. Even though the continuum does not mention XR directly, XR includes the AR, MR, and VR components of the framework.

The continuum by Milgram and Kishino was developed in terms of visual features, but the advancement of XR has extended the sensory information able to users to include audio, motion, and haptic features. As such, it is not simply the level of reality (or virtuality) that separates environments, but the technological features of the system and psychological characteristics of the experience. This includes elements like the degree of presence, the coherence of the system, and the fidelity of modeling of the real world [3, 16].

Fig. 1. Example augmented reality application. ("Home Made Augmented Reality" by T. Geersing is licensed under Creative Commons BY 2.0)

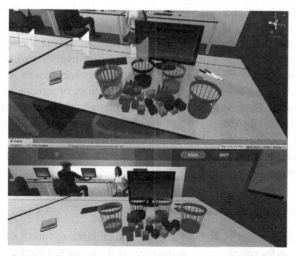

Fig. 2. Example virtual reality application. ("Tom Brown by The Glasgow School of Art is licensed under Creative Commons BY-NC-ND 2.0)

2.3 Characteristics of XR

The original reality-virtuality continuum [16] and more recent reviews of this framework [3] suggest that the XR experience can be described by both objective and subjective characteristics. Objective characteristics primarily reflect the features and functionality of the XR system, whereas subjective characteristics refer to the user's experience and psychological processes within the XR environment. Objective characteristics include immersion, coherence, and extent of world knowledge. Immersion reflects the level of realism in the XR environment, including the extent to which the technology reproduces the physical environment (e.g., physical fidelity) and supports valid actions by the user (e.g., psychological fidelity) [3]. Immersion arises when the technology produces an inclusive, self-contained environment, supports sensorimotor actions by the user, enables the user to effect change in the virtual setting, and contains rich images and content [11]. Coherence is defined as the extent to which the technology creates a unified, integrated experience as well as the level of consistency in which the system conveys this to the user [3]. Skarbez et al. [3] argue that coherence in VR typically relies on virtual objects interacting in predictable ways, while coherence in AR depends on virtual objects interacting with real-world objects and the user in predictable ways. Lastly, Milgram and Kishino [16] describe extent of world knowledge as the degree to which the system is aware of the real world, including the identification and location of the objects. For example, an AR device that is able to superimpose an image directly on a remotely viewed object would have higher extent of world knowledge than an AR device that requires the user to interact with the virtual object until it matches the physical objects location and positioning.

The most commonly discussed subjective characteristic of XR environments is presence. Presence is the feeling of "being there" that arises when users feel connected to their experience and suspend beliefs that they are in an augmented or virtual environment [11]. The psychological experience of presence is closely tied to the immersion and coherence of the XR system. XR environments that provide better recreations of the real-world environment and support typical behaviors by user are likely to engender feelings of presence [3]. Presence is argued to improve outcomes in XR by producing more meaningful experiences that connect users to the environment. Other subjective characteristics, which have received less attention in research, include embodiment (i.e., ability of user to adopt the perspective of the objects and entities), awareness, and replicated world and MR illusion [3, 17]. Overall, these characteristics highlight the unique aspects of XR and how well-designed XR can provide promising solutions for various aviation use cases.

2.4 Benefits of Using XR in Aviation

The task and skill demands as well as the safety and efficiency goals of aviation make XR a plausible solution for several applications ranging from task support systems to training. In aviation, tasks must be completed with the highest possible efficiency, or stated another way, in the quickest amount of time with minimal to no error. Personnel must also be able to respond accurately in low-probability, high-risk events that are not regularly practiced. As well, the advancing technology used in aircraft and aviation systems places additional demand on the workforce both in terms of the training they need and the on-the-job support required for completing tasks. Several reasons as to why XR technologies may be appropriate in aviation are described in the literature. These benefits can be attributed to the functionalities of the XR system, such as object recognition, motion tracking, and haptic feedback, and the immersive, interactive experiences provided by XR. A brief review of potential benefits for XR in aviation are discussed below.

In aviation inspection and maintenance, for instance, tasks involve a significant amount of manual steps, a variety of components that vary in shape and size, and extensive, detailed documentation. Eschen et al. [8] argue that when the time and effort of interaction with real-world objects (e.g., equipment, tools) is high, as is the case in maintenance, the benefit of XR increases. XR can improve the communication of procedures that are difficult to explain with traditional materials and provide novel support tools such as augmented manuals and illustrated part catalogues that support sequential steps and facilitate object identification [18]. XR also offers the potential for remote capabilities that support technicians during procedures through virtual images or remotely located subject matter experts.

XR can also augment human capabilities required by pilots and air traffic controllers. Visual augmentation systems (e.g., HMDs) have been developed to improve pilot situation awareness and collision avoidance [1]. Additionally, the manner and format in which information is presented to pilots can be enhanced through XR systems (e.g., AR cockpit) to reduce workload and improve displays. In the realm of air traffic control, Bagassi et al. [10] highlight that XR can enhance control tower operations by improving out-of-the-window scanning in low visibility conditions and reducing controller heads-down time. Similarly, XR systems can support the monitoring of ground and air traffic through visual and voice interactions [19].

The training of pilots, air traffic controllers, technicians, and other aviation personnel can benefit from XR as well. The immersive, interactive environments created via XR can create training scenarios that are meaningful, effective, and cost-effective. Compared to non-immersive methods (e.g., lecture, eLearning), XR can produce realistic three-dimensional environments that are immersive and elicit behaviors within the system that match what is required on the job. Training must also advance in step with the progression of aviation systems and XR can enable training that better meets the skill demands of aviation professionals [6]. Traditional high-fidelity training relies on physical simulators and physical mock-ups that are expensive and difficult to modify. Comparatively, XR software is easy to edit and cost-effective since less physical equipment is needed to create complex scenarios [9, 18]. However, ensuring the match between learning objectives, content, and XR device is necessary prior to using XR for training.

3 Scientometric Analysis

Scientometrics, or the measurement of science and scholarly literature, offers a way to examine existing research within a field through quantitative means. This methodology analyzes metrics such as co-citation networks and keyword trends. This approach relies on gathering a corpus and recording relevant bibliometric information, such as author, title, keywords, journal, and references, to visualize information about the field of interest. For this paper, the scientometric analysis provides a broad overview of the research landscape and explores various networks of sources, citations, and keywords to document the inter-relationships and development of XR research in aviation.

3.1 Method

A scientometric analysis was conducted to visualize connections in the published literature relevant to the topics of the current paper. Input data for these analyses were retrieved from the scientific database, Web of Science Core Collection, on December 11, 2021. The Boolean search parameters defining the search were:

ALL = (("augmented reality" OR "virtual reality" OR "mixed reality" OR "extended reality") AND "aviation").

Note that, for these analyses, no filter for the "publication year" data field was set, with the intention to illustrate trends in research over time. The resultant dataset contained a total of 144 records, with publication years spanning 1993–2021. VOSviewer software, version 1.6.17 © 2021, was used to create visualization networks (www.vosviewer.com; [20]).

3.2 Results and Discussion

Figure 3 illustrates a co-citation analysis using cited sources (i.e., journals) as the unit of analysis; the minimum number of citations was set to 15. This network depicts links between publications within academic journals that cite publications within other academic journals; that is, it illustrates the sort of cross-pollination of domains of research publishing articles on the topic of XR in aviation. The network reveals three major clusters of publications: one that may represent applied aviation research (in blue), one that may represent engineering research (in red), and one that may represent medical research (in green). While links between the three nodes exist, the greater distance between the green node and the blue and red nodes indicate that greater number and greater strengths of links exist between the blue and red (applied aviation and engineering) nodes. Additionally, the depicted size of the nodes reflect the total link strength of the nodes. Of the blue nodes (applied aviation), the journals *Aviation, Space, and Environmental Medicine,* and *Human Factors* are largest, with total link strengths of 1514, with 33 links and 152 citations, and 857, with 35 links and 62 citations, respectively. Of the red nodes, the journal *Applied Ergonomics* is largest, with a total link strength of 483, with 26 links and 41 citations. Of the green nodes, the journal *Surgical Endoscopy* is largest, with total link strength of 1155, with 30 links and 88 citations. Note that these nodes with highest link strength display citation across sub-domains, as in the case of *Applied Ergonomics*, with many links to both the blue and red nodes.

Figure 4 illustrates a co-citation analysis using cited references (i.e., articles) as the unit of analysis; the minimum number of citations was set to four. This network depicts links between publications and the publications referenced therein. The network reveals some of the most frequently referenced articles on the topic of XR in aviation, and is consistent with Fig. 4, above. There appear to be nodes representing medical research (in

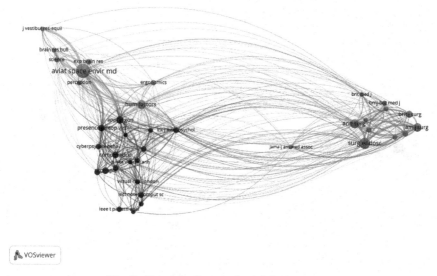

Fig. 3. Network of co-citation of cited sources.

green), applied aviation research (in red) and two nodes that may represent engineering (in yellow and blue).

Figure 5 illustrates a co-occurrence analysis using all keywords as the unit of analysis, and the "full counting" method; the minimum number of occurrences to be included set to five. This network depicts links between the 24 keywords that meet this threshold from the corpus of Web of Science data. An adjustment was made to change "augmented-reality" (with hyphen) to "augmented reality" (without hyphen) to ensure VOSviewer interpreted these keywords as the same.

Interestingly, the node for the keyword *virtual reality* showed a total link strength (aggregating all links) of 99, and appeared in 47 occurrences, with an average publication year of appearances of 2012.59. The keyword *augmented reality* showed a total link strength of 31, and appeared in 21 occurrences, with an average publication year of 2018.94. This suggests that AR may be a growing trend in research of XR in aviation, or, at least is a more recently occurring keyword.

Also of note is an apparent trend in applications in which keywords "training" and "performance" have an older average publication year (2011.88 and 2011.32, respectively), relative to the keyword, "education," with an average publication year of 2014.73. This supports a trend in the literature of task training once being a primary application of XR in aviation, but that seems to have grown into general education applications.

Similarly, there appears to be recent growth in publications involving applications of XR using the keywords "maintenance," "design," and "system." This may suggest growth in how XR is being applied within aviation, and a recent focus on engineering and maintenance.

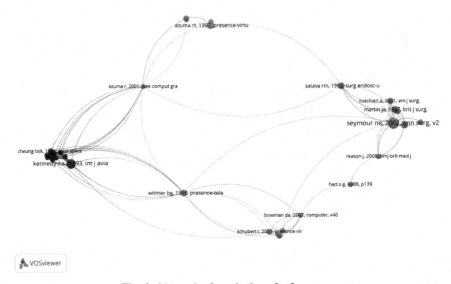

Fig. 4. Network of co-citation of references.

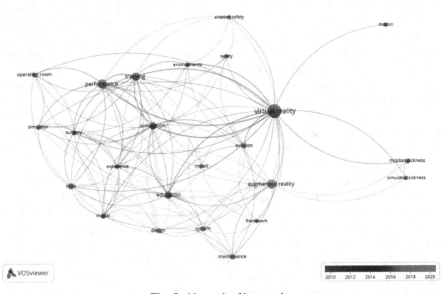

Fig. 5. Network of keywords.

Lastly, the keywords "motion sickness," and "simulator sickness" are associated with average publication dates of 2011.50, and 2007.20, which may suggest that issues regarding these factors are either largely understood, or largely addressed through more contemporary XR system design.

4 Qualitative Literature Review

4.1 Method

The purpose of the qualitative literature review was to identify research on the application of XR technology in aviation. Articles for this literature review were collected from Google Scholar, open-access archives (e.g., arXiv), and the Federal Aviation Administration library system. Results were limited to articles published since 2015 to evaluate the current applications of XR and aviation, not historical trends. In addition, given recent advancements in XR capabilities, limiting the search to recent years helps to ensure that findings are based on current technology and applications and not technology of the past. Databases were searched using keywords such as "extended reality", "augmented reality", "mixed reality", "virtual reality", "aviation", "aircraft maintenance", "pilot", and "air traffic control". Articles included in this review include peer-reviewed (refereed) journal articles, book chapters, conference proceedings, dissertations and theses, and government technical reports.

The inclusion criteria for this review were: (1) articles must contain the phrase(s) "extended reality", "virtual reality", "augmented reality", or "mixed reality", (2) make reference to the field of aviation and apply XR within an area of aviation, such as pilot training, air traffic control, and aircraft/system maintenance, and (3) describe, at least briefly, the type of XR technology used. Articles excluded were not relevant to aviation or did not explore the use or presence of XR technology.

Following a review of the identified articles, 37 met the inclusion criteria. Articles included empirical studies, demonstration/use cases, proposals, and reviews. Of note, this was not an exhaustive search, but the collected articles are a representative sample of XR and aviation research. Information was recorded about each article, including the aviation domain (e.g., pilot, air traffic control, maintenance), type of XR technology, the XR device type (e.g., headset, tablet), and the specific application and use case. Additionally, for empirical studies, additional data was collected on sample size, sample population, and independent and dependent variables.

4.2 Results and Discussion

The selected articles ($N = 37$) ranged in publication year from 2015 to 2021. Articles came from outlets such as *International Journal of Aviation, Aeronautics, and Aerospace, Human Factors, Sensors, Aircraft Engineering and Aerospace Technology, Aviation Psychology and Applied Human Factors, IEE Transactions on Learning Technologies,* and *International Symposium on Aviation Psychology.* Seven papers (18.9%) focused on a technology type (i.e., AR or VR), but did not assess a particular device type or form factor (e.g., HMD or smart phone), instead providing reviews (3) or surveys (4) of XR technologies overall.

Augmented, Mixed, or Extended Reality. Presents the user with some veridical, real-time environment augmented with additional virtual content (e.g., pathfinding, checklists, indicators). Table 1, below, displays key factors in the 24 articles exploring Augmented, Mixed, or Extended Reality (note that this table also includes articles that explored *both* AR and VR in the same article). Of note is the diversity of workgroups investigated in this domain. While many articles investigate aviation maintenance use cases, pilot, ergonomist, flight crew, passenger, drone operator, and others are explored as well. Additionally, many of these articles investigate the use of a head-mounted display (HMD) device type, with relatively few articles researching multimodal XR applications including gesture or voice, and similarly few articles researching other device types such as XR applications using smartphones or tablets; these variables may become more common in future research. Also notable is that only 7 of the 24 articles (29.2%) were empirical studies. As XR technologies mature, and as use cases and concepts of operation are developed, it may be the case that a greater proportion of empirical studies become common in the literature.

A few articles illustrative of the type of AR research being conducted aviation is work by Yong and Sung [21], Borgen et al. [23], and Gangabisson et al. [26]. Yong and Sung [21] demonstrate the use of an AR, marker-based application for supporting fan cowl door opening procedures. The AR application tracks the physical aircraft engine using the device's camera and presents the technician with step-by-step textual information and animations via the device's screen. Since this AR technology relies on the ability of the mobile device to recognize and track the aircraft engine, Yong and Sung [21] analyzed the impact of different camera angles on the modeling and found that the animations are visible at camera angles of 30 to 80°. Borgen et al. [23] compared an AR-based and traditional training format on a checklist procedure for an aircraft's auxiliary power unit. Prior to performing the actual procedure, participants (aeronautical engineering students) were provided either a paper-based checklist or AR-equipped device for training. Borgen et al. [23] found that time-on-task was consistently faster for participants who used the AR device in the training phase compared to the paper-based format. Interestingly, these authors found that participants spent more time interacting with the AR technology prior to the actual task than participants using the paper checklist suggesting potential gamification and novelty effects. Finally, Gangabisson et al. [26] investigated if AR improved engagement in emergency procedure training for cabin crews. The marker-based mobile application used image recognition and visual overlays of safety equipment to provide users with training content, tutorials, and virtual demonstrations. In general, Gangabisson et al. [26] found that users reported high levels of engagement with the AR device suggesting that it can potentially improve engagement during safety critical training. However, engagement with AR device was not compared engagement levels achieved with other training methods. Overall, these articles highlight the type of tasks and applications that AR is being used for within aviation and the positive evidence for its use.

Noteworthy articles exploring MR include work by Han et al. [19] and Siyaev and Jo [35]. Han et al. [19] present a four-dimensional (3D plus time) holographic MR system to support the visualization and management of air traffic by air traffic controllers. Using a HMD, the MR system allows controllers to switch between multiple displays using visual and voice interaction. The authors tested two different flight scenarios using the MR system. Based on feedback from two air traffic controllers, users provided positive feedback about the holographic MR device, but noted that the limited field of view of the HMD made it difficult to identify objects. This finding points to the potential perceptual limitations of XR capabilities for certain applications. Siyaev and Jo [35] explored the application of MR to maintenance training using smart glasses and speech recognition. The use of speech recognition enables trainees to use hands to manipulate and operate equipment as opposed to pressing buttons or using hand gestures. While Siyaev and Jo [35] did not directly investigate the effectiveness of the MR system for aircraft maintenance, they found that speech recognition feature to be highly accurate in recognizing both English and Korean speech providing evidence for the viability of this feature.

While there were fewer articles examining MR, the MR technology explored appears to fall in line with commonly held definitions indicating that MR is an extension of AR and provides greater levels of modeling and interaction (e.g., voice/speech recognition) with the real and virtual objects. Yet, the effectiveness of the additional features for task completion or training limited by a lack of empirical investigation.

Virtual Reality. Uses stereoscopic displays to create three-dimensional content that is not concurrent with a real physical world environment. In this paper, we have adopted, for ease of discussion, an operational definition of virtual reality as involving a display of a wholly 'synthetic' environment with no synchronization to a veridical representation of a real-time physical environment. We also operationally defined augmented, mixed, or extended reality (which, here, we've used relatively interchangeably) as involving a display of a veridical, real-time physical environment augmented with additional display elements such as pathfinding information, checklists, or indicators. As such, two articles that described their research as involving augmented reality, D'Anniballe, et al. (2020) [37] and Meister, et al. (2021) [38], as fitting our definition of *virtual* reality.

Table 2, below, displays key factors in 13 additional articles (bringing the total to 21 articles when including those mentioned above which explored both AR and VR) articles exploring Virtual Reality. In contrast to the diversity of workgroups investigated in Table 1, 11 of the 21 articles (52.4%) explore VR applications with pilot use cases, such as flight training. While many articles investigate aviation maintenance use cases, pilot, ergonomist, flight crew, passenger, drone operator, and others are explored with less prevalence. Interestingly, while HMD device types are, as we might expect, most common in Table 2, a greater number of motion tracking and gesture tracking aspects were explored, relative to the AR articles. Also notable is that 8 of the 21 articles (38.1%) were empirical studies.

Notable among these VR articles is work by Buttusi and Chittaro [12], and Chittarro, et al. [40], who conducted empirical studies of cabin crew and passenger populations, respectively. These studies compared training of procedural tasks, and compared VR applications to traditional paper cards (Buttusi and Chittaro [12] compared conditions

Table 1. Selected articles from the review of AR/MR/XR in aviation

Author(s)	Article Type	Workgroup	Application	XR Type	Device Type
Ceruti et al. [18]	Case studies	Maintenance	Engineering	AR	HMD
Yong and Sung [21]	Demonstration	Maintenance	Process guidance	AR	Smartphone
Hebert Jr. [22]	Empirical	Maintenance	Maintenance support	AR	HMD
Borgen, Ropp, and Weldon [23]	Empirical	Maintenance	Training	AR	HMD
Wang et al. [24]	Empirical	Maintenance	Training	AR	Not described
Papakostas, et al. [25]	Empirical/Model	Firefighters	Training	AR	HMD, Smartphone
Safi et al. [1]	Review	Maintenance, pilot, engineers, airport operations	Engineering, navigation, training, simulation	AR	HUD, HMD
Gangabissoon et al. [26]	Review	Flight crew	Training	AR	Mobile app
Moesl et al. [27]	Survey	Pilot	Training	AR	N/A (Survey of potential users)
Schaffernak et al. [14]	Survey	Pilot	Training	AR	N/A (Survey of potential users)
Anne et al. [28]	Review	Maintenance	Training	AR	N/A
Palmarini, et al. [7]	Review	Maintenance	Maintenance operations	AR	N/A
Brown [29]	Presentation	Pilot, maintenance	Training	AR, VR	HMD
Brown et al. [30]	Review	Ergonomics practitioners	Ergonomic assessment & design	AR, VR	N/A
Eschen et al. [8]	Review	Maintenance	Maintenance operations	AR, VR	HMD
Biggs et al. [31]	Review	Pilot	Training, navigation	AR, VR	HMD, HUD, simulator
Girdler & Georgiou [32]	Demonstration	Pilot	Training	AR, VR	HMD, gesture recognition

(*continued*)

Table 1. (*continued*)

Author(s)	Article Type	Workgroup	Application	XR Type	Device Type
Kim et al. [33]	Empirical	Drone operators	Navigation, training	AR, VR	HMD
Bagassi et al. [10]	Proposed Study	ATC	Control tower operations	AR, VR	HUD, HMD
Brown [34]	Review	Pilot, flight crew, maintenance	Training	AR, VR, MR	N/A
Siyaev and Jo [35]	Demonstration	Maintenance	Training	MR	Smart glasses, speech recognition, audio
Han et al. [19]	Empirical	ATC	Navigation	MR	HMD
Tsykunov et al. [36]	Empirical	Drone operators	Navigation	MR	HMD
Luisier et al. [15]	Survey	Logistics	Training	XR	N/A (Survey of users)

of HMD and smartphone device types as well). Findings were largely similar for the two studies: VR training applications yielded better transfer of procedural knowledge, faster task performance, and fewer errors than training with smart cards. This comparison of device types, and their suitability in different environments and for different tasks and use cases, provides valuable empirical support for training development and the adoption of new technologies in aviation.

Also of note among these VR articles is a study of maintenance training comparing legacy, desktop computer (i.e., a "flat" monitor display of information) based training with immersive, VR and gesture-based training (Bailey, et. al [11]). This study found that the desktop computer based training yielded more procedural (i.e., content) errors, whereas the VR training yielded more gesture (i.e., interface) errors, and that the desktop computer based training was less efficient overall. This highlights an important consideration when evaluating XR applications: some care must be taken in considering performance metrics that may be reflective of learning to use the XR device itself.

Similar to articles discussed in the AR section above, the articles investigating VR, broadly support the notion of VR technologies being particularly beneficial in the training of procedural knowledge. The immersive, egocentric perspective, and the potential for physical interaction with an environment, may create a rich, "hands on" training environment that is manipulable and repeatable.

Table 2. Selected articles from the review of VR in aviation (Note: See Table 1 for additional articles which investigated both VR and AR)

Author(s)	Article type	Workgroup	Application	XR Type	Device type
D'Anniballe et al. [37]	Case study	Accident investigators	Training, visualization	VR	HMD, Smartphone
Meister et al. [38]	Demonstration	Pilot	Training	VR	Smartphone
Buttussi and Chittaro [12]	Empirical	Cabin crew	Training	VR	HMD, Smartphone
Bernard et al. [9]	Empirical	Maintenance	Ergonomic assessment & design	VR	HMD
Landas [39]	Empirical	Pilot	Training	VR	Screen, Motion sensor
Chittaro et al. [40]	Empirical	Passengers	Training	VR	Smartphone, Paper cards
Oberhauser et al. [41]	Empirical	Pilot	Flight Test	VR	HMD, Tracking system
Thomas et al. [42]	Empirical	Pilot	Training	VR	HMD
Haritos and Fussell [43]	Presentation	Pilot	Training	VR	HMD
Geyer and Biggs [44]	Review	Pilot	Training	VR	HMD
Irvin et al. [45]	Review	Pilot	Training	VR	HMD, Gloves, Eye-tracking
Fussell and Truong [46]	Survey	Pilot	Training	VR	N/A (Survey of potential users)
Bailey et al. [11]	Empirical	Maintenance	Training	VR	Monitor, Motion sensor

5 General Discussion

This paper has described the technologies of virtual, augmented, mixed, and extended reality. A discussion of key review articles, as well as common applications of these technologies in the field of aviation was presented.

Scientometric networks of 144 articles published from 1993–2021 (Figs. 1–3, above) illustrated key journals, authors, and keywords in this research area. These networks appear to present three major clusters of research: a medical cluster, an applied aviation/human factors cluster, and an engineering/computer science cluster. A pattern that appears to emerge from these networks (see Fig. 3, especially) is that the research may have first appeared within the scope of aerospace medicine, but has more recently found application in engineering and aviation human factors domains. This is also reflected in more recent average publication dates for keywords like "education," "maintenance," and "design," relative to keywords such as "simulator sickness" and "training." This trend remains evident in an analysis of articles published since 2015 (Tables 1 and 2, above), as many of these articles were published in engineering journals, and none of the 37 articles we analyzed had a medical focus. However, engineering psychology and human factors were uncommon in this selection of articles. This may suggest a need or opportunity for more engineering psychology and human factors research to be conducted to investigate XR applications in aviation. Also of note was the low proportion, only 14 of the 37 articles (37.8%), being empirical studies. Similarly, 18.9% of the papers in this corpus did not assess a device type or form factor, instead reviewing or surveying at a more conceptual level the usefulness of XR applications. Of the empirical studies in this selection of articles, at least seven collected data from fewer than 20 participants. This suggests the need for empirical research, with sufficient statistical power to derive reliable inferences, that investigates and compares different technology/reality types, device types, form factors, in different combinations as most appropriate for different use cases and applications.

As research continues to explore the efficacy of XR and apply these technologies in innovate ways to improve performance and safety, it is imperative that research keep a critical eye on the appropriateness of XR as a remedy or solution. While XR poses numerous benefits to aviation, the lack of empirical research conceals the potential downsides that may arise using this technology. Oberhauser et al. [41] found that a VR flight simulator produced higher ratings of simulator sickness (e.g., nausea, disorientation) than a conventional simulator. Simulator sickness, also referred to as cybersickness, is often attributed to a mismatch between sensory and visual information, which reduces system immersion. As sensory capabilities in XR improve, sickness effects are likely to reduce. Attentional tunneling, or the excessive allocation of attention to virtual information, is a concern in environments where users must attend to both virtual and physical objects [47]. Since virtual and real-world objects carry important information in AR and MR settings, designing systems that reduce attentional issues is critical for safety-oriented tasks. Lastly, with any new technology, novelty effects have the potential to bias findings such that better performance or outcomes are achieved because the technology is new, not because the technology provides a better long-term solution.

The enthusiasm for XR across aviation is evident. The increasing affordability and availability of quality XR devices has the potential to transform the day-to-day tasks and training of those working in aviation, including pilots, air traffic controllers, and maintenance technicians. Given the widespread interest in these technologies, matching the cognitive and environmental demands of the task to the capabilities of the XR solution can safeguard against misapplications and optimize human performance and safety. XR holds substantial promise for the field of aviation and findings from this review can help guide future areas of research.

References

1. Safi, M., Chung, J., Pradhan, P.: Review of augmented reality in aerospace industry. Aircr. Eng. Aerosp. Technol. **91**(9), 1187–1194 (2019)

2. Cipresso, P., Giglioli, I.A.C., Raya, M.A., Riva, G.: The past, present, and future of virtual and augmented reality research: a network and cluster analysis of the literature. Front. Psychol. **9**, 2086 (2018)

3. Skarbez, R., Smith, M., Whitton, M.C.: Revisiting the Milgram and Kishino's reality-virtuality continuum. Front. Virtual Real. **2**, 647997 (2021)

4. Speicher, M., Hall, B.D., Nabelling, M.: What is mixed reality? In: CHI Conference on Human Factors in Computing Systems Proceedings Glasgow, Scotland, UK, pp. 1–15. ACM New York, NY, USA (2019)

5. Alizadehsalehiu, S., Hadavi, A., Huang, J.C.: From BIM to extended reality in AEC industry. Autom. Constr. **116**, 103254 (2020)

6. Brown, L.J.: Professional reflection – mixed reality to augment the next generation of aviation professionals. In: Kearns, S.K., Mavin, T.J., Hodge, S. (eds.) Engaging the Next Generation of Aviation Professionals, pp. 163–180. Routledge, New York, NY (2020)

7. Palmarini, R., Erkouncu, J.A., Roy, R.: A systematic review of augmented reality applications in maintenance. Robot. Comput. Integr. Manuf. **49**, 215–228 (2018)

8. Eschen, H., Kötter, T., Rodeck, R., Harnisch, M., Shüppstuhl, T.: Augmented and virtual reality for inspection and maintenance processes in the aviation industry. Proc. Manuf. **19**, 156–163 (2018)

9. Bernard, F., Zare, M., Sagot, J.: Using digital and physical simulation to focus on human factors and ergonomics in aviation maintainability. Hum. Factors **62**(1), 37–54 (2020)

10. Bagassi, S., De Crescenzio, F., Lucchi, F., Masotti, N.: Augmented and virtual reality in the airport control tower. In: 30th Congress of the International Council of the Aeronautical Sciences, pp. 1–8, Daejeon, South Korea (2016)

11. Bailey, S.K.T., Johnson, C.I., Schroeder, B.L., Marraffino, M.D.: Using virtual reality for training maintenance procedures. In: Interservice/Industry Training, Simulation, and Education Conference (I/TSEC) 2017, vol. 17108, pp. 1–11 (2017)

12. Buttussi, F., Chittaro, L.: A comparison of procedural safety training in three conditions: virtual reality headset, smartphone, and printed materials. IEEE Trans. Learn. Technol. **14**(1), 1–15 (2021)

13. Kaplan, A.D., Cruit, J., Endsley, M., Beers, S.M., Swayer, B.D., Hancock, P.A.: The effects of virtual reality, augmented reality, and mixed reality as training enhancement methods: a meta-analysis. Hum. Factors **63**(4), 706–726 (2021)

14. Schaffernak, H., Moesl, B., Vorraber, W., Koglbauer, I.V.: Potential augmented reality application areas for pilot education: an exploratory study. Educ. Sci. **10**(4), 86 (2020)

15. Luisier, J., Tsong, C. K., Yooyen, S.: XR training and confidence levels in undergraduate logistics management programs. In: 2nd Innovation Aviation and Aerospace Indsutry-International Conference, pp. 30–34 (2021)

16. Milgram, P., Kishino, F.: A taxonomy of mixed reality visual displays. IEICE Trans. Inf. Syst. **77**(12), 1321–1329 (1994)

17. Markowitz, D.M., Bailenson, J.N.: Virtual reality and emotion: a 5-year systematic review of empirical research (2015–2019). In: Nabi, R., Myrick, J. (eds.): Our Online Emotional Selves: The Link Between Digital Media and Emotional Experience. Oxford University Press (2021). (in press)

18. Ceruti, A., Marzocca, P., Liverani, A., Bil, C.: Maintenance in aeronautics in an Industry 4.0 context: the role of augmented reality and additive manufacturing. J. Comput. Des. Eng. **6**, 516–526 (2019)

19. Han, K., Shah, S.H.H., Lee, J.W.: Holographic mixed reality system for air traffic control and management. Appl. Sci. **9**, 3370 (2019)

20. Van Eck, N.J., Waltman, L.: Software survey: VOS viewer, a computer program for bibliometric mapping. Scientometrics **84**(2), 523–538 (2010)

21. Yong, S.W., Sung, A.N.: A mobile application of augmented reality for aircraft maintenance of fan cowl door opening. Int. J. Comput. Netw. Inf. Secur. **11**(6), 38–44 (2019)

22. Hebert Jr, T.: The impacts of using augmented reality to support aircraft maintenance. Master's thesis, Air Force Institute of Technology (2019)

23. Borgen, K.B., Ropp, T.D., Weldon, W.T.: Assessment of augmented reality technology's impact on speed of learning and task performance in aeronautical engineering technology education. Int. J. Aerosp. Psychol. **31**(3), 219–229 (2021)

24. Wang, Y., Anne, A., Ropp, T.: Applying the technology acceptance model to understand aviation students' perceptions toward augmented reality maintenance training instruction. Int. J. Aviat. Aeronaut. Aerosp. **3**(4), 3 (2016)

25. Papakostas, C., Troussas, C., Krouska, A., Sgouropoulou, C.: Measuring user experience, usability, and interactivity of a personalized mobile augmented reality training system. Sensors **21**, 3888 (2021)

26. Gangabissoon, T., Bekaroo, G., Moedeen, W.: Application of augmented reality in aviation: Improving engagement of cabin crew during emergency procedures training. In Proceedings of the 2nd International Conference on Intelligent and Innovative Computing Applications, pp. 1–8, September 2020

27. Moesl, B., Schaffernak, H., Vorraber, W., Braunstingl, R., Herrele, T., Koglbauer, I.V.: A research agenda for implementing augmented reality in Ab Initio Pilot training. Aviat. Psychol. Appl. Human Factors **11**(2), 118–126 (2021)

28. Anne, A., Wang, Y., Ropp, T.D.: Using augmented reality and computer-generated three-dimensional models to improve training and technical tasks in aviation. In: 18th International Symposium on Aviation Psychology, p. 452 (2015)

29. Brown, L.: The next generation classroom: Transforming aviation training with augmented reality (2017)

30. Brown, C., Hicks, J., Rinaudo, C.H., Burch, R.: The use of augmented reality and virtual reality in ergonomic applications for education, aviation, and maintenance (2021)

31. Biggs, A.T., Geyer, D.J., Schroeder, V.M., Robinson, F.E., Bradley, J.L.: Adapting virtual reality and augmented reality systems for naval aviation training (Report No. NAMRU-D-9-13), Naval Medical Research Unit Dayton (2018)

32. Girdler, A., Georgiou, O.: Mid-air haptics in aviation–creating the sensation of touch where there is nothing but thin air. arXiv preprint arXiv: 2001.01445 (2020)

33. Kim, D.H., Go, Y.G., Choi, S.M.: An aerial mixed-reality environment for first-person-view drone flying. Appl. Sci. **10**(16), 5436 (2020)

34. Brown, L.J.: Professional reflection–mixed reality to augment the next generation of aviation professionals. In: Engaging the Next Generation of Aviation Professionals, pp. 163–180, Routledge (2019)

35. Siyaev, A., Jo, G.: Towards aircraft maintenance metaverse using speech interactions with virtual objects in mixed reality. Sensors **21**, 2066 (2021)

36. Tsykunov, E., Ibrahimov, R., Vasquez, D., Tsetserukou, D.: SlingDrone: mixed reality system for pointing and interaction using a single drone. In 25th ACM Symposium on Virtual Reality Software and Technology, pp. 1–5, November 2019

37. D'Anniballe, A., Silva, J., Marzocca, P., Ceruti, A.: The role of augmented reality in air accident investigation and practitioner training. Reliab. Eng. Syst. Saf. **204**, 1–11 (2020)

38. Meister, P., Wang, K, Dorneich, M.C., Winer, E., Brown, L., Whitehurst, G.: Applying Augmented Reality Capabilities to Enhance General Aviation Weather Training. AIAA Aviation Forum (2021)

39. Landas, E.L.: The next generation of aviation maintenance training: game based and virtual reality augmented learning. Naval Postgraduate School Monterey United States (2018)

40. Chittaro, L., Corbett, C.L., McLean, G.A., Zangrando, N.: Safety knowledge transfer through mobile virtual reality: a study of aviation life preserver donning. Saf. Sci. **102**, 159–168 (2018)

41. Oberhauser, M., Dreyer, D., Braunstingl, R., Koglbauer, I.: What's real about virtual reality flight simulation? Aviation Psychol. Appl. Human Factors **8**(1), 22–34 (2018)

42. Thomas, R.L., et al.: Usability of the virtual reality aviation trainer for runway-width illusions. Colleg. Aviat. Rev. Int. **39**(2), 163–179 (2021)

43. Haritos, T., Fussell, S.G.: Implementing immersive virtual reality in an aviation/aerospace teaching and learning paradigm (2018)

44. Geyer, D.J., Biggs, A.T.: The persistent issue of simulator sickness in naval aviation training. Aerosp. Med. Human Perform. **89**(4), 396–405 (2018)

45. Irvin, W., Goldie, C., O'Brien, C., Aura, C., Temme, L., Wilson, M.: A virtual reality aviation emergency procedure (EP) testbed. In Virtual, Augmented, and Mixed Reality (XR) Technology for Multi-Domain Operations II, vol. 11759, p. 1175909. International Society for Optics and Photonics, April 2021

46. Fussell, S.G., Truong, D.: Using virtual reality for dynamic learning: an extended technology acceptance model. Virtual Real. **26**, 1–19 (2021). https://doi.org/10.1007/s10055-021-00554-x

47. Syiem, B.V., Kelly, R.M., Goncalves, J., Velloso, E., Dingler, T.: Impact of task on attentional tunneling in handheld augmented reality. In Proceedings of the ACM SIGCHI Conference on Human Factors in Computing Systems, pp. 1–14. Yokohama, Japan (2021)

Industrial Applications of VAMR

Assisted Human-Robot Interaction for Industry Application Based Augmented Reality

Haonan Fang$^{(\boxtimes)}$, Jingqian Wen, XiaoNan Yang, Peng Wang, and Yinqian Li

School of Mechanical Engineering, Beijing Institute of Technology, Beijing, China
ffanghaonan@126.com, {wenjq,yangxn,3220210403}@bit.edu.cn

Abstract. Augmented Reality provides more possibilities for industrial manufacturing to solve the current problems. However, previous researches have been focused on virtual scene visualization and robot trajectory prediction. The investigation of robotic real-time teleoperation using AR is limited, which is still facing great challenges. In this research, a novel method is presented for human-robot interaction for industrial applications based on AR, like assembly. Users can intuitively teleoperate a 6-DOFs industry robot to recognize and locate entities by multi-channel operation via HoloLens2. Augmented reality, as a medium, bridges human zones and robot zones. The system can transform user instructions from virtual multi-channel user interface to robots by communication module in AR environment. The above approaches and related devices are elaborated in this paper. An industrial case is presented to implement and validate the feasibility of the AR-based human-robot interactive system. The results provide evidence to support that AR is one of the efficient methods to realize multi-channel human-robot interaction.

Keywords: Human-robot interaction · Augmented Reality · Manufacturing industry

1 Introduction

With the advances of Industry 4.0, the manufacturing industry calls for a new generation of novel systems and technologies to reduce product development time and cost. As an important part of intelligent mechanical equipment, industrial robot has been the heart of the modern manufacturing plant, which is widely used in many operations, e.g. welding, assembly, machining. Within the usage of industrial robots, human-robot interaction (HRI) is developed as an essential technology. It provides efficient support and becomes an essential part of manufacturing, especially assembly operations [1]. A growing number of novel technologies have been developed for HRI. However, there are still some problems, such as lack of safety, complex operation process and few personnel with rich experience. Augmented reality (AR) is considered a promising method to resolve the above questions. It combines the physical manufacturing environment with the virtuality in cyberspace to provide a new tool to developers and customers of industrial systems. Therefore, it necessitates integrating the AR approach with the HRI application to offer a more natural and convenient method for the operator, which can also enhance the efficiency of human interaction with robot systems [2].

© Springer Nature Switzerland AG 2022
J. Y. C. Chen and G. Fragomeni (Eds.): HCII 2022, LNCS 13318, pp. 291–301, 2022.
https://doi.org/10.1007/978-3-031-06015-1_20

In parallel, there are multiple AR hard devices developed by companies, which can be divided into Head-mounted displays (HMDs), hand-held devices and spatial devices. Meanwhile, HMDs are considered to visualize 3D data most directly so that the users can observe a spatial display of detailed information, which supports understanding and choosing [3]. Besides, the advantage that frees users both hands from manual operations of head-mounted AR, like assembling, was considerably convenient in manufacturing. As a cutting edge of head-mounted AR, the Microsoft HoloLens2 provides a possibility to work remotely without any external interference by using gaze and gesture controllers [4].

Current applications of AR-HRI mainly apply to virtual reality fusion technology, assisting operators to see the virtual information in its real physical surroundings to augment the understanding of the real world by showing information. Previous studies include displaying operating instructions for non-experts, forecasting in advance the motion path, and observing potential pick location during grasping movement by HoloLens2 [5]. Nevertheless, using AR technology to build up real-time HRI has been rarely studied.

According to the above challenges and requirements, this paper presents a system to recognize and locate entities by multi-channel teleoperation via HoloLens2. The research in this paper assists users to teleoperate robots via the multi-channel in a fixed station that is not convenient to move, and have to accomplish a real-time selection of relevant components without interruption. Meanwhile, getting the correct component directly by using the robot vision with receiving the orders from AR, instead of manual measurements and searching, enables saving manpower and decreasing the workload of operation. This research builds a new channel for human-robot interaction with AR systems in the future.

2 Relative Work

2.1 Human-Robot Interaction in Manufacturing

In recent years, the focus of human-robot interaction has shifted from equipment to the demands of humans. Traditional HRI is mainly through an "interactive interface", such as a mouse, keyboard, and operation panel, to operate robots. Workers transfer decisions to robots by tapping the keyboard or clicking the touch screen [6]. After processing information, robots transfer it to users through the visual channel. The major concern of the above process is the accuracy of transmitted contents. However, the connection between the mentioned separate robot workspaces and the robot's physical environment can be unintuitive. Once robots are fixed, the freedom of the relevant operators is limited.

Recently, the advances of Industry 4.0 bring about methods of robotic implementation. The overwhelming transformation put forwards that, a long period of time in the future, eliminating the boundaries of information exchange will become a new development direction of HRI. Robots can actively adapt to the demands of users through multi-channel perception, and produce a more natural and convenient way to collaborate [7]. Working side-by-side with robots in close proximity simultaneously also enables informative and real-time communication [8].

2.2   AR-Based Operator Support System

The burgeoning world of augmented reality provides a new route toward addressing some of the challenges that have been mentioned above. AR can provide a new tool to developers and customers of industrial systems in the manufacturing industry. The combination of digital content with real working spaces creates a fresh environment, which can produce visible feedback during HRI. In the literature, abundant recent works have demonstrated their HRI systems on real industrial manufacturing tasks, where both aspects, control and visualization, are considered (see Fig. 1).

As one of the main advantages of AR, visualization exhibits extensive applications in safety and robotics trajectory planning. In 2019, Faizan Muhammad [9] outlined a system that allows the users to visualize the robot's sensory information and intended path in intuitive modalities overlaid onto the real world. And users can interact with visual objects, such as textual notes, as a means of communication with the robot. Similarly, an AR approach [3] was proposed to visualize the navigation stack. Therefore, relevant data including laser scan, environment map and path planning data are visualized in 3D within Hololens. Then the research was extended to an AR-based safety margins visualization system. Antti Hietanen [10] proposes a shared workspace model for HRI manufacturing and interactive UIs. It focuses on monitoring safety margins and unfolding the virtual zones to users with AR technology.

In the process of robots control and application, AR technology is presented and demonstrates to possess huge potential towards accurate HRI operations. In the process of motion prediction, Dennis Krupke [5] introduced a system in which users can intuitively control a co-located robot arm for pick-and-place tasks. In addition, an AR interface has been developed to show a preview of robot pick selection or trajectory to the operator. Similarly, Kenneth A. Stone [11] detailed an app to edit the code directly and teleoperate robotic motion via virtual keyboard and a virtual panel, which realized the visualization of target, path and visual robot within AR. Then an MR-based distributed system [12] has been proposed to evaluate the robots movements before execution. The planning focus is the use of cloud-based computing and control to find a collision-free path. In addition, Chung Xue Er [13] also proposed a demo to preview and evaluate the motion planned artificially, using a visual robot to detect collision automatically and interact.

During the process of inputting commands, Xi Vincent Wang [1] developed a feasible AR system with a novel closed-loop structure. Within the system, users can manipulate the virtual robot via gesture commands to determine the posture, trajectory and task. After confirming trajectory, the physical robot will duplicate the operation accordingly. What's more, Congyuan Liang [14] also introduced a system to allow operator to teleoperate a robot via capture gestures information.

To recap, despite the significant development of the AR-based HRI application in recent years, there is still a lack of a comprehensive design for AR-based robotics input commands system. But the channel of most previous works is gesture information. Workers using their hands for a long time will be tired and lower productivity. Thus in this research, a novel AR-based HRI system is proposed within multi-channel teleoperation.

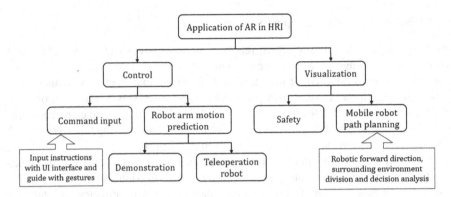

Fig. 1. The framework of AR-based HRI systems.

3 System Description

3.1 System Framework

To improve the efficiency and accuracy of the teleoperation between humans and robots, an AR-based framework is presented for assisted industry operations, as shown in Fig. 2. In this study, two separate workspaces, human zone and robot zone, are combined for assembly and other industrial operations by AR technology.

In the human zone, users, wearing the Microsoft Hololens2, could operate the AR user interface by gesture, voice and gaze. The multi-channel interaction could transform its input data to convey their orders and control the HRI system. In the robot zone, robots could receive the orders that transferred by the hardware device to gain the correct components. As a medium, AR technology connects the physical world and visual world between two zones.

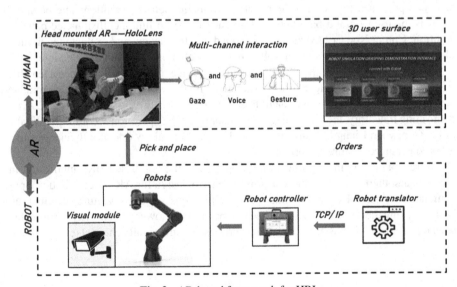

Fig. 2. AR-based framework for HRI.

Hardware Devices. The Hardware equipment contains Microsoft Hololens2 and a collaborative robot with an industrial camera.

With huge potential and advantages, HoloLens can mix images in the real world and related virtual images to display devices, giving users a powerful sense of immediacy. Scanning the real world and building real-time environment meshes, Hololens is capable of realizing world-scale positional tracking and spatial mapping of the virtual environment [15]. In this way, digital contents are allowed to be anchored to objects or surfaces wherever you are.

Hololens supports multiple modals to realize the interaction between humans and the virtual environment. Users remain focused on safely completing tasks error-free with hand tracking, built-in voice commands, eye tracking, spatial mapping, and large field of view. Specifically, Hololens understands precisely where you're looking to adjust its holograms to follow users' eyes in real time. Hololens adapts to both hands to fully execute hand tracking, touch, grasp, and move holograms in a natural way. Concurrently, built-in voice systems allow Hololens respond to the commands when users are occupied with a task and have no hands to quickly operate Hololens [16]. All above functions break through the space limitation of the two-dimensional interface and expand the human-robot interaction interface from two-dimensional to three-dimensional.

AUBO robots, as 6-DOF industrial robots, are used to interact with human. Cooperative robots that are also called workplace assistant robots or just "cobots", can cooperate with the operators on the same assembly line. The "partners" can fully give play to the efficiently of robots and human intelligence.

The type of AUBO robot used in this paper is the i3 series which has the range of motion of a sphere with a radius of 625mm. Meanwhile, as an HRI interface, AUBORPE (AUBO robot programming environment) displays on the touch panel of a teach pendant, which provides a visual operation interface to program and simulate the robot [17]. The system sets up two types of coordinate system for position control, including based on base or flange center coordinates. Equipped with an industrial camera of HIKROBOT, the robot will perform autonomously the operation of distinguishing, picking and handling[18]. Among the process, path planning is calculated and selected voluntarily through built-in scripts of the robot.

Software Device. The software setup contains unity to produce visual world and Vision Master to be used in visual positioning.

Unity3D is a comprehensive large-scale development tool for making interactive content such as scene visualization and 3D dynamic model. C# is used in Unity to be its primary language for developer scripting, which is a secure but straightforward language for beginners to cross the threshold [19]. The convenience of operation improves the productivity and problem-solving skills of experts and engineers.

Microsoft builds, without doubt, an open source cross-platform development kit, called Mixed-Reality Toolkit, to accelerate development of applications. Unity3D offers a sensible method for the development of the target hardware in Hololens. Building the virtual environment and virtual objects using Unity3D forms a portion of AR, such as research on collision detection and ergonomics analysis. The paper is mainly used for the establishment of the virtual user interface, as a way to interact with operators and transform native think into digital signals.

3.2 System Approach

The main goal of this project is to provide an example of the potential of AR technology applied to the world of industrial robots. The paper establishes communication and transfers information between users and robots via two 'middlemen', a multi-channel interactive user interface presented by HoloLens2 and the computer vision module of robots. The research emphases in this paper are the establishment of multi-channel AR user interface, computer vision recognition technology and the communication module.

Multi-channel AR User Interface. In this system, the user interface is used to complete interactive operation with special virtual digital contents through gaze, voice and gesture within the Microsoft HoloLens2 [20].

Users can interact with the menu page by multi-channel interactive operation, e.g. air-tap, bloom, hold and manipulation, to click, exit and flip the menu page. The above application enables to implement the several parts of complex interactive operation, setting buttons for users to click and activate. By the way, in the center of the user's field of vision is a white dot called the "gaze", which is emitted through the user's eyes [5]. Set colliders covering with cubes to collide with the above visual rays, and users can place their gaze on any cube they wish to interact with. About the voice, editing the setting and adding codes of the interactive cube can take actions after users say the corresponding words. The text on the button can be activated as a language instruction by a module called "SEE IT SAY IT" in Hololens.

The specific interaction methods and their combination modes can be formulated according to the actual scene. In this topic, the first step is to connect the robot with Hololens. Users gaze at the cube with "connect with Robot" for three seconds or say "connect" while gazing. The cube will highlight after the connection is successful. Then users perform an action of "hold" by two fingers toward the needed component, and the instruction can be transmitted to the robot. The cube with "SUCCESS" will highlight after successful choice. Communication technology will be commended in the next section (see Fig. 3).

Following these steps, users can select designated components and gain the corresponding information they need.

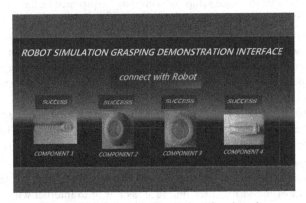

Fig. 3. Multi-channel AR user interface in unity

Communication Module. The communication module likes a "gap" to connect Hololens2 and the robot through the above multi-channel UI. Its framework and logical description are shown in Fig. 4.

The system uses C/S (Client-Server) architecture to solve the problem of user instructions' real-time transmission. HoloLens, as the server, can complete the functions of target information collection, model loading, spatial mapping and human-computer interaction, which enhances the mixing effect. The client, namely robot, completes the corresponding task according to the change of the system target information.

TCP/IP (Transmission Control Protocol/ Internet Protocol) is the data transmission protocol of the Internet in the whole system, which provides reliable service and plays an important role in guaranteeing network performances. When Hololens sends a connection request, the robot accepts data and returns data of successful acceptance to Hololens, which indicates successful communication. During transmission, the server and client are under the same Local Area Network (LAN).

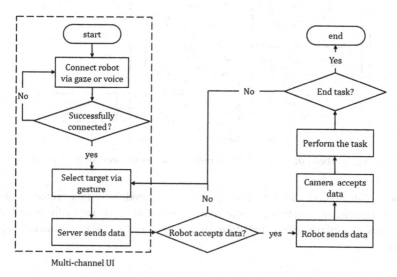

Fig. 4. The communication module of the system.

Robot Vision. After receiving the comments, the robot distinguishes and grabs the designated component by recognizing the size, shape or other characteristics through the visual sensor.

An image-based visual recognition control system was developed for the robot to recognize and grab the designated component. Through hardware design of the system, the image processing, and recognition technology, the recognition and location of the target are achieved.

The basic process is divided into two steps (see Fig. 5). The first step is to train and test the image samples collected as algorithm training models, so as to debug and verify the reliability and stability of the algorithm and continuously improve the fitting degree of the model. The operations of involved label image samples include distortion correction, target features extraction, build feature set and hand-eye calibration. Building target feature sets is usually a model training process. The other step is to classify and recognize the target image with the optimal model after training, which includes repetitive distortion correction, target features extraction, target recognition and calibration conversion [21]. Finally, the target coordinates of the base coordinate system are obtained.

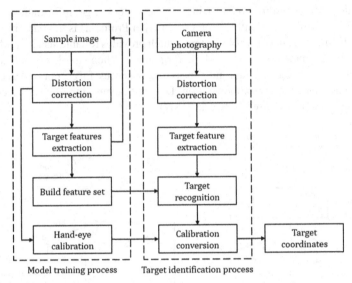

Fig. 5. The basic flowchart of the image-based visual recognition system

The architecture of the robotic computer vision module in this project is shown in Fig. 6. The camera matches the objective according to users' instructions and get its coordinates. The information is transmitted to the robot to grasp the target and accomplish the task.

3.3 Case Study

The AR-based human-robot instruction system is applied to the case study for a simple assembly process. As mentioned above, the HRI system consists of 3 parts: the human operator, an AR device (Hololens), a 6-DOF robot with a camera. Wearing Hololens, the human operator can catch sight of the virtual scene and control the robot anywhere as shown in Fig. 7.

During the task, for example, obtain a ball through teleoperation, which was developed to verify the application of the developed method. First, gaze at the cube with "connect with Robot". Then select the component magic representing the ball with a gesture. At last, the robot moved and grabbed the ball, as shown in Fig. 8.

The results provide evidence that AR is one of the efficient methods to realize multi-channel human-robot interaction. This application will help pave the way for future applications of augmented reality to practical, industrial, and other applications.

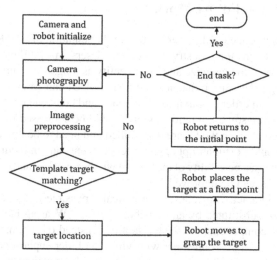

Fig. 6. The robotic computer vision module architecture

Fig. 7. The user operate virtual UI with Hololens

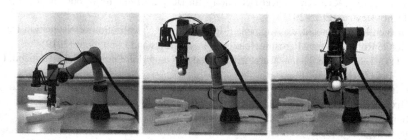

Fig. 8. The robot action process of ball grabbing

4 Conclusion and Future Work

In this paper, we introduced and presented the implementation of an AR-based human-robot interaction system for industry application. Users can intuitively teleoperate a 6-DOFs industry robot to recognize and locate entity as long as the entity are within the robotic visual range. The multi-channel interaction of UI can be defined according to the scene and tasks, in order to maximize efficiency and convenience.

However, there are some limitations, which could be addressed in the future work. For example, the contents in the UI are determined and need to be uploaded again once modified, which couldn't suit abrupt environmental events and individual habits.

In the future, the vast possibility of the project will be revealed, and certain limitations from current abilities can be improved.

The ability to interact with robot is theoretically possible to be more natural. The virtual UI could be substituted by an invisible interface. Wearing Hololens, operators select directly real components via their visual ray, instead of clicking pictures on the visual interface. This ray can intersect with virtual collider superimposed on the real object. Within the above improvement, selected parts will not stick in the virtual interface and the sight line will not be blocked in this way as well, which improves the safety and flexibility of assembling.

Additionally, according to personas of operators, the spatial auxiliary information in virtual world can present intelligently. The system recognizes the human activities and forecasts user intention. After that, it will present auxiliary information and robotic motions as outputs. Meanwhile, the system is worth verifying to combine with JCS (Joint Cognitive Systems) and to be used in remote collaboration with robot. Offer more value relevance information for users in every case, which will enhance the individuation and productivity of tasks.

We believe that AR technology is an ongoing pursuit in the field of HRI. The finding of this paper has provided a new paradigm for AR-based applications and imparted novel insight to HRI for industry.

References

1. Wang, X.V., et al.: Closed-loop augmented reality towards accurate human-robot collaboration. CIRP Ann. **69**(1), 425–428 (2020)
2. Guo, J., et al.: Real-time Object Detection with Deep Learning for Robot Vision on Mixed Reality Device. IEEE (2021)
3. Kästner, L., Lambrecht, J.: Augmented-Reality-Based Visualization of Navigation Data of Mobile Robots on the Microsoft Hololens - Possibilities and Limitations (2019)
4. Huang, J.: A non-contact measurement method based on HoloLens. Int. J. Performabil. Eng. **14**, 144 (2018)
5. Krupke, D., et al.: Comparison of Multimodal Heading and Pointing Gestures for Co-Located Mixed Reality Human-Robot Interaction. IEEE (2018)
6. Guhl, J., Nguyen, S.T., Kruger, J.: concept and architecture for programming industrial robots using augmented reality with mobile devices like Microsoft HoloLens. Institute of Electrical and Electronics Engineers Inc., Limassol, Cyprus (2017)
7. Perzanowski, D., et al.: Building a multimodal human-robot interface. IEEE Intell. Syst. App. **16**(1), 16–21 (2001)

8. Vahrenkamp, N., et al.: Workspace analysis for planning human-robot interaction tasks. IEEE Computer Society, Cancun, Mexico (2016)

9. Muhammad, F., et al.: Creating a Shared Reality with Robots. IEEE Computer Society, Daegu, Republic of Korea (2019)

10. Hietanen, A., et al.: AR-based interaction for human-robot collaborative manufacturing. Robot. Comput.-Integr. Manuf. **63**, 101891 (2022)

11. Stone, K.A., et al.: Augmented Reality Interface for Industrial Robot Controllers. Institute of Electrical and Electronics Engineers Inc., Orem, UT, United States (2020)

12. Guhl, J., Hügle, J., Krüger, J.: Enabling human-robot-interaction via virtual and augmented reality in distributed control systems. Procedia CIRP. **76**, 167–170 (2018)

13. Xue, C., Qiao, Y., Murray, N.: Enabling Human-Robot-Interaction for Remote Robotic Operation via Augmented Reality. Virtual Institute of Electrical and Electronics Engineers Inc., Cork, Ireland (2020)

14. Liang, C., et al.: Robot Teleoperation System Based on Mixed Reality. Osaka Institute of Electrical and Electronics Engineers Inc., Japan (2019)

15. Azuma, R.T.M.: Augmented Reality A Reality. San Francisco OSA - The Optical Society CA, United States (2017)

16. Microsoft HoloLens | Mixed Reality Technology for Business. https://www.microsoft.com/en-us/hololens. Accessed 28 Jan 2022

17. AUBO Collaborative Robot. https://www.aubo-cobot.com/public/. Accessed 28 Jan 2022

18. Meng, Y., Zhuang, H.Q.: Autonomous robot calibration using vision technology. Robot. Comput. Integr. Manuf. **23**(4), 436–446 (2007)

19. Fan, L., et al.: Using AR and Unity 3D to Support Geographical Phenomena Simu-lations. Institute of Electrical and Electronics Engineers Inc. Virtual, Nanjing, China (2020)

20. Furlan, R.: The future of augmented reality: Hololens - Microsoft's AR headset shines despite rough edges [resources-tools and toys]. IEEE Spectr. **53**(6), 21 (2016)

21. Wang, J., et al.: Research on automatic target detection and recognition based on deep learning. J. Visual Commun. Image Represent. **60**, 44–50 (2019)

AI-AR for Bridge Inspection by Drone

Jean-François Lapointe[1]([⊠])(iD), Mohand Saïd Allili[2], Luc Belliveau[1],
Loucif Hebbache[2], Dariush Amirkhani[2], and Hicham Sekkati[1]

[1] National Research Council Canada, Digital Technologies Research Centre,
Ottawa, Canada
{jean-francois.lapointe,luc.belliveau,hicham.sekkati}@nrc-cnrc.gc.ca
[2] Université du Québec en Outaouais, Gatineau, QC, Canada
{mohandsaid.allili,hebl08,amid01}@uqo.ca
https://nrc-cnrc.canada.ca, https://www.uqo.ca

Abstract. Good and regular inspections of transportation infrastructures such as bridges and overpasses are necessary to maintain the safety of the public who uses them and the integrity of the structures. Until recently, these inspections were done entirely manually by using mainly visual inspection to detect defects on the structure. In the last few years, inspection by drone is an emerging way of achieving inspection that allows more efficient access to the structure. This paper describes a human-in-the-loop system that combines AI and AR for bridge inspection by drone.

Keywords: Bridge · Inspection · AI · Artificial intelligence · Deep learning · AR · Augmented reality · UAV · UAS · RPAS · Drone · Remote guidance

1 Introduction

The recent tragedies caused by the collapses of the I-35W and Morandi bridges [4,26] illustrate the importance to conduct regular inspections of such transportation infrastructures. Until recently, these inspections were done on site by teams of inspectors who used mainly visual inspection to monitor the state of those infrastructures. The emergence of flying drone technology (a.k.a. Unmanned Aerial Vehicles - UAVs or Remotely Piloted Aircraft Systems - RPAS or Unmanned Aerial Systems - UASs) for civilian applications [5,10,38] combined with computer vision-based inspection [6] allows for an easier access to parts of civil infrastructures such as bridges that are often difficult to inspect [8,33,34].

Though it is clear that using drones is a promising way for automatic bridge inspection, it remains important to design systems to collaborate humans and drones to perform the inspection task in an efficient way. That is to say, drones

This project was supported in part by collaborative research funding from the National Research Council of Canada's Artificial Intelligence for Logistics Program.

J. Y. C. Chen and G. Fragomeni (Eds.): HCII 2022, LNCS 13318, pp. 302–313, 2022.
https://doi.org/10.1007/978-3-031-06015-1_21

should be guided in a way that reduces the flying time and collision risks, while enabling to assess about potential defects through real-time image analysis. For this purpose, the combination of drone navigation with AI and AR technologies has a huge potential to increase the efficiency of the inspection. This combination will integrate the benefits of an easier access to the structure, automatic detection and classification of defects while facilitating drone remote navigation by a technician [18].

In this paper, we propose a remote guidance approach [18] toward realizing such a system, by enabling an open-loop and interactive collaboration between one or several remote experts and an onsite technician with pilots locally a drone. The drone is equipped with a camera sensor that will capture live video streams that are sent to a ground station to perform real-time image analysis for visual scene understating and defect detection. Then, an AR module will synthesize useful high-level information that will be superimposed to the view of the technician through and AR headset in order to give the technician crucial information about the presence of defects, the progress of the inspection mission and the drone navigation state (e.g., 3D position, speed, energy consumption, etc.). Finally, another, web-based AR module will provide to one or several remotely-located experts (the inspectors) the images relayed by the drone camera augmented with the AI-detected defects. The concept is illustrated in Fig. 1 below.

This paper is organized as follows: Sect. 2 presents some related work about bridge inspection using drones. Section 3 presents the proposed inspection system. Section 4 presents a discussion about the proposed system.

2 Related Works

Several method are used to inspect bridges [39] and they can be classified as non-visual and visual inspection methods. Also some research has been done already on the use of drones and augmented reality (AR) for bridge inspection.

2.1 Non-visual Methods for Bridge Inspection

Different technique have been used to inspect bridges as an alternative for visual inspection. For example, acoustic techniques have been used to detect changes in sound pitch resulting from hitting the concrete surface with a hammer [11]. One of the advantages of these methods is cheapness, but they are less accurate in deep layer defect detection. They are also less applicable to non-concrete bridges [20]. Another group of bridge inspection techniques is ground-penetrating radar (GPR). In this method, inspectors use electromagnetic radiation to image the underlying layers and detect defects [7]. The disadvantage of this approach is its high energy consumption and the need for expertise to interpret the data. Another method is Half-Cell Potential which assesses the electrical potential difference between the reinforcement in concrete and a standard electrode for defect detection [29]. This method can detect corrosion in the early stages, but it incurs a high cost.

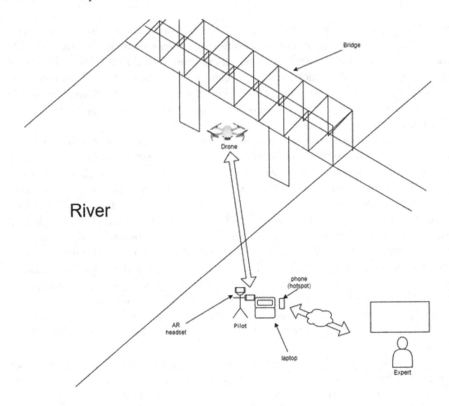

Fig. 1. Illustration of the concept

2.2 Visual Methods for Bridge Inspection

For visual inspection, methods have been proposed using different modalities of visual data. Most of existing methods for visual inspection are based on he visible spectrum, although infrared/thermal imaging can be used for detecting special defects such as delamination [37]. Until recently, statistical methods were the most used to detect defects on images. Image features such as edges, color and texture are first extracted. Then, pattern recognition techniques including clustering and classification are in defect detection [15]. Abdel-Qader et al. compared four well-known image processing techniques: Fast Haar transform (FHT), Fast Fourier transform, Sobel edge detector, and Canny edge detector to detect bridge cracks [1]. They stated that the accuracy of the FHT in detecting cracks is much higher than other methods. Salman et al. provided an automated method for detecting cracks based on the Gabor filter [32]. Talab et al. used Sobel's filter and Otsu method [2] to detect cracks [36].

2.3 Drones and AR for Bridge Inspection

The use of Augmented reality (AR) and/or drones are emerging methods of inspecting bridges. Drones allow access to hard-to-reach areas, eliminating the need for physical presence. Wells et al. [38] used drones to inspect bridges. They used different types of drones on eight bridges with different sizes, locations, and conditions to evaluate the effectiveness of drones in inspecting bridges. Dam et al. [6] Measured the effect of AR cue types (none, bounding box, corner-bound box, and outline) on discrete levels in prominent places of the search location with a signal detection task. They concluded that different AR cue types differ greatly in false alarm rates while the terms hits and misses have no effect. Kilic et al. [17] Described the benefits of using AR with a visual inspection, Ground Penetrating Radar (GPR), Laser Distance Sensors (LDS), Infrared Thermography (IRT), and Telescopic Camera (TC). Hu et al. [12] proposed a method using a combination of AR and GPR to inspect concrete bridges.

Nowadays, with the expansion of artificial intelligence, these methods have been replaced with deep learning models. In most recent research, neural networks have been used to detect defects more accurately than previous methods. Among the deep learning algorithms, convolutional neural networks (CNNs) have been shown to effectively detect defects in concrete bridges and tunnels [19,28,35] along with U-net model [21]. This paper presents the result obtained so far in our research project aimed at improving bridge inspections by combining the technologies of AI, AR and drones.

3   The Proposed System

The system is composed of a drone that flies nearby a bridge to inspect it, which is remotely piloted by an onsite pilot with a line-of-sight on it. The images relayed by the drone are analyzed by an AI module to detect potential defects and highlight them on the images seen by one or several remote experts (the inspectors) who can be located anywhere on the internet, thus providing an AR display. Finally, the pilot wears an AR headset which allows to augment the real view of the drone with relevant information (see Fig. 1). The network connection is provided by a smartphone which acts as a Wi-Fi hotspot.

This paper describes the various modules of this system as illustrated on the system architecture (Fig. 2). The architecture describes well the various modules of the system and their links with the actors (pilot, experts, drone).

3.1   The AI Module

The AI module uses three computer vision techniques to inspect the defects that can be found on bridges, namely: object classification, detection, and segmentation. A level of gravity is then assigned to each defect. This process usually has six steps as illustrated by Hüthwohl et al. [14] in Fig. 3.

The public datasets used to date are: CODEBRIM (COncrete DEfect BRidge IMage Dataset) and MCDS (Multi-Classifier DataSet for reinforced concrete bridge defects). CODEBRIM [25] is a multilabel dataset composed of six categories of defects: background (2490), crack (2507), spallation (1898), exposed bar (1507), efflorescence (833), and corrosion (1559). MCDS [14] is multilabel dataset

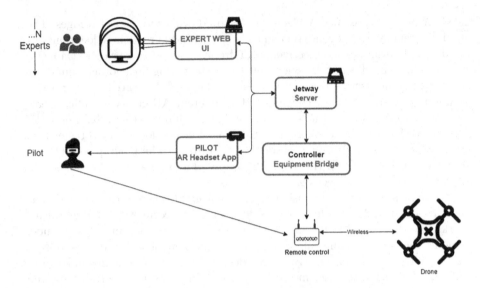

Fig. 2. System architecture

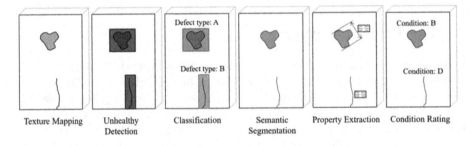

Texture Mapping   Unhealthy Detection   Classification   Semantic Segmentation   Property Extraction   Condition Rating

Fig. 3. Defects inspection steps [14].

defined by a hierarchy of classifiers which contains ten categories of defects: crack (789), efflorescence (311), scaling (168), spalling (427), general defects (264), no defects (452), exposed reinforcement (223), no exposed reinforcement (203), rust staining (355), and no rust staining (415).

A comparative study of current deep learning algorithms has been conducted to determine the most appropriate architecture for the classification and detection of defects from images. In particular, the ResNet, Inception, EfficientNet architectures and their variants are explored for classification. YOLO, SSD, Faster R-CNN and their variants are studied for detection. Finally, FCN, U-Net, and their variants are compared for the segmentation. The method used for learning is transfer learning and the fine-tuning of models is conducted on tested models to optimize performance [3].

For the experiment's environment, we used Google Colab Pro+, which provides 52 GB of RAM alongside 8 CPU cores and priority access to GPU P100.

We split the dataset CODEBRIM into training, validation, and test set with a ratio of 70%, 20%, and 10% respectively.

To evaluate the performance of the fine-tuned classification models, we used AUC-ROC metric which is the area under the receiver operating characteristic curve. This metric is one of the most robust evaluation metrics for classification tasks having the problem of imbalanced data which is the case of CODEBRIM dataset. Table 1 shows the comparison of defect classification results obtained with tested models against those of a previous study. We observe that our result obtained by ResNet50 outperforms the state of the art, so we chose to select this classifier for defect classification.

Table 1. Comparison of defect classification results.

Models	Our results	Previous results study [3]
VGG16	0.88	0.88
ResNet50	**0.96**	0.90
Inception-v3	0.87	0.89
EfficientNet-B0	0.89	–
DenseNet-201	0.95	–
InceptionResNet-v2	0.93	–

In the case of defect detection, to evaluate the performance of the detectors and compare it to other studies, we used the mAP (mean Average Precision) metric representing the mean value of the AP of all classes. The AP is the area under the precision-recall curve. Table 2 shows the comparison of defect detection results obtained with tested models against those of previous studies. We observe that our result obtained by YOLOX outperforms the state of the art in terms of accuracy and speed, so we chose to select this detector for defect detection. YOLOX is the latest version of YOLO models, improving the limitation in terms of speed and accuracy, and most recently it won the Streaming Perception Challenge at CVPR 2021's Automatic Driving Workshop. Since CODEBRIM is multi-label dataset, we used YOLOX as a multi-label detector which assigns more than one label for each bounding box. The Fig. 4 illustrates some early images from defect detection using YOLOX where we can see that the multi-label defects are represented by overlaid bounding boxes.

For the segmentation task, we plan in the future to create segmentation masks for the CODEBRIM dataset, and use semantic segmentation technique to label each pixel of an image with a corresponding defect.

Table 2. Comparison of defect detection results.

Studies	Method	mAP@0.5	Inference time (s)
Our study	**YOLOX**	**0.91**	**0.04**
	YOLOR	0.86	0.05
	SSD	0.41	0.06
	Faster R-CNN	0.36	0.14
Previous studies	Jiang et al. (YOLOv3) [16]	0.65	0.05
	Jiang et al. (SSD) [16]	0.64	0.06
	Zhang et al. (YOLOv3) [40]	0.80	0.05
	Zhang et al. (Faster R-CNN) [40]	0.74	0.14

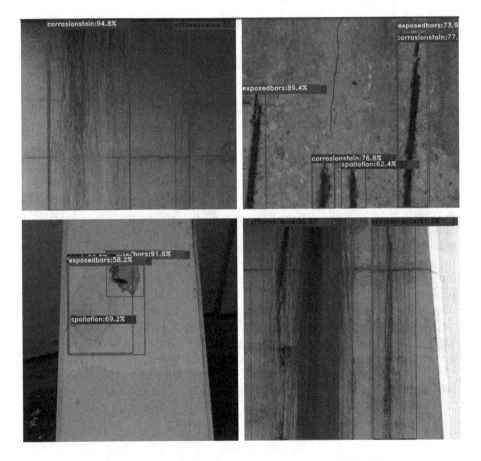

Fig. 4. Early images of defect detection using YOLOX

3.2   The AR Modules

The system will include two AR modules. The first AR module will augment the images seen by the experts (the inspectors) by highlighting the defects detected by the AI module. An early prototype of this AR module for inspection is illustrated in Fig. 5 that uses a YOLOv3 deep learning method to detect objects and people instead of bridge defects.

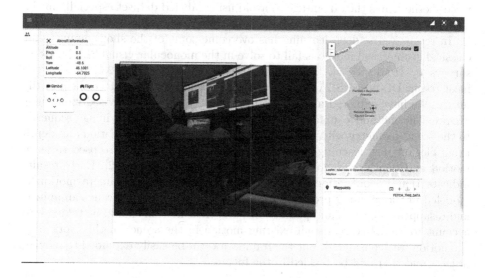

Fig. 5. Early prototype of the inspection AR module

Figure 5 also illustrates the possibility for the expert to control the yaw/pitch/roll parameters of the camera and to get some basic flight parameters such as the altitude. Finally, since many experts can be connected at once, the user interface allows each expert to request the control of the drone.

The second AR module will augment the images seen by the drone pilot with relevant information such as the video feed from the camera and battery life. This second module will try to palliate the current problem with drone remote guidance where the pilot must constantly share his/her visual attention between keeping a line of sight with the drone and looking at the remote control to gather useful flight information as well as the video feed from the drone's, a problem commonly referred as *head down time* [31]. As a result, the pilot will constantly keep a line-of-sight with the drone. Finally, additional information will be overlaid on this real view in the AR headset to improve the pilot's situational awareness [30].

3.3   Depth Estimation and Drone Trajectory Module

Estimating jointly depth map and motion cues, known by SLAM (Simultaneous Localization and Mapping) in the robotic community and by Structure-From-

Motion (SFM) in the computer vision community, starts to attract attention in recent learning methods. The use of monocular SLAM by deep learning is explored in our work to provide both motion trajectory of the mounted sensor on the drone and depth map of the scene. Using a single camera is less constrained whether to the weight or to the occlusions related to stereo or multiple cameras. However, depth inference is more challenging in the case of monocular than methods using stereo cameras or RGB-D in SLAM. Also, using unsupervised methods has the advantage to avoid using labeled dataset especially in the context of uncommon environments like bridges.

In recent years, deep learning has overcome some of the shortcomings that classical geometrical methods fail to solve in the monocular visual SLAM. Good surveys by Huang et al. [13] and recently by Metan et al. [23], present the most recent DL-based SLAM methods and the challenges that face them in the future. We have explored a new paradigm to solve the unsupervised monocular SLAM. The method couples the spatio-temporal variations in image sequence to the scene geometry with the goal to supervise both camera motion and depth in an elegant new learning framework. Two CNNs networks are used to learn motion and depth, and are trained using KITTI dataset [9,22]. Early results indicate that we outperform existing methods even if only camera motion is modeled in the learning process. Other moving objects in the scene can appear and disappear, like cars and pedestrians, and their motion should be taking into account to model correctly all existing motion in the scene. In this work only egomotion was considered, but the framework can be easily extended to moving objects and that will be tackled in the future.

4 Discussion

The purpose of the system described here is to assist, not replace, inspectors in performing their tasks so that they can achieve it in a better and faster way. Given their ability to quickly scan and acquire images of surfaces that can be hard to reach otherwise, drones are well suited to this task. In order to better understand the task itself and thus find better ways to fit the technology to the users, a task analysis is planned. Because of the current pandemic situation however, it is not completed yet. In fact, discussions with some bridge management authorities allowed us to collect some documentation on the task [24,27] but direct field interviews with inspectors have been delayed. Nonetheless, as discussed in Sect. 2 we already know that the inspection task itself is not always visual and that sometimes non-visual inspection methods are used.

Lab and field trials will allow to observe the performance of the whole system, including the possible image resolution and frame rate that can be transmitted in real-time over a cell phone connection. The available bandwidth at the inspected bridge site will mainly dictate those parameters. Also, field trials will allow us to compare the usability of the AR headset for the pilot as compared to the traditional way of flying the drone without an headset. Once assessed and optimized the system could be demonstrated to real bridge inspectors for further feedback, development and validation.

5 Conclusion

This paper described an advanced human-in-the loop system that combines AI and AR for bridge inspection by drone. Although still in development, this system is really promising and the multidisciplinary nature of the project team enriches it. Future works will be to complete user and system requirements by conducting a task analysis of the inspection task itself, as well as lab and field trials to test and refine the system usefulness and usability. We also plan to explore image segmentation for the detection of defects, in order to better characterize them. Finally, the possibility to automatically locate and document the defects also has a lot of potential to allow bridge inspectors to better perform their task and avoid other tragedies.

References

1. Abdel-Qader, I., Abudayyeh, O., Kelly, M.E.: Analysis of edge-detection techniques for crack identification in bridges. J. Comput. Civ. Eng. **17**(4), 255–263 (2003). https://doi.org/10.1061/(ASCE)0887-3801(2003)17:4(255)
2. Boulmerka, A., Allili, M.S., Ait-Aoudia, S.: A generalized multiclass histogram thresholding approach based on mixture modelling. Pattern Recognit. **47**(3), 1330–1348 (2014). https://arxiv.org/abs/2104.06456
3. Bukhsh, Z.A., Jansen, N., Saeed, A.: Damage detection using in-domain and cross-domain transfer learning. Neural Comput. Appl. **33**(24), 16921–16936 (2021). https://doi.org/10.1007/s00521-021-06279-x
4. Calvi, G.M., et al.: Once upon a time in Italy: the tale of the Morandi bridge. Struct. Eng. Int. **29**, 198–217 (2019). https://doi.org/10.1080/10168664.2018.1558033
5. Chen, S., Laefer, D.F., Mangina, E.: State of technology review of civilian UAVs. Recent Pat. Eng. **10**(3), 160–174 (2016). https://doi.org/10.2174/1872212110666160712230039
6. Dam, J.V., Krasne, A., Gabbard, J.L.: Drone-based augmented reality platform for bridge inspection: effect of AR cue design on visual search tasks. In: 2020 IEEE Conference on Virtual reality and 3D User Interfaces Abstracts and Workshops (VRW), pp. 201–204 (2020). https://doi.org/10.1109/VRW50115.2020.00043
7. Diamanti, N., Annan, A.P., Redman, J.D.: Concrete bridge deck deterioration assessment using ground penetrating radar (GPR). J. Environ. Eng. Geophys. **22**(2), 121–132 (2017). https://doi.org/10.2113/JEEG22.2.121
8. Feroz, S., Dabous, S.A.: UAV-based remote sensing applications for bridge condition assessment. Remote Sens. **13**(9), 1809 (2021). https://doi.org/10.3390/rs13091809
9. Geiger, A., Lenz, P., Urtasun, R.: Are we ready for autonomous driving? The KITTI vision benchmark suite. In: 2012 IEEE Conference on Computer Vision and Pattern Recognition (CVPR), pp. 3354–3361 (2012). https://doi.org/10.1109/CVPR.2012.6248074
10. Hassanalian, M., Abdelkefi, A.: Classifications, applications, and design challenges of drones: A review. Prog. Aerosp. Sci. **91**, 99–131 (2017). https://doi.org/10.1016/j.paerosci.2017.04.003

11. Hendricks, L.J., et al.: High-speed acoustic impact-echo sounding of concrete bridge decks. J. Nondestr. Eval. **39**(3), 1–12 (2020). https://doi.org/10.1007/s10921-020-00695-0
12. Hu, D., Hou, F., Blakely, J., Li, S.: Augmented reality based visualization for concrete bridge deck deterioration characterized by ground penetrating radar. In: Construction Research Congress 2020: Computer Applications, pp. 1156–1164. American Society of Civil Engineers Reston, VA (2020). https://doi.org/10.1061/9780784482865.122
13. Huang, B., Zhao, J., Liu, J.: A survey of simultaneous localization and mapping. ArXiv (2019). https://arxiv.org/pdf/1909.05214v1.pdf
14. Hüthwohl, P., Lu, R., Brilakis, I.: Multi-classifier for reinforced concrete bridge defects. Autom. Constr. **105**, 1–15 (2019). https://doi.org/10.1016/j.autcon.2019.04.019
15. Jahanshahi, M.R., Kelly, J.S., Masri, S.F., Sukhatme, G.S.: A survey and evaluation of promising approaches for automatic image-based defect detection of bridge structures. Struct. Infrast. Eng. **5**(6), 455–486 (2009). https://doi.org/10.1080/15732470801945930
16. Jiang, Y., Pang, D., Li, C.: A deep learning approach for fast detection and classification of concrete damage. Autom. Constr. **128**, 103785 (2021). https://doi.org/10.1016/j.autcon.2021.103785
17. Kilic, G., Caner, A.: Augmented reality for bridge condition assessment using advanced non-destructive techniques. Struct. Infrast. Eng. **17**(7), 977–989 (2021). https://doi.org/10.1080/15732479.2020.1782947
18. Lapointe, J.-F., Molyneaux, H., Allili, M.S.: A literature review of AR-based remote guidance tasks with user studies. In: Chen, J.Y.C., Fragomeni, G. (eds.) HCII 2020, Part II. LNCS, vol. 12191, pp. 111–120. Springer, Cham (2020). https://doi.org/10.1007/978-3-030-49698-2_8
19. Li, S., Zhao, X.: Image-based concrete crack detection using convolutional neural network and exhaustive search technique. Adv. Civ. Eng. **2019**, 1–12 (2019). https://doi.org/10.1155/2019/6520620
20. Lin, S., Meng, D., Choi, H., Shams, S., Azari, H.: Laboratory assessment of nine methods for nondestructive evaluation of concrete bridge decks with overlays. Constr. Build. Mater. **188**, 966–982 (2018). https://doi.org/10.1016/j.conbuildmat.2018.08.127
21. Liu, Z., Cao, Y., Wang, Y., Wang, W.: Computer vision-based concrete crack detection using U-net fully convolutional networks. Autom. Constr. **104**, 129–139 (2019). https://doi.org/10.1016/j.autcon.2019.04.005
22. Menze, M., Geiger, A.: Object scene flow for autonomous vehicles. In: 2015 IEEE Conference on Computer Vision and Pattern Recognition (CVPR), pp. 3061–3070 (2015). https://doi.org/10.1109/CVPR.2015.7298925
23. Mertan, A., Duff, D.J., Unal, G.: Single image depth estimation: an overview. ArXiv (2021). https://arxiv.org/abs/2104.06456
24. Ministère des Transports, de la Mobilité durable et de l'Électrification des transports: Manuel d'inspection des structures. Gouvernement du Québec (2017). http://www3.publicationsduquebec.gouv.qc.ca/produits/ouvrage_routier/guides/guide24.fr.html
25. Mundt, M., Majumder, S., Murali, S., Panetsos, P., Ramesh, V.: Meta-learning convolutional neural architectures for multi-target concrete defect classification with the COncrete DEfect BRidge IMage dataset. In: Proceedings of the IEEE/CVF Conference on Computer Vision and Pattern Recognition (CVPR 2019), pp. 11196–11205 (2019). https://doi.org/10.1109/CVPR.2019.01145

26. National Transportation Safety Board: Collapse of I-35W highway bridge, Minneapolis, Minnesota, 1 August 2007 (2008). http://www.dot.state.mn.us/i35wbridge/pdf/ntsb-report.pdf
27. Public Works and Government Services Canada: Bridge inspection manual. Government of Canada (2010)
28. Ren, Y., et al.: Image-based concrete crack detection in tunnels using deep fully convolutional networks. Constr. Build. Mater. **234**, 1–12 (2020). https://doi.org/10.1016/j.conbuildmat.2019.117367
29. Rhazi, J.O.: Half-cell potential test from the upper-side and the lower-side of reinforced concrete slabs: a comparative study. In: NDTCE 2009, Non-Destructive Testing in Civil Engineering (2009)
30. Ruano, S., Cuevas, C., Gallego, G., Garcia, N.: Augmented reality tool for the situational awareness improvement of UAV operators. Sensors **171**(2), 297–313 (2017). https://doi.org/10.3390/s17020297
31. Safi, M., Chung, J., Pradhan, P.: Review of augmented reality in aerospace industry. Aircr. Eng. Aerosp. Technol. **91**(9), 1187–1194 (2019). https://doi.org/10.1108/AEAT-09-2018-0241
32. Salman, M., Mathavan, S., Kamal, K., Rahman, M.: Pavement crack detection using the Gabor filter. In: Proceedings of the IEEE Conference on intelligent transportation systems (ITSC 2013), pp. 2039–2044 (2013)
33. Seo, J., Duque, L., Wacker, J.: Drone-enabled bridge inspection methodology and application. Autom. Constr. **94**, 112–126 (2018). https://doi.org/10.1016/j.autcon.2018.06.006
34. Spencer, B., Jr., Hoskere, V., Narazaki, Y.: Advances in computer vision-based civil infrastructure inspection and monitoring. Engineering **5**, 199–222 (2019). https://doi.org/10.1155/2019/6520620
35. Słoński, M.: A comparison of deep convolutional neural networks for image-based detection of concrete surface cracks. Comput. Assist. Methods Eng. Sci. **26**, 105–112 (2019). https://doi.org/10.24423/cames.267
36. Talab, A.M.A., Huang, Z., Xi, F., HaiMing, L.: Detection crack in image using Otsu method and multiple filtering in image processing techniques. Optik **127**, 1030–1033 (2016). https://doi.org/10.1016/j.ijleo.2015.09.147
37. Vaghefi, K., Melo e Silva, H., Harris, D., Ahlborn, R.: Application of thermal IR imagery for concrete bridge inspection. In: PCI National Bridge Conference, PCI/NBC, Salt Lake City: UT (USA), pp. 1–12 (2011)
38. Wells, J.L., Lovelace, B., Kalar, T.: Use of unmanned aircraft systems for bridge inspections. Transp. Res. Record **2612**(1), 60–66 (2017). https://doi.org/10.3141/2612-07
39. Yaghi, S.R., Dabous, S.A.: State-of-the art practices in bridge inspection. Int. J. Civ. Environ. Eng. **9**(10), 1344–1347 (2015). https://doi.org/10.5281/zenodo.1109619
40. Zhang, C., Chen Chang, C., Jamshidi, M.: Concrete bridge surface damage detection using a single-stage detector. Comput. Aided Civ. Infrastruct. Eng. **35**(4), 389–409 (2020). https://doi.org/10.1111/mice.12500

Spatial Augmented Reality (SAR) System for Agriculture Land Suitability Maps Visualization

Hanhan Maulana[1,2(✉)], Toshiki Sato[1], and Hideaki Kanai[1]

[1] School of Knowledge Science, Japan Advanced Institute of Science and Technology, 1-1, Asahidai, Nomi, Ishikawa, Japan
hanhan@email.unikom.ac.id

[2] Department of Informatics Engineering and Computer Science, Universitas Komputer Indonesia, Jl. Dipatiukur no 112-114, Bandung 40134, Indonesia

Abstract. The purpose of this Study is to visualize Agriculture land suitability maps using Spatial Augmented Reality (SAR). This research has three main stages. The first stage collects map data from open data sites and processes it with GIS software. The second stage is the land suitability evaluation using the weighted overlay method. The Last stage is the visualization of the land suitability map. The visualization process begins with the creation of a 3D map taken from DEM data. Then the land suitability map generated in the previous stage is projected onto the 3D map model. SAR visualizes a land suitability map to a 3D object with projectors. The calibration process uses the Procam library using Open CV. This study compares the projection map with the land suitability map in the form of a raster file (Tiff file format) to evaluate the projection results. Then used qualitative methods to get user responses to the system. This study concludes that SAR provides a new way to visualize maps. SAR makes it easy for map users to obtain information on the map. This system is expected to assist farmers in understanding the resulting land suitability map.

Keywords: Land suitability evaluations · Spatial augmented reality · Projected map · Weighted overlay method · Agriculture land suitability

1 Introductions

The ability of farmers to understand land suitability maps is crucial [1, 2]. This capability can help farmers increase the productivity of agricultural commodities. Data to support land suitability map development is available on various open data sites [3, 4]. Unfortunately, farmers are still not able to utilize this data optimally [5]. It's because (1) The data available have different formats; (2) The land suitability maps development has a complex process; and (3) For making land suitability maps requires large amounts of data. It requires not only tabular data but also spatial data [5]. The Indonesian government uses a geographic information system to facilitate land evaluation. Geographic information systems (GIS) can map land conditions, weather, and other factors for the

J. Y. C. Chen and G. Fragomeni (Eds.): HCII 2022, LNCS 13318, pp. 314–328, 2022.
https://doi.org/10.1007/978-3-031-06015-1_22

land evaluation process [6–8]. Furthermore, GIS can analyze geospatial data. So, it is easier for farmers to evaluate land suitability. In Indonesia, GIS implementation for agriculture is still not optimal [9]. That's because only a few farmers can read maps [10]. In addition, analogizing the map to the real world requires spatial thinking skills. 3D maps provide topographical shapes similar with the real world. Therefore, 3D maps are relatively easier to understand than 2D maps. Laksono et al. conduct research that focuses on visualizing topographic maps in 3D [9]. The study concluded that 3D maps increase user understanding of the information on the map. The Spatial Augmented Reality (SAR) is also an alternative in displaying maps to make them easier to understand. Kundu et al. used an augmented reality sandbox to improve students' understanding of geography [11]. However, it is hard to create real-world topography using sand.

The motivation behind this study is the application of augmented reality (AR) sandbox to visualize 3D maps with sand media. AR Sandbox is a learning medium in geology, hydrogeology, and geography [11]. Furthermore, from a cartographic point of view, AR Sandbox is an effective way to introduce the basic concepts of topography [12]. Many researchers claim AR sandbox as an effective learning medium because it provides a real-time experience [11–13]. AR sandbox uses sand as a medium, the camera's depth sensor detects the surface of the sand, and computer devices control the visualization and simulation. AR sandbox is effective for use as a medium for early learning and simulations [11]. However, it is still difficult to simulate a real topographic map. It is hard to form topographic reliefs that are appropriate and accurate with real-world conditions [11]. This Study replaces the sand media with 3D objects created from DEM data. The resulting map has an accurate topography according to the contours of the real world.

This study collects geographic data from various open data sites. First, this study creates a thematic layer based on the criteria used for land evaluation. Second, create nine thematic map layers to develop a land suitability map. Last, this study uses Spatial Augmented Reality (SAR) to visualize land suitability maps. This study uses Blender 3D to model 3D maps from digital elevation model (DEM) data. Due to the large size of the map, Blender 3D divides the map into a smaller size. This process makes it easier to print 3D map models using a 3D printer. This study uses the Unity 3D game engine to visualize the land suitability map. Unity 3D scene imports 3D objects (Obj File) for base maps and land suitability maps (images) for texturing 3D objects. Azure Kinect deep camera detects 3D objects. The projector projects the maps into a 3D map. The calibration process of this study uses the OpenCV library. With the map projected into 3D, the land suitability map has an identical visualization with the real-world topography. This system is expected to assist farmers in understanding the resulting land suitability map.

2   Related Work

Spatial Augmented reality (SAR), or projection mapping, makes it possible to augment the real world with virtual information using light emitters such as video projectors [11, 12, 14–16]. One of the main advantages of SAR is that the user can see the real-world object and not on a screen like the original augmented reality, thus making the computer presence perfect. Today, this technology is applied and used for industry, arts, cultural heritage, and others [16, 17].

The essence of SAR is the superimposition of a digital image onto a real-world object using projected light [18]. SAR utilizes a digital projector to display graphic information onto physical objects. The main difference in SAR is that the view is separated from the user of the system [19]. Because output views are not related to each user, SAR naturally scales to groups of users. It allows collocation collaboration between users. SAR enhances the physical world with perspective-correct computer-generated graphics using a digital projector. SAR requires the surface of a physical object to project virtual information [16]. The physical can be anything. Projection is not limited to custom-made walls or screens. Interaction with virtual objects can improve the user experience level and user performance. SAR places computer-generated information directly onto real-world objects in the real world. Group of users can see and interact with the system. It makes SAR the ideal choice for collaborative tasks [11].

AR Sandbox is a learning medium in geology, hydrogeology, and geography [11]. Furthermore, from a cartographic point of view, AR Sandbox is an effective way to introduce the basic concepts of topography [12]. Many researchers claim AR sand-box as an effective learning medium because it provides a real-time experience [13].

3   Research Framework

This study consists of three main stages. The first stage is processing map data. The map data are collected from open data sites and then processing the data with GIS software. The map processing starts from the clipping process. This process cuts the map from a larger size to a more specific map showing the study area. After doing clipping, the second process is to provide georeferenced on the map. Geo reference is the transformation of raster map coordinates from scanner coordinates to real-world coordinates. The last process is the map transformation process to adjust the reference coordinate used in the study area.

The second stage is to carry out the process of determining the land suitability map using the weighted overlay method. At this stage, all thematic map layers are converted into Raster files. Then the raster data were classified based on the guidelines for conducting land evaluations for commodities cultivated in Indonesian regions. The weighting process is carried out using an online group discussion with members of the Indonesian Agricultural Forum. There are ten farmers involved in the weighting process.

The third stage is the visualization of the land suitability map. The visualization process begins with the creation of a 3D map taken from DEM data. Then the data is converted into a 3D object (obj file), and then the 3D object is printed using a 3D printer. Figure 1 describes the research framework used in this study.

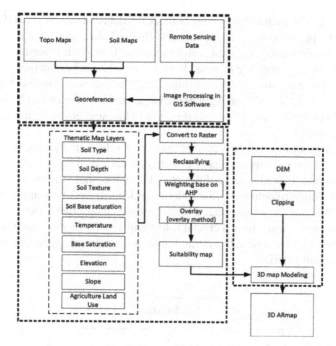

Fig. 1. Research framework

4 Result and Discussion

4.1 Land Suitability Map Development

This study selects the Bandung district as the study area. This is because Bandung Regency has promising agricultural potential. According data from Bandung district agriculture office, 70% of the Bandung district area is agriculture area [20]. Figure 2 describe Bandung district and the agriculture areas.

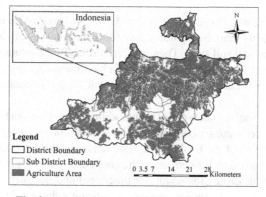

Fig. 2. Bandung district and the agriculture areas.

In Indonesia, open-data sites provide both spatial data and tabular data [10]. Indonesia's geospatial portal provides spatial data, while the Indonesian site has one data for tabular data. Unfortunately, the data is still in various formats. It is hard to use it without going through a processing process. In this study, the land evaluation process uses several criteria that are the key to land suitability. The key is considered based on the guidelines issued by the Food and Agriculture Organization of the United Nations (FAO) and the land suitability guidelines issued by the Indonesian government's Ministry of Agriculture [21, 22].

This study processes and converts the dataset into the same format. It can make it easier to build a land suitability map. Furthermore, each map layer is classified based on the land suitability parameters published by the Indonesian Ministry of Agriculture. The land suitability guidelines by the Indonesian Ministry of Agriculture have many parameters. This study limits the criteria factors and uses three criteria factors. According to FAO, these three factors have a crucial role compared to other factors. Furthermore, these three factors have nine sub-criteria. Figure 3 describes the hierarchical structure of criteria and sub criteria.

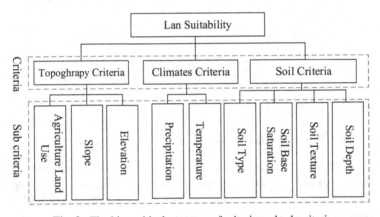

Fig. 3. The hierarchical structure of criteria and sub criteria

Based on the hierarchical structure in Fig. 3, this study uses nine thematic layers to create a land suitability map. Soil criteria have four sub-criteria; soil depth, soil texture, soil base saturation, and soil type. Then temperature and precipitation are sub-criteria for climates criteria. Last, the topography criteria have elevation, slope, and agricultural land use sub-criteria. Figure 4 describes nine thematic layers for create a land suitability map.

In this study, we analyze six types of commodities. Based on data from Bandung district agriculture office, these six commodities have higher productivity than other. Table 1 describes the weights of the final criteria for each agriculture commodity. This study uses online discussions with farmers using the zoom app to determining weight of each criterion. Based on the discussion result, for tuber commodities such as sweet potatoes, cassava and onions, the soil factor has a more significant influence than topography. For

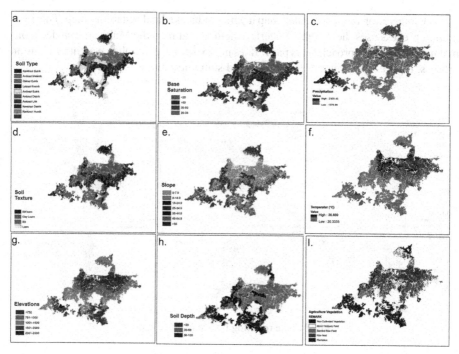

Fig. 4. The nine thematic layers to create a land suitability map.

potato and cabbage plants, the climate factor is more important than other factors. Table 1 describes the final weights for each commodity.

Table 1. The final weights for each commodity

Criteria	Sub criteria	Final weight for commodity					
		Rice	Onion	Cassava	Potatoes	Cabbage	Sweet potatoes
Soil	Soil depth	0.08	0.09	0.17	0.10	0.10	0.15
	Soil texture	0.10	0.11	0.16	0.12	0.10	0.15
	Soil base Saturation	0.09	0.09	0.11	0.09	0.13	0.11
	Soil type	0.11	0.15	0.17	0.13	0.13	0.15
Climate	Temperature	0.12	0.11	0.07	0.15	0.12	0.09
	Precipitation	0.15	0.15	0.06	0.13	0.13	0.07
Topography	Elevation	0.11	0.09	0.10	0.13	0.11	0.10
	slope	0.09	0.08	0.09	0.09	0.9	0.08
	Agriculture land use	0.15	0.13	0.07	0.06	0.9	0.10

The integration of the weighted map layers produces a land suitability map. This integration process uses the weighted overlay method that uses the Multi-criteria decision-making (MCDM) approach. This paper does not explain the complete weight calculation process. Figure 5 describes the resulting land suitability map.

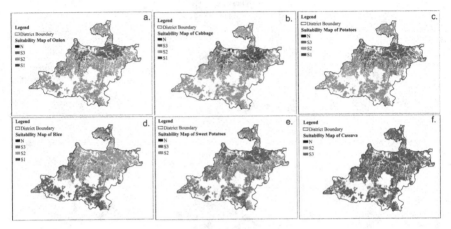

Fig. 5. The resulting land suitability map

4.2   3D Map Processing

This study creates a 3D map to visualize the actual relief of the earth. The process of creating a 3D map begins by taking digital elevation model (DEM) data. The Indonesian government provides DEM data through the Indonesia Geoportal (https://tanahair.indonesia.go.id/demnas/#/demnas). DEM data from Indonesia Geoportal is in Tiff file format. DEM file size is relatively large. This portal divides the DEM file into smaller pieces to make it easier to download data.

This study downloads the DEM file that intersects with the Bandung regency area. Seven raster files make up the Bandung regency area. QGIS software processes the seven DEM files to be merged and cropped according to the study area. QGIS software is open source-based software. After combining the raster data, the second step is to clip the raster data according to the Bandung district. This study clipped the combined raster files from the DEM file using the Shp file for the Bandung district boundaries. Then uses Qgis2TreeJS Plugin to export DEM into 3D maps. This study saves the converted maps into an OBJ file. OBJ files make it easy to process 3D maps using 3DBlender. Based on research conducted by Kundu et al. and George et al., the ideal size for displaying spatial augmented reality is about one meter [11, 12]. The problem is that it is hard to print large 3D maps at once. That's because the size of the printer plate is limited. This study divides the 3D Maps into elevens parts with accurate size. Like a puzzle, this study generates a connector on each part of the map to connect one to another. Figure 6A describes a complete 3D map, and Fig. 6B. shows the dividing part of the 3D maps.

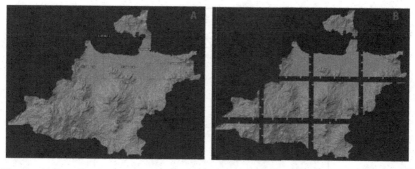

Fig. 6. A. describes a complete 3D map, and B. shows the dividing part of the 3D maps.

Blender 3D converts OBJ files into STL files. 3D Printer prints one part at a time using the STL file using the slicer application. The entire map printing process took two weeks to complete. Figure 7A describes one of the processes of the STL file slicer, while figure B shows the result of printing a 3D Map using a 3D printer.

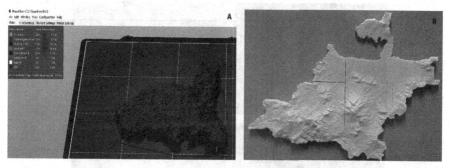

Fig. 7. A describes one of the processes of the STL file slicer; B shows the printed 3D maps.

4.3 System Development and Evaluations

This research uses a projector and a computer that controls the map to display it on 3D objects. Figure 8 illustrates the spatial Augmented reality (SAR) Component.

This study builds a system using the Unity 3D game engine. A 3D map object in the form of a file (.obj) combined with a map layer as a texture. This study built a menu to control the map layer visualizations. Currently, the menu is limited for managing map layers and displaying land suitability based on suitability class. SAR uses a computer to control the entire system. The system uses a projector to visualize the suitability map on the printed 3D Map. In contrast with the augmented reality sandbox, this system uses 3D objects to visualize accurate topographical shapes the Kinect 3D camera is mounted in the same direction as the projector's output. It will detect the distance and shape of the printed 3D map model. Figure 9A show the process of system development using Unity 3D, Fig. 9B is a projector setting, Fig. 9C shows the process of parameter calibration settings, and Fig. 9D illustrates the camera projector calibration process.

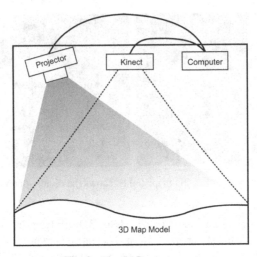

Fig. 8. The SAR component

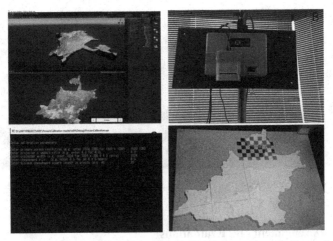

Fig. 9. A. System development using Unity 3D; B. Projector setting, C. Parameter calibration settings; and D. The camera projector calibration process.

SAR projects a land suitability map to a 3D object. The calibration process uses the Procam (Projector camera) library using Open CV (Fig. 9C and Fig. 9D). SAR can project land suitability maps properly onto 3D objects. SAR makes the map displayable to a larger area and can show the topography relief. Figure 10 describes the projection map from various points of view.

This study uses two methods to evaluate the system. The first evaluation method this study compares is the projection map with the land suitability map in a raster file (Tiff) extension to test the projection results. The results of the comparison show that the projection results are relatively accurate. Projected maps can wrap well-printed 3D maps. SAR does not change the composition of the projection map even though the projection

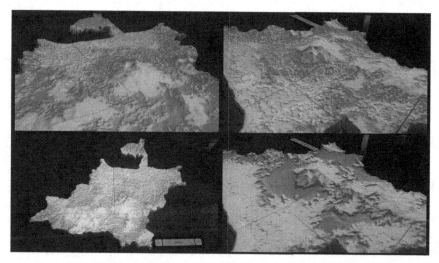

Fig. 10. The projection map output from various points of view

plane has a contour (not a flat plane). SAR projects smooth and precise output following 3D topography. Figure 11 describes the comparison between original land suitability maps with Projected land Suitability maps.

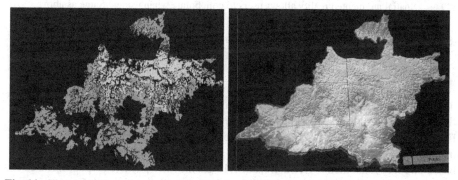

Fig. 11. The comparison between original land suitability maps with Projected land Suitability maps.

In the second evaluation method, this study used qualitative methods to get user responses to the system. Currently, farmers are still unable to use the SAR system directly. That's because of the limited activity due to the covid pandemic. This study distributes the system documentation and demonstration videos that explain the SAR system. The system documentation and demonstration videos can give information about the feature and how the system work. After that, this study conducts online discussions to discuss the system. Then farmers fill out a questionnaire related to the system. This study designed ten statements related to map visualization using SAR. Table 2 describes the statements in the questionnaire.

Table 2. The statements in the questionnaire

No	Statement	Response item
S1	Printed 3D maps can represent the actual topography of the real world	Strongly agree Agree Neutral Disagree Strongly disagree
S2	3D maps model is more helpful than 2D Maps in understanding topography shapes	Same as above
S3	Spatial Augmented Reality displays a map on the topography model accurately	Same as above
S4	Spatial Augmented reality can visualize the land suitability map well	Same as above
S5	Data visualization through Spatial Augmented reality makes it easier to understand	Same as above
S6	SAR Map information visualization is easier to understand	Same as above
S7	Visualizing the Land suitability maps using Spatial Augmented reality makes it easy for users to interact with the map	Same as above
S8	Spatial Augmented Reality makes it easier for farmers to understand the land suitability maps	Same as above
S9	Spatial augmented reality allows users to collaborate when using maps	Same as above
S10	In general 3D Maps are easier to read than 2D Maps	Same as above

Twenty-six respondents were involved in filling out the questionnaire. Figure 12 describes the overall response of the user to the system.

Based on the questionnaire recapitulation result, we draw the following conclusions: First, there is no negative response (Disagree or Strongly Disagree) to the statement. It means that SAR has a positive influence in presenting land suitability maps. Second, based on Fig. 1, statements S1, S2, S6, and S10 get the most positive response. Based on these responses, we concluded that SAR is able to visualize maps well. Last, statement S8 got the most neutral answers. We conclude that farmers still have difficulties in understanding the map. It's because farmers have not used the system directly. Therefore, the system still needs further evaluation. The farmers should use the SAR directly. In this way, farmers' understanding of land suitability maps will be increased.

4.4 Discussion

This study displays a map using spatial augmented reality. The motivation behind this research is the application of augmented reality sandbox to visualize 3D maps with sand media. AR Sandbox is a learning medium in geology, hydrogeology, and geography [11, 12]. Furthermore, from a cartographic point of view, AR Sandbox is an effective way to

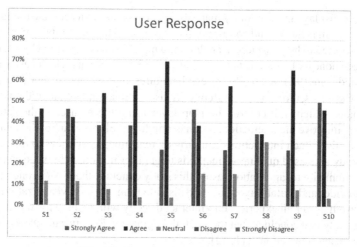

Fig. 12. The overall response of the users

introduce the basic concepts of topography [12]. Many researchers claim AR sandbox as an effective learning medium because it provides a real-time experience [13]. AR sandbox uses sand as a medium, the camera's depth sensor detects the surface of the sand, and computer devices control the visualization and simulation. AR sandbox is effective for use as a medium for early learning and simulations [11]. However, it is still difficult to simulate a real topographic map. It is hard to form topographic reliefs that are appropriate and accurate with real-world conditions. This research replaces the sand media with 3D objects created from DEM data. The resulting map has an accurate topography according to the contours of the real world. Figure 13 describe comparison between 3D maps with 2D contour map; A. 3D printed map, B. 2D map with contour lines.

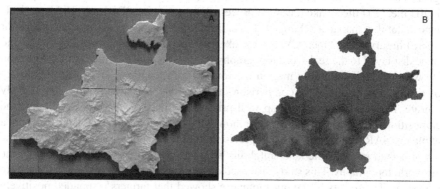

Fig. 13. The comparison between 3D maps with 2D contour map

SAR can display land suitability maps to objects that have an accurate topographical shape. This result is the second contribution of this research. Land suitability maps using SAR are expected to help farmers in analogizing maps. This is supported by the research that has been done by Laksono et al. concludes that 3D maps can make it easier for users to understand maps [9]. Even so, this research requires improvement from various aspects as future research. Currently, the system only uses animation to change the map layer. The computer system can control the map layer using the mouse. In the future, it is necessary to improve the interaction. As an example, developers can implement hand or gesture detection. Such interactions can provide real-time experiences to map users.

This study also used qualitative methods to get user responses to the system. Based on the questionnaire recapitulation result, this study conclude that SAR is one of the new ways to provide land suitability maps. SAR is able to make good visualization. SAR is also can give the user an experience to interact directly with maps. This result is in line with other study that conclude that the Spatial Augmented Reality can give a good maps visualization and interactions [11, 12].

5   Conclusion and Future Research

This study processes soil, climate, and topographic data to create a land suitability map. First, this study collects map data from open data sites and processes it with GIS software. Then uses the weighted overlay method to analyze land suitability. The weighted overlay method is a method of analyzing spatial data using the overlay technique. This method uses several raster maps related to the factors that influence the vulnerability assessment of a problem. This study uses three criteria and nine sub-criteria. AHP method generates weights for the nine sub-criteria. Based on the overlay results, the study area has suitable (S2) for cultivating onions, cabbage, and potatoes. Last, this study uses Spatial Augmented Reality (SAR) to visualize land suitability maps. This study uses Blender 3D to model 3D maps from digital elevation model (DEM) data. This study also uses Qgis2TreeJS Plugin to export DEM into 3D maps. Then save the converted maps into an OBJ file. OBJ files make it easy to process 3D maps using 3DBlender. SAR projects a land suitability map to a 3D object. The calibration process uses the Procam (Projector camera) library using Open CV. SAR makes the map displayable to a larger area and can be displayed to the real-word topography relief. This study compares the projection map with the land suitability map in the form of a raster file (Tiff)To test the projection results. The results of the comparison show that the projection results are relatively accurate. Projected maps can wrap well-printed 3D maps. SAR does not change the composition of the projection map even though the projection plane has a contour (not a flat plane). SAR projects smooth and precise output following 3D topography. With the map projected into 3D, the land suitability map has an identical visualization with the real-world topography. This study also used qualitative methods to get user responses to the system. The results of the questionnaire showed that farmers responded positively to the statement given. This study concludes that SAR provides a new way to visualize maps. SAR makes it easy for map users to obtain information on the map. This system is expected to assist farmers in understanding the resulting land suitability map. Even so, this research requires improvement from various aspects as future research.

Currently, the system only uses animation to change the map layer. In the future, it is necessary to improve the interaction on SAR Systems. With better interaction methods, the collaborative use of maps can be maximized.

References

1. Maulana, H., Kanai, H.: Multi-criteria decision analysis for determining potential agriculture commodities in Indonesia. J. Eng. Sci. Technol. **15**, 33–40 (2020)
2. Herzberg, R., Pham, T.G., Kappas, M., Wyss, D., Tran, C.T.M.: Multi-criteria decision analysis for the land evaluation of potential agricultural land use types in a hilly area of Central Vietnam. Land **8**(6), 1–25 (2019)
3. Tzvetkov, J.: Relief visualization techniques using free and open-source GIS tools. Polish Cartogr. Rev. **50**, 61–71 (2018)
4. Jiamin, Y., Hua, Z., Shuai, L., Zhonghao, W., Wencheng, X.: Application of open-source GIS technology in seismic analysis and forecasting system. In: 4th International Conference on Systems and Informatics, ICSAI 2017 January 2018, pp. 1621–1624 (2017)
5. Maulana, H., Kanai, H.: Multi-criteria decision analysis for determining potential agriculture commodities in Indonesia. J. Eng. Sci. Technol **15**, 33–40 (2020)
6. Bandyopadhyay, S., Jaiswal, R.K., Hegde, V.S., Jayaraman, V.: Assessment of land suitability potentials for agriculture using a remote sensing and GIS based approach. Int. J. Remote Sens. **30**, 879–895 (2009)
7. Ostovari, Y., et al.: GIS and multi-criteria decision-making analysis assessment of land suitability for rapeseed farming in calcareous soils of semi-arid regions. Ecol. Indic. **103**, 479–487 (2019)
8. Yohannes, H., Soromessa, T.: Integration of remote sensing, GIS and MCDM for land capability classification in Andit Tid watershed. Ethiopia. J. Indian Soc. Remote Sens. **47**, 763–775 (2019)
9. Laksono, D., Aditya, T.: Utilizing a game engine for interactive 3D topographic data visualization. ISPRS Int. J. Geo-Inf. **8** (2019)
10. Maulana, H., Kanai, H.: Development of precision agriculture models for medium and small-scale agriculture in Indonesia. In: IOP Conference Series on Materials Science and Engineering, vol. 879 (2020)
11. Kundu, S.N., Muhammad, N., Sattar, F.: Using the augmented reality sandbox for advanced learning in geoscience education. In: Proceedings of 2017 IEEE International Conference on Teaching, Assessment and Learning for Engineering TALE 2017, 13–17 January 2018 (2017)
12. George, R., Howitt, C., Oakley, G.: Young children's use of an augmented reality sandbox to enhance spatial thinking. Child. Geogr. **18**, 209–221 (2020)
13. Woods, T.L., Reed, S., Hsi, S., Woods, J.A., Woods, M.R.: Pilot study using the augmented reality sandbox to teach topographic maps and surficial processes in introductory geology labs. J. Geosci. Educ. **64**, 199–214 (2016)
14. Leutert, F., Herrmann, C., Schilling, K.: A spatial augmented reality system for intuitive display of robotic data. In: 2013 8th ACM/IEEE International Conference on Human-Robot Interaction (HRI), pp. 179–180. IEEE (2013)
15. Hod, Y., Twersky, D.: Distributed spatial Sensemaking on the augmented reality sandbox. Int. J. Comput. Support. Collab. Learn. **15**(1), 115–141 (2020). https://doi.org/10.1007/s11412-020-09315-5
16. Olwal, A., Gustafsson, J., Lindfors, C.: Spatial augmented reality on industrial CNC-machines. Eng. Reality Virtual Reality **6804**, 680409 (International Society for Optics and Photonics, 2008)

17. Uva, A.E., Gattullo, M., Manghisi, V.M., Spagnulo, D., Cascella, G.L., Fiorentino, M.: Evaluating the effectiveness of spatial augmented reality in smart manufacturing: a solution for manual working stations. Int. J. Adv. Manuf. Technol. **94**(1–4), 509–521 (2017). https://doi.org/10.1007/s00170-017-0846-4

18. Bimber, O., Raskar, R.: Spatial Augmented Reality: Merging Real and Virtual Worlds. AK Peters/CRC Press, New York (2019)

19. Carrera, C.C., Asensio, L.A.B.: Landscape interpretation with augmented reality and maps to improve spatial orientation skill. J. Geogr. High. Educ. **41**, 119–133 (2017)

20. Bandung, B.: Kabupaten Bandung Dalam. Angka **1**, 1–68 (2021)

21. FAO.: An Overview of Land Evaluation and Land Use Planning, pp. 1–19. The Food and Agriculture Organization, Rome (1976)

22. Ritung, S., Nugroho, K., Mulyani, A., Suryani, E.: Petunjuk Teknis Evaluasi Lahan untuk Komoditas Pertanian (Edisi Revisi). Balai Besar Penelitian dan Pengembangan Sumberdaya Lahan Pertanian, Badan Penelitian dan Pengembangan Pertanian (2011)

Multimodal Augmented Reality and Subtle Guidance for Industrial Assembly – A Survey and Ideation Method

Nicole Tobisková[✉], Lennart Malmsköld, and Thomas Pederson

Department of Engineering Science, University West, 461 86 Trollhättan, Sweden
{nicole.tobiskova,lennart.malmskold,thomas.pederson}@hv.se

Abstract. Industrial manual assembly is a relatively established use case for emerging head-mounted Augmented Reality (AR) platforms: operators get visual support in placing pieces depending on where they are in the assembly process. However, is vision the only suitable sensory modality for such guidance? We present a systematic review of previous work done on multimodal guidance and subtle guidance approaches, confirming that explicit visual cues dominate. We then outline a three-step method for generating multisensory guidance ideas intended for real-world task support based on task observation that led to identification of 18 steps in truss assembly, brainstorming AR guidance approaches related to assembly and maintenance, and mapping of brainstorming results to the observed task. We illustrated the use of the method by deploying it on our current mission in producing AR guidance approaches for an industrial partner involved in designing and assembling wooden trusses. In this work, we went beyond the standard visual AR guidance in two ways, 1) by opening for guidance through auditory, tactile, and olfactory sensory channels, 2) by considering subtle guidance as alternative or complement to explicit information presentation. We presented a resulting set of multisensory guidance ideas, each tied to one of the 18 steps in the observed truss assembly task. To mention a few which we intend to investigate further: smell for gradual warning about non-imminent potential hazardous situations; 3D sound to guide operators to location of different tools; thermos-haptics for subtle notifications about contextual events (e.g., happening at other assembly stations). The method presented helped us to explore all modalities and to identify new possibilities. More work is needed to understand how different modalities can be combined and the impact of different modality distractions on task performance.

Keywords: Augmented reality · Guidance · Multimodal interaction · Subtle cues · Industrial assembly

1 Introduction

Despite a dramatic increase in automation and digitalization of industrial production processes in the last 2–3 decades, some production activities are still characterized by

---

The original version of this chapter was revised: the chapter contains a typographical error: "Quidance" instead of "Guidance". The correction to this chapter is available at
https://doi.org/10.1007/978-3-031-06015-1_26

© Springer Nature Switzerland AG 2022, corrected publication 2022
J. Y. C. Chen and G. Fragomeni (Eds.): HCII 2022, LNCS 13318, pp. 329–349, 2022.
https://doi.org/10.1007/978-3-031-06015-1_23

a combination of automatic and semi-automatic machines controlled and monitored by human operators. Augmented Reality (AR) technology offers a unique platform for mediating and exploring ways of facilitating the tasks of these human operators, given that the immense data available about the state of relevant machines and processes are filtered and presented in a cognitively suitable way. The discussion in this paper is presented in connection with a bigger project – designing an assistive guidance system for operators in wooden house industry in Sweden, based on head-mounted AR technology.

Current Solution: The task of the operators is to assemble wooden truss components, sometimes several meters long and weighing up to 30 kg each, using metal nail plates at predefined locations (Fig. 1a). Paper printouts showing the locations of these fixation points and types of wooden components are currently complemented by visual guidance in the shape of laser marks projected from lasers mounted in the ceiling, based on Computer aided design (CAD) data (Fig. 1b). The wooden pieces are organized into the shape of the final truss using heavy metal pedestals as a support (Fig. 1c). The final product – a wooden truss is shown in Fig. 1d. The complete sequence of 18 tasks an operator does is presented in the Sect. 4.2.

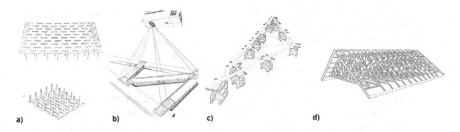

a)   b)   c)   d)

Fig. 1. Wooden truss assembly: a) metal nail plates, b) laser projector guidance to attach nail plates, c) pedestals to support wooden components, d) wooden truss.

In the project, we focus on dealing with distraction and guiding attention to support operators in assembly in a smooth and effective way. The task itself is primarily visual and therefore we tend to use visual guidance as a core for the design. We argue, based on principle of multitasking – humans have a hard time multitasking on the same channel [1, 2]. However, people can multitask well on two separate channels [2, 3] and, therefore, for a complex task like this we should not rely only on vision. We need to explore other modalities such as auditory, tactile and olfactory, and their suitable combinations to prevent high cognitive load of the user [2]. As we discovered in the systematic review of previous work, the majority of guidance in AR focuses on vision (see Fig. 2) We also reviewed how different modalities are typically combined and found that visuo-audio guidance dominates (see Fig. 3). From our review of subtle guidance approaches, we also intend to use some of them in our future system design.

The gap where we aim to contribute is how the different modalities can be combined (in particular non-visual) and also to a higher degree rely on subtle stimuli for AR guidance in assembly tasks.

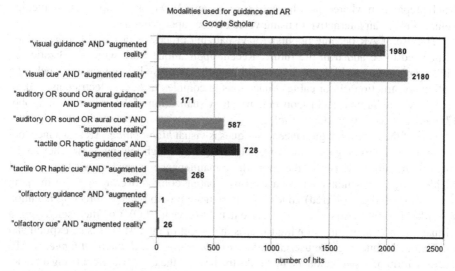

Fig. 2. Number of scientific publications on combination of Augmented Reality and single-modality guidance (visual, auditory, tactile).

2   Related Work

Providing guidance is the act of helping and giving advice about how to do something [4]. While the classical situation would be a human expert guiding a human novice, digitalization, and advances in the development of context-aware artificial intelligence (AI) - powered systems, "guidance" is likely to encompass situations where humans are the experts and machines the novices, or perhaps more frequently the other way around: AI systems guiding humans.

While the typical truss assembly operator we design for, by no means can be regarded as a novice (in fact, they are per definition experts), we focus on the latter kind of guidance scenario simply because the system could potentially usefully guide a human thanks to its access to more and different relevant information than any single unassisted operator has. Human action tends to be situated [5] and operators will always care most about what they happen to have in front of them here and now. Obviously, the human's and system's ability to contextualize current situations differently opens for a potentially better human-machine system if only the views can be adequately combined. Head-Mounted Display (HMD) is a promising interaction platform for doing exactly this.

2.1   Visual Guidance Techniques

AR applications typically add information to real-world objects. The spatial tracking of these objects can be facilitated through markers, e.g., Quick-Response (QR) codes placed on the objects [6, 7], but more recently marker-less approaches have emerged through advanced sensor technologies and image recognition algorithms. Industrial applications, therefore, attract opportunities to replace current solutions using AR, an example can be batch preparation where - pick by AR [8] - uses an HMD to guide operators in picking components as an alternative to using voice call or paper printouts.

The use of AR became popular for visualizing processes or parts that are hidden or planned to be added in the future. Recent applications work with visualization of hidden areas of a machine and inner machine processes like [6], hidden areas behind a wall in construction [9], or cable connections in complex tasks for electricians [10]. In settings where humans and robots collaborate, visualization of the trajectory of a robot [7] increases security of the workplace.

One of the traditional guidance techniques is visual *highlighting*. AR assistance tool for an industrial folding machine for hotel linen [6] uses highlighting of switches on the machine to guide the user to the spot where maintenance is needed. Another kind of highlighting [7] is guidance using a semi-transparent colored overlay, e.g., for marking safe (green) and unsafe (red) zones. We investigate possibilities of directing attention towards important parts outside of current field-of-view (FOV) of the user. Using a virtual *arrow* dynamically moving towards the object of interest [11] is an explicit and efficient technique to guide user attention [6]. *Omnidirectional attention funnel* (OAF) [12] is a form of visual guidance that links the head of the user to a target using a tunnel of frames. This approach proved to decrease mental workload and visual search time compared to visual highlighting [12, 13]. In research, OAF has been used, for example, in batch preparation [8] where the picker is guided to the right bin by the 3D tunnel. *Spherical wave-based guidance* (SWAVE) [11, 14] uses semi-transparent concentric waves moving towards a target providing information about both the position of the target and distance from the target in more subtle way. From a scenario in virtual reality where participants were asked to assembly a bird house, dynamically moving arrows performed as the fastest guidance method compared to OAF and SWAVE [11].

Normally a novice is trained by shadowing a professional performing the task. Replacing the professional with an *avatar* as in [15] saves the time of an expert and allows the novice to follow and perform the task simultaneously.

2.2 Beyond (Evident) Visual Guidance

Our investigation for potentially supporting the truss assembly operators in their task using a head-mounted AR solution has its outset in the idea of replacing the existing projected laser marks (see Fig. 2b) with similar visual information shown on the AR display, reducing existing need for regular laser calibration and to potentially facilitate the training of novice truss assemblers. However, given that future wearable AR hardware likely will have more extensive capabilities of both sensing human behavior and providing stimuli, we naturally want to investigate AR support beyond the evident visual guidance which seems to dominate related work.

We find two research directions particularly interesting: 1) to complement or replace the visual AR modality with other system output modalities such as auditory, tactile, and olfactory; 2) to complement or replace directly perceivable (evident) guidance approaches with more subtle ones.

Multimodal Guidance. Transferring information presentation from some of the visual modalities to others can lead to less distraction and faster reaction time as in a haptic interface on the wrist presented in [2] showing its potential to replace notifications given by a mobile phone display while the user being busy with a visual searching task. The prototype uses three spots on the downside of a wrist to provide the user with a haptic pattern using different intensity and sequence. SensFloor [16] is a floor sensor that can detect persons, falls, or allow the use of foot gestures to give input. This can be useful for assembly operators to easily confirm actions in the system with their hands being busy in a loud environment. Thermal bracelets [17] and rings [18] are other wearables that can be used for alerts with minimal interference with the current task [17]. Design of the thermal ring in [18] uses four spots on the finger with a combination of hot and cold input.

To get more understanding of multimodal guidance in AR, namely, the representation of different modality combinations in current literature, how different modalities are combined in the applications and what are the results of comparing different multi-modal approaches, we systematically reviewed the previous work. We used Google Scholar as a search engine. The search strings consisted of:

- "Multimodal guidance" AND "augmented reality" (50 hits)
- "Multi-modal guidance" AND "augmented reality" (11 hits)
- "Multimodal cue" AND "augmented reality" (63 hits)
- "Multi-modal cue" AND "augmented reality" (11 hits)
- "Multimodal cueing" AND "augmented reality" (37 hits)
- "Multi-modal cueing" AND "augmented reality" (8 hits).

We reviewed the set of 180 papers first based on their abstract and the parts that included the searched terms (e.g., "multimodal cue") in the paper. If needed, we read the whole paper to identify its relevance. We typically excluded publications that: contained the searched terms only in the reference list; focused on VR (Virtual Reality) instead of AR with no explicit applicability to AR; mentioned the search terms e.g., only in related work section or introduction without any further application; thesis work and reports.

The final set of 20 publications is shown in Table 1. We investigated the modality combinations presented in the publications, the general purpose of the paper, in case the publication compared or collected feedback on different modality combinations, we captured the data as well. We use abbreviations for multimodal cue combinations: VA (visuo-auditory), VT (visuo-tactile), AT (audio-tactile), VAT (visuo-audio-tactile).

Modality Combination Effect on Task Performance. In the experiment in [31] users were more precise when using multimodal combinations. Proximity-transition cues examined in [29] show usefulness of tactile transition cues where visuo-tactile cue performed 63% faster reaction and audio-tactile cue 65% faster reaction to incoming out-of-view augmentations than visuo-audio cue. In [26], exploring different designs for shifting attention to out-of-view objects, combination of animated visual and no audio had shorter reaction times compared to combination of non-animated visual cue and audio. In [19] tactile component correlated with faster take over and information processing. Both games focusing on physiotherapy presented in [25] received, however, low user preference of multimodal option, only 10% of users preferred the combination over no clue

Table 1. The final list of 20 publications on combination of multimodal guidance (cue) and augmented reality.

Publication title	Reference	Multimodal cue	Purpose of the paper	Modality comparison result
Takeover requests for automated driving:...	[19]	VA, VT, AT, VAT	Support vehicle takeover	Signals with a tactile component: faster takeover, information processing
BurnAR:...	[20]	VA	Cross modal transfer	x
Rendering visual events as sounds:...	[21]	VA	Visual to auditory transfer	x
Pseudo-Haptics:...	[22]	VT	Framework	x
Using visual and auditory cues to locate out-of-view...	[23]	VT	Location of out-of-view objects, adding spatial audio cues to targets location	x
Toward AI-enabled AR to enhance the safety...	[24]	VAT	Multimodal notifications on-spot to enhance safety	x
Multimodal Cueing in Gamified Physiotherapy:...	[25]	VA	Engagement and entertainment for gamified physiotherapy	In both games only 10% preferred audio-visual
Where to Look: Exploring Peripheral Cues...	[26]	VA	Shifting attention to out-of-view objects	Animated visual cue + no audio had shorter reaction times than non-animated visual cue + audio
Audio-visual AR to Improve Awareness of Hazard Zones...	[27]	VA	Warning about entering hazard zones	x
Augmented-Reality Multimodal Cueing for Obstacle Awareness:...	[28]	VAT	Obstacle avoidance and awareness for pilots	x, feedback on user's preference collected but results not clear from the paper

(continued)

Table 1. (*continued*)

Publication title	Reference	Multimodal cue	Purpose of the paper	Modality comparison result
Multisensory Proximity and Transition Cues...	[29]	VA, VT, AT	Proximity-transition cues to compensate for narrow field of view	Visual-Tactile: 63% and Audio-Tactile: 65% faster reactions than Visual-Audio
Multimodal Motion Guidance:...	[30]	VT	Motion guidance	x
Experimental evaluation of multimodal...	[31]	VA	Target tracking	Users more precise using multimodal combinations (6–16%)
Implementation of Educational Drum...	[32]	VAT	Drum training	x
Read-It...	[33]	VA	Reading support for kids	x
Multimodal AR assembly guidance...	[34]	VT	AR guidance to assembly operators	x, users suggested adding audio
A self-aware and active-guiding...	[35]	VAT	Worker-centered training and assistance	x
TutorialLens:...	[36]	VA	Authoring interactive AR tutorials	x
Dialogue Enhanced Extended Reality:...	[37]	VA	Worker transition to new processes	x
Facilitating Workers' Task Proficiency...	[38]	VA	Context-sensitive assistance	x

and single-modality options. Design of AR guidance in [34] was bimodal, but users suggested adding audio.

Most Common Modality Combination. From the Venn diagram in Fig. 3 we can see that visuo-auditory interfaces were, as expected, most of the reviewed work. To our surprise many publications focused on tri-modal interfaces.

Applications for Industrial Operator Support. Surprisingly many multimodal interfaces focused specifically on the production setting. Interface in [27] targeted warning about entering hazard zones around robots. Visuo-tactile interface [34] aims to provide guidance for assembly operators. Tri-modal interface in [35] provides worker-centered training and assistance. Interactive system for the operator 4.0 from [37] provides worker support in transition to new processes. AR based assistance that adapts to workers individual cognitive task proficiency is presented in [38].

Modality Terminology Confusion. The terminology of what is a certain modality varies in the publications. For example, [31] distinguished between positional sound and distance sound and perceives the combinations of graphics and positional sound vs. graphics and distance sound as two different multimodal combinations. To be able to generalize and compare different publications in Table 1, in our view, both are providing visuo-auditory guidance. Similarly, [20] refers to proprioception as one of the multimodal inputs of their system, however, we perceive the guidance provided by the system as visuo-auditory. TutorialLens presented in [36] considers text to be a different modality but we see it as a form of visual guidance. From [30] to vibrotactile and pneumatic we both refer to as tactile.

Reasons for Multimodality. Some of the reasons for using modality combinations found in the publications were: to support visual guidance by other modalities [36]; increase confidence of the operators [37]; reducing slowdown in finding a target [23]; to create sensation on another channel [20]; compensate for narrow field of view [29].

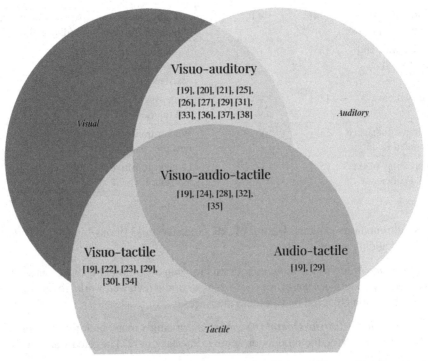

Fig. 3. Venn diagram showing what publications belong to which modality combination category.

Guidance Through Subtle Cues. Human attention is a scarce resource and the increased number of digital systems calling for it in everyday life – on top of sometimes an al-ready complex real-world situation – has spawned a huge interest within the Human-Computer Interaction discipline to try to make future interactive systems less disruptive. It turns out that by relying on modalities not currently in use and in other ways to care for the use situation, interactive systems can be designed to become operable and useful without demanding almost no attentional brain resources. This is the essential idea behind Peripheral Interaction [39]. While much work in this area has focused on using audio and haptic modalities for "seamlessly" mediating information to users occupied by predominantly visual tasks [39, 40], prototypes for providing subtle visual cues to affect human perception and ultimately behavior also exist [41].

To get more understanding of how subtle guidance is designed in augmented reality, we systematically reviewed previous work. We used Google Scholar as a searching engine to collect a sample of data. Initially, we collected synonyms for the word guidance and included them in the search as well, such as:

- Implicit/subtle hints
- Implicit/subtle modifications
- Implicit/subtle changes
- Implicit/subtle stimuli.

However, these searches resulted in being too far from the definition of guidance [4]. For example, *implicit* or *subtle hints* often referred to intonation of speech in the publications found.

We therefore included only 5 variants of the query:

- "Subtle guidance" AND "augmented reality" (27 hits)
- "Implicit guidance" AND "augmented reality" (47 hits)
- "Implicit cue" AND "augmented reality" (33 hits)
- "Subtle cue" AND "augmented reality" (47 hits)
- "Subtle gaze direction" AND "augmented reality" (66 hits).

From this set of 220 publications, we searched for each of the separate terms (e.g., *subtle guidance, augmented reality, implicit cue* etc.) and deleted publications that were not relevant. We also excluded publications where: the term occurred only in reference list; the term occurred only in the introduction/related work section without reflection on it later; concerned VR instead of AR without any implications to AR.; discussed the terms separately in the publication without relation to the work presented in the paper, for example, discussed *augmented reality* and *subtle guidance* in distinct parts of the publication without creating a connection; the publication was a thesis work or a report.

The resulting set of 19 relevant publications is presented in Table 2. For each publication we collected the information about the task the guidance is used for and the design of the cue.

Differences in Designs of the Subtle Stimuli. Most of the previous work reviewed is in the visual domain of subtle guidance. In [47] the subtle cue is described as almost invisible

Table 2. The final list of 19 publications using subtle cue/guidance in augmented reality.

Publication title	Reference	Task	Subtle cue/Guidance design
Empathy glasses	[42]	Remote collaboration (empathic connection between collaborators)	Facial expression tracking to show comprehension
Problems people with dementia have with kitchen tasks...	[43]	Drawing attention to certain location	Flashes to enhance explicit cues
Head-worn displays for healthcare and industry workers...	[44]	Navigation in Healthcare/ Industry related task	Adding not in the space available information necessary for task competition
Effects of AR Object and Texture Presentation...	[45]	Walking Guidance	Guide by placing objects in space to make people walk alongside the objects
Behavioral Research and Practical Models of Drivers' Attention	[46]	Guiding a driver towards hazards or crucial elements	Shadows of pedestrians, thin lines converging on pedestrians
Subtle Cueing for Visual Search in Head-Tracked HWD	[47]	Visual search for a known target	Adjusting opacity of a white square surrounding a black cross target, almost invisible towards the background
Evaluating subtle cueing in head-worn displays	[48]	Visual search for a known target	Same as [47]
A Visual Interaction Cue Framework...	[49]	Visual guidance in a game environment with implications for use in AR	Examples to guide through one of 3 doors: make the other doors appear closed; darken the undesirable entry ways + illumine desired path; make it appear as there is only one door; placing cleaning signs to 2 of the doors; places blocking objects in the path of two of the paths
A Browser – Based Perceptual...	[50]	Searching for a virtual object embedded in AR	Like [47] but different contrast levels of subtle cue

(continued)

Table 2. (*continued*)

Publication title	Reference	Task	Subtle cue/Guidance design
Attributes of Subtle Cues...	[51]	Visual search for virtual cues in a person's field of view	Same as [47]
AR as a New Media Experience	[52]	Interaction between interactive characters in AR	One character would turn towards the other to show he´s not available
Look Out! A Design Framework...	[53]	Directing people's attention to potential hazards	A flicker in the viewer's periphery triggering his eye movement
Dynamic Tactile Feedback in HCI	[54]	Dynamically revealed target selection	"It could provide a very subtle cue of the direction of the information without letting the surrounding people to know what the user is doing."
Shared Gaze Visualizations ...	[55]	Remote setting	Gaze visualizations as a subtle cue of attention
Parsimony & Transparency in Ubiquitous Interface Design	[56]	Piece confirmation in a board game	Visual projection to a bord game gives player a subtle cue about present computational entity
Directing Attention and Influencing Memory with Visual Saliency...	[57]	Attention direction	Increased saliency of unattended regions to shift attention there
Enhancing Art History Education Through ...	[58]	Controlling attention	Brightening certain parts of virtual version of a painting in hand-held AR
Guiding Attention in Controlled Real-World Environments	[59]	Gaze manipulation	Subtle luminance change of the scene using a projector
Subtle Cueing for Visual Search in AR	[60]	Visual search	Like [47] but with 3 contrast levels

in comparison to an explicit cue and achieves that by the design shown in Fig. 4., a black cross-shaped target surrounded by a white low-opacity square. The same design idea but presenting different opacity levels and therefore different levels of the subtle cue can be found in [50, 60]. A visual interaction cue framework from [49] describes the importance that a subtle cue fits in the environment - both visually and contextually. The paper presents 5 different designs of how to, in subtle way, guide through one of three doors in VR and uses that as an inspiration for AR environments. Other designs include flickers [53] in the viewer periphery, flashes [43], brightening certain parts [58], luminance change [59], and increasing saliency of unattended regions to shift attention there [57]. An interesting approach suggested both by [45] and [49] is placing virtual objects in the scene so users will walk alongside the objects. The only tactile subtle cue was found in [54] and the work stresses the cue not being noticeable for others. This is in line with one of the uses of subtle interaction – hiding the interaction from others, found based on a review of subtle interaction in Human-Computer Interaction publications by [61].

Ways of Use: In most cases from the publications reviewed, subtle guidance is used for shifting attention in various tasks such as towards desired location or element. It can be locations in kitchen [43], hazards or crucial elements while driving [46], unattended regions [57], or a specific spot in a painting [58]. Subtle cue can be used as a substitute for explicit cue in cases where explicit cue would cause, for example, distraction or clutter [47, 48], or can enhance the explicit cue [43]. Works in [45, 49] present subtle guidance as indirectly persuading user to choose a specific trajectory.

Why Subtle Cue? Subtle cue can be an alternative to explicit cue in cases of distortion, occlusion, clutter, and distraction [48] that explicit cues can cause in certain cases. They can also function well as a complement to strengthen the effects of an explicit cue as in [43].

Implicit Cue Outliers. A couple of publications found referred to approaches as being implicit which we regard being non-subtle. A facial expression recognition component in [42] pairs a facial expression of a local user with an emoji and presents the emoji to the remote user to show comprehension. This is presented in the paper as an implicit cue of comprehension. Similar, in [44] a hand of a patient is overlaid by a picture of how it can look inside the hand to guide clinicians' tool in the hand.

Explicit cue   Implicit cue   No cue

Fig. 4. The design of implicit cue that occurred the most frequently in the publications. A black target surrounded by a white square with low opacity so almost invisible towards the background [47, 48, 51].

3   Method

Our method for ideating alternative modes of guidance consisted of initial observation of the operators performing wooden truss assembly, followed by brainstorming connecting related work and the case of wooden truss assembly from task and modality point of view and in the end matching the wooden truss assembly task to the found possible guidance approaches using a wider spectrum of modalities.

3.1   Observations

As a starting point we visited our industrial partner and discussed future opportunities and inclusion of AR in their processes with managers. This approximately 2-h-long discussion has been followed by visiting the shopfloor and observation of operators assembling wooden trusses. In the end, we produced 18 truss assembly process steps (see Sect. 4.2) which we discussed and further edited with the managers.

3.2   Brainstorming Sessions

To find relevant modalities for our AR-guidance task, we (the authors) brainstormed about the related work described in the previous sections in a structured way using a table with predefined categories (see Table 3). The table consisted of four main columns based on modality (visual, auditory, tactile, and olfactory) divided each into two sub-parts (explicit and subtle for each of the modality categories). In the rows, we identified the main purposes for guidance relevant for assembly-related tasks. In two 1-h long sessions, we filled in relevant ideas about how the modality can be used for each of the specific tasks identified in related work. The goal was to fill in all the spots, but we identified places where we were not able to find any suitable ideas.

Table 3. Raw outcome of brainstorming: Examples of head-mounted AR guidance types potentially mediated through different sensory modalities and through clearly noticeable (explicit) and less obtrusive (subtle) stimuli.

Modality/guidance purpose	Visual	Auditory	Tactile	Olfactory
Facilitating spatial alignment	*Explicit*: Existing laser, superimposing CAD data, OAF [12], prevent misalignment *Subtle:* SWAVE [11], high/lowlighting areas of interest/irrelevant	*Explicit:* Click sound for right position, frequency based on distance, 3D sounds from source *Subtle:* Increasing importance – increasing intensity	*Explicit:* Wrist band – impulse when truss component on its right place *Subtle:* Gradually increase temperature using band or ring	*Explicit:* *Subtle:*

(*continued*)

Table 3. (*continued*)

Modality/guidance purpose	Visual	Auditory	Tactile	Olfactory
Making abstract information perceivable	*Explicit*: Quality info about the handled truss component Counter showing how many to do /done *Subtle:*	*Explicit:* "Hurry up" To synchronize with contextual processes *Subtle:*	*Explicit*: Notification about leaving safety zone [27] *Subtle*: Wristband signal. the state of processes at other workstations (cold, hot) [18]	*Explicit*: Transform odor-free dangerous gas leaks to smellable *Subtle:*
Showing perceptually obstructed objects	*Explicit*: Show nail plate below the truss [44] *Subtle:*	*Explic*it: *Subtle:* To make important feedback sounds to not get obstructed	*Explicit:* *Subtle:*	*Explicit:* *Subtle:*
Suggesting object manipulation	*Explicit*: Adjust for predicted unplanned dislocation -e.g., nail plates *Subtle*:	*Explicit:* *Subtle:*	*Explicit:* *Subtle:*	*Explicit:* *Subtle:*
Attracting attention	*Explicit*: Arrows, pointers etc *Subtle*: System draws attention to next object of interest [43, 47, 48] Enlighten important [58, 59]	*Explicit:* spatial sound *Subtle:* Important sounds get a volume boost, irrelevant get filtered out as in [38] Present a comfortable sound environment (bird song etc.) Gradual noise increase	*Explicit*: Error notification via a wearable bracelet *Subtle:* Make picking the right plate more comfortable in the hands than the wrong one	*Explicit*: *Subtle:* Signalize time for a break via smell of coffee
Distracting attention	*Explicit:* *Subtle:* Smooth out edges for not important areas, or make them transparent, shadowed [49]	*Explicit*: Remove unwanted noise, system moderate modality landscape to simplify focus *Subtle:* Same as for attention attraction	*Explicit:* *Subtle:*	*Explicit:* *Subtle:*

3.3 Matching

We later linked the findings from the brainstorming sessions (see Table 3) to the task of wooden truss production to identify suitable modality options. This modality map will help us to better see the possibilities of different modality combinations for our application. Our approach builds on the existing sequence when introducing the AR guidance, but we are aware that using AR can change the sequence a lot potentially.

In the next section, we present the resulting set of AR – related ideas for industrial applications and the final set of 18 steps in wooden truss assembly each liked to different modality alternatives on how the operator can be guided with the use of augmented reality.

4 Discussion

4.1 Results from Brainstorming

The output from the brainstorming session is presented in Table 3 and it consists of examples for each modality and manual operation. Creating the modality table gave us a base for further pairing the different modalities with the steps in wooden truss production. We struggled to find use of olfactory modalities for our case, but we found one useful, making inodorous dangerous gas leaks smell and therefore inform about possible danger.

4.2 Modality Alternatives for Wooden Truss Assembly Task

Here, we connect each of the 18 sub-tasks identified during observation with ideas that came out of the brainstorming sessions. We are aware of the new technology shaping the way work is done but as mentioned before, the purpose of this is to map the possibilities rather than to design a final solution at this point.

1. Identify the job number and get a drawing of the truss from a manager:

    - Visual: Pop-up notification, OAF [12] or SWAVE [11].
    - Auditory: A message mentioning a room number.
    - Tactile: A wrist band with a pattern for this notification as in [2].

2. Set up the laser using computer in the production hall: To be replaced by AR projection.

3. Position pedestals approximately:

    - Visual: Superimpose the information from CAD data on the floor using HMD, highlight the place where pedestals should be placed, color codes for right or wrong position, arrows to show direction.
    - Auditory: A click sound when pedestals are placed right, cues about the right direction using different frequency.
    - Tactile: Directing using vibration and temperature (ring, band) using patterns. Haptic feedback when placed wrong or right.

4. Get the correct set of nail plates:

   - Visual: OAF [12] or SWAVE [11] to guide to pick the right nail plates, show amount for each type.
   - Auditory: Pick by voice as in [8], navigating from where, what type and what amount to pick.
   - Tactile: Notification if one needs to collect more. Can be combined with a scale weighting the kit and notifying when the kit is complete.

5. Put bottom nail plates on pedestals: Similar as 3.
6. Place the wooden components and adjust the pedestal cylinders (stops)

   - Visual: guiding the alignment, highlighting the cylinders to remind, highlight place on the wood where nail plates should be attached.
   - Auditory: Navigate alignment by voice, remind to use cylinders.

7. Adjust pedestals more carefully together with nail plates (align with laser): As 3.
8. Fix components better using hammer and nails: Tacit knowledge, hard to include.
9. Recalibrate laser to project position of top nail plates: Replaced by AR, can be complemented by tactile or audio confirmation of repositioning (e.g., "Now guidance for top nail plates").
10. Put the top nail plates: Same as 5, can be complemented by highlighting a place on the top of the wood where the nail plates are placed under the wood.
11. Use the press machine to attach nail plates to the wood:

    - Visual: OAF [12] or SWAVE [11] or arrow to guide to the machine. Subtle color overlay to guide where to use the machine.
    - Auditory: 3D sound cue where the machine is located. Click sound when reached the right spot to use the machine.
    - Tactile: Guide approx. – forward, left, … using spots on the wrist as in [2].

12. Verify the finished truss with a drawing:

    - Visual: Project CAD data on the truss to check alignment, highlight misalignments.
    - Auditory: Sound confirmation to notify the user that everything is OK.

13. Write the truss number on the truss (e.g., T1) on the first in sequence of same ones.
14. Lift the truss to a temporary storage for finished trusses: Notify to mark (visual, auditory, tactile).
15. Recalibrate after 50 trusses (in case of doing more than 100): Replaced by AR.
    When all trusses are done in the set:
16. Take green packing straps to pack all trusses together:

    - Visual: highlight where to strap, attract attention to the spot with straps.

17. On the last truss write details about the job (job number, customer, etc.): Notify to do that (visual, auditory, tactile).
18. Push out the truss package by hand/tool/forklift: notify in a subtle way that operator should be done soon (truck driver is waiting), e.g., by increasing haptic stimuli.

Smooth transition between the steps can be accomplished by the system drawing visual attention using subtle cues to the next object/area of interest according to the current phase in the activity sequence to eliminate uncertainty of what to do next using, for example, the design from [47, 48].

Every work happens in a context and therefore we explore the connection between the task and the surroundings. This modality landscape consists of distractions caused by the environment - the sounds from different machines or people moving. Operators use hearing protection but there is a need to hear sound input such as a fire alarm, communicate with others in the team or hear sound-based guidance in e.g., using 3D sound to help with location of a machine or tool. We suggest giving important sounds a boost and filtering out not important ones as in [38].

AR opens for mediating otherwise imperceivable phenomena in the surroundings to the operator, e.g., notifying about an order to be picked up soon by a haptic band or subtle colour illumination around their watch [62]. Communication can be done using different spots on a haptic wristband associated with people involved in the process as in [2] and by using different patterns (e.g., Morse code or different temperature). Less important areas or objects can be made actively less visible and important ones highlighted by using colour overlays [7] or blurring edges. Smell can also be moderated similarly, e.g., by transforming inodorous dangerous gas leaks to become smellable.

Some of the possible modalities can directly influence the operator's efficiency, mood, or comfort. The distraction caused by uncomfortable smells can be controlled by neutralizing or covering them by something comfortable for the operator. To enhance productivity, a system for taking breaks can be implemented e.g., by a coffee smell or by giving an input perceivable only when the operator is not occupied with another task e.g., by notifying him or her on the periphery of his or her vision [39] or via a pneumatic compression band [63] offering a persistent stimulus until the users realizes.

5   Conclusions

In this paper, we have presented our initial steps towards developing a multimodal AR-based guidance system for assembly operators in industry. Specifically, we report on our idea generation method and how we tried to go beyond the standard explicit visual stimuli approach which we found to be dominating in our systematic literature review. The method helped us explore the space of all modalities (including non-visual) and identify new possibilities. More work is needed to better understand the technological possibilities of combining modalities and the impact of different modality distractions on task performance due to cognitive and perceptual human factors.

Acknowledgments. The authors would like to thank Derome AB for valuable discussions and the possibility to do observations in the production facilities and the project "Tillverka I Trä" (ID-nr 20201948) that is funded by Region Västra Götaland and Swedish Agency for Economic and Regional Growth.

References

1. Rubinstein, J., Meyer, D., Evans, J.: Executive control of cognitive processes in task switching. J. Exp. Psychol. Hum. Percept. Perform. **27**, 763–797 (2001)
2. Lee, S., Starner, T.: BuzzWear. In: Proceedings of the 28th International Conference on Human Factors in Computing Systems - CHI 2010 (2010)
3. Schumacher, E., et al.: Virtually perfect time sharing in dual-task performance: uncorking the central cognitive bottleneck. Psychol. Sci. **12**, 101–108 (2001)
4. Cambridge Dictionary (2021). https://dictionary.cambridge.org/dictionary/english/guidance
5. Suchman, L.: Plans and Situated Actions: The Problem of Human-Machine Communication. Cambridge University Press, New York (1987)
6. Heinz, M., Büttner, S., Röcker, C.: Exploring augmented reality training for automated systems. In: Workshop "Everyday Automation Experience" at ACM CHI Conference on Human Factors in Computing Systems (CHI 2019). ACM (2019)
7. Michalos, G., Karagiannis, P., Makris, S., Tokçalar, Ö., Chryssolouris, G.: Augmented reality (AR) applications for supporting human-robot interactive cooperation. Procedia CIRP. **41**, 370–375 (2016)
8. Hanson, R., Falkenström, W., Miettinen, M.: Augmented reality as a means of conveying picking information in kit preparation for mixed-model assembly. Comput. Ind. Eng. **113**, 570–575 (2017)
9. NCC: VR-VirtualReality (2021). https://www.ncc.com/our-offer/customer-values/digital-construction/virtual-reality/
10. Boeing: Paul Davies (Boeing): Evolution of the Boeing AR Kit, & Its Application to Airplane Manufacturing (2019)
11. Renner, P., Pfeiffer, T.: Attention guiding techniques using peripheral vision and eye tracking for feedback in augmented-reality-based assistance systems. In: 2017 IEEE Symposium on 3D User Interfaces (3DUI) (2017)
12. Biocca, F., Tang, A., Owen, C., Fan, X.: The omnidirectional attention funnel: a dynamic 3D cursor for mobile augmented reality systems. In: Proceedings of the 39th Annual Hawaii International Conference on System Sciences (HICSS'06) (2006)
13. Danielsson, O., Holm, M., Syberfeldt, A.: Augmented reality smart glasses for operators in production: survey of relevant categories for supporting operators. Procedia CIRP **93**, 1298–1303 (2020)
14. Renner, P., Pfeiffer, T.: Attention guiding using augmented reality in complex environments. In: 2018 IEEE Conference on Virtual Reality and 3D User Interfaces (VR) (2018)
15. Cao, Y., Qian, X., Wang, T., Lee, R., Huo, K., Ramani, K.: An exploratory study of augmented reality presence for tutoring machine tasks. In: Proceedings of the 2020 CHI Conference on Human Factors in Computing Systems (2020)
16. SensFloor System - Future-Shape EN. https://future-shape.com/en/system/
17. Bolton, F., Jalaliniya, S., Pederson, T.: A wrist-worn thermohaptic device for graceful interruption. interaction design and architecture(s) J. IxD&A **26**, 39–54 (2015)
18. Zhu, K., Perrault, S., Chen, T., Cai, S., Lalintha Peiris, R.: A sense of ice and fire: exploring thermal feedback with multiple thermoelectric-cooling elements on a smart ring. Int. J. Hum. Comput Stud. **130**, 234–247 (2019)
19. Huang, G., Pitts, B.: Takeover requests for automated driving: the effects of signal direction, lead time, and modality on takeover performance. Accid. Anal. Prev. **165**, 106534 (2022)
20. Weir, P., et al.: Burnar: involuntary heat sensations in augmented reality. In: 2013 IEEE Virtual Reality (VR) (2013)
21. Stone, S., Tata, M.: Rendering visual events as sounds: spatial attention capture by auditory augmented reality. PLoS ONE **12**, e0182635 (2017)

22. Pusch, A., Lécuyer, A.: Pseudo-haptics. In: Proceedings of the 13th International Conference on Multimodal Interfaces - ICMI 2011 (2011)

23. Binetti, N., Wu, L., Chen, S., Kruijff, E., Julier, S., Brumby, D.: Using visual and auditory cues to locate out-of-view objects in head-mounted augmented reality. Displays **69**, 102032 (2021)

24. Sabeti, S., Shoghli, O., Baharani, M., Tabkhi, H.: Toward AI-enabled augmented reality to enhance the safety of highway work zones: Feasibility, requirements, and challenges. Adv. Eng. Inform. **50**, 101429 (2021)

25. Haghbin, N., Kersten-Oertel, M.: Multimodal cueing in gamified physiotherapy: a preliminary study. In: Proceedings of the 7th International Conference on Information and Communication Technologies for Ageing Well and e-Health (2021)

26. Gruenefeld, U., Löcken, A., Brueck, Y., Boll, S., Heuten, W.: Where to look. In: Proceedings of the 10th International Conference on Automotive User Interfaces and Interactive Vehicular Applications (2018)

27. San Martín, A., Kildal, J.: Audio-visual AR to improve awareness of hazard zones around robots. In: Extended Abstracts of the 2019 CHI Conference on Human Factors in Computing Systems (2019)

28. Miller, J., Godfroy-Cooper, M., Szoboszlay, Z.: Augmented-reality multimodal cueing for obstacle awareness: towards a new topology for threat-level presentation. In: Vertical Flight Society's 75th Forum (2019)

29. Trepkowski, C., et al.: Multisensory proximity and transition cues for improving target awareness in narrow field of view augmented reality displays. IEEE Trans. Visual Comput. Graph. **28**, 1342–1362 (2022)

30. Schönauer, C., Fukushi, K., Olwal, A., Kaufmann, H., Raskar, R.: Multimodal motion guidance. In: Proceedings of the 14th ACM International Conference on Multimodal Interaction - ICMI 2012 (2012)

31. Obrenovic, Z., Starcevic, D., Jovanov, E.: Experimental evaluation of multimodal human computer interface for tactical audio applications. In: Proceedings. IEEE International Conference on Multimedia and Expo (2002)

32. Kweon, Y., Kim, S., Yoon, B., Jo, T., Park, C.: Implementation of educational drum contents using mixed reality and virtual reality. In: Stephanidis, C. (ed.) HCI 2018. CCIS, vol. 851, pp. 296–303. Springer, Cham (2018). https://doi.org/10.1007/978-3-319-92279-9_40

33. Weevers, I., Sluis, W., van Schijndel, C., Fitrianie, S., Kolos-Mazuryk, L., Martens, J.-B.: Read-It: a multi-modal tangible interface for children who learn to read. In: Rauterberg, M. (ed.) ICEC 2004. LNCS, vol. 3166, pp. 226–234. Springer, Heidelberg (2004). https://doi.org/10.1007/978-3-540-28643-1_29

34. Wang, X., Ong, S., Nee, A.: Multi-modal augmented-reality assembly guidance based on bare-hand interface. Adv. Eng. Inform. **30**, 406–421 (2016)

35. Tao, W., Lai, Z., Leu, M., Yin, Z., Qin, R.: A self-aware and active-guiding training & assistant system for worker-centered intelligent manufacturing. Manuf. Lett. **21**, 45–49 (2019)

36. Kong, J., Sabha, D., Bigham, J., Pavel, A., Guo, A.: TutorialLens: authoring Interactive augmented reality tutorials through narration and demonstration. In: Symposium on Spatial User Interaction (2021)

37. Serras, M., García-Sardiña, L., Simões, B., Álvarez, H., Arambarri, J.: Dialogue enhanced extended reality: interactive system for the operator 4.0. Appl. Sci. **10**, 3960 (2020)

38. Neumann, A., Strenge, B., Schalkwijk, L., Essig, K., Schack, T.: Facilitating workers' task proficiency with subtle decay of contextual AR-based assistance derived from unconscious memory structures. Information **12**, 17 (2021)

39. Bakker, S.: Design for peripheral interaction, Ph.D. thesis. Technische Universiteit Eindhoven (2013)

40. Bolton, F., Jalaliniya, S., Pederson, T.: A wrist-worn thermohaptic device for graceful interruption. Interact. Des. Archit. **26**, 39–54 (2015)
41. Bailey, R., McNamara, A., Sudarsanam, N., Grimm, C.: Subtle gaze direction. ACM Trans. Graph. **28**, 1–14 (2009)
42. Masai, K., Kunze, K., Sugimoto, M., Billinghurst, M.: Empathy glasses. In: Proceedings of the 2016 CHI Conference Extended Abstracts on Human Factors in Computing Systems (2016)
43. Wherton, J., Monk, A.: Problems people with dementia have with kitchen tasks: the challenge for pervasive computing. Interact. Comput. **22**, 253–266 (2010)
44. Schlosser, P., Matthews, B., Sanderson, P.: Head-worn displays for healthcare and industry workers: a review of applications and design. Int. J. Hum. Comput. Stud. **154**, 102628 (2021)
45. Isoyama, N., Sakuragi, Y., Terada, T., Tsukamoto, M.: Effects of augmented reality object and texture presentation on walking behavior. Electronics **10**, 702 (2021)
46. Kotseruba, I., Tsotsos, J.: Behavioral research and practical models of drivers' attention. ArXiv. abs/2104.05677 (2021)
47. Lu, W., Feng, D., Feiner, S., Zhao, Q., Duh, H.: Subtle cueing for visual search in head-tracked head worn displays. In: 2013 IEEE International Symposium on Mixed and Augmented Reality (ISMAR) (2013)
48. Lu, W., Feng, D., Feiner, S., Zhao, Q., Duh, H.: Evaluating subtle cueing in head-worn displays. In: Proceedings of the Second International Symposium of Chinese CHI on - Chinese CHI 2014 (2014)
49. Dillman, K., Mok, T., Tang, A., Oehlberg, L., Mitchell, A.: A visual interaction cue framework from video game environments for augmented reality. In: Proceedings of the 2018 CHI Conference on Human Factors in Computing Systems (2018)
50. Feng, D., Weng, D., Lu, W., Sun, C., Do, E.: A browser-based perceptual experiment platform for visual search study in augmented reality system. In: 2013 IEEE 10th International Conference on Ubiquitous Intelligence and Computing and 2013 IEEE 10th International Conference on Autonomic and Trusted Computing (2013)
51. Lu, W., Duh, H., Feiner, S., Zhao, Q.: Attributes of subtle cues for facilitating visual search in augmented reality. IEEE Trans. Visual Comput. Graph. **20**, 404–412 (2014)
52. MacIntyre, B., Bolter, J., Moreno, E., Hannigan, B.: Augmented reality as a new media experience. In: Proceedings IEEE and ACM International Symposium on Augmented Reality (2001)
53. John, B., Kalyanaraman, S., Jain, E.: Look out! A design framework for safety training systems a case study on omnidirectional Cinemagraphs. In: 2020 IEEE Conference on Virtual Reality and 3D User Interfaces Abstracts and Workshops (VRW) (2020)
54. Ahmaniemi, T.: Dynamic tactile feedback in human computer interaction. Dissertations. Aalto University (2012)
55. D'Angelo, S., Schneider, B.: Shared gaze visualizations in collaborative interactions: past, present and future. Interact. Comput. **33**, 115–133 (2021)
56. Wren, C., Reynolds, C.: Parsimony & transparency in ubiquitous interface design. In: Proceedings of the 2002 International Conference on Ubiquitous Computing (UBICOMP) (2002)
57. Veas, E.E., Mendez, E., Feiner, S.K., Schmalstieg, D.: Directing attention and influencing memory with visual saliency modulation. In: Proceedings of the SIGCHI Conference on Human Factors in Computing Systems (2011)
58. McNamara, A.M.: Enhancing art history education through mobile augmented reality. In: Proceedings of the 10th International Conference on Virtual Reality Continuum and Its Applications in Industry - VRCAI 2011 (2011)

59. Booth, T., Sridharan, S., McNamara, A., Grimm, C., Bailey, R.: Guiding attention in controlled real-world environments. In: Proceedings of the ACM Symposium on Applied Perception (2013)
60. Lu, W., Duh, B.-L.H., Feiner, S.: Subtle cueing for visual search in augmented reality. In: 2012 IEEE International Symposium on Mixed and Augmented Reality (ISMAR) (2012)
61. Pohl, H., Muresan, A., Hornbæk, K.: Charting subtle interaction in the HCI literature. In: Proceedings of the 2019 CHI Conference on Human Factors in Computing Systems (2019)
62. Pohl, H., Medrek, J., Rohs, M.: ScatterWatch. In: Proceedings of the 18th International Conference on Human-Computer Interaction with Mobile Devices and Services (2016)
63. Pohl, H., Brandes, P., Ngo Quang, H., Rohs, M.: Squeezeback. In: Proceedings of the 2017 CHI Conference on Human Factors in Computing Systems (2017)

Virtual Reality Assembly of Physical Parts: The Impact of Interaction Interface Techniques on Usability and Performance

Ketoma Vix Kemanji[✉][ID], Rene Mpwadina, and Gerrit Meixner[ID]

Heilbronn University, UniTyLab, Max-Planck-Straße 39, 74081 Heilbronn, Germany
{ketoma-vix.kemanji,rmpwadin,gerrit.meixner}@hs-heilbronn.de

Abstract. In the last few years there has been increased interest in Virtual Reality technology application in the professional context. The technology is used in industry for training. There are several reported successful pilot applications in the industrial training of assembly of physical parts. However, our understanding of how interaction techniques affect performance on these tasks is still limited. In this research, we study the usability of three common hand-based interaction methods: controllers, camera-based hand tracking, and dataglove interaction in the virtual assembly of physical parts. We investigate how performance on the task is affected by the interaction method. We measure the usability, task time, task accuracy, and interaction errors in a study with 12 participants ($n = 12$) - with and without prior Virtual Reality experience. The results show that users rate the usability of controllers higher than camera based tracking, while datagloves are rated lower than camera tracked solutions. Users also complete the task faster, and with fewer interaction errors when using a controller, than when using a camera-tracking solution, or dataglove. However users execute actions more precisely when using a dataglove. Participants gender does not play a significant rule on the reported usability or task performance. However, as participants experience with Virtual Reality increases they can become less precise at executing actions with the controller, and more precise with the dataglove. The results of this study can help to design systems for the Virtual Reality assembly of physical parts, and to make decisions on which interaction method is suitable based on which aspects of the system are most important.

Keywords: Virtual Reality · Interaction techniques · Industrial assembly tasks · Usability · Performance

1 Introduction

For some years now, an increasing development of new technologies in the field of Virtual Reality (VR) has been observed. At the latest since the introduction of the Oculus VR head-mounted-display (HMD) - the topic of VR has seen

© Springer Nature Switzerland AG 2022
J. Y. C. Chen and G. Fragomeni (Eds.): HCII 2022, LNCS 13318, pp. 350–368, 2022.
https://doi.org/10.1007/978-3-031-06015-1_24

increased interest in research and industry, progressing to the "Slope of Enlightenment" in the Gartner Hype Cycle for Emerging Technologies. VR technology has reached a new level that is strongly focused on the consumer market. To be successful with the general public, it is important for developers and researchers to create an optimal user experience (UX). Input technologies are a crucial part of the VR system as they allow the user to interact and perform tasks in the virtual world. The choice of input technology is therefore crucial for the UX, as it strongly influences the performance and the way the user perceives and interacts with the virtual world. It is therefore important to investigate different input technologies within a VR system to better understand how they affect user interaction, performance, and to provide developers with the necessary data to improve the UX. Despite recent advances in consumer VR technologies, there is still a need for more scientific studies that directly investigate these approaches in applied scenarios, and improve our understanding of how these interaction modalities affect the user's performance while performing a task in the virtual world.

The aim of this research is to investigate different interaction interfaces in a single VR system and to determine how these interfaces affect a user's work performance. The results of this work can be used as a basis for further research to improve user interfaces and their UX. To achieve this goal, a VR application was developed in which a user can perform the same task with three different interaction technologies. In this study, the user is asked to construct a predefined object on a table in a virtual space using building blocks. The interaction is mainly hand-based; therefore, three different types of interaction technologies were chosen: glove-based (SenseGlove DK1), controller-based (HTC Vive controller) and camera-based (Ultraleap Leap Motion). In order to study and evaluate these interaction technologies, various objective data are recorded by the application during the execution of the task: the duration of the task, interaction errors, assembly accuracy. Qualitative data was also collected with the Post-Study System Usability Questionnaire (PSSUQ) from all twelve participants. An observation and analysis was conducted using both quantitative and qualitative data as described.

The remainder of this paper is structured as follows: in Sect. 2, we discuss the current state of the art, and other research and development effort. We also discuss some industry cases where VR has been used for the training and assembly of physical parts. In Sect. 3 we present the research questions for this study. Section 4 describes the experimental study. We present the experimental procedure, tasks, and measures. In Sect. 5, we present the results of the experiment as well as the qualitative and quantitative data analysis. Section 6 discusses the results and contributions. We discuss the results in the light of the experimental procedure, observations during the study, and user feedback after the study. We also discuss the results in relation to state of the art, strengths and weaknesses. In Sect. 7 we recap this paper with the main issues, main contributions, possible implications of the results, and an outlook for our future work.

2   State of the Art

There is increasing interest in research and development on the use of VR technology for skill and behaviour training [4, 19]. Use of VR technology for training provides several advantages: costs saving, reduced exposure to risky situations, a safe virtual environment, rapid testing and optimization of procedures, easy and quick deployment of training in multiple locations [9].

A study conducted at Yale University School of Medicine and Queens University [16], to investigate the impact of VR training on operating room performance and transfer of technical skills to the operating room environment, found that: Surgeons who used VR training for 2 h improved their work time by 83% and were more than 70% "more efficient" in movements and measurements. They made fewer mistakes and were likely to make consistent progress throughout the procedure. Another study conducted by Shannon K. *et al.* [3] on the use of VR for training in maintenance procedures, comparing effectiveness of VR-based and computer-based training, and two different input methods for interacting with the VR environment. Participants were assigned to one of three conditions: computer-based simulation, gesture-based VR, or voice-based VR - and were trained in maintenance procedures for a system to decelerate and break aircraft upon landing. Results showed that mistakes made by trainees during training were significantly different between conditions, suggesting that computer-based training may be less effective than VR training.

The global car manufacturer - Audi AG - used VR technology to train employees on the assembly of its new electric sports car the Audi eTron GT, saving on time and costs when building cars is a very dynamic plan [2]. Other manufacturers like *e.g.* , Volkswagen and Airbus have also explored the use of this technology for training and process improvement[1] [5]. Despite wide interest, there are still several challenges concerning the development of the technology for effective use in the training context. Several research efforts are being conducted to investigate approaches for the effective use of this technology in the professional context for training. In this paper we focus on hand-based interaction in the virtual assembly of physical parts.

Several research efforts acknowledge the need to study the effect of interaction interfaces when performing tasks in VR [6–8]. Gusai E. *et al.* [8] investigated user interaction with the HTC Vive controllers and the Leap Motion on a gamified task to place 12 three-dimensional objects (different in color and shape) inside corresponding holes. The goal was to investigate which device was preferred for the task by measuring the time to execute the task, and the score obtained by the user. The results indicated that users performed better when using the controller than when using the Leap Motion, re-positioning 0.3 (less than one) element(s) on average during the task execution while users re-positioned on 3.4 elements on average when executing the task with the Leap Motion. Users also required less time to complete the task with the controller than with the Leap Motion. Open discussions with the users also showed that 73% of users preferred the controllers

---

[1] https://bit.ly/3urrmEY.

over the Leap Motion (13%). However, the task was not an assembly task and the usability evaluation was not based on any formal usability questionnaire. Figueiredo L. *et al.* [7], conducted a similar study with the Leap Motion and HTC Vive controller exploring near and far object interaction, and using the System Usability Scale questionnaire. The results showed that users preferred natural interaction with the Leap Motion for near interactions, but not for interaction with distant objects due to instability of the tracking leading to reduced ray-cast selection accuracy. Navarro D. and Sundstedt V. [14] also explored the usability of both these devices in a study with 20 participants in game play. Results also showed that player performance decreased with the Leap Motion. Participants also reported interaction with the HTC Vive controllers was more reliable than with the Leap Motion.

A study conducted by K Tanjung *et al.* [6,18] with 20 participants investigated three interaction interfaces: the HTC Vive, Leap Motion, and Senso Glove. The study task here was to allow users interact with an anatomical learning system. When the user grabs a bone structure from a virtual skeleton, name of the grabbed bone is displayed. The authors compared the interactivity, ease of learning, and comfort of translation movement. Participants were asked to rate the interaction interfaces on a likert scale. Results show that the HTC Vive controller was most preferred of the three followed by the Leap Motion, and the Senso Glove was the least preferred. However the haptic feedback provided by the dataglove was rated higher above the other two interaction interfaces. The authors do not use any standard evaluation usability evaluation scale, and also do not track any objective performance data.

3   Research Questions

In the previous section we discussed the current state of the art, and presented some industry cases where VR is used in assembly training. We also discussed some research effort and results that investigate the usability of virtual reality hand-based interaction interfaces. However some of these research studies do not directly address the issues of assembly of physical parts in VR which is a common use case in industry training applications. Some studies also do not use standard usability evaluation methods and scales that have been tested and proven by other researchers. As new interaction methods are developed by startups and the continued interest in using VR in industry, we also want to investigate how interaction interfaces affect performance in the assembly of physical parts. Therefore we formulate the following research questions to investigate in this study:

1. Does the interaction interface method have an effect on performance in the VR assembly of physical parts?
2. What is the effect of different VR interaction interface techniques on usability in the VR assembly of physical parts.
3. What effect does a user's experience with VR technologies have on their performance and usability rating of VR interaction interface techniques in the VR assembly of physical parts?

In this study, we evaluate three hand-based VR interaction techniques: controller based, camera-based hand tracking, and glove-based interaction. We use the HTC Vive controller, the Leap Motion controller, and the SenseGlove DK1 for each of these categories respectively.

4   Experiment

In this section, We report the experiment procedure according to Ko *et al.* structure for reporting experiments in the field of Human-Computer Interaction [10].

4.1   Method

A within subjects Usability Lab Study was conducted to study the usability of three different VR hand-based interaction interfaces and the effect of these interfaces on task performance in the virtual assembly of physical parts. The within subject variable is interaction technique/interface, and the three conditions are: interaction with controllers, camera-based hand tracking, and datagloves. Participants performed all conditions; executing the assembly task with a controller, camera-based hand tracking, and a dataglove.

4.2   Procedure

In this section, we discuss the study procedure, from participant recruitment to post-study debriefing. Figure 1 shows an overview of the study procedure.

Recruitment.   Participants were required to be at least 16 years old and have some experience in the use of electronic devices. A total of 12 recruited participants successfully completed the study: 5 female and 7 male, with ages ranging from 25 to 37 years old and an average age of 28.33 years ($\mu = 28.33, \sigma = 4.52$). Of the 12 recruited participants, 6 participants never experienced VR and this study was their first experience with VR, while the other 6 participants had some previous VR experience, and had used VR at least three times in the last 24 months preceding this study.

Fig. 1. Study process

Consent. At the beginning of the study each participant had to read and sign a consent document. This document contained all the conditions of participation, risks, potential inconveniences, and instructions related to the study. Participants were eliminated if the previously had health problems or other inconveniences using VR, only participants who met the requirements and signed the consent document were allowed to proceed with the study. During the execution of the study, the participants had the right to stop the experiment in case they had a health problem or other inconvenience. Participation was voluntary without any financial benefits or costs to the participants.

After signing the consent document, participants filled a questionnaire collecting demographic data and previous experience with VR and related technologies. All data collected in the study was kept anonymous and handled in compliance with the relevant local data protection regulations.

Group Assignment. As mentioned above a within-subjects design was adopted for this study, with three conditions corresponding to three different VR hand-interaction interfaces. Participants were asked to perform the experiment tasks in all three conditions; therefore, there was no group assignment. However, to minimize errors due to learning effect; participants were randomly assigned to begin the study with one of the three conditions (interaction interface).

Training. To familiarize participants with use of the devices, they where shown prerecorded videos before performing the experimental tasks in each of the three conditions. The prerecorded videos showed participants how to use the device and how to perform the study task with the device. Participants watched the video for each interface, just before using the interface to perform the experimental tasks.

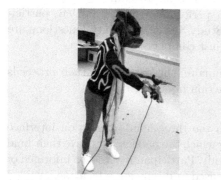 

(a) Participant with SenseGlove DK1 during the Study procedure.

(b) Work Space in the Virtual Environment.

Fig. 2. Virtual environment work space and participant in laboratory.

Tasks. The task was to build a predefined structure in the virtual world, using block pieces. After watching the example video for an interaction interface, the participants could perform the task as demonstrated in the video. Participants performed each of the following tasks three times, once for each of the three within-subjects experimental conditions:

1. *Watch video for the interface*: Participant is shown a video of the hand-interaction interface which will be used in the condition.
2. *Use the interface to build structure in VR*: The participant is placed in the VR environment, and participant builds the predefined structure with the current VR interaction interface. Participants have to collect block pieces and build a block structure, as shown in Fig. 3a, consisting of nine block pieces, and with matching colors. The task was specifically designed to capture a wide range of interaction actions including: translational movement of objects, rotation, pulling, pushing, and button press.

   Fig. 2a shows a participant during the study, while Fig. 2b shows the workspace where the task was executed in the virtual environment. A sample of the completed predefined structure (Fig. 3a) was placed on the table for participants to see, and use as a guide for constructing a similar structure. A relatively simple structure/task was chosen to avoid influence of participants technical or vocational experience.

   The user was expected to perform the following tasks:
   - Press the red button to indicate start of the procedure.
   - Pull open a table drawer.
   - Pickup block pieces from inside the drawers.
   - Use blocks retrieved from the drawer to construct the structure. The table could be used to temporarily place construction pieces. Participants were asked to construct an identical structure with matching position and colors of the blocks.
   - Press the red button again to indicate end of procedure.
3. *Complete usability questionnaire*: After performing the task in VR, participants were asked to fill the IBM Post-Study System Usability Questionnaire (IBM PSSUQ) for the task which was just completed.

After completing the usability questionnaire, the participant then proceeds to the next condition, with another interaction interface.

Debrief. After completing the task with the three hand-interaction interface types, a debriefing session was held, during which the participants gave their final remarks and general appreciation of the study. Participants were also informed of the study goals and how the data will be used, a discussion which was avoided before the start of the study in order to evade influencing the reaction and response of participants.

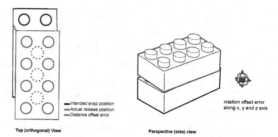

(a) Template of structure to construct.

(b) Task precision errors. (*block length: 12.50cm, width: 6.25cm, height: 5.00cm*

Fig. 3. Structure to construct and task precision errors.

4.3   Outcome Measures

Quantitative and qualitative data was collected in the experimental procedure to investigate the effect of the virtual interaction interface types on the virtual assembly of physical parts. Quantitative data was collected automatically during the study task with programmed trackers implemented in the VR application, while qualitative data was collected by means of a questionnaire issued to the participant after performing each experimental condition.

Quantitative Data from Performance Trackers

1. *The Duration*: The time spent to complete the task was recorded. This time corresponds to the time from when the participant was immersed in the virtual environment and pressed the red button to begin the task to when the participant pressed the red button again to indicate task completion.
2. *Interaction error*: While completing the task, users could grab block pieces and other objects by performing a grab gesture with the interaction interface. When a grab gesture was performed, but the grab was not successful, this was counted as a grab failure. For the Leap Motion and SenseGlove DK1 a grab is performed by at least two fingers, including the thumb, while for the controller users have to insert the controller in the object and press the trigger button.
3. *Assembly Precision*: The precision of the assembly of the physical parts is important for some application use cases. Therefore, in this study we wanted to investigate the impact of each interface on the precision/accuracy (*i.e.* proper alignment of the blocks) of interactions performed by users during the assembly task. To measure this property, the following two metrics were automatically logged and analysed (Fig. 3b illustrates the two types of task precision errors):
   - *Distance*: When constructing the structure with Lego block pieces, blocks can only fit in specific positions on another block, constrained by the sockets on the blocks. Users therefore need to place blocks only in these

exact positions for the blocks to lock (snap) in place. Therefore, a "distance error" is the positional difference between the final position where the user actually placed the block (where the block is released) and the actual locking position where the user intended to place the block. This difference measures, how precisely the user positions the block in place. This value is logged every time the user places a block in place.

- *Orientation*: Similar to the "distance error" described above, the user also needs to place the block flat and in correct alignment to snap it on another block. The "orientation error" here measures the angle difference (offset) along the x, y and z axis of the block when the user finally releases the block in place, and the intended actual alignment.

Qualitative Data

Usability Questionnaire: Usability is a major factor in the use of VR interfaces. It can have significant effects on the execution of VR tasks and acceptance. Therefore, the study was designed to collect usability measures of the different interaction interfaces. After executing the study task with each interface type, participants responded to the IBM PSSUQ [11, 12] questionnaire for the interface type which was used.

5 Results

In this section we present the results of repeated measures ANOVA analysis of the experimental data, described in Sect. 4.3 above. For all results presented below (unless stated otherwise): significance level is 0.05, confidence intervals are 95.0%, and for sphericity assumed. The symbol μ represents the mean, and σ the standard deviation.

5.1 Interaction (Grab) Errors

As described in Sect. 4.3, grab errors occur when the user performs an unsuccessful grab action on an object. Figure 4 shows the mean grab errors for all participants with the three VR interaction interfaces. The chart, shows that the most failed attempts were recorded when users performed the task using the "SenseGlove", followed by the "Leap Motion", and the HTC Vive controller.

The mean grab errors when the task was completed with the controller is 1.58 ($\mu = 1.58$, $\sigma = 2.15$), with the Leap Motion 2.83 ($\mu = 2.83$, $\sigma = 3.01$), and with the SenseGlove DK1 10.83 ($\mu = 10.83$, $\sigma = 5.79$).

There was a significant main effect of the interaction interface used on the grab errors, $F(2, 16) = 33.63$, $p < .001$. Contrasts revealed that the overall grab errors for the HTC Vive controller was significantly less than the SenseGlove DK1 ($F(1, 8) = 52.68$, $p < 0.001$), and during execution of the task with the Leap Motion the grab errors were significantly less than with the SenseGlove DK1 ($F(1, 8) = 31.78$, $p < .001$).

There was no significant effect of the participant's gender ($F(1, 8) = 0.24$, $p = .637$). Participant's previous experience with VR also did not have a significant effect on the grab errors ($F(1, 8) = .001$, $p = .974$).

There was no significant interaction effect between the interaction interface used and the gender ($F(2, 16) = 1.10$, $p = .357$), or previous VR experience ($F(2, 16) = .257$, $p = .776$) on the grab errors.

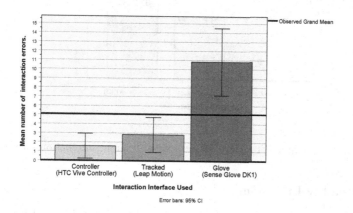

Fig. 4. Mean interaction (grab) errors during task execution.

5.2   Task Duration

Figure 5 shows the mean time participants took to complete the task. The time recorded is the time from when the user is immersed in VR and presses the red button to begin the task, and ends when the user presses the red button again to stop the task. Figure 5 shows that participants required more time to complete the task with the SenseGlove DK1. The mean time needed to complete the task with the controller was 177.03 s ($\mu = 177.03s$, $\sigma = 83.43$), with the Leap Motion 347.90 s ($\mu = 347.90s$, $\sigma = 113.99$), and with the SenseGlove DK1 555.20 s ($\mu = 555.20s$, $\sigma = 235.08$).

There was a significant main effect of the interaction interface used on the time needed to complete the task, $F(2, 16) = 24.20$, $p < .001$. Contrasts revealed that completing the task with the HTC Vive controller required significantly less time than with the SenseGlove DK1 ($F(1, 8) = 29.54$, $p < 0.001$), and executing the task with the Leap Motion required significantly less time than with the SenseGlove DK1 ($F(1, 8) = 15.40$, $p = .004$).

There was no significant effect of the participant's gender ($F(1,8) =$ 0.07, $p = .802$). Participant's previous experience with VR also did not have a significant effect on the time required to complete the task ($F(1,8) = .25$, $p = .629$).

There was no significant interaction effect between the interaction interface used and the gender ($F(2,16) = 1.166$, $p = .221$), or previous VR experience ($F(2,16) = 1.225$, $p = .320$).

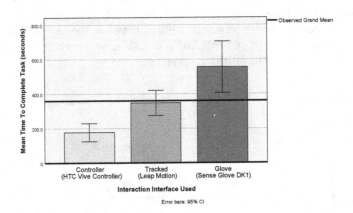

Fig. 5. Time required to complete task with different interaction interfaces.

5.3   Assembly Precision

Distance Error: Distance errors (as described in Sect. 4.3, and illustrated in Fig. 3b) measure the distance offset when the user releases a block in a snapping position. The chart in Fig. 6a shows the results of recorded distance offset errors in centimeters (cm). The mean distance offset for the HTC Vive controller was 1.67 cm ($\mu = 1.67$ cm, $\sigma = 0.24$), with the Leap Motion the mean distance offset was 1.06 cm ($\mu = 1.06$ cm, $\sigma = 0.20$), and 0.93 cm ($\mu = 0.93$ cm, $\sigma = 0.23$) with the SenseGlove DK1. This means that users placed the block pieces more accurately with the SenseGlove DK1, followed by the Leap Motion and then The HTC Vive controller.

There was a significant main effect of the interaction interface on the distance precision error, $F(2,16) = 56.55$, $p < .001$. Contrasts revealed that executing the task with the HTC Vive controller led to significantly less precise snapping distance than with the SenseGlove DK1 ($F(1,8) = 84.49$, $p < 0.001$), and executing the task with the Leap Motion led to significantly less precise snapping distance than with the SenseGlove DK1 ($F(1,8) = 5.55$, $p = .046$).

There was no significant main effect of the participant's gender ($F(1,8) =$ 0.012, $p = .915$). Participant's previous experience with VR also did not have a significant main effect on the snap distance error ($F(1,8) = .160$, $p = .699$).

There was no significant interaction effect between the interaction interface used and participants' gender ($F(2,16) = .307$, $p = .740$). However, there was a significant interaction effect between the interaction interface used and participants' previous VR experience $F(2, 16) = 3.792$, $p = .045 (< .05)$. Figure 6b shows that participants are equally as precise when using the Glove whether they have previous experience with VR or no previous experience with VR. However, participants with more VR experience are significantly more likely to be less precise when using a controller for such an assembly task.

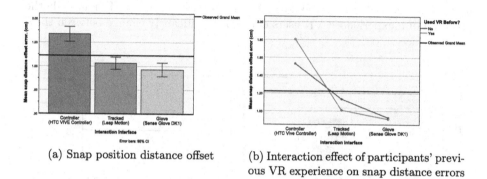

(a) Snap position distance offset

(b) Interaction effect of participants' previous VR experience on snap distance errors

Fig. 6. Construction task - snap distance precision.

Orientation Error: The orientation (rotation) precision error (also described in Sect. 4.3, and illustrated in Fig. 3b) was recorded. Figure 7 presents the results of orientation angle offset errors (in degrees); Fig. 7a - the mean overall offset for all axes, and Figs. 7c, 7d, and 7e the mean offset errors along the x, y and z axis respectively.

The mean snap angle offset error when the task was completed with the controller is 3.44° ($\mu = 3.44°$, $\sigma = .43$), with the Leap Motion 2.58° ($\mu = 2.58°$, $\sigma = .54$), and with the SenseGlove DK1 2.30° ($\mu = 2.30°$, $\sigma = .60$)

There was a significant main effect of the interaction interface used on the snap angle offset error, $F(2, 16) = 27.91$, $p < .001$. Contrasts revealed that executing the task with the HTC Vive controller led to significantly less precise snapping orientation angles than with the SenseGlove DK1 ($F(1, 8) = 102.85$, $p < .001$). However, executing the task with the Leap Motion did not lead to a significant difference in snapping orientation angles compared to the SenseGlove DK1 ($F(1, 8) = 3.65$, $p = .092$) for all participants (Fig. 7a).

There was no significant main effect of the participant's gender ($F(1, 8) = 1.23$, $p = .299$). There was also no significant interaction effect between the interaction interface used and participant's gender ($F(2, 16) = .206$, $p = .816$).

Participant's previous experience with VR did not have a significant main effect ($F(1, 18) = .031$, $p = .865$). However, there was a significant interaction effect between the interaction interface used and participants' previous experience with VR ($F(2, 16) = .6.84$, $p = .007$ (< 0.05)). Figure 7b shows that when using the HTC Vive controllers, experienced VR users are less precise compared to users with no prior VR experience. While both groups of users are least precise with the HTC Vice controller, the precision of experienced VR users is better with the SenseGlove DK1 than with the Leap Motion while the precision of inexperienced VR users does not significantly change between these two interfaces.

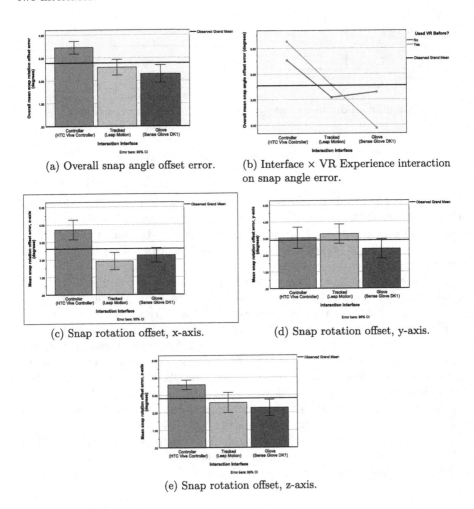

(a) Overall snap angle offset error.

(b) Interface × VR Experience interaction on snap angle error.

(c) Snap rotation offset, x-axis.

(d) Snap rotation offset, y-axis.

(e) Snap rotation offset, z-axis.

Fig. 7. Construction task - snap angle precision.

5.4 Usability - IBM PSSUQ

The PSSUQ [11,12] measures the usability of a system using a rating scale with positive questions. Participants can rate their satisfaction on a scale from 1 to 7 where 1 is "Strongly Agree" (most satisfied), and 7 is "Strongly Disagree" (least satisfied). PSSUQ measures usability along four scales: "System Usefulness", "Information Quality", "Interface Quality" and "Overall Rating". However in this study, we are most interested with the "Interface Quality". Figure 8 shows the results of the "Interface Quality", and "Overall Rating" ratings. Note that lower ratings mean better (more satisfied), while higher ratings mean less satisfied.

PSSUQ Interface Quality Rating. The mean PSSUQ interface quality rating when the task was completed with the HTC Vive controllers is 2.17 ($\mu = 2.17$, $\sigma = 1.71$), with the Leap Motion 2.25 ($\mu = 2.25$, $\sigma = 1.12$), and with the SenseGlove DK1 3.42 ($\mu = 3.42$, $\sigma = 1.68$).

There was a significant main effect of the interaction interface used on the PSSUQ interface quality rating, $F(2,16) = 4.09$, $p = .037$. Contrasts revealed that the PSSUQ interface quality rating for the HTC Vive controller was significantly lower than for the SenseGlove DK1 ($F(1,8) = 5.52$, $p = 0.047$), and while executing the task with the Leap Motion the interface quality rating was significantly lower than with the SenseGlove DK1 ($F(1,8) = 6.76$, $p = .032$).

There was no significant effect of the participant's gender ($F(1,8) = 0.25$, $p = .633$). Participant's previous experience with VR also did not have a significant effect on the PSSUQ interface quality rating ($F(1,8) = .02$, $p = .899$).

There was no significant interaction effect between the interaction interface used and the gender ($F(2,16) = 0.79$, $p = .469$), or previous VR experience ($F(2,16) = 1.30$, $p = .299$) on the PSSUQ interface quality rating.

PSSUQ Overall Rating. The mean PSSUQ overall rating when the task was completed with the controller is 2.18 ($\mu = 2.18$, $\sigma = 1.51$), with the Leap Motion 2.50 ($\mu = 2.50$, $\sigma = 1.17$), and with the SenseGlove DK1 3.69 ($\mu = 3.69$, $\sigma = 1.59$).

There was a significant main effect of the interaction interface used on the overall PSSUQ rating, $F(2,16) = 4.80$, $p = .023$. Contrasts revealed that the overall PSSUQ rating for the HTC Vive controller was significantly lower than the SenseGlove DK1 ($F(1,8) = 6.57$, $p = 0.034$), and while executing the task with the Leap Motion the PSSUQ rating was significantly lower than with the SenseGlove DK1 ($F(1,8) = 8.14$, $p = .021$).

There was no significant effect of the participant's gender ($F(1,8) = 0.028$, $p = .871$). Participant's previous experience with VR also did not have a significant effect on the PSSUQ overall rating ($F(1,8) = .001$, $p = .976$).

There was no significant interaction effect between the interaction interface used and the gender ($F(2,16) = 0.65$, $p = .534$), or previous VR experience ($F(2,16) = 1.31$, $p = .297$) on the overall PSSUQ rating.

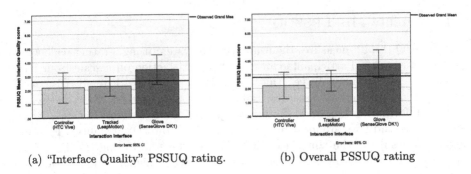

(a) "Interface Quality" PSSUQ rating.   (b) Overall PSSUQ rating

Fig. 8. Results of PSSUQ usability scores for the three interaction interfaces.

6   Discussion

In the previous Sect. 5 we presented the results of the experimental study. In this section we discuss the results, in relation to our research questions, state of the art, and observations during the study and post-study debriefing feedback from participants.

Addressing our first and second research questions on the effect of interaction interfaces on virtual assembly tasks and the impact on usability. The study results show that using the HTC Vive controller to complete the task was most reliable, and least reliable with the SenseGlove DK1. Users encountered grab interaction errors about twice as much (1.8) with the Leap Motion than with the HTC Vive controllers, and about four times as much (3.8) with the SenseGlove DK1 than with the Leap Motion. Users also required significantly more time to complete the task with the SenseGlove DK1 than with the HTC Vive controller and the Leap Motion; requiring about twice as much time (1.96) to complete the task with the Leap Motion than with the HTC Vive controller, and about 1.6 times more time to complete the task with the SenseGlove DK1 as with the Leap Motion. Gusai E. *et al.* [8] obtained similar results when investigating the HTC Vive controllers and the Leap Motion, showing that users performed fewer errors (repositioning of objects) when using the HTC Vive controller than when using the Leap Motion. However, the authors recorded only objective performance measure. In this study we also performed a usability study with the PSSUQ usability questionnaire. The results of the PSSUQ usability evaluation presented in the previous section also confirm the findings from the objective measures. Users reported similar "Interface Quality" and "Overall" PSSUQ ratings for the three interfaces. Users preferred the HTC Vive controller with a PSSUQ interface quality rating of 2.17, over the Leap Motion with a rating of 2.25 and the SenseGlove DK1 with a rating of 3.42. The study by Figueiredo L. *et al.* [7] obtained contrary results when comparing the HTC Vive controllers and the Leap Motion. In this study users were asked to interact with the user interface in VR, and users reported preference for the Leap Motion. However, since users were performing a different type of task in contrast to the study of Figueiredo L. *et al.* [7], it may be the case that the user preference for a specific interaction method depends on the task which is performed. When users interact with user interface elements in VR, natural hand interaction with a camera tracked solution such as the Leap Motion may be preferred. For tasks requiring the user to interact and manipulate 3D objects in VR, such as the virtual assembly of physical parts which we study here, controllers are preferred for the more reliable performance. It is important to note that the preference of controllers is mainly due to the reliability (fewer interaction errors). If camera tracked solutions or datagloves which offer a more natural interaction would be just as reliable or more reliable than a controller, then they might not only be preferred for tasks such as VR assembly of physical parts, but might also offer an increased sense of virtual body ownership [1,13]. In our observation during the study, users had problems using the glove: successfully grabbing an object only after a few tries, and also releasing the object after performing the release gesture a few times. This was also confirmed by users in the debriefing and post-study discussion. Users reported that the Leap Motion, and SenseGlove DK1 were more natural, but the controller was more reliable and stable for performing not only grab actions, but also push and pull actions when interacting with the table drawers (opening the drawers to collect block pieces and closing the top drawers to access lower drawers).

Investigating the effect of user's prior experience with VR technologies is an important factor in designing such systems for use by a diverse group of users (our third research question). In this study half of participants had no prior experience with VR, while the other 50% of participants had previous VR experience, with at least three VR experiences in the last 24 months preceding the study. The results showed that user's experience with VR technologies had no significant effect on the usability rating of the three interaction interfaces, or interaction (grab) error and required time to complete the task. However, participants' experience with VR had a significant interaction effect with the interaction interface used on the level of precision with which the task was executed. When completing the VR assembly of physical parts with the HTC Vive controller, experienced VR participants were less precise than non-experienced participants; making a mean distance error of 1.8 cm and 1.5 cm respectively, and a mean orientation angle error of 3.6° and 3.3° respectively. This precision error drops for both groups when performing the task with the Leap Motion to: 1.0cm distance error and 2.6° orientation angle error for the experienced users, and 1.1 cm distance error and 2.5° orientation angle error for the non-experienced group. The distance error drops even further when executing the task with the SenseGlove DK1 for both groups to approximately 0.9 cm. However while the orientation angle error for the experienced group drops to 1.9° with the SenseGlove DK1, orientation angle error for the inexperienced group stays approximately the same at 2.6°. As illustrated in Figs. 6b and 7b, participants' precision error dropped similarly - approaching the same value, only differing with the SenseGlove DK1 orientation angle error. This indicates two things: first, all users are likely to be more precise with interaction interfaces that offer a more natural interaction modality.

Secondly, this also shows that users are more likely to be less precise with the controller when their experience with VR increases. However when performing the task with interaction interfaces that offer a more natural interaction such as the Leap Motion and SenseGlove DK1, users' precision in interaction does not change with increased VR experience (users interact similarly with natural interaction interfaces).

Despite these results, we are keen to point out a few points. First, the results show that users encountered more interaction errors with the Leap Motion and SenseGlove DK1. These errors could be mostly software related. Manufacturers of these devices do provide a software development kit (SDK) which is used by developers for implementing interactions in VR applications. In this study we used the SDK provided by the device manufacturers for use in the Unity game engine. If the software algorithms are improved, the experience and performance of users could be different. Secondly, one of the major goals of dataglove manufacturers is to provide force- and tactile-feedback when interacting with objects in VR. In this study we did not consider this feature of datagloves, in fact this feature was turned off for the SenseGlove because we wanted to evaluate only the interaction features. These results show that camera tracking and dataglove solutions would provide a much better interaction experience if the manufacturing effort would not only be focused on providing the additional (force- and tactile feedback) features, but also on improving the interaction experience. We also note that in the study we used specific devices that were currently the most advanced devices available in the community (still, the SenseGlove DK1 is a development kit and not a full product). However there is continued active development and innovation in this field which means that the results of the study may be different when conducted with "improved" devices in the future. For example, shortly after this study was conducted a newer version of the Sense-Glove was released by the manufacturer (the SenseGlove Nova). However, these studies are still relevant to guide future development of interaction interfaces, and interaction interface choices during design and development of VR applications to serve a diverse group of users.

7   Conclusion and Future Work

In this study we investigated the effect of three VR hand interaction interface types: controller, camera hand tracking, and dataglove - on usability and performance when performing VR assembly of physical parts. We chose the devices HTC Vive controller, Leap Motion, and SenseGlove DK1 for each of these categories. Results showed that when users perform the VR assembly of physical parts with the HTC Vive controller, they encounter fewer interaction errors, require less time to complete the task, and rate the usability of the controller above the Leap Motion and SenseGlove DK1. However, users are more precise in their interactions when using the Leap Motion and SenseGlove DK1 than with the HTC Vive controller, been most precise with the SenseGlove DK1. We also found that there is a significant interaction effect between the interaction interface and users' experience with VR technologies. VR experienced users execute

VR assembly tasks less precisely with the controller than non-experienced users. The distance precision in snapping objects together in an assembly task is the same irrespective of users' prior experience with VR technologies, *i.e.* inexperienced users are just as precise as experienced users with natural interaction interfaces.

The implications of this result is that when designing a system for virtual assembly of physical parts, if precision when executing the task is a primary concern, then it will be best to use the Leap Motion (a camera hand tracked solution), or the SenseGlove DK1 (a dataglove) for best precision in task execution. Also when designing a VR system for the assembly of physical parts, using an interaction interface that offers a natural interaction modality (such as the Leap Motion or SenseGlove) ensures consistent accuracy in performance for all types of users (VR experienced and non-experienced).

Recruited participants in this study were mostly in the same age group 25–38 years (median = 26.5 years). However, studies have reported mixed results on performance of different age groups on VR assessments *e.g.* no significant difference was found between seniors and young adults in a VR shopping memory assessment task [15], yet others have found a significant difference between age groups in VR way finding tasks [17]. Therefore in further studies, we would like to investigate the effect of different age groups on VR assembly tasks. Future research should also investigate these effects with professionals in the manufacturing and maintenance industry, in this case a more industrial task can be selected for the study. In a further research work we would also like to conduct the study with industry ready devices such as the SenseGlove Nova.

References

1. Argelaguet, F., Hoyet, L., Trico, M., Lécuyer, A.: The role of interaction in virtual embodiment: effects of the virtual hand representation. In: 2016 IEEE Virtual Reality (VR), pp. 3–10. IEEE (2016)
2. Audi AG: With virtual reality into the electric era: Audi makes technicians worldwide fit for the e-tron — audi mediacenter (2019). https://www.audi-mediacenter.com/en/press-releases/with-virtual-reality-into-the-electric-era-audi-makes-technicians-worldwide-fit-for-the-e-tron-11658
3. Bailey, S.K., Johnson, C.I., Schroeder, B.L., Marraffino, M.D.: Using virtual reality for training maintenance procedures. In: Proceedings of the Interservice/Industry Training, Simulation and Education Conference (2017)
4. Berg, L.P., Vance, J.M.: Industry use of virtual reality in product design and manufacturing: a survey. Virtual Reality 21(1), 1–17 (2016). https://doi.org/10.1007/s10055-016-0293-9
5. EPIC: Beyond the manual: VR training on aircraft maintenance (2019). https://www.unrealengine.com/en-US/spotlights/beyond-the-manual-vr-training-on-aircraft-maintenance?sessionInvalidated=true
6. Fahmi, F., Tanjung, K., Nainggolan, F., Siregar, B., Mubarakah, N., Zarlis, M.: Comparison study of user experience between virtual reality controllers, leap motion controllers, and senso glove for anatomy learning systems in a virtual reality environment, vol. 851, p. 12024. IOP Publishing (2020)

7. Figueiredo, L., Rodrigues, E., Teixeira, J., Teichrieb, V.: A comparative evaluation of direct hand and wand interactions on consumer devices. Comput. Graph. **77**, 108–121 (2018). https://doi.org/10.1016/j.cag.2018.10.006

8. Gusai, E., Bassano, C., Solari, F., Chessa, M.: Interaction in an immersive collaborative virtual reality environment: a comparison between leap motion and HTC controllers. In: Battiato, S., Farinella, G.M., Leo, M., Gallo, G. (eds.) ICIAP 2017. LNCS, vol. 10590, pp. 290–300. Springer, Cham (2017). https://doi.org/10.1007/978-3-319-70742-6_27

9. Kalkan, Ö.K., Karabulut, Ş, Höke, G.: Effect of virtual reality-based training on complex industrial assembly task performance. Arab. J. Sci. Eng. **46**(12), 12697–12708 (2021). https://doi.org/10.1007/s13369-021-06138-w

10. Ko, A.J., LaToza, T.D., Burnett, M.M.: A practical guide to controlled experiments of software engineering tools with human participants. Empir. Softw. Eng. **20**(1), 110–141 (2013). https://doi.org/10.1007/s10664-013-9279-3

11. Lewis, J.R.: Psychometric evaluation of the post-study system usability questionnaire: the PSSUQ (1992)

12. Lewis, J.R.: IBM computer usability satisfaction questionnaires: psychometric evaluation and instructions for use. Int. J. Hum.-Comput. Interact. **7**(1), 57–78 (1995)

13. Lougiakis, C., Katifori, A., Roussou, M., Ioannidis, I.P.: Effects of virtual hand representation on interaction and embodiment in HMD-based virtual environments using controllers. In: 2020 IEEE Conference on Virtual Reality and 3D User Interfaces (VR), pp. 510–518. IEEE (2020)

14. Navarro, D., Sundstedt, V.: Evaluating player performance and experience in virtual reality game interactions using the HTC Vive controller and leap motion sensor, pp. 103–110. SciTePress (2019). HTC Vive is more reliable than Leap Motion.
Reduced performance when using Leap Motion

15. Plechatá, A., Sahula, V., Fayette, D., Fajnerová, I.: Age-related differences with immersive and non-immersive virtual reality in memory assessment. Front. Psychol. **10** (2019). https://doi.org/10.3389/fpsyg.2019.01330

16. Seymour, N.E., et al.: Virtual reality training improves operating room performance: results of a randomized, double-blinded study. Ann. Surg. **236**(4), 458 (2002)

17. Taillade, M., et al.: Executive and memory correlates of age-related differences in wayfinding performances using a virtual reality application. Aging Neuropsychol. Cogn. **20**(3), 298–319 (2013). https://doi.org/10.1080/13825585.2012.706247. pMID 22901081

18. Tanjung, K., Nainggolan, F., Siregar, B., Panjaitan, S., Fahmi, F.: The use of virtual reality controllers and comparison between vive, leap motion and senso gloves applied in the anatomy learning system. J. Phys.: Conf. Ser. **1542**, 12026 (2020). https://doi.org/10.1088/1742-6596/1542/1/012026

19. Zimmermann, P.: Virtual reality aided design. A survey of the use of VR in automotive industry. In: Talaba, D., Amditis, A. (eds.) Product Engineering, pp. 277–296. Springer, Dordrecht (2008). https://doi.org/10.1007/978-1-4020-8200-9_13

Multi-person Collaborative Augmented Reality Assembly Process Evaluation System Based on HoloLens

JingFei Wang, YaoGuang Hu, and XiaoNan Yang[✉]

Industrial and Systems Engineering Laboratory, School of Mechanical Engineering, Beijing Institute of Technology, Beijing, China
{hyg,yangxn}@bit.edu.cn

Abstract. With the development of products in the direction of products in complexity and sophistication, assembly process planning becomes a complex and time-consuming issue in manufacturing. Augmented reality (AR), especially collaborative augmented reality, can be used to aid the design of assembly processes, help efficiently evaluate and improve the designed assembly process from multiple perspectives. This paper presents a methodology and the associated system for enhancing assembly process scheme evaluation in assembly process plan stage using collaborative augmented reality. It first describes the overall scheme of the system that based on a role-based multi-person collaboration method. Subsequently, system features like: AR collaborative environment (synchronization of multiple AR devices), AR assembly simulation (virtual model manipulation, collision detection), AR assistant evaluation tools (AR observation tool, visualize performance data, AR evaluation table) are described. Finally, this paper illustrates possible usages and potential benefits of how collaborative AR helps evaluate the assembly process and helps find the bottleneck of assembly step through a use case study.

Keywords: Multi-person collaboration · Augmented reality · Assembly process evaluation

1 Introduction

In the era of globalization, with the development of products in the direction of complexity and customization, assembly complexity is surge increasing sharply. The assembly design and process planning have become a time-consuming and important element that directly impact on the final quality of the product. Product assembly simulation and evaluation technology is considered as one of the key technologies in the complex product assembly design and process planning in manufacturing [1]. Simulation software, such as DELMIA, CARTIA, has been widely used in current manufacturing systems to simulate assembly process with computers. It helps to find possible problems in the assembly process before being put into production, and optimize the design and assembly process

© Springer Nature Switzerland AG 2022
J. Y. C. Chen and G. Fragomeni (Eds.): HCII 2022, LNCS 13318, pp. 369–380, 2022.
https://doi.org/10.1007/978-3-031-06015-1_25

plan. However, existing computer-based simulation software that offer assembly process plan either limited to evaluation of clearances or lack of natural human operation.

With the development of virtual reality (VR) technology, many assembly simulation systems based on the VR environment have been developed [2, 3]. Even though using a VR based simulation offers the integration of natural human interaction and intuitive feedbacks with 3D models to assembly planning, there are still deficiencies: (1) there is still a gap between assembly simulation with the real operation environment [1]. (2) user's perception will be limited in a purely virtual environment [2].

Augmented reality (AR) technology could be more suitable to address these issues. The AR assembly system can give users a way to directly manipulate the virtual model in real environment without restricting their perception. Ong et al. [4] Proposed a bare-hand interaction augmented assembly system (BHAA), in which users can effectively complete the simulated assembly process by manipulating the model with bare hands in the real environment, and evaluate the assembly process through collision interference and assembly stability [5, 6]. However, Ong's system only supports a single user, and does not consider the scenario of multiple people such as designers and on-site workers in collaboration for assembly process plan and evaluation. The assembly process designer is both an executor and an evaluator, which will limit the designer's comprehensive review of the assembly process to a certain extent.

In fact, collaborative AR can bright a wide range of benefits to assembly tasks [7], for example, integrating the knowledge and experience of multiple people, increasing problem context understanding and awareness. Liu et al. [8] proposed an intelligent collaboration assembly system (ICAS) combining a real-time data driven method with AR technology, to provide support for multi-person collaborative aerospace equipment assembly work. Chantziaras et al. [9] proposed an augmented reality platform in which remote supervisor could uses intuitive digital annotations that enrich the physical environment of the workplace to facilitate the execution of on-site worker's tasks. The collaborative AR interactive interface has been widely used in assembly guidance and training currently, but it is rarely used in assembly simulation. Therefore, a multi-person collaborative AR assembly simulation system is proposed in this study. The system provides a role-based collaborative AR environment for multi-users, assisting them to cooperate with each other to complete the test and evaluation of the assembly process scheme.

2   Overall Scheme

As explained in research done by Wang Z.B. [10], the assembly process plan in AR could be decomposed in three steps: design, simulate, and evaluate. Figure 1 presents the detailed workflow. The first step is to design the initial assembly process plan based on the part structure. There are many methods that can be used, including the method based on knowledge and experience, and the automated algorithms. Then, the designer needs to manually test the assembly process scheme on the virtual prototype, to eliminate infeasible solutions and evaluate feasible solutions. Finally, the designer selects the assembly process scheme, according to optimization objective, such as performance data, ergonomics and so on. In the proposed system, AR is used in the second steps. In the AR assembly environment combining virtual and real, the assembly process is tested and evaluated on virtual prototypes instead of real prototypes, saving the time and cost of manufacturing prototypes.

1-Design the initial assembly process plans
- Design from experience
- Design based on automated algorithms
- Relying on human-computer interaction to design

2-Evalute the assemblability designed assembly process
➢ Manually test and evaluate the designed assembly process schemes on the virtual prototype

3-select the assembly process scheme
➢ compare the evaluation indices of different feasible assembly to select the best scheme

Fig. 1. The workflow of the assembly process plan in AR

Different from the above workflow, the main objective of the proposed system is to test and evaluate the assemblability of the assembly process collaboratively. Therefore, a role-based collaborative method is proposed, as shown in Fig. 2. In the work process, users need to play two kinds of roles: operator and evaluator. The operator has the authority to manipulate the virtual model to perform the virtual assembly process. Evaluators have authority to read performance data and use AR assisted evaluation tools to observe and evaluate the assembly process of the operator. The role of each user can be changed in the actual work process. Users complete the evaluation for each step of the assembly process collaboratively by the workflow of selecting roles, performing tests, and observing and evaluating.

To apply the proposed collaborative method, the proposed system consists of three modules: AR collaborative assembly environment, AR assembly simulation and AR assembly evaluation. The AR collaborative assembly environment module is mainly responsible for providing a common augmented reality assembly environment for collaborators. The AR assembly simulation module mainly provides support for the operator. It integrates the technology of manipulating the model by hand and the technology of simulating real collision contact. The AR assembly evaluation module mainly provides support for the evaluator. It contains AR assistant evaluation tools, such as visual observe tool, visual performance data and visual evaluation form. The detailed design of each module of the system will be introduced in the following sections.

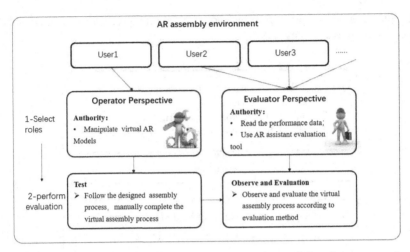

Fig. 2. The role-based collaborative method for the multi-person collaborative augmented reality assembly system

3   AR Collaborative Assembly Environment

This section is going to describe how the augmented reality assembly environment is constructed. It explains how to ensure display content is consistent when multiple users wear different AR display devices. This is the foundation of the multi-person collaborative augmented reality assembly system.

The architecture for managing collaboration is shown in Fig. 3. This architecture requires at least one server and two AR devices. The server deals with data which needs to be synchronized (models' position, rotation, …) Every user's AR device run a client application, which manages the interaction and send request to the server to synchronize them for every other client application connected.

Moreover, in an AR application for single user, there is only one space coordinate system. However, in a collaboration AR application, all coordinate systems in different AR devices need to unify, to ensure the objects that each user sees are at the same point in space. The coordinate system uniform method based on the marker-based is used for this problem in the system. This method can be divided into three steps:

- Reference device setting. In a collaborative AR application, the space coordinate system of one device will be designated as the space coordinate system of the entire system, which is namely the reference device. By default, the first device running the client terminal is used as the positioning reference device.
- Mark position recognition. Place three markers in certain places in the space (such as the desktop). Then, based on the camera and image recognition algorithm of each AR device, the space coordinates of markers could be recognized.
- Conversion matrix calculation. Except for the reference device, all other AR devices perform calculations based on the recognized coordinates and the reference device coordinates to solve the 4×4 coordinate conversion matrix. When changing the

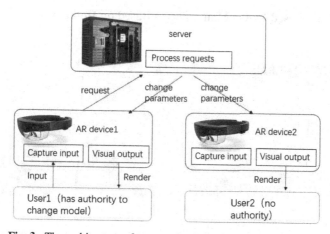

Fig. 3. The architecture of proposed collaborative AR environment

position and posture of the virtual object, the server will calculate the change value with the conversion matrix of each AR device, and give different change instructions for each AR device. This ensures that content rendered by multiple AR devices are consistent in time and space.

4 AR Assembly Process Simulation

This section introduces how to realize the simulation of the virtual assembly process. It describes the method of manipulating the model with bare hands, which is based on HoloLens2 sensor data. Then, the Collision detection algorithm used in the system is also introduced. The combination of the two methods will make the virtual assembly process simulation bring as close to the real experience as possible. The AR assembly environment for operator is shown in Fig. 4.

Fig. 4. Augmented reality assembly environment

4.1   Bare-Hand Based Model Manipulation Based on HoloLens2

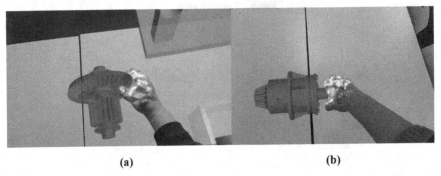

(a)   (b)

Fig. 5. Natural virtual model manipulation gestures. (a) Grab the disc-shaped portion of the model. (b) Grab the shaft-shaped portion of the model.

The Hololens2 sensor supports real-time tracking of the position and posture of the hand joints. Based on the tracking data, a virtual model manipulation gestures have been developed for natural hand movements. Users can naturally make holding gestures to manipulate virtual parts, as shown in above Fig. 5. The model manipulation method requires two steps:

- Manipulate object selection. Virtual models are registered at key nodes of the hands for each frame, based on tracked position and pose data. A virtual object is being selected by the user only when all virtual models registered on the fingertips are both in contact with the virtual object. The user can deselect a virtual object by enlarging the distance between all fingertips to such that some or all virtual models are not in contact with the virtual object. When the virtual object is being manipulated by the user, the spatial relationship between the virtual objects and a hand coordinate system established on the user's hand is recorded and maintained.
- Manipulation intention recognition. In terms of driving the model motion, the virtual manipulation force calculation method proposed in the research done by Wang X. and Ong S.K. [5] is used in this research. Based on a springer-damper model, the motion of the hands is converted into a virtual manipulation force or torque to drives the exact direction and distance of movement of the model.

4.2   Virtual Model Collision Detection

In the process of simulating assembly, collision detections between virtual models are essential for assemblability checking. In this research, the collision detection algorithm proposed in the literature [11] is applied and integrated. This algorithm is divided into three stages, the rough bounding box detection stage, the triangle patch extraction stage that needs to be detected, and the fine triangle patch detection stage. This makes the algorithm have better performance in real-time and accuracy.

Based on the collision detection algorithm, the state of contact and interference between virtual objects will be detected on every frame. In addition, approximate models at the identified key node positions of the hands are registered, so the collision between the hands and the parts that are not assembled will also be detected. When the operator is manipulating the AR models to simulate assembly process in proposed system, if his actions are significantly different from the right assembly method, then the virtual model collision will be detected and recorded, and indicated by a color change, which will prompt him to pay attention to the assembly operation to rationalize it.

5 AR Assembly Process Evaluation

This section is going to describe in detail the evaluation method of the assembly process in the system. It introduces a fuzzy comprehensive evaluation method, and the evaluation of assembly process is completed based on this method. Then, it also described the AR assistance tools of the system to help the evaluator complete the evaluation.

5.1 Assembly Process Operation Evaluation Method

In the current widely used design for assembly (DFA) method, the factors that affect the assembly process are divided into several aspects: geometry, physics, connection and operation [12]. Among them, the geometric, physical and connection can be derived from the analysis of the designed part structure. However, the operation, which involves manual factors, are difficult to be directly quantitatively analyzed. Therefore, the evaluation of the assembly process operation is the objective of the proposed multi-person collaborative augmented reality assembly system. And the fuzzy evaluation method is adopted in this research.

According to the evaluation method in [10] and [13], five factors that have an impact on the assembly process operation are considered, namely visibility and operation space, translation, rotation and position. And their respective weight values are shown in Table 1. Each influence factor has five fuzzy levels, and the specific membership determination method for each level is described in Table 1.

$$R = \begin{bmatrix} u_1^1 & u_1^2 & \ldots\ldots & u_1^n \\ u_2^1 & u_2^2 & \ldots\ldots & u_2^n \\ u_3^1 & u_3^3 & \ldots\ldots & u_3^n \\ u_4^1 & u_4^4 & \ldots\ldots & u_4^n \\ u_5^1 & u_5^5 & \ldots\ldots & u_5^n \end{bmatrix} \qquad (1)$$

$$A = [0.19, 0.19, 0.12, 0.19, 0.38] \qquad (2)$$

$$B = A \bullet R = [b_1, b_2, \ldots\ldots, b_n,] \qquad (3)$$

Table 1. The fuzzy evaluation table for the assemblability of the assembly process.

Assemblability factor	Weight value	Fuzzy level
Visibility (u1)	0.19	0 completely invisible during assembly
		1 Need to adjust sight frequently
		2 Need to adjust sight sometimes
		3 Need to adjust sight occasionally
		4 fully visible
Operation space (u2)	0.19	0 can't operate
		1 the hand collides with the rest parts frequently
		2 the hand collides with the rest parts sometimes
		3 the hand collides with the rest parts occasionally
		4 fully plenty space
Translation (u3)	0.12	0 Unable to perform translation operation
		1 There are more than a dozen discontinuous translation operations
		2 There are several discontinuous translation operations
		3 The translation operation is continuous
		4 No need to translate
Rotation (u4)	0.19	0 Unable to perform rotation operation
		1 There are more than a dozen discontinuous rotation operations
		2 There are several discontinuous rotation operations
		3 The translation operation is continuous
		4 No need to rotate
Position (u5)	0.38	0 Unable to position
		1 takes very long time to position
		2 takes a long time to position
		3 takes a short time to position
		4 No need to position parts

5.2 AR Assistant Evaluation Tools

During the work of evaluators, AR assembly process evaluation tools will support their work. These tools give full play to the enhanced information characteristics of AR and expand the ability of evaluators to observe. There are three main tools: AR observation tool, visualization data and AR evaluation table.

AR Obervation Tool. The AR observation tool mainly expands the evaluator's observation ability and prompts the content that needs attention. When the evaluator needs it, he can turn on these tools to assist his work. AR observation tools mainly include the following three types:

– Visualize assembly path. As shown in Fig. 6(a), the movement path of the virtual model being assembled will be displayed with green lines, and the location node where the collision occurs will be rendered with green dots, prompting the evaluator to observe the movement (translation and rotation) of the assembly model;
– Visualize field of sight. As shown in Fig. 6(b), the field of view of the assembler will be displayed in a rendered cone. The virtual model within this range will change in color, which will prompt the evaluator of the objects that the assembler can observe, assist the evaluation for visibility of the assembly operation.

(a)   **(b)**

Fig. 6. AR assistant evaluation tools. (a) The visualize field of sight, models within range will be colored. (b) The visualize model movement path, the purple path in the figure indicates that there is a collision in the path.

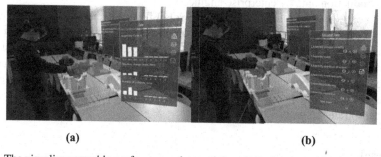

(a)   **(b)**

Fig. 7. The visualize assembly performance data and the AR Evaluation table. (a) The visualize assembly performance data in AR. (b) The visualize AR assembly evaluation form

Visualize Assembly Performance Data. Some assembly process performance data is collected and displayed visually in the form of an AR bar graph, as shown in Fig. 7(a). These data include the actual execution time of the assembly for each assembly step, the number of times the substrate was oriented during assembly for each assembly step, and the number of collisions between hands and environmental parts during assembly for each assembly step. These data will be used to assist the evaluation of the assemblability factors like: operation space, position.

AR Evaluation Table. The AR evaluation table is an interactive AR interface designed for the fuzzy evaluation. as Fig. 7(b) shows. After the evaluator completes the evaluation of an indicator, he can use the "click" gesture of HoloLens2 to click the virtual button in the AR evaluation table to confirm the score of this indicator. After all the evaluation indicators are completed, the final evaluation score will be calculated and shown by the system according to the calculation method.

6 Use Case Study

The proposed augmented reality collaboration tool was used and tested among students who are in major of mechanical engineering. The experiment was followed by a training session in use of this system.

6.1 Use Case Description

The use case is based on the models and assembly process of the reducer of an automobile company. There were 10 participants, between 20 and 30 years old, randomly divided into five groups. Each group of two persons, and cooperated to complete the reducer assembly process evaluation task.

The objective of every group is to discover issues of assemblability in the current assembly process through a collaborative evaluation. There are eleven kinds of components and three standard parts in the assembly process that were divided into seven assembly steps. The reference evaluation results are corresponding to the analysis of specific production data by enterprise engineers.

Group of participants first assigned their roles. Two collaborators wear Hololens2 and work together, to perform tasks corresponding according to the different roles in augmented reality environment. The operator completed the assembly process simulation according to the current assembly process in AR assembly environment, and the evaluator completed the evaluation based on the virtual assembly process, with reference to the assembler's comments. Once done, users are filling the System-Usability-Scale questioner to rate the proposed system.

6.2 Results

All of these groups have found the bottleneck assembly process, which is the fifth process, installing the end cap of the output shaft. They all marked the process as the lowest fuzzy evaluation score. Among these groups, three groups accurately identified that the bottleneck process had problems in position, assembly orientation and assembly visibility. In fact, augmented reality systems are effective for evaluating assembly processes and finding assemblability issues.

Moreover, during the collaboration, we can observe the benefits of the division of roles. The operator's subjective experience and the evaluator's objective observations are combined to evaluate the assembly process. In the evaluation of the third assembly process, many groups of operators gave feedback to the evaluators that the operation was difficult, and the evaluator would accurately determine that the problem were in the part positioning and visibility, because he observes a lot of adjustments of the operator's sight and long positioning time during assembly. If this evaluation is entrusted to a single person who must complete both the assembly simulation and the evaluation, and the complex task will cause omissions.

A usability evaluation method of SUS was used [14], to collect and quantify participants' assessments for the usability of the proposed AR system. The SUS evaluation obtains a mean score of $71(\sigma = 14)$. According to the reference value [15], the usability of the proposed multi-person collaboration AR system is qualified as "good". We suppose that these results could be improved with a more intuitive interface and interaction paradigm.

7 Conclusion

This paper presents a methodology and the associated system, multi-person collaborative augmented reality assembly process evaluation system, for enhancing evaluation making in assembly process using collaborative augmented reality.

First, we identified how collaborative AR is used in an assembly process evaluation. Then the architecture of such a system and functions to collaborative work is described. Finally, we evaluate the system usability in a use case study. It reveals that the AR helps to find the bottleneck of the assembly process scheme and take into account ergonomics and assemblability issues.

Future works will first focus on improving interaction paradigms and evaluating the proposed system with a larger cohort of users in order to assess the case study results obtained. Secondly, we will work on an in-depth integration within with widely used computer aided design tools (CAD) of this collaborative AR assembly evaluation system in order to allow data exchange with CAD and AR tools.

References

1. Qiu, C., Zhou, S., Liu, Z., Gao, Q., Tan, J.: Digital assembly technology based on augmented reality and digital twins: a review. Virtual Reality Intell. Hardw. **1**(6), 597–610 (2019)
2. Ji, P., Choi, A.C., Tu, L.: VDAS: a virtual design and assembly system in a virtual reality environment. Assembly Autom. **22**, 337–342 (2002)
3. Gonzalez-Badillo, G., Medellin-Castillo, H.I., Lim, T.: Development of a haptic virtual reality system for assembly planning and evaluation. Procedia Technol. **7**, 265–272 (2013)
4. Ong, S.K., Wang, Z.B.: Augmented assembly technologies based on 3D bare-hand interaction. CIRP Ann. **60**(1), 1–4 (2011)
5. Wang, X., Ong, S.K., Nee, A.Y.C.: Real-virtual components interaction for assembly simulation and planning. Robot. Comput. Integr. Manuf. **41**, 102–114 (2016)
6. Wang, Z.B., Ong, S.K., Nee, A.Y.C.: Augmented reality aided interactive manual assembly design. Int. J. Adv. Manuf. Technol. **69**(5), 1311–1321 (2013)
7. Wang, X., Ong, S.K., Nee, A.Y.C.: A comprehensive survey of augmented reality assembly research. Adv. Manuf. **4**(1), 1–22 (2016). https://doi.org/10.1007/s40436-015-0131-4

8. Liu, X., Zheng, L., Shuai, J., Zhang, R., Li, Y.: Data-driven and AR assisted intelligent collaborative assembly system for large-scale complex products. Procedia CIRP **93**, 1049–1054 (2020)

9. Chantziaras, G., Triantafyllidis, A., Tzovaras, D.: An augmented reality-based remote collaboration platform for worker assistance. In: International Conference on Pattern Recognition, pp. 404–416 (2021)

10. Wang, Z.B., Ng, L.X., Ong, S.K., Nee, A.Y.C.: Assembly planning and evaluation in an augmented reality environment. Int. J. Prod. Res. **51**(23–24), 7388–7404 (2013)

11. Smith, A., et al.: A simple and efficient method for accurate collision detection among deformable polyhedral objects in arbitrary motion. In: Proceedings Virtual Reality Annual International Symposium 1995, pp. 136–145, NC USA (1995)

12. Dochibhatla, S. V. S., Bhattacharya, M., Morkos, B.: Evaluating assembly design efficiency: a comparison between Lucas and Boothroyd-Dewhurst methods. In: International Design Engineering Technical Conferences and Computers and Information in Engineering Conference, vol. 58165, p. V004T05A012. Ohio, USA (2017)

13. Liu, T.H., Fischer, G.W.: Assembly evaluation method for PDES/STEP-based mechanical systems. J. Des. Manuf. **4**(1), 1–19 (1994)

14. Jordan, P.W., Thomas, B., McClelland, I.L.: Usability Evaluation in Industry, 2nd edn., p. 1996. CRC Press, London (1996)

15. Bangor, A., Kortum, P., Miller, J.: Determining what individual SUS scores mean: adding an adjective rating scale. J. Usabil. Stud. **4**(3), 114–123 (2009)

Correction to: Multimodal Augmented Reality and Subtle Guidance for Industrial Assembly – A Survey and Ideation Method

Nicole Tobisková, Lennart Malmsköld, and Thomas Pederson

Correction to:
Chapter "Multimodal Augmented Reality and Subtle
Guidance for Industrial Assembly – A Survey and Ideation
Method" in: J. Y. C. Chen and G. Fragomeni (Eds.):
Virtual, Augmented and Mixed Reality: Applications
in Education, Aviation and Industry, **LNCS 13318,**
https://doi.org/10.1007/978-3-031-06015-1_23

In the version of this chapter that was originally published the heading contains a typographical error. This has now been corrected.

The updated version of this chapter can be found at
https://doi.org/10.1007/978-3-031-06015-1_23

Author Index

Printed in the United States
by Baker & Taylor Publisher Services